The Alchemy of Wolves

MW01068162

The literature on psychological trauma and traumatic attachment has progressed over the past few decades; however, issues of coerced and internalized perpetration have not been fully explored and deconstructed. This book presents a synthesis of relational and archetypal psychology, trauma and dissociation theory, and highly relevant child soldier literature, to offer new clinical perspectives to assist psychotherapists and trauma patients to achieve more successful therapy outcomes.

The Alchemy of Wolves and Sheep offers instructive, cautionary and innovative therapeutic approaches to help transform the lives of survivors of complex trauma. The book deconstructs the origins and permutations of coerced perpetration and its effects on the psyches and lives of many trauma victims.

Chapters include:

- trauma, dissociation, and coerced perpetration
- the child soldier as a model of internalized perpetration
- relational concepts in the treatment of trauma and dissociative disorders
- treatment trajectory
- archetypal constructs as a vehicle for integration.

This book provides valuable new perspectives on the psychodynamic challenges and opportunities for mental health professionals treating internalized perpetration in survivors of complex trauma, and will prove essential reading for psychotherapists, psychoanalysts and postgraduate students as well as researchers, sociologists, theologians, legal scholars and policy makers.

Harvey L. Schwartz is a clinical psychologist, psychotherapist and consultant with more than 25 years experience treating complex trauma survivors and training psychotherapists in relational approaches to the treatment of trauma and dissociative disorders, and is the author of *Dialogues with Forgotten Voices: Relational perspectives on child abuse trauma and treatment of dissociative disorders*.

The Alchemy of Wolves and Sheep

A relational approach to internalized perpetration in complex trauma survivors

Harvey L. Schwartz

Routledge
Taylor & Francis Group
LONDON AND NEW YORK

First published 2013
by Routledge
27 Church Road, Hove, East Sussex, BN3 2FA

Simultaneously published in the USA and Canada
by Routledge
711 Third Avenue, New York, NY 10017

First issued in paperback 2015

Routledge is an imprint of the Taylor & Francis Group, an informa business

British Library Cataloguing in Publication Data
A catalogue record for this book is available from the British Library

Library of Congress Cataloging in Publication Data
Schwartz, Harvey L., 1955-
The alchemy of wolves and sheep : a relational approach to internalized
perpetration in complex trauma survivors/Harvey L. Schwartz.
    page cm
ISBN 978-0-415-64470-9 (hardback)–ISBN 978-0-203-07933-1 (ebook)
1. Psychic trauma in children–Complications–Treatment. 2. Post-traumatic stress
disorder in children–Complications–Treatment. 3. Dissociative disorders in children–Treatment. 4. Child soldiers–Social aspects. I. Title.
RJ506.P66S39 2013
618.92′8521–dc23   2012041694

ISBN13: 978-1-138-93238-8 (pbk)
ISBN13: 978-0-415-64470-9 (hbk)

Typeset in Galliard
by Cenveo Publisher Services

Contents

Preface

The intention of this book is to expand the interdisciplinary dialogue between the psychoanalytic and trauma/dissociation communities, while drawing a wider circle to include stakeholders advancing international justice and the rehabilitation of survivors of orchestrated violence and subjugation. By supporting a further cross-pollination of multidisciplinary perspectives, this work hopes to better elucidate, and thereby counter, one of the most hidden and disturbing aspects of the treatment of many complex trauma survivors – internalized perpetration.

Herein are integrated-treatment insights and caveats that synthesize the most valuable contributions from the clinical and theoretical systems that have shaped my effectual psychotherapeutic interventions and responses. This book does not offer clinicians a formula for conducting psychotherapy or a new list of techniques, nor does it promulgate a particular theoretical agenda for dissociative patients whose trauma is compounded by coerced and internalized perpetration. Presented here are useful perspectives on psychological transformation for seemingly intractable cases that have resisted redemption through other psychotherapeutic methods. The highest aim of this work is to raise my lantern alongside my courageous colleagues who strive to illuminate the connections between treating severely traumatized individuals and resolving the deep social and political problems of human exploitation and suffering. In the darkness of trauma's most remote outposts, may even a single candle inspire hope.

Acknowledgements

This book could not have been completed without the generosity and contributions of colleagues, friends and patients. First, my heartfelt thanks to Leonard Cetrangolo for his insightful feedback, outstanding editing, and for significant refinement of the final manuscript. I am grateful for the dedication and valuable clinical and editorial perspectives of Susanne Chassay and Cal Gough – contributions essential to the quality and completion of the book. Many thanks to Lisa Cardyn for her thorough and superb editorial comments, inspiration, and essential references. I am very appreciative of David Wasserman's and Karen Peoples' time, energy, and careful review of several chapters during various phases of the project. Thoughtful input, support, and general suggestions from my colleagues Melissa Farley, Larry Edwards, Anne Uemura, Martha Monetti, Jay Rosenblatt, Bobby Weinstock, Grace Furst, Catherine Miller, and James Kovacs have been important assets to this project. I would like to thank my editor, Jane Harris, and the editorial/publishing staff at Routledge for their support of this project, and for streamlining the entire publication process in a most collaborative and respectful manner. Finally, I would like to extend my deep appreciation to all the patients who for the past three decades have trusted me with stewarding their healing journeys, witnessing their trauma and transformation, and receiving their wisdom.

Chapter 1

The alchemy of wolves and sheep

> The shepherd drives the wolf from the sheep's throat, for which the sheep thanks the shepherd as his liberator, while the wolf denounces him for the same act as the destroyer of liberty.
>
> Abraham Lincoln

Overview

An unfortunate legacy of some unimaginably cruel childhoods – those in which children have been subjected to prolonged mind-altering immersion in malevolent familial, cult, criminal, and paramilitary systems – is inculcation into a culture of brutality, to the point of internalizing their perpetrators' identities and values. One of the worst transgressions against a victim occurs when a perpetrator systematically confuses the victim about his or her true identity through the victim's coerced violence against a third party. This traumatically bonds the child in forged complicity to his or her perpetrator. Even as theories and practices presented in the psychological literature on traumatic attachment have progressed over the past few decades – from acceptance of the Stockholm Syndrome onward – issues of coerced and internalized perpetration have yet to be fully elucidated and deconstructed.

Many dissociative trauma patients (e.g., severe child-abuse survivors, child and adult soldiers, gang members, prostitutes, trafficked individuals, and cult victims) report coerced perpetration as the most difficult aspect of their trauma histories and recoveries. When these victims do find their way to treatment, they often vehemently reject and undermine opportunities for liberation by re-enacting the confusion, threats, betrayals, and sadism of the pathological social systems wherein they were raised and indoctrinated. The acute, yet defiantly self-protective, deformation of a person's identity along with eruptions of dissociated aggression can destabilize the patient–therapist relationship in ways few clinicians have been adequately prepared to anticipate or manage. The well-documented plight of child soldiers who have been abducted into armed cartels and political revolutionary groups, or who have "volunteered" under a range of psychosocial and economic pressures in conflicts throughout the world, provides a valuable model of parallel processes resulting in perpetrator identity states. These children (and the adult survivors of child soldiering) lend important insights into the rehabilitation process of victims of coerced perpetration.

This book illuminates the psychological terrain at the far end of the spectrum of traumatic attachment and "identification with the aggressor" to provide valuable new perspectives on the psychodynamic challenges and opportunities for mental health professionals treating internalized perpetration in survivors of complex trauma. By standing on the shoulders of groundbreaking pioneers, whose insights into the processes and rehabilitation of child soldiers have informed my perspective, I present a systematic investigation of the parallel clinical profiles of Western trauma and dissociative disorders patients. In turn, my relational perspective may prove valuable to clinicians and policy makers designing protocols for child soldiers and others ensnared in victim–perpetrator–collaborator matrixes.

This book offers instructive, cautionary, and innovative therapeutic approaches grounded in relational psychoanalytic and archetypal theory to help transform the lives of survivors of complex trauma.

Introduction

The potential to become a perpetrator exists in every human being. When perpetration is cultivated in the psyches of traumatized children, numerous maturational processes are disrupted and deformed. Because of "successful" self-protective cover narratives, compensations, and dissociative self-organization, adult survivors of complex trauma[1] suffer a profound sacrifice of psychological, emotional, and spiritual development. This condition coincides with the emergence of alternate pathways of psychological development where defensive precocity, resilience, and degeneration appear in unusual combinations, including: activation of primitive impulses and concretization of aggressive fantasies; mobilization of precocious abstraction abilities and survivalist cognitive functions such as hypervigilance and hypermnesia; institutionalization of omnipotent thinking; and the management of emotional, sensory, and identity challenges with resourceful dissociative strategies (Kluft, 1999; Putnam, 1997; Schore, 2002, 2009; Van der Kolk *et al.* 1996). Those whose trauma experiences involved being forced to perpetrate extreme abuse against others carry an exceptionally heavy burden with them into treatment. Although this book addresses the treatment of internalized perpetrator identification in adult survivors of coerced perpetration in childhood, many of the underlying psychodynamics and treatment perspectives discussed here also apply to individuals whose identification with perpetration occurred through indirect (nonviolent), unconscious, intergenerational transmission, as well as to adult posttraumatic stress disorder patients – including war veterans, gang members, former prison inmates, victims of sex trafficking – who have been involved in acts of severe violence (and betrayal) against others in service to sub-cultural instructions and imperatives.[2]

Coerced, and then internalized, perpetration is one of the most challenging forms of psychic damage to heal psychotherapeutically. The difficulty with treating internalized perpetration is rooted in the paradoxes of survival mechanisms under tyrannical interpersonal conditions. Challenges derive primarily from the complex process of attachment to, and identification with, aggressors (A. Freud, 1936; Ferenczi, 1933).[3] This includes the self containing and internalizing terrifying alien objects, resulting in the antilibidinal ego or "internal saboteur" (Fairbairn, 1954). Further treatment complications involve the delicate intricacies required by the treatment of all complex dissociative disorders – especially victims of torture and mind control (Lacter, 2011; Miller, 2012; H. Schwartz, 2000), where overwhelming affects and frequent dangerous enactments threaten to undermine the basic therapeutic alliance. Psychotherapy for patients afflicted with the conflation of victim and perpetrator experiences naturally overlaps with broader psychotherapeutic approaches, yet must be designed along independent lines of inquiry and intervention.

By its nature, internalized perpetration tenaciously insists on remaining hidden.[4] The truth of coerced and internalized perpetration is not only sequestered in the psyche of the patient, but it is also unseen in the training of the majority of psychotherapists[5] and for the most part concealed in our culture at large. Prejudice and disgust are not uncommon professional attitudes toward victims of organized child abuse (where most coerced perpetration trauma occurs) and many professionals who treat these patients are subjected to, or fear, collegial skepticism. When internalized perpetration does reveal itself in therapy, the way it presents itself can be alarming and intimidating and it stubbornly resists treatment. A perpetrator personality state often provokes threats and actions against others (and the self) as re-enactments of the cruelty and betrayals of the pathological social systems in which victims were raised and indoctrinated.

Perpetrator alters are motivated by some of the same intrapsychic, attachment, and trauma-based stressors that inspire the development of the well-documented "hostile" or "persecutory" alter phenomenon in dissociative identity disorder (DID) patients (Kluft, 1984; Putnam, 1989; C. Ross, 1997). However, perpetrator alters and self-states tend to have a greater narcissistic investment in separateness (Kluft, 1984; 1999), and demonstrate more deeply entrenched pseudodelusionality (Kluft, 1987; 1996). They are more intensely organized around the severe dissociation-mobilizing affect states of disgust, shame, helplessness, rage, terror, and hopelessness, and maintain a deeper commitment to perpetrator protection and perpetrator ideology. Abuser personalities have long been understood as part of most severely dissociative patients' systems and mostly all clinicians and theorists encourage an appreciation of their protective function in the patient's life, regardless of their initial presentation. Some clinicians (Blizard, 1997; Curtis, 1997; H. Schwartz, 2000) have noted the existence of psychopathic or criminal self-states that wish only for their own power, find pleasure in deception, provocation, and "duping delight" (Salter, 1995; 2003) and chillingly embody archetypal demonic identifications.

Several authors (e.g., Lacter, 2011; Miller, 2012; Sinason, 1994; H. Schwartz, 2000; Vogt, 2008) have described the existence of perpetrator-engineered (i.e., not self-generated) and implanted self-states conjured under conditions of torture-based mind control extending to identifications with antisocial, criminal, and diabolical behaviors. Underscoring the differences between perpetrator self-states and other dissociative phenomena in complex trauma survivors, Vogt (2008) describes perpetrator states as demonstrating: startling unpredictability and intractability; shocking betrayals; choleric and coercive internal and interpersonal pressure; a pattern of quick, impulsive and violent actions followed by rapid withdrawals; and causing chronic mental confusion. Treating perpetrator states in violent, dissociative children, Marks (2012) has observed these children feel utterly demoralized and intimidated by their own unpredictable perpetrator behaviors and identities. When therapists try to deal with perpetrator introjects as if they were normal dissociative identities, Marks notes there is often a backlash in the therapy office, exasperating the therapist and patient alike. Perpetrator introjects can remain elusive and unresponsive to traditional trauma/dissociation treatment methods; unlike other self-states, they may circumvent normal processes of integration, sometimes moving underground only to emerge at full force at a later stage of treatment (Marks, 2012).

Traumatic attachment of victims to abusers and the misdirection of aggression in posttraumatic stress disorder patients have been well researched, however the particular dynamics that give rise to traumatically-induced perpetrator states have yet to be thoroughly excavated and studied. This deficiency of investigation is exacerbated by the fact that violent acts of coerced perpetration are often kept secret by adult patients as self-protection against incredulity, shame, and criminal liability. The child soldier phenomenon – the mechanics of their abduction/ recruitment/enlistment and the tentative paths to their rehabilitation – provides parallel patterns derived principally from non-Western contexts for understanding and treating perpetrator states in DID[6] patients, specifically adult survivors of severe child abuse who have been subjected to prolonged mind-altering immersion in criminal, familial, paramilitary, and cult systems where unspeakable deeds were coerced from the child both as a perverse end in itself and to forge an enduring allegiance.

Interview excerpts

Child soldiers

These interview fragments are based on excerpts of testimony from child soldiers who have at some point entered the demobilization process.

> I was attending primary school. The rebels came and attacked us. They killed my mother and father in front of my eyes. I was 10 years old. They took me with them [...] they trained us to fight. The first time

I killed someone, I got so sick, I thought I was going to die. But I got better […] My fighting name was Blood Never Dry.[7]

D., 16-year-old, Sierra Leonean male

The rebels told me to join them, but I said no. Then they killed my smaller brother. I changed my mind.[8]

L., 7-year-old, Sierra Leonean male

The rebels attacked my village. All the huts were burned and many people were killed. The RUF [Sierra Leone] rounded up those who lived. Then they took some young boys to go with them. They said they would kill us if we did not go. They gave me a rifle and told me to kill this woman […] she was my relative [aunt] and I didn't want to hurt her. They told me to shoot her or I would be shot. So I shot her […] I did it to survive.[9]

16-year-old, Sierra Leonean male

Everybody was gathered. They talked about us newly abducted children and they said: "You look like people who plan to escape and we are going to make you rebels now." They told us to lie down. Now we were surrounded by 40 rebels. They said: "Do not raise your head or we will kill all of you." We had to stretch our hands forward and put our foreheads to the ground. They started beating my back. Three hundred-fifty strokes were given on my back and buttocks. After a while the pain was so big that I felt that it would be better if I was dead. It was just too much to bear. Cold-ness started creeping into my body. And the trembling started. And then it happened again. I looked at my body from outside. I knew I would die. I saw death. It was in me. Death takes people's soul. My soul was already outside my body. I could feel pain, deep pain, but it was not from my back, from the strokes, it was everywhere inside me now […] I couldn't hear anything. I also didn't realize when it was that they had stopped beating me. But then I heard a loud voice: "Get up." I tried, but I couldn't sit. I kneeled for almost one hour. It felt like a very long time. I realized that all other children around me had died in the beating. I could see them lying still and not breathing. They were lying all around me. Their bodies were swollen and full of blood all over. The rebels dragged their bodies and dumped them into the nearby river.[10]

O. B., abducted at age 14 by Lord's Resistance Army, Ugandan male

I think I joined freely. All my friends were already part of this group, even my uncle and many of my cousins […] it didn't take me long to decide. In those days I was frightened since our home was attacked almost every night by bandits and other rebel groups as well. What did I have to lose? Also my parents were too poor to send me to school anymore. My mind was made up fast, I joined my friends and from that day I never went home to my parent's house again. I know you think, how can I not think of home, but I never did. I was totally there in the forest with the rebels, I only thought of today and the drugs we got there. One time my parents tried to find me and buy me out with a goat, but I didn't even look at them. Home did not exist anymore, you know, I was always under drugs from that day onwards. Also we had a purpose [...] many people come and want to rule us, they come and want our riches and we need to fight that, we need to fight for our freedom and to fight for our village. Our commander used to talk to us about this every morning when we met for morning assembly.[11]

> K.G., joined at 13-years-old, interviewed at 16-years-old
> male, Democratic Republic of Congo

I'm proud of what I learned – how to speak to groups, organize people, command, use weapons. I never got this from (the) government. How else am I supposed to have a future? If I had to do it again, I'd join again.[12]

> 16-year-old female commander in Sierra Leone

Dissociative identity disorder patients (perpetrator alters)

These interview fragments are taken from sessions with patients who are dissociative survivors of, among many traumas, coerced perpetration.

I am not a person. I am a creation of them [the abusers]. I am a cube posing as a person. I've been allowed to have a life providing I play by the rules and instructions book. If I don't I can be recalled. If I am recalled, I have to be broken down all over again. That would be a pain I could not survive.

> Alex, 42-year-old DID male

My father gave me two choices for disobeying him and having bad thoughts about the family. Either my new puppy, the one he had just bought for me, could die a slow and painful death at his hands or he said I could kill it quickly and put it out of its misery. He said if I loved him and I loved the puppy I should kill it quickly. After I killed it he had sex with me and told me what a good girl I was and after that he bought me ice cream and after that he told me that I was going to be of great use to the family some day and that the family had many enemies that I would enjoy killing.

> Sonja, 48-year-old DID female

If I tell you all my dirty secrets, I'll blow up, I'll explode, I'll bleed away, I'll bleed out.

> Jen, 52-year-old DID female

I'm afraid to think about it [the training to kill] or say it out loud. If I say it I might become it. If I tell you what they taught me I might become what they taught me – again. My head is not a safe place. It can make me turn into someone else.

Mike, 43-year-old DID male

Once you've crossed that line into hell you can never come back and you can never belong in this world again.

Steve, 44-year-old DID male

Don't you get it? I hated some of what I had to do or did; I just endured some, and yes I also liked some of it. Yeah, it was a mix. All right, there, I've said it. Do you still want to sit in the room with me?

John, 48-year-old DID male

Conflation of victim and perpetrator dynamics

Trauma and posttraumatic conditions have been widely documented and researched for decades, yet like the subject of dissociation, trauma continues to have its diagnostic-definitional challenges. Spiegel's (1990) description of trauma[13] is particularly useful because he speaks to both subjective and objective dimensions of the experience: "Trauma can be understood as being made into an object; the victim of someone else's rage, of nature's indifference, or of one's own physical and psychological limitations" (p. 251). Highlighting the assault and overwhelm of an individual's defenses, Spiegel (1990) and Herman (1992) describe the essence of trauma as including: unbearable helplessness; fragmentation in the sense of self and a view of the self as damaged or contaminated by the terror, humiliation, and pain that the events imposed; an inability to assimilate the event into one's own identity or cognitive framework; and "a realization that one's will and wishes have become irrelevant to the course of events" (Spiegel, 1990: 251).

Severe, ongoing trauma has been variously associated with "soul murder" (Shengold, 1989), "puncturing" (Howell, 2011) and "fragmentation of the psyche" (Herman, 1992; Kluft, 1984), and "altering the operation, functioning, and patterning of the brain" (Nijenhuis, 2003, 2004; Schore, 2002). Distinguishing between that which is unpleasant, disturbing, anxiety-provoking, and traumatic, Bromberg (2011) emphasizes that trauma consists of disorganizing hyperarousal that destabilizes significant relationship experience and overwhelms the mind's ability to reflect or cognitively process feelings, events, and meanings; this trauma-based dysregulation actually threatens the individual with annihilation of the continuity of selfhood.

Chronic extreme stress has the greatest potential to adversely affect cognitive and emotional development during childhood and adolescence when the mind and brain are particularly vulnerable and plastic (Putnam, 1997; Schore, 2002; Terr, 1990; Van der Kolk, 1996, 2005). Consistent exposure to significant stressors during sensitive developmental periods may cause the young brain to develop along a stress–responsive pathway – predominantly organized in a way to facilitate survival in a world of deprivation and danger, enhancing the individual's capacity to rapidly and dramatically shift into intense/angry/aggressive or fearful/fleeing/avoiding states when threatened (Herman, 1992; Schauer and Elbert, 2010; Van der Kolk, 1996, 2005).

According to Van der Hart *et al.* (2006), chronic trauma causes both a compartmentalization and an opposition of two basic psychobiologically-mediated self-organizing mental systems – those devoted to daily life and those devoted to defense. Overreacting, shutting down, under- and over-functioning, tendencies toward overgeneralizations and under-discrimination (Kluft, 2000; Putnam, 1997; C. Ross, 1997), and emotional and somatic flashbacks are products of this loss of integration. The impact of chronic traumatic environments in childhood has also been associated with adult deficits in critical and reflective thinking – a breakdown in the capacity to think about one's own mental states, processes, feelings, beliefs and interactions with others, i.e., loss of, or failure to develop, meta-cognitive functions (Fonagy *et al.*, 2002). Witnessing murder and committing violence against others are among the most serious, detrimental life events[14] that may cause all biologically mediated subsystems of attachment, learning, impulse control, affective regulation, and information processing to be adversely affected.

Because trauma changes not only the personality but the brain itself, victims' relationships with perpetrators and abusive caretakers become intricately interwoven with the trauma-based alterations in the brain's memory, shut-off, flight/fight, and bonding systems (Nijenhuis *et al.*, 2004). Like a malfunctioning fuse box, the psychologically traumatized neurobiological system contains counterintuitive irregularities, causing it to overreact or underreact to situations by way of distorted perspectives on the past (Stout, 2001). For survivors of chronic trauma, many dangers are misinterpreted as non-threatening, while neutral situations can be interpreted as dangerous (Herman, 1992; Kluft, 1984). Numbing responses and overreactions alternate unpredictably (Van der Kolk, 1989), and "not caring," apathy, and hope-aversion emerge as coveted defensive strategies offering transient relief from pain and a compelling illusion of freedom. It is always fundamentally easier for the child victim to introject the perpetrator than to be aware of his or her own victimization (Herman, 1992; Ross, 1989). Yet, when sadistic trauma fragments the personality, the victim is reduced to a state where primitive survival instinct and predatory/sadistic impulses are activated, making the victim's psyche highly porous to abuser training/directives.

Research has consistently shown that chronic exposure to trauma in the formative years may affect the maturation of the central nervous system and the neuro-endocrine system, with particular negative impact on the hippocampus[15] (Bremner *et al.*, 1997; Schore, 2002, 2009; Van der Kolk, 1996, 2005). Traumatically-induced alterations of cortical homeostasis seem to result in dysregulation of cognitive and narrative memory, while disruptions to the limbic system often result in emotional memory impairments. Biological defense mechanisms such as depersonalization, derealization, numbing, and in extreme cases catatonia and "tonic immobility"[16] are activated by the chronically stressed central nervous system (Marx *et al.*, 2008; Perry and Pollard, 1998). Although dissociation allows the traumatized child to survive psychologically and physically, over time dissociative defenses often become maladaptive, emerging at inappropriate times in neutral situations that may trigger nonverbal/bodily memories of earlier trauma; or in situations of true danger, self-protective cognition and behaviors may be blocked (Kluft, 1985; Putnam, 1989; C. Ross, 1997). Kluft (1990) refers to this latter aspect of dissociative disorders patients' dilemma as "sitting duck syndrome." As Bloom (1997) states, the cognitive consequence of all of this confusion and reversal is that chronically traumatized people cannot predictably count on their emotions to provide the proper evaluative information; they can no longer trust what they feel or think. Activities that might normally provide pleasure may instead evoke terror, rage, or despair. Experiences that normally incite fear and dread may become pleasurable and addictive. Numbness and deadness may be soothing and longed for, while expansiveness, joy, and serenity may be perceived as uncomfortably unreliable or dangerous. In this inversion of comfort and dread, villains may become heroes and rescuers frightening enemies.

Children who have learned to cope with trauma by dissociating may fail to develop other age appropriate defensive patterns. Over-reliance upon dissociative adaptations disrupts information processing and cognitive and emotional integration, often leading to problems with discernment, affect regulation, and self-protection (Joshi and O'Donnell, 2003; Putnam, 1997). Deployment of dissociative defenses, anticipatory dread, avoidance, and unconscious re-enactment of trauma may become a way of life. Almost all relationships become unconsciously charged with a propensity for replications of victim–perpetrator dynamics (Herman, 1992; Kluft, 1999; C, Ross, 1997; Van der Kolk, 2005).

Echoing research by LeDoux (1996; 2000)'s,[17] Steele, Van der Hart, and Nijenhuis (2009)'s model of "structural dissociation of the personality" emphasizes that traumatic material is registered differently and apart from benign experience as it occurs. When an individual experiences aversive stimuli, threat, or danger, Steele *et al.* posit that mental representations and behavioral instincts are activated to escape threats. These experiences are registered in emotional parts of the personality with psychobiological functions separate from the system used to integrate normal or appealing stimuli. In the face of chronic trauma, double binds and/or unpredictable primary attachment figures, the healthy separation and dedication of the two psychobiological systems affecting memory and attachment can become dangerously muddled.

Sophisticated perpetrators make use of these confusions to exploit a victim's pliability under conditions of terror, pain, helplessness, and captivity – conditions over which they position themselves as the masters. As Vogt (2008) describes, weaker and more vulnerable traumatized individuals must resort to dissociation

to switch off unbearable feelings and sensations, and the victim's self-develop-
ment becomes informed by the perpetrator(s)' position over the victim. As a
function of social imprints embedded in our species, cognitive orientation/
worldview is copied from the "superior object" (abuser/perpetrator/caretaker)
in order to maximize the possibility of survival.[18] In search of a relief from this
extreme alienation, the survivor/coerced-perpetrator transmutes the annihilating
assault on subjectivity into a form of inclusion and comfort. The victim's
cultivated helplessness becomes a psychological platform, from which coerced-
perpetration can be staged.

> The psychopathic moment is a virtually universal moment in all lives. When
> we are faced with intolerable, uncontainable dread, the natural tendency is to
> identify with the persecutor, becoming the agent of doom as the only way of
> controlling it. Evil is the attempt to inflict one's doom on others, becoming
> doom, rather than living subject to it. In this sense evil is bad faith, the lie
> that one could escape one's fate by inflicting it on others.
>
> Alford (1997:58)

Lacter (2011) raises the question of whether torture actually enhances
the brain's capacity not only for dissociation but for storing information in
pristine form. She goes on to describe how the central mechanisms that facilitate
the efficacy of torture-based mind control can force a victim's psyche to form
new, readily programmable self-states,[19] separated from the "front" personality
by amnesic barriers that can be exploited to hold and hide directives, skills, and
information. Both coerced perpetration and torture-based mind control may
lead to the creation of new, compliant personality states, the manufacture of
which bypasses the victim's self-protective mechanisms and exploits dissociative
adaptive survival mechanisms.

Regressing into perpetration

New identifications with diabolism, domination, righteousness, and
idealized-evil drive the victim/coerced-perpetrator's violent behavior and paranoid and megalomaniacal worldviews.[20] The chain of perpetration links the
perpetrator to the victim and establishes a social norm in groups giving rise to
what Grand (2000:17) has termed "malignant dissociative contagion." Malignant
dissociative contagion refers to the intrapsychic and interpersonal network of
influence between perpetrators, bystanders, and victims (Grand, 2000).

The same capacity for dissociative encapsulation that enabled the victim's
survival leaves self-protective aspects of his or her personality walled off and
unavailable for later healing and integration. Under conditions of chronic terror
and torture, dissociative compartmentalizing of the self may be one of the psyche's
alternatives to the formation of an indiscriminate, and wholesale, corrupt character
structure. Howell (2011) believes that dissociative self-protection (the dissociation

of rageful and terrified states) can facilitate the preservation of the capacity to love, in spite of how seemingly obliterated that capacity to love might have become through immersion in pathological interpersonal matrices. An essential function of perpetrator self-states in dissociative trauma survivors may be to hold ruthlessness and ambition (for potential later integration), along with actulazing needs for recognition and validation from cruel, inconsistent caretaker/abusers, for prosocial parts of the patient's self. This compartmentalization allows a modicum of positive interpersonal functioning and potential to be realized.

Extreme adaptations to trauma may present clinically as unitary pseudo-integration of the personality or as dissociative states that consistently undermine the individual's efforts to organize a new life based on good object relations. With survivors of extreme terror and environmental failure,[21] some psychoanalysts (Bion, 1967; Klein, 1975; Meltzer, 1973/2008; Rosenfeld, 1971) describe severe regressions where primitive envy, psychotic processes, and the death instinct infiltrate into healthy parts of the patient's personality. Victims of "regressions through destructiveness" confuse the internal and external world, exhibit "manic denial" of external reality, and live in persecutory dread that annihilates the potential for trust, tenderness, or productive intrapsychic conflict (Meltzer, 1973/2008).

Similarly, De Masi (2003) describes pathological deformations of the personality under stress that lead to the absolute elimination of anxiety, guilt, and shame. These perversions represent a mixture of excitation and indifference that replaces real human relational engagement. Eroticization of power and cruelty may become a "stabilizing" focal point in a pathological restructuring of the personality. Instead of rage at bad or threatening objects, there is idealization. This developmental (or perhaps anti-developmental) tract echoes the perverse exploitation of larger social collapse and disorder by fascistic and fundamentalist leaders to who take over fragile communities. Rosenfeld's (1971) compelling portrait of "destructive narcissism" shows how the patterns within many perpetrator groups are present in the psyches of many trauma patients whose dissociative structures have been co-opted by their abusers.

> The destructive narcissism of these patients appears often highly organized, as if one were dealing with a powerful gang dominated by a leader, who controls all the members of the gang to see that they support one another in making the criminal destructive work more effective and powerful. However, the narcissistic organization...has a defensive purpose to keep itself in power and so maintain the status quo. The main aim seems to be to prevent the weakening of the organization and to control the members of the gang so that they will not desert the destructive organization and join the positive parts of the self or betray the secrets of the gang to the police, or the protecting super-ego, standing for the helpful analyst, who might be able to save the patient.
>
> (p. 174)

Describing a breakdown of the personality at the far end of the trauma continuum, Goldberg (2000) suggests that some patients may suffer a complete disintegration both of meaning and its psychological containers. He describes an emergent self, rising from the ashes of catastrophic environmental and psychic failure that is inured to human pain. Often this pattern of personality reorganization is accompanied by a hyper-rational mind that is simulating sanity, morality, and coherence, but is frantically devoted to the destruction of all signs of hope in the world and all manifestations of love of life. Goldberg notes that such extreme adaptations to trauma create likely insurmountable obstacles to integration and reconciliation.

Goldberg (2000) draws an important connection between the social patterns leading to a community's decay and the breakdown of the personality in advance of its malevolent transformation. He posits the dynamics of evil are not solely in aberrations of the personality or endogenous conflicts, but moreover in the catastrophic failure of the broader environment to support healthy development. Degradation of vital components of the social matrix – prominently family, community, religious and political-economic structures – creates fault lines in the collective containers that may precipitate the collapse of normative values. This disintegration may explain how ordinary people under conditions of societal deterioration are susceptible to the ingratiation of evil. For approaching evil within psychoanalysis, Goldberg distinguishes destructiveness based on conflict and relatedness from destructiveness originating from a nihilistic drive to eradicate life and purposefulness. "Helping patients differentiate *being* evil from *imitating* evil in order to survive encounters with evil is a labor-intensive process" (H. Schwartz, 2000:412).

Traditional training of therapists, even within trauma-oriented professional organizations, does not adequately prepare clinicians for these menacing encounters with internalized perpetrator dynamics.[22] Navigating the revolving and superimposed positions of victim and perpetrator in the psyche of one individual can be overwhelming in the profoundly dissociative and in less fragmented forms. Through a variety of coercive processes, the perpetrators have entered the patient's mind and their representations will inevitably enter the therapy relationship, challenging it at its core. Aspects of a trauma survivor's personality will endeavor doggedly to undermine the treatment in a manner tantamount to having the original perpetrators themselves in the room facing off against the therapist. The therapist's awareness, knowledge and skill in handling this particular aspect can make or break a treatment.

Perpetrator self-states

All perpetrator personality states represent traumatic encapsulations of perpetrator approved, imitated, and/or coerced behavior (Vogt, 2008). Based on her observations of aggressive, dissociative children, Marks (2012) reports that the most common introjects are violent, sexualized, controlling, suicidal and homicidal introjects. Perpetrator alters in adult DID patients have a wide range of tasks, skills, and motivations (e.g., couriers, informers, torturers, sexual sadists, actors in pornography films, executioners, overseers, priestesses, and group leaders). Alter personalities of highly dissociative patients are motivated primarily by survival at their root, but this can be aggravated into motives of power, status, relief of pain and anxiety, narcissistic gratification, and revenge impulses. Because coerced perpetration disrupts normative developmental advancement, the reworking of all coerced perpetration trauma is a rehabilitation of an individual's developmental capacities.

According to Vogt (2008), the relative severity of dissociative self-systems may be described using comparative measurements along three dimensions: (1) degree of dissociation, (2) degree of availability for modification, and (3) the degree to which the patient was "switched off" (chemically, traumatically, hypnotically, etc.) during the creation of the personality state. The spectrum progresses from the mild and more easily observed perpetrator internalization, through the progressively more obdurate introject-states,[23] then finally to the most difficult and intractable implant- and programmed-states.

The intentional cultivation of dissociative identity disorder in child victims whose multiple perpetrator-loyal states (with separate but overlapping motivations and functions) co-exist in service to authoritarian perpetrators most often include strategies to avoid detection by the larger community. According to several researcher/clinicians (Lacter, 2011; Miller, 2012; Vogt, 2008) some introject, implants, and most programmed states are under the executive control of the perpetrator(s). In the extreme, the patient experiences him or herself as being remotely controlled, with completely ego-alien feelings, thoughts, beliefs, impulses, commitments, and agendas that stand apart from his or her everyday self.[24]

Based on the social organization seen in the Jewish ghettos of World War II in Eastern Europe, Frankel and O'Hearn (1996) created a compelling classification system for the hostile and perpetrator-identified personalities found within most DID patients. Most split-off aggression is located in what they call the "anti-bonding force" which consists of four subsets of dissociated identities:

- *Enforcers*: Arrogant, challenging, persecutory personalities, anesthetized to pain, who have amnesia for the circumstances surrounding their original emergence in the self-system. They control by force, threat, intimidation, and inciting acts of self-harm.
- *Deniers, self-blamers, and approval seekers*: Diverting and misleading the clinician, they seek to prevent or distort the disclosure of newly emerging traumatic material. They may facilitate re-engagement with perpetrators, and foster denial inside and outside the system. Using self-blame, self-derogation and other confusion tactics, they create doubt.
- *Internal leaders*: Remaining hidden behind other alters, they strategically discourage bonding with the therapist for fear it will put the entire system

in danger. They distort and reframe information and experience to match perpetrator ideology and belief systems.

- *Independent forces.* "Independently" self-directed, these alters trust no one inside or outside of the dissociative system – including any of the sources to whom they report. Their observational acuity is potentially useful to the therapy, however they generally provoke disruptions in treatment, and at times they impersonate other alters. They leverage distrust as a survival strategy.

Virtually all perpetrator-identified alter personalities are the terrorized, shame-ridden, desperate, and ruthless child aspects of the personality. When perpetrator identities enter the treatment process, they can undermine all prior psychotherapy progress with threats of premature termination, suicide, and/or blackmail. Unprepared therapists will understandably be alarmed and conflicted by how to parse their responsibilities to themselves and to their patient. Untreated perpetrator states leave some patients at risk of criminal behavior and re-engagement with their perpetrator(s). It is essential that the therapist is familiar with the psychological literature on thought reform and group violence, and have a grasp of the history of extreme victimization across cultures to assist patients in understanding their traumatic experiences in larger social and historical (external) contexts. Because most traumatic subjugation experiences occur in isolation, linking victims' personal histories to the longer historical record of abuse and liberation struggles provides an objective frame through which patients can approach their own deprogramming, destigmatization, and recovery.

The therapist's capacity to lead a fearless and detailed inquiry into the feelings, specific events, and mechanics of perpetration experiences (e.g., torture) is imperative for successful treatment outcomes. This investigation must include the full unearthing of perpetrator-loyal belief systems, perpetrator-identified states, the indoctrination techniques, and the threatened consequences of "betraying" the perpetrator. Unflinching examination of all the details of coerced perpetration and mind control demonstrates strength and courage, by therapist and patient, in confronting material that most people would be inclined to disbelieve or shun. Perpetrators count on disbelief and avoidance of abhorrent behavior as a tactical obstacle to discovery and credibility. Tolerating the uncomfortable feelings that accompany witnessing the specifics of a victim's revelations is an indispensable requisite for healing.

Interview excerpts

Child soldiers

I raised my gun and pulled the trigger, and I killed a man. Suddenly, as if someone was shooting them inside my brain, all the massacres I had seen since the day I was touched by war began flashing in my head. Every time

I stopped shooting to change magazines and saw my two young lifeless friends, I angrily pointed my gun into the swamp and killed more people. I shot everything that moved until we were ordered to retreat because we needed another strategy.[25]

Ishmael Beah, rehabilitated child soldier, Sierra Leone

It's like magic. I kill people and it doesn't stick to me. I still go to heaven.[26]

Bad Pay Bad, age unknown, Sierra Leonean male child soldier

It's easier the second time. You become indifferent.[27]

L., 15-year-old Columbian male

Last night I fired a rocket-propelled grenade against a tank. The Americans are weak. They fight for money and status and squeal like pigs when they die. But we will kill the unbelievers because faith is the most powerful weapon.[28]

M., 12-year-old Iraqi male

At age 11, I remember the commander coming home to the house early and I had not cleaned-up yet. He beat me severely for that. From that day onwards he would do it regularly. Sometimes so much that I had to go to hospital, but the rebels always took me out again forcefully and brought me back before my wounds were healed. One day when I was 12 years old we saw how children in a school were forced to eat their own teacher by the LRA; apparently the man had resisted giving food to the rebels. At age 14 years, the commander started raping me and told me that I am now his wife. A few months later I had my first baby. It was a beautiful child, but I did not know how to look after him, so he died soon. In the same year, there was a fierce battle with the UPDF [Uganda People's Defense Force], an air attack, where many of our people in the settlement died. At age 16, I gave birth to another baby. The next morning when I woke up, also he had died. He had been tiny and weak and he probably died from the cold night air, since I had nothing to cover him. One day soon after this we saw how the Lutugu people got hold of enemies and poured boiling water over their bodies until they died. At age 18, I had to take part in a raid on Lira IDP camp. We were trying to get new abductees and food, but people resisted, so 18 of them were killed by our group. At age 20, I gave birth to George in the bush. He is weak, but he is still alive, I so much hope that he will grow up. That same year during an attack by government soldiers – the rebels, including my husband, left me behind. I guess I was a burden to them, since we women with small children were not able to run fast.[29]

V.A., abducted by Lord's Resistance Army, 20-years-old at time of interview, Ugandan female

Dissociative identity disorder patients (perpetrator alters)

After some time and a lot of sexual abuse, and some training with hurting and killing animals and babies, they brought a young boy about my age for me to spend time with. I don't know where he came from. Probably one of those lost or stolen or throwaway children, you call them, I think. They let me bond with him. I did. He was like a friend, but something was wrong with him so he was not like a normal kid. Still, I was so lonely and he was like a friend. Then one day they did stuff to try to get us mad at one another. They gave us drugs and provoked us. I know now it was a set up but I did not know that back then. They put a gun in my hand. I don't know how it all happened but I shot him and killed him. He was my friend. They told me I was a very good boy and a brave boy. They taught me that he was born to die and I was born to live and kill. They said that's how it is, that I should get used to it.

Mike, 43-year-old DID male

You have no idea how precious it is to not care about anything or anybody anymore.

Sarah, 45-year-old DID female

My fury contains my terror because without my rage and hatred I would just be swallowed up by my nothingness.

Val, 39-year-old DID female

I don't want to be helped and I don't want to be loved. I just want to be left alone. If I am continuously mean to you [the therapist] and torment you the way I have been doing in here then maybe I will make you hate me and then you will make me go away, and then that will be that – I won't have anything to be worried about anymore – I'll be through with all of this. If I trust you I have to feel, and I don't want to feel anything. It could kill me.

Jared, 42-year-old DID male

I had to wreck my therapy, or try to wreck it anyway, in order to find out if it could take me where I need to go [...] I feel so vile and unlovable and I hate you for thinking you could see me differently, that you could find compassion for me, find me worth anything. Something in me needs to attack you for that.

Anna, 52-year-old DID female

With all your [therapist's] hard work, there's still no real danger of breaking through. Don't let yourself think that anyone is worried that you are even getting close. It's like they're still dancing in the ballrooms of Berlin and you haven't even landed your troops at Normandy yet.

John, 48-year-old DID male

My system is like a set of non-intersecting terrorist cells. Each one thinks it's the only one, and each has no idea of the existence of the others. But the whole system is like a hierarchy, but not a vertical up and down hierarchy, a sphere hierarchy, kind of like a dandelion, with a black center in the middle that controls everything and the rest are duped on one level or another, expendable, and replaceable. As long as the black center orb stays intact, there can be more cells produced and the system could go on ad infinitum.

Keith, 57-year-old DID male

Child soldiers and dissociative trauma survivors

Although I have been working with the subjects of traumatic attachment, mind control, thought reform, coerced-perpetration, and complicity for three decades, it was not until I had read a haunting memoir of a former child soldier that I became inspired to consider a renewed methodology of relational psychotherapy for the treatment of coerced-perpetration in complex trauma. Ishmael Beah's *Long Way Gone: Memoirs of a Boy Soldier* details his harrowing journey in Sierra Leone from childhood innocence through his complete corruption in the savagery of child soldiering, then ultimately to his miraculous redemption via a unique set of therapeutic settings, processes, and relationships. From a brutal childhood in one of the world's most gruesome civil wars to the zigzagging process of demobilization treatment in a United Nations rehabilitation center, Beah is the first child soldier to give voice to one of the most bizarre and disturbing phenomena that has thankfully been under the lens of international human rights organizations since the last years of the 20th century (Boyd, 2007).

Beah's experiences in the African civil war are replete with sociopathic rebel leaders and national army forces inflicting diabolical cruelties, mostly on civilians. These included participation in the slaughter of innocents from his own region, as is a common initiation practice in the training of child soldiers (Schauer and Schauer, 2010; P. Singer, 2006; Wessels, 2006). Reading Beah's book, I was inspired by the unwavering compassion and sustained love from those who battled to extricate him from his degenerated life.

Many of the severely dissociative trauma patients I have treated, or consulted on, over the past three decades – especially those who have reported involvement in destructive familial, criminal, cult systems – have endured violations comparable to the gruesome forms of organized child abuse found in Beah's accounts. Pimps, pedophiles, charismatic cult leaders, militia commanders, and other ruthless narcissistic predators know how to exploit a child's vulnerability to traumatic attachments and identity reconfiguration. They know how to foster and exploit silencing, complicity, and incredulity in both victims and larger communities. They understand how to destroy innocence – how to suffocate it in unbearable shame. This tactical cunning allows many opportunistic perpetrators to operate without restraint. With the harnessing and perversion of healthy human bonding, successful predators are able to turn victims into devoted allies. By a systematic disabling of the victim's capacity for self-protection and discernment, the perpetrator becomes the only source of guidance and protection available.

In some situations of chronic exploitation, a child's hurt and anger are purposefully not recognized or brutally punished. Many child victims are fed religious or spiritual justifications for their abuse, such as God is choosing them, loving them, punishing them, or abandoning them by way of the traumatizing events. Many of my patients have spoken of radical splits in their dissociative systems between "day and night" selves, or "left and right" selves, and insist on keeping these separate long after their active submission in perpetrator groups has ended. The ability of a child to sustain symbiotic loyalty to perpetrators will come to depend on the dissociative compartmentalization of aggression or its redirection toward other victims (including the self). In such circumstances the child comes to see his or her own aggression as threatening rather than that of the perpetrator (Howell, 1997). This process results in the idealization of the perpetrator and the devaluation of the self; the self is exalted only when honoring or imitating the perpetrator.

This counterintuitive form of captor/captive bonding was first given a name in 1973[30]: Stockholm Syndrome (Soskis and Ochberg, 1982). This condition embodies several of the essential attachment paradoxes (Graham, 1994): gratitude for the perpetrator having spared the victim's life, the leveraging of small kindnesses, false mediation and "resolution" between captor and hostage through coerced sympathy for the ideological agenda of the perpetrator, and won-over identification with the devaluation of perpetrator enemies. These attachments compensate for the larger picture of the perpetrator's cruelty. Graham (1994) maintains that prolonged terror and isolation can result in a situation whereby the victim's sense of self is experienced exclusively through the eyes of the abuser. Many pimps have skillfully mastered this technique to efficiently manage large numbers of prostitutes by exploiting their victims' desire to please them (Schwartz et al., 2007). The effects of a pimp's mind-control on prostitutes hinge on classical identification with the aggressor. Stockholm Syndrome is merely the outer (and consensually validated) layer of a more complex configuration for personality alteration in the hands of perpetrators who have more prolonged influence over victims.

Patients from intergenerational, interfamilial and criminal cults and cartels describe specific child-rearing practices that involve the use of pain and fear (e.g., starving, burning, beating, sensory deprivation, overexposure to severe heat and cold, sexual sadism, electrical shock torture) (Lacter, 2011; Miller, 2012; Noblitt and Perskin, 2000; Sinason, 1994). Such experiences, which trigger and then institutionalize dissociative responses at an early age, can disrupt the usual differentiation of self- and other-representations; concurrently it creates a storehouse of rage that can be harnessed and redirected by perpetrators and programmers.

The most insidious victim–perpetrator dynamic occurs when a child is coerced into perpetration against other innocents. Encountered in almost every case of child soldiering, ritual abuse[31] (M. Smith, 1993; Noblitt and Noblitt, 2008;

Noblitt and Perskin, 2000; R. Schwartz, 2011; Sinason, 1994, 2011a; Young *et al.*, 1991), and spiritual abuse (Sinason, 2011b), coerced perpetration sabotages the free will and moral conscience of the child for the perpetrator's agenda; yet it is framed by the adult, and experienced by the child, as a choice. Grand (2000) uses the term "bestial gesture" (p. 113) to describe situations in which trauma victims are offered the perpetrator(s)' "approving embrace" following the victim's coerced moral transgressions. Such approbation may include rewards, affection, drugs, sex, or simply cessation of the victim's suffering. When isolated victims' most devastating experiences have occurred without cohorts with whom to commiserate, and the only outlet for reparative gestures has been the perpetrator, the victim must invent an empathic other in the perpetrator who is then only a mirroring object, the victim's only human link. Resulting perpetrator-sponsored personality deficiencies may completely eradicate victims' capacities for healthy guilt and remorse. When a dissociative individual (often through a child-alter) remembers predating on others – inflicting pain on, or having to perform sex acts with, other children, luring or kidnapping them to be victimized and sometimes killing them, having to select which child would be tortured or killed, defecating on a Bible, "spitting in the face of God", or torturing and dismembering animals – he or she experiences him or herself as irredeemably "bad" and "evil," and even retrospectively as an adult is locked into a false perception of voluntary participation. Some dissociative patients' self-damnation can slow the therapy's integration process down for an extended period, or worse become a permanent impediment to the completion of healing.

Perpetrator-identified self-states, including alter personalities,[32] may be more common in severely dissociative patients than has previously been appreciated. Perpetrator alters may be the rigid organizing principle in extreme cases of "disorganized attachment" (Blizard, 2003; Hesse and Main, 1999). These alters may also serve a variety of psychodynamic functions (i.e., maintaining narcissistic equilibrium, rescue fantasies, ambivalence, conflict evasion, ruthlessness, ambition, and avoidance of grieving) for the rest of the dissociative patient's self-system. When attempting to identify and engage these self-states, therapists are likely to encounter intractable forms of avoidance, distraction, and counterattack – all of which are likely to provoke a disruption in treatment. Like other components of the dissociative personality system, these self-states are part of an intricate self-protection system (Kluft, 1984, 1999; Putnam, 1989, 1997; C. Ross, 1997). Perpetrator ego-states must manage the anxieties inherent in what R. Schwartz (2011) calls the ever-present double threat of therapy: either the therapist is seen to be luring or seducing the patient into a trap, like others in the patient's life have previously done, or the therapist's authentic engagement in a benevolent relationship is experienced as a threat to the attachment to the abuser(s) and the perpetrator system.

Perpetrator-identified states transfer responsibility from themselves and the original perpetrators onto the victim.[33] Some dissociative survivors have other non-violent alter personalities that believe their internal perpetrator alter is the mastermind perpetrator. For these deeply confused and highly dissociated alters, the discernment between internal and external danger has completely broken down. Perpetrator alters may even be "best friends" of the actual perpetrator; in this role they serve as excellent blockades to criminal and legal recourse. Treatment can be repeatedly undermined as the mechanisms of the trauma, such as malice, humiliation, and betrayal are compulsively re-enacted. This type of sabotage is likely if the patient is revealing secrets or begins significant developmental progress by building trust with the therapist.

Although treatment involves connecting with one unique individual at a time, it benefits the therapist and patient to contextualize the journey of healing in the broadest historical and mythological context of heroic power struggles. Coerced, and then internalized perpetration is one of the darkest shadows of the human experience. However, this sinister pall also holds the archetypal[34] potentials inherent in all human struggles. Archetypal potentials serve to hold a space for the possibility of an unexpected return to wholeness after the collapse of all hope. This is inherent in all archetypal narratives where the inner landscape of fear, self-doubt, and self-betrayal must be traveled concurrently with the outer physical world's treacherous terrain,[35] populated with morally ambiguous shape-shifters.

Interview excerpts

Child soldiers

Most times I dream, I have a gun, I'm firing, I'm killing, cutting, amputating. I feel afraid, thinking perhaps that these things will happen to me again. Sometimes I cry […] When I see a woman I'm afraid of her. I've been bad with women; now I fear that if I go near one she'll hit me. Perhaps she will kill me.[36]

Z., 14-year-old Liberian male

When I came out of the bush, I didn't know what I would do, how I would live – nothing. I didn't know if it's possible to live in the village or maybe I should go fight again. But I was so tired of fighting; I decided to try another way. When I was a little boy, my grandfather helped me build things […] Now I am learning to be a carpenter and I know what to do.[37]

Child soldier, age-unknown Sierra Leonean male

When I was out in the forest I was feeling nothing. I was drugged all the time. But after I had come out and now since I stay in this transit center, I get these terrible nightmares. They are always about the children we killed, especially their crashed skulls and I hear the voice of my commander telling me to do things. I wake up and get so frightened. My heart is beating strong these days and something in my head is so wrong. On one hand, I have a new life and I have left the forest behind and also all the hardship of those days. On the other, I think of the times and especially the drugs we had. Sometimes at night I walk out of the building, especially when I get the dreams and stare at the sky. I would just wish that my head gets normal again.[38]

K.K.G., 16 years old at time of interview,
Democratic of Congo, Mai-Mai fighter, male

After crossing that line, I was not a normal kid [...] I became completely unaware of the dangerous and crooked road that my life took. In fact, most of the horrible events that I went through didn't affect me until after I was taken out of the army and put in a psychosocial therapy home years later. At the psychosocial therapy, I began to experience my trauma. I had sleepless nights. Every night I recalled the last day that my childhood was stripped away from me. I felt I had no reason for staying alive since I was the only one left in my family. I had no peace. My soul felt corrupted and I was lost in my own thoughts, blaming myself for what happened to me. The only time I found peace with myself was when I began writing songs about the good times before the war. Through these writings, as well as the help of the staff in my psychosocial therapy home, I was able to successfully overcome my trauma. I once again found my childhood that was almost lost. I realized that I had a great determination to survive.[39]

I., 14-year-old country-unknown, male

Dissociative identity disorder patients (perpetrator alters)

The part I am most afraid to say is about the rush, the zap, the adrenalin. It's a power. You wouldn't understand. You haven't killed anyone. Not that I know anyway. You probably wouldn't tell me if you had. I can tell though you haven't. I can tell these things about people. You're not like me. We are like marked people. We can see each other. We know it's not all bad. There is a rush, and something feels good seeing the life go out of somebody and you did it. You made it happen. And then it feels awful, and then it goes numb, and then sometimes it feels good again. Sometimes that's where the drugs come in. They help. Do you really think there's a cure for people like me?

Jared, 42-year-old DID male

For some parts of me even the sight of blood makes me sick and for other parts the sight or taste of blood makes us numb [...] but for other parts, the ones I am most afraid of, the taste of blood feels good and makes them feel powerful. They like it. A lot. No matter what you [the therapist] say, I don't believe you would feel the same about these different parts of me. You couldn't be that nice, that fair, that neutral, and I don't deserve it anyway.

Carrie, 46-year-old DID female

I want to hurt you and then again I don't want to hurt you. This is why I may not be able to stay in therapy. This is my dilemma. You always said I could talk about everything but I have been too scared to talk about wanting to kill you for fear that I would kill you just by talking about wanting to. Like the babies I had to kill and the children I had to hurt with them [...] in this case you are the baby and I am the killer and I do not want to do that to anyone ever again. The more I talk about wanting to kill you, directly, from the place in me that wants or thinks it wants to really kill you, the more I realize that I am not going to do that, and that this may be a safe place to be.

> Mike, 43-year-old DID male

I don't have to do their [the perpetrators'] dirty work anymore. I don't have to stay in their boxes or anyone's boxes. My mind and spirit were broken but that's not the whole story or the whole of me. I know you know I am quivering as I say this.

> Toni, 45-year-old DID female

One day it happened. Unexpectedly. I heard a voice in my head saying "you are not a trauma survivor anymore." It was not like old denial or perpetrator voices. No, it came from a loving place deep inside, from before and beyond and including the trauma and suffering, saying "you are much more than that, you are a human being and you deserve to live and to love, to occupy your own life."

> Fran, 55-year-old DID female

Basic clinical perspective

In recent years, psychoanalytic and trauma theorists have begun to ask whether psychotherapy can effectively address the problem of evil. Perpetration's annihilation of subjectivity is a quintessential vehicle for the transmission and enactment of evil. Coerced perpetration along with coerced complicity represent major elements contributing to what Grand (2000) termed "the reproduction of evil." Incremental advances in understanding the structure and treatment of psychological adaptations to coerced perpetration trauma can add to the professional discourse on treatment of survivors of extreme malevolence, to offer measured hope to clinicians and patients facing one of the most obscured and poorly understood terrains of psychological trauma: the propagation of evil.

Throughout this book are important concepts and principles drawn from five overlapping clinical traditions: trauma/dissociation theory, contemporary/relational psychoanalysis; archetypal (e.g., Jungian, Buddhist psychology, transpersonal psychology); cult, ritual abuse and mind control treatment; and child soldier demobilization. Each of these traditions offers unique perspectives – at times opposing or overlapping – for confronting the aftermath of acts of evil.

In synthesizing these traditions, I was motivated by a commitment to interdisciplinary discourse and the value of cross-fertilization of clinical perspectives. The challenging clinical dilemmas of coerced and internalized perpetration will benefit from the wisdom of multiple therapeutic and philosophical perspectives. The phenomena of coerced perpetration is perversely adaptive (i.e., resistant) so an integrated multidisciplinary approach to recovery is an advantageous fortification of resources.

Therapeutic action

The essential elements of therapeutic action proposed throughout the book include:

- Establishing safety and stabilization
- Sustaining affective attunement
- Compassionate witnessing
- Limit-setting, boundary maintenance, confrontation of attitudes and behaviors that undermine the therapeutic alliance
- Holding, containing, detoxifying
- Empathic, "experience-near" interpreting
- "Interpreting both trauma-based and characterological patterns embedded within dissociative self-organization"
- Welcoming linear and non-linear narratives, dreams and anomalous experiences
- Deconditioning: traumatic hypo- and hyper-activity and traumatic relational paradigms
- Linking/bridging self-states, modeling the principle of inclusivity
- Fostering dialogue through encouraging mutuality and negotiation
- Facilitating inquiry, the cultivation of introspection and curiosity
- Benevolently disrupting fixed ideas, encapsulated states, pathological attachments and rigid belief systems including deprogramming all indoctrinations and perpetrator ideologies
- Engaging in "reverie" (after Bion,1965; 1967), ongoing transformational emotional exchanges between the mind of the patient and the mind of the therapist, aimed at metabolizing previously unmanaged, undigested, and unknown elements of the patient's psyche and experience
- Sharing the experience of the patient's impact on the therapist, and encouraging the patient to share his or her experience of the therapist's impact on him or her
- Confronting and repudiating destructiveness and analyzing patterns of duping, betrayal, and intimidation
- Facilitating confession, and understanding responsibility for ethical transgressions
- Reiteration of informed consent at different junctures and passages

- Analyzing enactments to generate insight and increase competency in affect regulation
- Engaging healthy aggression, self-protection, self-assertion and healthy defiance
- Recontextualizing: psycheducation, bibliotherapy, cinema-therapy, storytelling, linking the personal with the political, the historical, the literary, and the spiritual
- Cultivating mindfulness, observing ego functions and critical thinking
- Creating an atmosphere of improvisation and authentic relatedness to promote creativity and communication as valid alternatives to repetitions of traumatic relational paradigms

In alignment with the clinical perspectives presented throughout this book, Draijer and Van Zon (2013, in press) have reported on their use of a transference-based/object-relations approach with asylum seeking former child soldiers. While underscoring the importance of empathic attunement and interpretations of posttraumatic relational dynamics for successful treatment outcomes, Draijer and Van Zon caution against the imprudent application of traditional cognitive-behavioral posttraumatic stress disorder (PTSD) treatment methods. They highlight these patients' intense fears of, and aggression toward, therapists (including entrenched beliefs in the use of violence and intimidation as legitimate means of achieving goals) as constituting significant interference in their abilities to absorb and process new information. If the clinical focus remains solely on patients' symptoms and new skills' acquisition and is not extended to analysis and interpretation of relationship dynamics (with the goals of modulating aggression and tolerating intimacy and vulnerability), only limited or situational aspects of survivors' difficulties can be addressed. For these patients' underlying fearful and controlling dispositions to be treated, Drajier and Van Zon emphasize that the patient's murderous self must be engaged, respected, appreciated for its contributions, and brought into a meaningful relationship with the rest of the survivor's self. Violent urges and fantasies, and past experience of perpetration must be welcomed into the therapy dialogues while the patient is held accountable for preventing regressions to violence and for utilizing creative communicative outlets and non-destructive modes of expression.

A crucial strategy for clinicians and coerced-perpetration survivors lies in striving for the "middle path" or "middle way"[40] between seemingly oppositional tactical positions: compassion and confrontation (Kalsched, 1996); collision and negotiation (Bromberg, 2011); stabilization and therapeutic disruption; protection from overwhelm and exposure to unmetabolized psychological experience. Therapists mindfully walk the shifting line between excessive empathy (which can foster regression) and premature challenging or excessive limits (where the patient's defenses can inhibit the emergence of deeper traumatized aspects of the self – those most adhesively identified with perpetrator behavior and ideology). Clinicians must recognize that the deadened, shame- and rage-filled, encapsulated states of survival do not easily respond to language, or the activation of reflective awareness (Benjamin, 1999; Nachmani, 1995). Where significant mind control programming was used in the trauma events, perpetrator-engineered obstructions may present a potential minefield within all meaningful interpersonal communication. These implanted resistances can obstruct the patient's revelations, attachment to the therapist, or autonomy of mind and actions (Lacter, 2011; Miller, 2012; H. Schwartz, 2000).

Compassion is essential for accessing and processing the core of internalized perpetration and for a successful treatment outcome. However, empathy and human kindness have the potential to be misappropriated by the internalized perpetrating system. Benevolent reception from the therapist can threaten the patient with the loss of the internal representations (around which the self has become organized and identified), precipitating flight-fight responses, sudden termination, depression, and suicidal acting out. Programmed "fail-safes" may be triggered, prompting hostility and self-destructive diversions (Miller, 2012). Confrontation, limit-setting, or repudiating destructiveness all have the inherent potential to become distorted by the patient (through his or her own natural defensiveness or through programmed reactivity and resistances). The dissociative survivor may experience confrontive clinical interventions as violations – as shaming, or vengeful punishment – or as proof of the therapist's "corrupt" motivations *rather* than the therapist's beneficial intervention into the perpetrators' agenda. "Reparenting" strategies and "overnurturant countertransference" responses run the risk of innocently functioning as collusion with the hegemony of sequestered perpetrator states, controlling the patient's therapy process from behind the dissociative curtain.

The therapist's emotional states are often fluctuating across intense feelings – devotion, skepticism, revulsion, admiration, nurturance, psychological and somatic overwhelm, helplessness, sorrow, excitement, horror, dread, and avoidance – along with fantasies of escape and rescue. When properly understood, and used for creative commentary negotiating the meaning of enactments, these feelings can become vehicles of transformational psychotherapy. The mind of the therapist must have a semi-permeable quality (Ferro, 2005) as he or she remains open to unnerving or uplifting surprises. Sometimes traumatized patients' material exceeds the capacity of the therapist's own psyche, causing therapeutic containment and interpretive functions to break down. Vicarious traumatization and secondary posttraumatic stress represent liabilities and fodder for potential breakthroughs in this work (Pearlman and Saakvitne, 1995).

As Ferro (2005) indicates, there are benefits regarding a therapist's absorption of the patient's emotional turbulence and projective identifications: "If we abandon our state of impermeability and become more available for assumption and 'contagion,' we generate a completely new and transformed *Gestalt*" (p. 67). Then that which had been unthinkable and unmanageable for the patient – expressed only in symptoms, suffering, or acting out behavior – can be transformed through an encounter with the therapist's mind (Bion, 1967, 1970;

Ferro, 2005), body (Chassay, 2012), and improvisational capacities (Bromberg, 2011; H. Schwartz, 2000). The resulting influence on the therapeutic field can facilitate communion where the lack of commonalities had previously failed. "The 'non-thinkable' becomes a shared account by way of a series of emotional vicissitudes [enactments] whereby a name can be given to what was previously not representable" (Ferro, 2005:61).

Recognition of, and joining with, what Winnicott (1947) and Grand (2000) refer to as "objective hatred" or "object-related hatred," supports the patient's development of healthy guilt, remorse and concern. When therapists guide patients through object-related hatred (i.e., non-vindictive repudiation, distinct from unbounded hatefulness), they reinforce a shared well-boundaried field, a container of authenticity. In this protective yet rage-activated field or "potential space" (Ogden, 1989), a safe holding environment is created and made useful for penetrating the resistant walls encapsulating perpetrator states. The essential therapeutic postures/strategies of repudiating destructiveness (and object-related hatred) can operate in various ways: subtle shifts in the therapist's internal world; bold inquiries; humorous, ironic, and intuitive comments; empathy instruction; limit-setting; therapeutic outrage; storytelling and psychoeducation; forceful confrontation; or complete renegotiation of the therapeutic alliance and contract.

Bion's (1963) principle of "negative capability" represents the counterintuitive value of confusion, ambiguity, and not-knowing. Rather than imposing preconceived beliefs or self-assurances onto ambiguous emotional challenges, the therapist should examine the therapeutic use of uncertainty. The poet John Keats first used the term "negative capability" while searching for higher-order truths in the natural world. The philosopher Roberto Unger (2004) used the term to explain his opposition and resistance to rigid social divisions and hierarchies, and in support of creating new forms of identity and social structure. Emphasizing tolerance for ambiguity, "negative capability" can help prevent the premature collapsing of doubts, and fend off the deceptive security of easy stances, in service to patiently allowing transcendent perceptions to emerge out of the discomfort of uncertainty.

Attention to the therapeutic potential in ambiguity should also extend to how language can function to both undermine and advance the treatment process. All dissociative survivors are unwittingly bound with thoughts (language) that keep them "stuck." The language of their own narratives is often contaminated by the thoughts and injunctions of their perpetrators. Counterproductive shame and guilt, as dictated by popular culture, have also likely been co-opted as scaffolding in their identity construction.

Because language is the primary vehicle for psychotherapy, inclusive of silence and non-verbal gesture, the therapist should be attentive to the three differing angles from which language can be deployed to undermine or advance the treatment process. First, there is the domain where language is used by the victim for survival. Inherently survivor narratives are fragmented and lack internal coherence. Here a patient's language can sooth away the distress of self-doubt, yet pre-empt the potential for revision and growth. Beyond a survival tactic, the perpetrator(s)' language may have been absorbed by the patient to unwittingly sustain his or her own subjugation to the perpetrator (and pathological system). Here there is a tenacious attachment to entrenched implanted self-deceptions; the patient must be coaxed into preparation for casting off these signifiers. Until then, their inner-dialogue, and by extension their therapy dialogue, tacitly reinforces the domination of the perpetrator. Ultimately, there is the emergence of the transformational language to activate liberation. Surfacing up out of the relational dyad, a new zone for language can support the conquest of fragmented dissociative patterns that chain patients to their past, to then progressively develop thought forms that lead to a new construct of their histories and open a previously untapped potential for restorative integration.

Chapter 2

The child soldier as a model of internalized perpetration

> We survived by becoming like them. We stole. We cheated. We lied.
> We hated ourselves and each other. And we trusted no one.
>
> Teeda Butt Mam
> Survivor of The Khmer Rouge[1]

The child soldier phenomenon

The subject of child soldiers seeped into the awareness of The West in the mid 1970s with reports of the atrocities put upon the Cambodian people under the rule of the Khmer Rouge. The Khmer Rouge contorted idealized political reform to inhuman extremism. In service to a radical re-envisioning of society, the political leaders drew a tactical demarcation between children and adults. The Khmer Rouge believed parents were tainted with capitalism. Consequently, children were separated from parents and indoctrinated in communism and taught torture methods with animals (Jackson, 1992). Children became "dictatorial instruments of the party" and were given leadership in torture and executions (Boyden and Gibbs, 1997; Jackson, 1992; Pran, 1999). One of the party's mottos, in reference to the citizens deemed politically and ideologically contaminated, was: "To keep you is no benefit. To destroy you is no loss" (Mam, 1999:13).

The horrific social upheaval carried out under the Khmer Rouge was accomplished by exploiting the developmental vulnerabilities inherent in children. By the age of eight, most children were sent away to live with other children in communal work camps under two or three senior Khmer Rouge officials. Under extremely harsh conditions their adhesive commitments to the state was programmed while destroying traditional community loyalties. Special espionage units, composed mainly of children, were used to spy and report on adults including parents, other relatives, and neighbors. In a surreal Twilight Zone-esque reversal of rational social structure, children served as official judges, punishers, and executioners; the children were forced to denounce and kill adults and their violence was rewarded (Boyden and Gibbs, 1997). "Children rose quickly up the ranks of the Khmer Rouge [...] Camps run by these children became notorious for the extreme and arbitrary violence inflicted on the inmates.

Children, even more than adults, appeared particularly cruel. Even after Cambodia was liberated in 1979 by the Vietnamese, there remained a 'residual fear of children' in the country" (p. 98).

The United Nations estimates child soldiers have been exploited in 85 countries and territories; are involved in 75% of the armed conflicts around the world; 60% of non-state military forces made use of child soldiers; Myanmar is presently the largest state user of child soldiers (Coalition to Stop the Use of Child Soldiers, 2008). According to numerous researchers (Elbert *et al.*, 2006; Schauer and Elbert, 2010; P. Singer, 2006; Wessells, 2006), children are targeted for "recruitment" in warfare because of their inherent malleability. They represent a quick and low-cost way for armed organizations to increase their troops. Children operate in many roles beyond warriors or porters: they serve as laborers, field medics, landmine deactivators, cooks, and sex slaves. They are also used for human target practice and as the casualty of human sacrifices offered before battle.

Children can be highly efficient on the battlefield because of their limited ability to assess risks, or extrapolate long-term consequences or comprehend moral jeopardy (Brett and Specht, 2004) along with their inherent resilience and predisposition to "follow." Unexpected in civilized societies, the fierceness and fearlessness of child combatants, sometimes amplified by psychoactive drugs, are aspects that make them unexpectedly productive tools of warfare. It is this counterintuitive component that leverages traumatized children wielding AK-47s to create shock value in the eyes of the enemy (P. Singer, 2006; Wessels, 2006). These factors, along with their ready availability and expendability, have made children a useful commodity in wars throughout the world (Coalition to Stop the Use of Child Soldiers, 2008; Drumbl, 2012; Human Rights Watch, 2003; Schauer and Elbert, 2010; P. Singer, 2006).

Trained to blunt their own inhibiting shame, disgust, and fear responses, the survival strategies of child soldiers are co-opted by their military leaders to maximize their obedience, dependency, and capacity for brutality. Children's formative developmental periods are disrupted by repeated exposure to chronic traumatic stress from witnessing and participating in atrocities of the worst kind; this compounded trauma further complicates their eventual social re-integration, often rendering them less than fully functional community members (Wessels, 2006). Describing the particular vulnerability of children of war and child soldiers, Schauer and Schauer (2010) explain that survivors must cope with repeated and ongoing traumatic life events including: combat exposure; chronic life threatening events; torture and rape; violent death of relatives and friends; witnessing loved ones being tortured, injured, and raped; separation from family and community; abduction/detention; insufficient adult care; lack of drinking water and food; inadequate shelter; exposure to explosive devices and dangerous building ruins; marching or being transported in crowded vehicles over long distances; spending months in transit camps; and being deprived of education and health care.

For female child soldiers, rape and sexual slavery are integral aspects of induction into military life. Sexual violence is used as a mechanism for demonstrating control and ownership of child soldiers and for severing attachments to their lives prior to conscription. Female adolescent soldiers[2] face serious health risks from multiple rapes, sexually transmitted diseases, forced sterilization surgeries, difficult pregnancies, forced abortions, and birthing without assistance (McKay and Mazurana, 2004; United Nations, 2003). The attachment adolescent females have to babies born to them – babies who were often conceived during individual or gang rapes, and who are raised to become future soldiers – makes even a passing fantasy of real autonomy implausible (Schauer and Schauer, 2010).

The ethos of impunity in which child soldiers are inculcated is very difficult to reverse (P. Singer, 2006). The unrelenting kill-or-be-killed atmosphere in which they are steeped breeds an addiction to violence. Spiteful pride replaces healthy remorse, such that any challenge to the legitimacy of violent murder does not move the individual toward contrition and reparation; instead this provocation activates the urge for still more violence. For most of these children driven to coerced perpetration, survival has become inseparably dependent on the violent control wielded over other people. For many, the possession of a weapon was their only means of certain access to food, self-direction, and a sense of power (Honwana, 2008). So compelling is this addiction to violence and power over others that many child soldiers do not want to leave their militarized lives when alternatives are presented (N. Ball, 1997; Huband, 1998; Wessels, 2006).[3]

A child soldier's self-concept may become wholly dependent on those of the captor-leaders.[4] Their coercively-grafted ego structures are wholly dependent on violent domination and extreme power arrangements (P. Singer, 2006). When they do escape, children are easily drawn back into soldiering, sometimes in the middle of therapeutic interventions (Beah, 2007; Wessels, 2006). Most of those who have grown up fighting find it difficult to imagine exactly what a non-violent life would be or how they would function in a peaceful society (P. Singer, 2006).

P. Singer (2006) presents three categories of motivation – coercive, remunerative, and normative – that help sustain participation in physically and emotionally violent systems. Coercive motivators are punishments, threats of harm, torture, and demotions to less desirable ranks. Remunerative motivators include rewards such as food, money, drugs, sexual activities, and promotions to more prestigious ranks. Normative motivators are based on psychosocial dynamics including peer pressure, and threats of abandonment. Wessels (2006) adds that many psychological pressures are at work to sustain perpetrator behavior in child soldiers: survival impulses, fear and admiration of authority, normalization of violence, catharsis derived from killing, and indoctrination into an ideology that manipulates specific meaning structures to justify killing (e.g., social justice, religious redemption, or revenge).

The use of human sacrifice is a link between the indoctrination experiences of child soldiers and those of some survivors of syndicate child abuse in the West.

Coerced participation in human sacrifice activates primitive tendencies and imposes criminal identities, all the while creating adhesive bonds with perpetrators. Cannibalism and the drinking of blood are often endowed by the perpetrators with "magical" powers, spiritual and mortal protection, and to void one's feeling of remorse (Honwana, 2006). Another disturbing parallel link in indoctrination experiences is the use of rape, forced pregnancy, or abortions as tools of social control, and for a supply of future group members/soldiers (Wessels, 2006).

Many perpetrating systems prevailing methods of "recruitment" involve non-consensual means, such as outright abduction or blackmail against villages. According to both Wessels (2006) and P. Singer (2006), these organizations sweep through orphanages, schools, youth groups, geographic areas with large numbers of street children, even public bazaars, targeting children by age and size. Some children are "recruited" individually, others in small groups. Sometimes, adults and village leaders are held hostage by criminal cartels and military groups and must offer children between the ages of 7–14 to the militia to spare their own lives or those of other villagers.

P. Singer (2006) acknowledges that desperate life conditions lead some children to join military groups seemingly of their own volition. Wessels (2006) and Honwana (2008) discuss the wide range of complex motivations (e.g., safety, money, self-esteem, power, food, clothing, shelter, medical care, revenge, family pride, protection, and vocational needs) that lead severely impoverished children, struggling to survive in areas ravaged by civil strife, to "choose" to enter military life as a reasonable accommodation to prevailing circumstances. The issue of a child's free will or his ability to make a choice to enter soldiering is an unviable proposition; a child's inability to comprehend the scope of responsibilities that await him or her – especially in the face of few or no alternatives – nullifies the prospect of consent.

Drumbl (2012) cautions against viewing the child soldier as a helpless, passive victim. He recommends a less-generalized, more-heterogeneous approach to honor the unique journeys and individual experiences of each child soldier, and to include non-culturally stigmatic perspectives that might speak to the circumstances of a child soldier that motivated enlistment. Whenever victimization includes alterations in identity – from child soldiers to trafficked sex workers and other traumatically-induced DID individuals acting out coerced criminality – the perplexing issues of free will and accountability tend to defy consensus by lawmakers, caregivers, policy makers, and survivors.

Drumbl (2012) has analyzed the international discourse that sometimes reduces child soldiers to a variety of potentially dehumanizing caricatures. Most common is the portrayal of a guileless naïve victim who is, without doubt, awaiting rescue by humanitarians. Although this rendering frames child soldiers' suffering as a human rights issue and communicates easily with the Western public, this objectifying depiction is primarily arranged around subordinating the child (or former child) to a pawn position as more powerful groups jockey for advantage on legalistic policies. Another overly-simplistic representation of the child soldier is as a courageous hero who has fought with valor for patriotism or in resistance to political oppression. This caricature risks the valorizing of military violence and exalting hyper-aggression as an honorable masculine virtue. In counterpoint to this stereotype is another, where child soldiers are irredeemable and irreparable "damaged goods." A variation on the inherently incurable soul is the ticking time-bomb with an unstoppable bloodlust to kill. These facile pigeonholes carry the potential to reinforce racial stereotypes and the urge to pathologize entire cultures while ignoring the plight of girl soldiers entirely. Such broad-brush stigmas help Western stakeholders to manage guilt and anxieties, yet may retraumatize former soldiers and inadvertently discourage investment in rehabilitation programs.

Case study of a child soldier: Ishmael Beah

Part 1: Descent

Prior to the publication of Ishmael Beah's memoir, little was known about child soldiers' experiences because the vast majority – hundreds of thousands – are simply swallowed up in the murderous chaos of warfare, never to be heard from again. Beah's memoir offers invaluable case material to illuminate the similarities in breakdown and recovery for all victims of coerced perpetration, regardless of context, geography or perpetrator ideology.[5]

Ishmael was raised in a relatively happy family in a traditional rural village in Sierra Leone. He came of age during one of Africa's most gruesome civil wars. As a child, he showed a gift for memorizing and reciting Shakespeare as entertainment for the villagers. As he approached adolescence, he became a creative lighthearted boy in love with hip-hop music and dance. In a sudden turn, Ishmael lost his entire immediate family to the senseless brutality of national conflict, and he found himself wandering aimlessly through the forests and the decimated landscapes of his country in search of food, shelter, and safety. By the age of 12, his life had been shattered. Caught in the middle of a bloody civil war, the motivations and meanings of which he could scarcely comprehend, he faced impossible survival dilemmas. By the age of 13 Ishmael became a "voluntary" child soldier, he had begun a degenerate life of drug addiction, sadistic violence, and killing sprees.

Unlike many child soldiers with early lives of abject circumstances, Ishmael came from an intact family and village, he had consistent nutrition and education, possessed keen intelligence, and received considerable social acceptance and validation. Prior to the war, he had excellent physical and mental health. His initiation into soldiering did not involve extensive torture or abuse. Undoubtedly, these factors significantly affected his resilience, enabling him eventually to benefit from treatment and triumph over tremendous adversity.

Ishmael's loss of innocence and his descent into hell began while he was walking, along with his older brother and a close friend, to perform in a talent show in a neighboring village. A rebel strike sent the boys running into the bush for their lives. War had been raging in Sierra Leone for a number of years. The boys were well aware that both government and rebel forces had been abducting local boys into soldiering with the threat of death. The boys never made it to the talent contest. Instead of singing and dancing, the brute will to survive would become the preoccupation of their young lives. The boys were continuously on the run, often lost, dodging violence and forced conscription.

When news reached the boys that their own village might have been attacked, it struck fear into their hearts. As Ishmael and his mates traveled aimlessly through the forests, they encountered terrible scenes of brutality and suffering – the dead, the dying, and the dispossessed littered the countryside. The boys shifted back and forth in classic posttraumatic cycling from traumatic overwhelm to memorizing hip-hop lyrics in order to numb and distract themselves and fantasizing reunification with family members. Fleeing from village to village, exhausted and on the verge of starvation, Ishmael became separated from his older brother and never saw him again. Timidly hopeful, he finally arrived at his family home only to find it smoldering. His beloved village had been destroyed – its inhabitants were wounded, dead, or displaced. Ishmael moved desperately from body to body, looking for familiar faces. He described the soil of the village as running red with blood. The charred remains of villagers were arrayed in rows in the middle of the road, no longer recognizable. He was confronted by the fact that his family had been slaughtered and his childhood world had been obliterated. Flooded with grief and rage, Ishmael had to find cover in the bush in case the marauding rebel soldiers were hunting for survivors.

Stumbling on alone, sometimes for weeks at a time, hungry, wracked with pain and anguish, Ishmael continued to be completely traumatized by his encounters with human depravity and the gruesome sights of civilian massacres: scorched women carrying dead babies on their backs; packs of dogs eating the remains of massacred elders; entire villages denuded of life; broken, and many other displaced people wandering aimlessly through the forest. While hiding, he witnessed the arrogant glee and "high fives" of violence-intoxicated rebel soldiers, one of whom "carried the head of a man which he held by the hair" (p. 96). He overheard a group of adolescent rebel soldiers blustering about the impressive way they had carried out their commander's orders to execute every living person in three villages.

Ishmael found his way to the safety of a government-protected village where he was eventually recruited. Besieged with nightmares, migraines, and a host of other posttraumatic symptoms, Ishmael was well-positioned for successful grooming by Sierra Leone government forces. Unlike many child soldiers who were coerced or abducted, Ishmael's preliminary military training began less abusively. The government's army leaders forced him to choose between staying and training to fight the rebels or striking out again on his own. No overt threats were made in his case, but Ishmael knew he had no workable options.[6] Having made this "choice," Ishmael's military training began in earnest with indoctrinations aimed specifically at exploiting the young recruit's retaliatory rage at the enemy rebels who killed his family.[7] His new military mentors keep constant in their refrains:

> Now is your time to revenge the death of your families and to make sure more children do not lose their families [...] The rebels have lost everything that makes them human. They do not deserve to live. This is why we must kill every single one of them. Think of it as destroying a great evil. It is the highest service you can do for your country.
>
> (p. 108)

The military leaders deftly manipulated Ishmael's posttraumatic anxieties: his rage, numbness, despair, terror, loneliness, and fantasies of vengeance. They would say, "visualize the enemy, the rebels who killed your parents, your family, and those who are responsible for everything that has happened to you." (p. 112). They were fed a daily diet of Rambo movies and mind-altering drugs, in particular "brown brown" an intoxicating mixture of cocaine and gunpowder. Ishmael and his comrades moved from target practice on banana trees to the accompaniment of propaganda to tentative combat experiences. In a matter of weeks, Ishmael was successfully transformed into a grim killer capable of casual mass slaughter. "We all wanted to be like Rambo. We couldn't wait to implement his techniques [...] The idea of death didn't cross my mind at all and killing had become as easy as drinking water." (p. 121). Beah described eventually losing all human feeling and compassion for fellow humans. He only cared about his weapon, his military group's conquests, and survival.

Increased drug use intensified his fearlessness and pride in killing. This enabled wholesale village massacres, brutal retaliatory public executions of rebel soldiers, and led finally to maniacally gleeful killing sprees.

> A lot of things were done with no reason or explanation. Sometimes we were asked to leave for war in the middle of a war movie. We would come back hours later after killing many people and continue the movie as if we had just returned from intermission. We were always either at the front lines, watching a war movie or doing drugs. There was not time to be alone or to think. When we conversed with each other, we talked only about the war movies and how impressed we were with the way either the lieutenant, the corporal, or one of us had killed someone. It was as if nothing else existed outside our reality.
>
> (p. 124)

Commentary

The transformation of an innocent child into a violent offender is unexpectedly simple to accomplish. Completely cut off from their previous lives and communities and with their captors/leaders as their only source of protection and comfort, the children construct new identities and internalize meaning structures that conform to the group's rules and code of respect. The harmonious relationships with elders, community, ancestors, and spirit world that would normally constitute significant psychological containers are gone. The obliteration of these traditional forms of intrapsychic and interpersonal functioning is as central to the creation of dissociative states as is the cold-blooded violence. In the absence of traditional elder authority, the perpetrators step in to fill the vacuum with new socio-psycho-dynamics in the service of a righteous cause. The creation of perpetrator identities includes systematic desensitization, operant and classical conditioning techniques, implosion/shock treatment, double binds, peer pressure, and forced choices with life-and-death consequences (P. Singer, 2006). Classic methods for "breaking in" new recruits entail political and spiritual indoctrination, constant intimidation through humiliation, psychotropic drugs, death threats, gang rapes (particularly of females),[8] sleep deprivation, compulsory participation in public and/or ritualized murder, cannibalism, drinking the blood of murdered or tortured victims, and a constant state of fear. Leaders of violent groups often equate drinking of human blood (or eating body parts) with power, protection, and other magical qualities, among them its supposedly talismanic effect against feelings of remorse (Honwana, 2006). The regular ingestion of human flesh and blood has also been observed to blunt the feelings young recruits might otherwise experience at the sight of blood and gore, and thereby bolster courage on the battlefield (P. Singer, 2006). Participation in death or sex-death rituals also helps new recruits overcome their instinctual fear of mortality at the same time it fosters a primitive psychological merger with group identity and power.

Initiatory spectacles of defilement are enacted against other children and sometimes against adults familiar to the child, including family members (Huband, 1998; P. Singer, 2006; Schauer and Schauer, 2010; Wessels, 2006). These strategies contribute to the critical mass of stress on the child recruit, inducing more-extreme internal responses and posttraumatic management strategies. Once individual identity has been stomped-out, further indoctrination is designed to supplant the recruit's former civilian identity with a new military self (P. Singer, 2006; Wessels, 2006). This conversion is often accomplished with a combination of physical branding of the recruit with the group's name or insignia, and/or the creation of alternative personas with new names such as "Rambo," "Cock and Fire," or "Blood Never Dry." Singer goes on to describe one group of child soldiers from Sierra Leone who called themselves "Cyborgs," proud killing machines named after creatures from the Hollywood movies they had watched repeatedly as part of their training.

Like all forms of cult mind control,[9] the techniques are chosen to produce a moral and psychological disconnection within the child from his or her former identity, destroy any sense of autonomy, eliminate avenues of escape or betrayal of perpetrators, and normalize violence thorough deracinating the victim/trainee's relationship with the sanctity of life (Hassan, 1990; P. Singer, 2006). The stress on female child soldiers who endure greater sexual violence and medical complications including childbirths, and experience more complex role demands may surpass those for most male soldiers; hence the likelihood of development of more severe dissociative conditions may be greater. Significantly fewer female child soldiers receive treatment, consequently gender-specific evaluations and comparisons of the dissociative processes have yet to be fully researched. Based on dissociative patterns occurring in Western trauma patients, we would expect former child soldiers with factors such as less positive pre-war social and psychological functioning, greater trauma in the initiation process (i.e., abduction versus volunteer), more severe task demands, and longer periods with perpetrators (and time in war zones) to be at a higher risk for dissociative self-organization.

In spite of the dedicated efforts of military perpetrators, a small number of child soldiers find their way to peacekeeping forces and treatment centers. Surprisingly, yet importantly, this rescue is not a fate for which most child soldiers have been secretly longing. For most child soldiers who have crossed out of ordinary reality into the archetypal realm of survival, chaos, and power, the idea of civilian life or a redemptive future is seen as betrayal and abandonment. This is precisely how many perpetrator-identified alter personalities in Western dissociative survivor patients view ending up in a therapist's office.

Part 2: The return

One day a United Nations Children's Fund (UNICEF) truck with four relief workers pulled up to Ishmael and his troops. For unclear reasons, the lieutenant ordered Ishmael and a few other boys to climb into the truck with them. Seeing himself as a soldier, not a civilian, Ishmael was not at all relieved to be rescued. In fact, he felt confused and humiliated by his lieutenant's abandonment. His weapon was not easily relinquished because possession of a weapon was the source of his dignity, food, safety, and power. He was outraged at having to take orders from civilians. Demobilization promised no "valuable rewards" and portended a return to intolerable posttraumatic anxieties. Furthermore, the end of soldiering life means loss of "family and community" for a second time, before treatment had even begun.

On the first day of his rehabilitation, the United Nations (UN) staff naively mixed a group of rebel and government child soldiers together in the same dining area, mistakenly believing that all child soldiers were basically the same and all would be well once these boys were removed from the warzone. "It hadn't crossed their minds that a change of environment wouldn't immediately make us normal boys. We were dangerous, and brainwashed to kill." (Beah, 2007:135). Violence broke out at the rehabilitation center as the boys of opposing political camps wielded knives attempting to inflict as much damage as possible on their former enemies. Ishmael tossed a grenade that he had smuggled in into a group of Rebel boys. Six boys were killed instantly. Military police (MPs) tried to control and subdue the conflict, but the boy soldiers overcame the MPs. The child soldiers stripped the MPs of their guns and began firing at the government-backed boys. The first group of MPs fled the scene. Reinforcements appeared, shooting guns in the air to take control and restore order. Eventually, the back-up forces subdued the adolescents. Ishmael and his peers were then closely guarded by MPs to prevent further violence. The boys celebrated the most recent round of violence to "cheer themselves up after a whole day of boring traveling and contemplation about why their superiors had let them go" (p. 136).

Ishmael was soon transferred to a new rehabilitation center, where he began to suffer intense symptoms of withdrawal from the drugs and violence to which he had become emotionally and physiologically addicted. Craving the violence of warfare, Ishmael and many of his peers regularly assaulted the staff and sought fresh victims to abuse from a neighboring village whose inhabitants gathered their daily water from the common well. The staff displayed remarkable patience and persistence in engaging the demobilized soldiers in the beginning phase of treatment, which included medical checkups, orientation, socialization, and counseling. Initially the adolescents met the staff's efforts with ardent rejection, and hostility:

> At the end of every meal, the nurses and staff members came to talk to us […] as soon as they started speaking, we would throw bowls, spoons, food, and benches at them. We would chase them out of the dining hall and beat them up. One afternoon, after we had chased off the nurses and staff members, we placed a bucket over the cook's head and pushed him around the kitchen until he burned his hand on a hot boiling pot and agreed to put more milk in our tea.
>
> (p. 138)

The constant message from the staff throughout the treatment process was a proclamation and reinforcement of the former combatant's innocence – in spite of the soldiers' prior offenses or extent of their posttraumatic behavior or beliefs. The demobilized soldiers hated and resisted the staff's tenacious therapeutic interventions aimed at reinforcing the boys' innocence, and at undermining the boys' attachments and commitments to perpetrator identities. In a poignant description of the encounter with a staff member, Poppay, who a group of demobilized adolescent soldiers brutally attacked. Beah writes (p. 140):

> Poppay returned during lunchtime, limping, but with a smile on his face. "It is not your fault that you did such a thing to me," he said, as he strolled through the dining hall. This made us angry because we wanted the "civilians," as we referred to the staff members, to respect us as soldiers who were capable of severely harming them. Most of the staff members were like that;

they returned smiling after we hurt them. It was as if they had made a pact not to give up on us. Their smiles made us hate them all the more.

After a couple months in rehabilitation, the boys' withdrawal symptoms subsided, and their violent outbursts became fewer and farther between. They had started on the road back to the ordinary world. Educational and recreational activities were considered essential during the next phase of treatment, though the boys only minimally cooperated. To foster participation in activities, staff used no force or coercion. Nonverbal rather than verbal expression of feelings was utilized. Intrusive posttraumatic symptoms such as mental and somatic flashbacks intensified as "the fastened mantle of our war memories slowly began to open" (p. 145). After days spent playing soccer or table tennis and feigning interest in school, nighttime still held their terrors:

> [A]t night some of us would wake up from nightmares, sweating, screaming and punching our own heads to drive out the images that continued to torment us even when we were no longer asleep. Other boys would wake up and start choking whoever was in the bed next to theirs; they would then go running into the night after they had been restrained. The staff members were always on guard to control these sporadic outbursts. Nonetheless, every morning several of us were found hiding in the grasses by the soccer field. We didn't remember how we had gotten there.
>
> (p. 149)

Meanwhile, acting out did not entirely cease – the boys went from burning their books and school supplies to selling them on the black market. The staff's attempts to create a "holding environment" were consistently undermined. Importantly, the staff never lost patience or retaliated against the boys. The staff members slowly curtailed access to the black market and imposed gentle but consistent limits while creating simple systems of rewards to motivate behavior change; trips to the city being most prized. Superficial cooperation for some boys led to incrementally deeper involvement in the healing process. While for others, going AWOL and returning to their lives as soldiers seemed to be their only goal. Deeply embedded addictions to re-enacting corruption, betrayal, and violent domination over others appears to be more defying to a recovery process than recovery from addiction to drugs.

Successful treatment of survivors who are victim-perpetrators involves an integration of many elements: a therapeutic/non-violent community with elders and trustworthy and consistent leadership, reliable safety in the environment, recreation and educational opportunities, flexible limits, supported withdrawal from drug addiction, and deconditioning/deprogramming of violent compulsions and perpetrator identifications. Most essential to the treatment is an intimate human connection. Ishmael's healing journey progressed due to an unexpected relationship with Esther, a nurse whose small kindnesses coupled with her indefatigable insistence that he confide the details of what happened to him (how he got his scars and wounds). He forged a humanizing connection that could begin to replace the bonds he'd lost with his family and those he felt with some of his military superiors. "I told her the whole story [...] not because I really wanted to, but because I thought that if I told her some of the gruesome truth of my war years she would be afraid of me and would cease asking questions" (p. 155).

Even after some productive time had passed within the therapeutic relationship, it is important to note that Ishmael's conscious motivations for dialogue with confessions were based on his desire to perpetuate the dynamics of intimidation and alienation – not the desire for understanding or redemption. This motivation system and enactment pattern within relationships is also commonly found early in treatment with perpetrator-identified states of Western dissociative trauma survivors. Even perfunctory human contact may unconsciously ignite longings for recognition and tenderness, but for survivors, perpetrator conditioning also associates human contact with unbearable vulnerability, igniting compelling reiterations of bravado and defensive isolation.

Esther eventually engaged Ishmael in regular individual sessions where his war experiences and his posttraumatic dreams could be shared. At first, little discussion took place. Esther listened and bore witness to Ishmael's revelations, often with tears in her eyes. She said little beyond "None of what happened was your fault. You were just a little boy, and anytime you want to tell me anything, I am here to listen." (p. 160). Her openness was disarming to Ishmael. Esther's intuitive persistence in underlining Ishmael's innocence and her relative non-intrusiveness models an essential therapeutic approach for working with trauma and perpetration experiences in the early stages of treatment. Ishmael's ongoing revelations and therapeutic dialogues with Esther activated his longings and aversions. His posttraumatic rage and contemptuousness was given a non-military context as his yearnings for human bonding emerged.

Ishmael somewhat reluctantly continued to communicate with Esther, who in turn began to take small emotional risks like putting an arm around him or the other boys in the bus, tickling them playfully, joking, and elbowing. She bought small but meaningful gifts for the boys, including a Walkman, Bob Marley cassettes, and pens and notebooks for Ishmael. Beyond her own vulnerability and affection, Ester's generosity, flexibility, and creativity with limits and boundaries were essential in the eventual dissolving of the hardened carapace encapsulating internalized perpetration identifications. Their sessions began to include a mix of sharing war stories and singing. In addition to serious conversations, Ishmael would perform the latest set of lyrics of Bob Marley songs he had memorized. Even though he could not fully trust Esther, or anyone for that matter, Ishmael began to look forward to the therapy sessions, and his behavior began to look like that of a noncombatant teenage boy.

Commentary

As the addictions and posttraumatic reactivity of the child soldier's nervous system wane, and as time and distance accrue from the corrupting influence of the military, individual and group psychotherapeutic work take on the more demanding tasks of recovery, specifically, P. Singer (2006) describes:

- Overcoming dispositions toward distrust and aggression
- Developing capacities for remorse, empathy, and frustration tolerance
- Developing an understanding of the contexts and dynamics in which the demobilizing soldier had been trapped
- Cultivating age-appropriate self-soothing, self-esteem, and affect regulation skills
- Family/village reunification

It is highly recommended that child soldiers be exposed to non-intrusive therapeutic means for expressing their feelings in the early and middle stages of healing, as both P. Singer (2006) and Wessels (2006) emphasize. Methods typically include song, dance, art, theater, and indirect inquiry. This can reduce stress and aid in self-regulation before full verbal expression, confession, and any detailed memory work, if any, are conducted. Verbal narratives and confession should eventually be part of the healing process in most cases, yet such expressions may be most effective and transformative in group or culturally-sanctioned settings. P. Singer (2006) describes how children asked to talk in front of the community about their experiences in a non-judgmental and accepting atmosphere can attain relief from guilt and shame, validation for their suffering, and spiritual purification from the contamination of immersion in violence and war (Honwana, 2006; 2008).

Most demobilized soldiers view traditional rituals for healing and spiritual cleansing (from their native culture) as greatly helpful. These rituals are restorative of the damaged relationship with community; ancestral spirits hold potentials for redemption according to the traditions of the child soldier's pre-military life. Through these events, the psycho-spiritual pollution carried by returnees, which is often seen as a collective threat to communal integrity by both villagers and the former child soldiers, is ceremoniously released (Honwana, 2006; 2008). Although dyadic healing relationship experience may be seen as helpful, the archetypal damage sustained by many child soldiers and the cultural factors defining the terms of healing and recovery favor utilization of communal and metaphysical containers for complete transformation and integration.

This clinical and community-based approach views the children (and helps them view themselves) as pawns rather than as premeditated perpetrators, however depraved the child's experiences (P. Singer, 2006). Child soldier demobilization treatment conceives reconciliation of the soldier's innocence and corruption within the processes of forgiveness. Integral to this model is a community of elders whose clarity about the culpability of the original perpetrators and the innocence of the child soldier supports the restoration of emotional and spiritual harmony within the psyche of the former soldier, the community, as well as the community of ancestors and benevolent spiritual forces (Honwana, 2006, 2008; Schauer and Schauer, 2010; P. Singer, 2006). In such a facilitating environment, the survivor's struggle to integrate (internally and socially) is witnessed and shared by the larger society. When trauma and healing are understood in this way, the survivor is never completely abandoned to shame, confusion, or self-hatred, nor permitted to serve as a permanent receptacle for the disowned shadow projections of the larger society.

"Welcoming and purification" are two central healing rituals described in the literature, aspects of which are sometimes combined. A team from Christian Children's Fund Angola (CCF/Angola) describes what commonly occurs when a village attempts to help a child to re-integrate and engage fully with the cultural resources of the tribal system.

> Women prepare themselves for the greeting ceremony [...] Some of the flour used to paint the women's foreheads is thrown at the child. A respected older woman of the village throws a gourd filled with ashes at the child's feet. At the same time, clean water is throw over him as a means of purification [...] The women of the village dance around the child, gesturing with hands and arms to ward away undesirable spirits or influences [...] They each touch him with both hands from head to foot to cleanse him of impurities [...] When the ritual is complete the child is taken to his village and the villagers celebrate his return. A party is held in his home with traditional beverages [...] the child must be formally presented to the chiefs by his parents [...] The child sits beside the chiefs, drinking and talking with them, this marks his change of status in the village.
>
> Wessels (2006:197–198)

Shamans or local healers must participate in specific purification ceremonies when a soldier has been involved in extensive killing, due to concerns about haunting by angry spirits of the murdered people. Wessels and Monteiro (2004) describe a classic ritual that begins with the local healer burning sacred herbs to create a safe space inaccessible to bad spirits. Former soldiers then breathe the fumes of carefully selected herbs. Their chests and backs are scrubbed with roots believed to expunge bad spirits and prevent their re-entry. Around the perimeter of the safe space, the healer makes offerings – which include liquor, traditional food, and a sacrificed chicken – to appease the spirits. The closing of the ritual is made official when the demobilized soldier ritualistically leaves the room by jumping through the door. This theatrical exit signifies the former soldier has left all impurities behind and is now fit for village life.

The powerful positive effects of these rituals on the former soldiers' social identities cannot be overstated: community members view the youth as having been reborn and thus able to re-enter civilian life. The former soldiers usually feel spiritually cleansed and freed, and now can safely re-engage with villagers and their families and thus hereby re-engage and continue the progress of the developmental tasks of adolescence and young adulthood and fulfill responsibilities to the community. In concert with these efforts, most authorities on the subject of child soldier rehabilitation (and legal processes) strongly advocate for the essential role of economic and vocational rehabilitation in the recovery process – sometimes placing this centrally, above and beyond the necessity of reparative psychotherapeutic processes – for successful demobilization (Drumbl, 2012; Schauer and Schauer, 2010; P. Singer, 2006; Wessels, 2006).

Turning points in all treatments are often unexplainable. They can be more a matter of "critical mass" than brilliant interpretation or riveting insights. Sometimes a turning point arises from a single gesture or a seemingly irrelevant detail.

Part 3: Transformation

After months of counseling sessions, in the wake of one of his disturbing dreams, Esther engaged Ishmael in conversation about the life he had lived before the war. By intuitively providing "linking functions" (Bion, 1965), Esther helped Ishmael connect his village life with his war experiences and his ongoing recovery. At the end of the session discussing his pre-war life, Esther reiterated, in her usual stern tone, the mantra "None of these things are your fault."

> Even though I had heard that phrase from every staff member – and frankly I had always hated it – I began that day to believe it. It was the genuine tone in Esther's voice that made the phrase finally begin to sink into my mind and heart. That didn't make me immune from the guilt that I felt for what I had done. Nonetheless, it lightened my burdensome memories and gave me strength to think about things. The more I spoke about my experiences to Esther, the more I began to cringe at the gruesome details, even though I didn't let her know that. I didn't completely trust Esther. I only liked talking to her because I felt that she didn't judge me for what I had been a part of.
>
> Beah (2007:165–166)

As Ishmael's healing progressed and his acting out subsided, depression set in. Ishmael was still trying to understand himself without his family or former community, and he knew he had blood on his hands. It was yet another turning point in his treatment where the larger existential aspects of his journey could be felt and addressed for the first time. Esther's interventions established a familial-like bond as well as a therapeutic relationship. She made herself available to Ishmael as a surrogate sister as well as a caregiver and healer. Therapeutic authority was balanced with camaraderie and communality. Esther seemed to intuitively understand that defensive encapsulation of perpetrator identities can only be relinquished slowly over time. With a mix of playfulness, affection, and commitment to his recovery, Esther was able to penetrate most of Ishmael's defenses and re-engage his healthy developmental strivings. Ishmael's depression was contextualized and normalized as a necessary passage in the recovery process. The disorientating rupture of perpetrator-based encapsulated states (in child soldiers and Western dissociative survivors) is often first accompanied by severe depression.

When representatives of the UN and other non-governmental organization (NGO) staff arrived at the rehabilitation center, Ishmael performed a monologue from Shakespeare's *Julius Caesar* and a hip-hop play he had written (with Esther's encouragement) about the redemption of a child soldier. Not long after that, the rehabilitation center located an uncle Ishmael did not know very well, and here began Ishmael's repatriation process. Meanwhile, Ishmael was nominated for a special UN project to bring Sierra Leonean children to the USA under the aegis of Children Associated with War (CAW) to raise awareness about the plight of child soldiers. His first visit to the USA in late adolescence mesmerized him. He was moved listening to the other children recount their experiences in front of the UN.

After returning to Africa and the death of his uncle, Ishmael realized it was virtually impossible to make a new life for himself; his country had become too dangerous for him to sustain the gains of treatment. Other losses and challenges eventually led Ishmael back to the USA. His emigration journey involved many dangerous passages through the same terrifying conditions that had led to his transformation into a soldier. It may not always be so, but in Ishmael's case, emigration was essential to full recovery. An American woman in New York City, who was a writer and storyteller, eventually adopted Ishmael, a storyteller himself from early childhood. A couple of years later as an undergraduate college student, he was shocked by Americans' general lack of awareness of conditions in West Africa: most had no idea where Sierre Leone was on the map. He became highly motivated to write a memoir and educate the world on the plight of child soldiers through his experiences. Ishmael's voluntary immersion in the psychological and historical material of his past for the purposes of awakening collective awareness was both retraumatizing and redemptive. Although he continued to struggle with posttraumatic symptoms and cross-cultural adjustments, a degree of normalcy and happiness returned to his life. Though his book *A Long Way Gone*, Ishmael gained international literary prominence. He went on to become a UNICEF ambassador and liaison, bringing significant awareness and promise for healing to child soldiers throughout the world.

In the last stages of writing this book, I had the opportunity to hear Ishmael Beah give a public talk at a local International Club. He was now 32 years old. He discussed his past trauma and recovery with great humility, maturity, and a refined sense of humor. He spoke of his posttraumatic struggles as an ongoing process, rather than as a completed project. He spoke about learning to live with overwhelming life events, finding a wider emotional and intellectual perspective in which to hold these experiences in relationship to his entire life's journey.

As a UNICEF ambassador, Beah is currently involved in facilitating the rescue and repatriation of many child soldiers, including controversial negotiations directly with warlords to obtain the release of young soldiers, and in continuing to raise awareness and funding for projects related to demobilization and reparation. When asked for his final comments, Beah made two moving statements. He underscored the power of small acts of kindness as a crucial force to stem the rippling effects of violence. Beah shared that his life had been saved by the courage and generosity of a few individuals taking a few significant risks. He urged the audience not to underestimate the value and potential power of even the smallest act of generosity toward other human beings. With sincere humility, Beah went on to say the rest of his life would be committed to service to others. He insisted that he would write more books but he wanted to write fiction and develop material entirely unrelated to his violent past – for me, his desire to "move on" in total marked his completed transcendence of his trauma.

One of the most resonant statements from Beah was his desire to return to his homeland and to eventually raise his children there rather than in the USA. He noted a distinct difference in the relationship with violence he saw between the two societies which to him favored the safety of raising children in Sierra Leone. Beah felt that Americans are to a great extent enamored with, and perplexed by, violence. He said Americans have not yet completely rejected violence, whereas most of his countrymen – having seen the worst of human depravity and destructiveness materialized in their lifetimes – have the clear-minded discernment to shun violence.

Chapter 3

Dilemmas of dissociative survival

> To a man utterly without a sense of belonging, mere life is all that matters. It is the only reality in an eternity of nothingness, and he clings to it with shameless despair.
>
> Eric Hoffer

Dissociation

Dissociation has been classically viewed as "the escape when there is no escape" (Putnam, 1992:104). Understood as a major feature of psychological life (Bromberg, 1994; 1996), dissociation may be the underpinning of many psychiatric disorders above and beyond posttraumatic stress and the dissociative disorders (Bromberg, 1998; Howell, 2005). Pathological or defensive dissociation is associated with "a failure of integration of ideas, information, affects, and experiences" (Putnam, 1989:19). Van der Kolk *et al.* (1996) highlight the compartmentalization of experience when overwhelming experiences cannot be integrated into a unitary sense of self. Describing dissociation as the protective activation of altered states of consciousness in reaction to overwhelming traumatic experience, Loewenstein (1996) claims that dissociation is an essential and inherent element of the human psychobiological trauma response. Bloom (1997) likens dissociation to "an internal plaster cast the brain places around 'broken' emotions to protect the break from further harm." Within this analogy, she views the emotions as restricted and immobilized, unavailable for normal use. "When one leg is broken, muscles in the other leg often become hypertrophied or enlarged, throwing the usually well-balanced system out of alignment. With broken emotions, a similar experience occurs because other emotions fill in for the dissociated feelings" (p. 36).

Much has been written about the easily misunderstood process of dissociation, however, a few major themes merit review as background for understanding dissociation's function as a substrate for internalized perpetration. In general, dissociation can operate both adaptively and maladaptively (Bromberg, 1994; Kluft, 1984; Putnam, 1989; C. Ross, 1997). Dissociation can be:

- overt and covert
- process and structure
- cause and effect
- self-protective and self-destructive
- solution and problem
- automatic and over-learned
- spontaneous and rehearsed
- enhancing creativity and constricting imagination and expression
- camouflaged/subtle and feigned/dramatic
- fostering personality stability and instability
- occurring with and without multiplicity

Dissociation may be a description of an individual (i.e., psychic structure) and a continuum of behavior and psychological functioning describing aspects of all people to varying degrees (Bromberg, 1996; Dell and O'Neill, 2009; Kluft, 1984; Putnam, 1989, 1997; C. Ross, 1997; Spiegel, 1990; Tarnopolosky, 2003; Van der Hart *et al.*, 2006). A given individual can use adaptive and maladaptive forms of dissociation simultaneously and/or intermittently. It can range from the mildest form of "spacing out" and daydreaming to trauma-induced flashbacks, blackouts, and re-enactments, and in its extreme form as programmed alter personalities and perpetrator installed "possession" states. Dissociative part-selves in traumatized children have been most commonly found to consist of unexpressed feelings, unprocessed sensory experiences, fragments of overwhelming physical or emotional experience, unexpressed body movements (i.e., fight/flight responses) from time of the trauma, solutions to overwhelming life challenges, unmet needs, abuser/perpetrator introjects, and internal helpers (Marks, 2012; Putnam, 1997).

Echoing the work of major theorists within relational psychoanalysis, Bromberg (1994) portrays dissociation as an "intrinsically adaptational talent representing the very nature of what we call consciousness" (p. 521). Viewing the human mind as a system of discontinuous and shifting states of consciousness from birth to death, Bromberg states, "the psyche does not start as an integrated whole, but begins and continues as a multiplicity of self-states that maturationally attain a feeling of coherence that overrides the awareness of discontinuity" (Bromberg, 1993:162).[1] The adaptive value of dissociation lies in its ability to facilitate traits of fluidity and flexibility in moving through life's joys and challenges, simultaneously negotiating both change and character stability. In contrast, maladaptive dissociation is associated with an overreliance on the constrictive and rigidifying aspects of the dissociative capacity of the mind (i.e., numbing, deflection, switching, disconnecting, compartmentalizing) to cope with states of traumatic overwhelm.

This inflexible repetitive use of dissociation often leads to rigid psychological systems characterized by a lack of linkages between symbolic and concrete modes of experience, alterations in mind–body connections, and disturbances in perception and meaning-making (Bromberg, 1994; 1998; Kluft, 1985, 1999; C. Ross, 1997).[2] What once had preserved life and sanity now compromises the quality of life and constricts the breadth and scope of mindfulness and life potential. Bromberg (2011) poses the pivotal question: is the psychological overprotection against (potential) retraumatization offered by dissociation worth the high price paid? Describing how this inevitable debate initially plays itself out in disputes among the patient's panoply of alter personalities and self-states, Bromberg explains that in this polarized field, some self-states demand only affective safety, while others advocate for what is life-enhancing, even though such choices involve risk. Because therapists inevitably become embroiled in their patient's self-state wars, therapists have the opportunity to participate empathically, enactively, and improvisationally in dissociative patients' complex relationship with their own tormentuous internal worlds, as they slowly but steadily assist patients to renegotiate their overreliance on dissociative solutions to real and imagined danger. (Bromberg, 1994; Chefetz and Bromberg, 2004; Pizer, 1992; 1998; H. Schwartz, 1994; 2000).

Dissociation involves adaptational discontinuities related to managing severe threats and challenges to identity, awareness, attachment, meaning, and responsibility. Bromberg (2006) stresses that defensive dissociation involves a constant watchfulness for repetitions of trauma and an unbearable conflict between different versions of the self (i.e., the competing aspects of "me"). He views dissociation as a vehicle not solely for disavowing disturbing mental contents and experiences, but also as a way an individual may become alienated from aspects of him or her self that are inconsistent with the experience of selfhood (or identity) at any given point in time. Along these lines, Bromberg (1994) suggests that dissociation differs from fragmentation, citing Ferenczi's (1933) insight that fragmentation may not be a dismantling consequence of trauma as much as it is a healing adaptation to it.

> In dissociating to cope with trauma, the psyche may be enlisting its inherent adaptational capacity to compartmentalize, freeze, and disconnect. Instead of remaining a passive, helpless victim to a fragmentation experience, the protective wisdom of the dissociative capacity of mind [...] reclaims the fragmentation – orchestrating it, personifying it, and camouflaging it. Then, forever dancing on the edge of annihilation, the dissociatively organized individual creates and deploys a kind of controlled fragmentation while in fantasy avoiding, and in some corner of the mind perpetually reliving, the horrendous visitations to the psychological sites of the original traumatically disintegrating experiences. Anticipating disaster [while] sustaining a life that is itself a disaster zone, and ultimately remaining a psychological disaster in some ways wards off [a much larger] disaster – loss

of the attachments to perpetrators and loss of self-as-disaster, the only self there is.

H. Schwartz (2000:140)

The dissociative process is the ultimate intrapsychic and interpersonal trickster.[3] Dividing both the self and patterns of object relations (Gabbard, 1993), while preserving and suspending elements of the dynamic relational unconscious in parallel self-states and parallel fragments of consciousness, the dissociative process allows these elements to be sequestered and personified by a variety of fantasy operations and external shaping influences. Once dissociative adaptation to trauma and posttraumatic living is operative, coping with non-traumatic emotional and developmental challenges may also become dissociatively managed. Eigen (1996) describes the myriad psychic possibilities inherent in splitting, identification, and dissociation processes:

> Good or bad aspects of the self can be identified with good or bad aspects of the object, and good or bad aspects of the object can be identified with good or bad aspects of the self. If one adds dislocations and amalgams of affect, the clinical possibilities become mind-boggling. Ego, object, and affect can be taken apart and put together in myriad permutations. Bad ego can hate good ego, good ego can love bad ego, bad object can hate good object loving good ego, good ego can love bad ego hating good object, bad object can hate bad ego loving good object, good ego can hate bad ego hating good object, and on and on.
>
> (p. 31)

Dissociative disorders

Severe dissociative disorders most often arise from internalizing dynamics of domination, coercion, and sacrifice (Rivera, 1996; H. Schwartz, 1994). Relying excessively on dissociative solutions, traumatized individuals become lost in their own dissociative matrices in an attempt to master and transcend the damage caused by untrustworthy caretakers and malevolent authorities. In order to protect survival, severely traumatized individuals may turn to their capacities for camouflage and self-deception. By displacing consciousness and rearranging memories of childhood terror and misery with more benign histories, they achieve survival by emotionally abandoning themselves.

Dissociated identities, based in the pseudo-delusion of separateness (Kluft, 1985; 1998) exist in what Kluft (2000) called the third reality – a closed and somewhat impenetrable system, an inner world that is felt, heard, visualized and experienced as real. Kluft describes alter personalities[4] as characterized by trance logic, inhabiting separate compartments of behavior, affect, feeling, sensation, memory, attachment, and meaning, and eluding logical critique or the recognition of contradiction. Brittle, defensive self-sufficiency characterizes the dissociative organization of such individuals. The dissociative internal world contains multiple subjectivities, glaring inconsistencies and illogicalities, and a striking absence of normal intrapsychic conflict (Bromberg, 1994). The dissociative self-system is a house divided, oblivious to the true nature of its own inner turmoil. In the cases where internalized perpetration has been a significant factor in structuring the victim's dissociative system, aspects of the individual may also be at war with anyone his or her perpetrator(s) have labeled as enemies. Unfortunately, this designated enemy population often includes therapists, other helping professionals, and autonomy-seeking aspects of the self.

Internalized perpetration reaches its epitome in the intrapsychic architecture of dissociative identity disorder (DID). Representing the extreme end of the spectrum of dissociative disorders, DID[5] may be viewed as a complex posttraumatic stress disorder, a variable and mixed character disorder syndrome, a consciousness disorder, a complex attachment disorder, and a disorder of self- and other-representation. In its purest form DID occurs when a traumatized child creates another version of him or herself to hold traumatic or conflictual experience and/or to represent the wish to have been unaffected by trauma or conflict (Kluft, 1996). Many also believe that DID can be systematically created or enhanced by sophisticated perpetrators through the use of mind control and by the exploitation of vulnerabilities inherent in the psychobiology of victims' attachment and perceptual systems (Lacter, 2011; Miller, 2012; Ross, 2000; H. Schwartz, 2000). The psychological map of DID patients represents an internalization of the dynamic patterns of intimate interpersonal violence and betrayal. The structure of DID and alter personality templates have been viewed (Davies and Frawley, 1994; Kluft, 1985; Howell, 2011) as conforming to the classic Karpman (1968) drama triangle composed of victim, rescuer, and perpetrator. In this notion of cascading permutations of drama triangles organizing the internal world of DID individuals, the unrecognized problem of identification with collusion (ostensibly the fourth side of the trauma square at the intrapsychic, familial, and cultural levels) is the strongest factor for driving and sustaining elaborate dissociative self-organization.

DID can be conceptualized as a disorder of internalized domination and failed recognition. Because it is a disorder based in caretakers/authorities' misuse of power potentiated through social complicity, what is reflected in DID symptomatology is the quintessence of malevolent hierarchy and authoritarian power imbalances (Rivera, 1996; H. Schwartz, 1994; 2000). From C. Ross's (1991) and hooks's (1995) perspective, forms of internalized domination reflect, and are reinforced by the patterns of, power enactments in the dominant culture. One significant effect of combining social complicity with traumatic impacts is the feigning of a unitary self commonly seen in severely dissociative patients. Gaps between survivors' social persona and their increasingly camouflaged traumatized self-experience can be exacerbated by two forces of invalidation: perpetrators, and factions of the professional communities and media who have difficulties accepting traumatic realities and dissociative disorders. Aside from further fragmenting awareness, such invalidation leads to cognitive and consciousness organizations that occlude possibilities for experiencing/tolerating paradox, inclusivity, and ambiguity. From a relational psychoanalytic perspective, DID represents a pattern of traumatically-induced collapse in transitional and dialectical experiencing in both intrapsychic and interpersonal life. When coerced perpetration, mind control, or ritual abuse trauma are part of the survivor's history, DID can precipitate a form of psychic slavery.

Case example: Sara

Sara was one of twelve children raised in an impoverished community in the Midwest. Her violent and sexually abusive family was involved in a multi-state cult with both Nazi and satanic ideologies. Following years of multiple-perpetrator sexual abuse and involvement in child prostitution and pornography, including private "performances," Sara was drugged, tortured, and pressured to perform violent acts on an infant and on a young child in front of a group of cult members. When after considerable torment she refused to comply, the group leaders brought out her younger sister, placed her on a sacrificial alter and threatened to rape and murder her in front of Sara if she continued to resist. With this climatic episode, the remaining integrity of her identity came apart and an alter personality capable of harming others materialized to protect her sister. These acts were filmed and the films subsequently used to manipulate Sara into further perpetrator-allegiant crimes.

I met Sara decades after these life-altering events in a locked unit of a psychiatric hospital. She was being closely monitored for self-injury as memories of her gruesome childhood secrets had begun to emerge. Despite close monitoring on a locked ward, Sara continued to slip back into sadistic perpetrator alter personalities carving blocks of pentagrams on her arms in odd numbers until she reached the number thirteen at which time she began all over again. No one, not even Sara herself, could figure out how she was obtaining sharp objects to mutilate herself on such a tightly monitored locked ward.

Initially, I tried to be patient and inquiring. I maintained a non-judgmental attitude as best as I could, attempting to avoid the seductive traps of becoming overly concrete or directive in the face of her self-mutilations. Sara, myself, and the hospital staff had become mired down in a set of vicious transference-countertransference enactments. Each time Sara succeeded in self-mutilation, the hospital staff (somewhat contemptuously but with a posture of "clinical appropriateness") placed her in four-point or five-point restraints for long periods of time. Unaware of Sara's deep childhood involvement in sadomasochistic rituals, when aspects of her trauma history were revealed, many staff members were incredulous or dismissive. The symbolic and traumatic-related underpinnings of Sara's behavior were inconceivable to them. Many preferred to label Sara as an extreme borderline personality and favored treating her "accordingly." Entrenched biases against the validity and use of the DID diagnosis had also contributed to the complex triangulation that took place among hospital staff, Sara, and myself.

The enactments between Sara and the staff escalated daily with escalating mutual distrust and rage. Each side of the polarization and re-enactment had their moments of dark triumph. Sara's perpetrator alters were barely able to contain their glee (which was dissociated by the rest of Sara's self-states) at their cunning victory in baffling the staff in preventing sharp objects from ending up in her hands, while the staff barely camouflaged their excitement while protecting/punishing Sara with longer and more coercive confinement in four- and five-point restraints and injections of Haldol. In the midst of all of the systemic uproar, I attempted to maintain a protective container for daily exploratory psychotherapy without reducing the treatment solely to management and control of the cutting behavior. Managing my countertransference surges of helplessness, dread, and anger at both staff and Sara became at times overwhelming.

At times, both Sara and I were equally confused about the cascade of symptoms. Many of the hard-line hospital staff viewed me as too lenient, placating, and susceptible to Sara's manipulation and control. But Sara saw me as the only person not playing mind games with her, the only person not determined to control her, the one trying to help her understand herself. Meanwhile I continued to strain at juggling the various enactments, misperceptions, projections, and legitimate frustrations of all the people involved in the psychotherapy and institutional transferences and countertransferences, without leaning too far in any one direction for fear of the entire therapy project capsizing and breaking down. Her perpetrator alters presented as cagey and cunning; they used hit-and-run and bait-and-switch forms of relating with me and constellated the interpersonal patterns of an archetypal trickster figure. Periodically I wondered out loud with Sara how much of her perpetrator alters' rage (and her own anger, split off into them) at me for getting at Sara's deepest secrets and disrupting her attachments to her abusers (or other hurts, angers, disappointments with me) were being played out and deflected onto the hospital staff. I also wondered aloud with her if some form of the "good cop/bad cop" set-ups she had described from her childhood were being recreated among all of us at the hospital.

Within this matrix of double binds and enactments I often found myself in the position of the humiliated, pitiful rescuer racing the clock to save a life that could not be saved. Many days (and some sleepless nights) were filled with reflections on, and confusion about, Sara's actual innocence vs. her corruption, her actual responsibility vs. her true helplessness, and for what she could and could not be held accountable. Was I the noble warrior fighting for good and protection of the innocent? Or was I the buffoon who had become the instrument of a diabolic consciousness masquerading as a fragmented trauma survivor? I knew I was gaining access to Sara's inner torment and unmetabolized trauma history, but at times I became too vicariously traumatized by Sara myself to make use of my own reflective capacities. Was this only secondary trauma I wondered, or was this type of confusion part of the dance of traumatic enactments, an aspect of the evil of her childhood revealing itself? At the time, I was less experienced in the ways of the severely traumatized and my heart was in empathic knots for Sara and her predicament. Sometimes it seemed as if Sara were stealing compassion for her victimized self from me and a few others while her perpetrator alters were orchestrating the hospital staff to simultaneously violate her, humiliate me, and cover the tracks of her perpetrator identified system.

From these reflections on my countertransference experiences, the process began to take on the feel of some of the satanic cult rituals Sara had described in cathartic outpatient sessions prior to this hospitalization. Disturbing questions arose in my mind: Was the hospital staff alternatingly perpetrating and abandoning Sara in wild unbridled unconscious enactments, or were we all somehow Sara's prey and was she the wicked predator *par excellence*? Was this broken shell of a woman capable of such complex manipulations? Were there pieces to the story that had not yet been revealed due to Sara's conscious avoidance or due to masked patterns within her complex multi-layered dissociative matrix?

Sara sometimes welcomed alternative dynamic perspectives on the situation. We began to link what we knew about her past trauma with what was taking place in the hospital. At other times she was completely overwhelmed, shutdown, and unable to reflect in any meaningful way. Sara alternated between states of indifference and clinging to me for dear life. Her hostile and perpetrator alters shifted back and forth between silencing, threatening, and teasing with morsels of potentially useful information and revelation. Sara was not yet ready to appreciate all the perspectives on what she considered to be the worst aspects of herself (by refusing to hear and remember what her perpetrator alters were revealing) or the legitimate feelings and perspectives of hospital staff. After the crisis abated, Sara became integrated enough to reflect on some of the meanings of the enactments we had lived through together. The hospital had become an institutional holding environment where Sara could play out the extremes of child-like dependence, self-absorbed oblivion, deceit, and untraceable, intractable malice. This was the precise recipe I would use to describe the dynamic ambience of her family of origin.

However patient and reflective I may have succeeded in being during that period, I was also anxiously watching the clock, quite aware I had limited time to turn the situation around. Unbeknownst to Sara, some of the staff wanted to transfer her to a maximum-security psychiatric facility. One turning point in Sara's treatment came when I decided to share my feelings of helplessness and anger in the situation. I was careful to not precipitate an abandonment crisis but vulnerable enough to help Sara to understand the impact of the totality of her behavior on me. I also explained that some of the hospital staff were preparing to have her transferred to a state institution as a final statement of their "concerns" for her welfare and my protestations might not be enough to prevent it.

To her credit, Sara was eventually able to tolerate my confrontations of the multifarious seductions and enactments her DID system was co-creating with all the staff, including me – to rescue, withdraw, hate, retaliate, go numb, and/or to give up on her entirely. She was most receptive when I shared how these diverse reactions had been stirred in me (not just the hospital staff). Articulation of my own reactions (e.g., doubly bound, coerced helplessness, frustration, worry, confusion) without siding with any one position in particular as the only truth seemed to facilitate Sara's capacity for witnessing her own multiplicity. This allowed her to briefly rise above the ricocheting victim, complicity, and perpetrator positions in which she had become ensnared. Prior to my more emphatically repudiating Sara's destructiveness and irresponsibility in the situation, Sara was unable to imagine or empathically relate to the enormous negative impact these escalations were having on me – a form of enactment involving objectification and exploitation dynamics of her childhood. As her empathic and mutuality capacity became more engaged in our dialogues, a noticeable decrement in her use of emotional abdication and dissociative flight occurred.

I was able to help Sara see how her omnipotent rescue fantasies were colliding with her enactments of the impossibility of rescue (which she had lived out during much of her childhood when protective adults had ever even minimally interfered with her extensive trauma and exploitation experiences). She began to see how her internal schisms were playing out with hospital staff and me, but this awareness took some time to fully integrate. It also helped Sara advance when she saw me express my helplessness and uncertainty in the face of not being able to prevent the staff from reacting so aggressively to her, and my limitations in helping her stop the self-mutilation. Her shift was also facilitated by my helping Sara to understand a difficult fact: much as I was devoted to her care, protection, and treatment, beyond a certain point there would be nothing more I could do for her if she did not find a deeper alliance with the healing process that was strong enough to put an end to the cutting behavior. I (moreover, *we*) could not begin to repair some of the negligence and betrayal of her childhood without a deeper level of cooperation. I delivered this communication with a preamble, underlining how similar to her childhood perpetrator double binds this might feel to her. Yet despite the surface similarities, the meanings, and implications of "forced choice" in the present situation were different than the deadly double binds of her childhood.

As I shared my grief at the impending premature ending of our work together and the sadness I felt at not being able to help Sara reach the next step in her healing journey, Sara's defenses seem to finally relax. Something more coherent and continuous seemed to finally awaken in her. This awakening – as if from a nightmare presented options parallel yet different from the dreadful choices Sara faced in her childhood. Rather than precipitating an abandonment crisis or a backlash of rage and derision, Sara responded positively to my expression of vulnerability and frustration and became more open to my descriptions of the interlocking double binds in which we found ourselves. Sara seemed to find a renewed sense of safety and containment. Most notably, there was a slight reduction in her extreme anxiety, self-mutilation, massive memory loss, and her cascading dissociative states. Lost in a world of action and reaction, Sara was not used to mental health professionals having affectionate feelings (or emotional struggles on her behalf) or expressing them. Her perpetrator alters were not familiar with power and vulnerability existing in the same person, and my honesty and deep feelings of concern and helplessness seemed to disarm them. Although I could not possibly follow all the threads of this tapestry as it was being woven, multiple unconscious therapy tests had evidently been administered and satisfactorily passed.

Amidst the gross enactments and dissociative chaos, Sara had to make a choice. Would she take responsibility and take a stand on the side of life? Instead of wanting her own death (for wanting life) – a key dynamic articulated in Grand's (2000) insightful analysis of the dynamics of survivors of human evil – Sara had to choose life and therapy (healing) for wanting life. She, at least temporarily, had to reject toying with lethality and self-mutilation as a way of maintaining some semblance of her integrity in the wake of her dim memories of her betrayal enacted against others.

Another issue that emerged at this time was Sara's unconscious belief that she deserved brutal punishment. Sara was confronted with a difficult set of choices at that point in her treatment. She could keep cutting and lose her relationship with me; her perpetrator alters could escalate the already intense institutional transferences and try their luck at a state hospital, or "they" could risk placing the madness, murder, and mayhem in the container of intensive outpatient therapy – without the bulwark of a hospital to provoke simultaneous longings and contempt with her oscillating needs for protection and punishment. Sara's non-perpetrator alters chose to fight to preserve the therapy relationship and deepen the attachment bond with me. Her perpetrator personalities faced an important reckoning with the double binds they had co-created with hospital staff while simultaneously negotiating an ongoing humanizing relationship with me. A fortuitous combination of fear, attachment, limits, humility, and negotiation brought all the parts of Sara into a rare, temporary alignment to solve the crisis.

Sara made a leap of faith. She sided with the promise of vulnerability, uncertainty, and relationship. Her perpetrator alters felt I was no match for them so they claimed they were not worried about the long-term plan. At least I didn't use drugs and restraints and they "were getting tired of how dumb the hospital staff were." At the eleventh hour, the pentagram carving activity subsided. This pleased a few staff members, mystified others, and, of course, disappointed a few of the hospital workers with whom she had been most at odds. With Sara, I directly and playfully promoted the idea of locating the transference (all of it) into our outpatient relationship. Somehow she came to believe that I might be able to handle all of her (and that they could handle all of me!).

Eventually, interpretations of transference-countertransference dynamics helped Sara realize (and integrate) that there were significant parallels to various aspects of her disowned childhood experience (and internalized object relations) represented by my, the staff's, and her own positions in the complex dramas that had been unfolding. The most challenging psychic elements Sara had to eventually face as an outpatient were the existence of extremely diabolical perpetrator states that had proudly risen to power in her cult and that possessed sophisticated capacities for engineering passion plays of destruction that sucked others into maelstroms of violence, betrayal, and confusion. As Sara became increasingly able to own and embody her own destructiveness and ruthlessness in a unitary consciousness – including facing her desire for acceptance and praise from her perpetrators – she disabled much of the unconscious motivating force that had been sustaining her perpetrator-identified and perpetrator-indoctrinated self-states.

Sara eventually made great strides through many years of treatment as she reintegrated most of her perpetrator-identified alters into her larger self-system. She broke off almost all contact with her family of origin, although this limit did not prevent their many attempts to breach her boundary. Two important disturbing mysteries – unknown to Sara and me during the hospitalization crisis – eventually become clear some time later in outpatient treatment. First, Sara's dissociative self-system had indeed been hi-jacked by perpetrators using mind control and torture to implant and create an entire hierarchy of alter personalities with complex jobs, tasks, skills, and interrelationships with one another. This system was buried beneath, yet somehow intertwined with Sara's own self-generated dissociative self-system. Teasing the two systems apart became a complicated but essential aspect of her treatment. Second, following preliminary outpatient treatment of some of Sara's more accessible perpetrator identities, these alters revealed that during the hospitalization on the locked unit, a pay phone (for patients' legal rights) was available for both incoming and outgoing calls. Unbeknownst to me and to Sara's conscious mind, Sara's family members and perpetrators had been calling her and signaling her to call them during the entire self-mutilation escapade. Once revealed, it seemed painfully obvious, and I felt dumbfounded and embarrassed that I had failed to consider it:the direct intrusion of perpetrators into the treatment process. In my work with survivors since then (and in the writings of many clinicians who treat ritual abuse survivors in particular), I became aware of a disturbing but important factor one must always keep in mind[6]: That is, what contact might the dissociative survivor be having with perpetrators and their collaborators, through perpetrator-engineered dissociative "black holes" and perpetrator-protective self-states cultivated in the DID system during years of childhood captivity. Sara's psyche had been under more pressure than I had ever understood at the time of the self-mutilation crisis. Sara had been sandwiched between her love-hate and hide-and-seek traumatic transferences with me, unconscious enactments with hospital staff, her two intersecting dissociative systems, and actual real-time intentional "triggering" (silencing, self-doubting, self-injurious) from members of the perpetrating system.

Like other professionals who have noted this problem, I am aware that the possibility of perpetrator-interference in treatment may be enough to induce paranoia and/or incredulity in many mental health professionals (or complete avoidance of these cases altogether). However, it is essential for clinicians treating victims of coerced perpetration to understand that these survivors remain vulnerable to interference from actual perpetrators as well as from internalized perpetration, particularly once they enter treatment. This applies to a spectrum of patients: child soldiers threatened with interference and recapture by former commanders; religious or political former cult members facing re-recruitment and kidnapping by cult leaders and active members; or dissociative survivors facing re-accessing, intrusions, and threats to their therapy and attempts at freedom. Potentials for behavior patterns implying such interference must be evaluated and addressed (Miller, 2012).

Throughout her years of outpatient treatment, Sara learned to balance stabilization and disruption with non-violent self-soothing. All forms of domination and complicity, and all forms of sadism toward, and abdication of, the mind and body were systematically challenged and interpreted. Sara's tolerance for internal conflict, ambiguity, and interpersonal stress dramatically improved. Just prior to completing a very long treatment, Sara – then in her late forties – died of medical complications from physical injuries sustained during years of torture. I was present in Sara's hospital room at the time of her death. In contrast with the many horrific deaths she had witnessed and participated in, her death was one that occurred in a state of grace. The grief I felt at seeing her life end too early was offset by knowing Sara had attained a previously inconceivable liberation by having thrown off the collection of psychological and spiritual programming that had enslaved her in self-hatred and self-destruction.

Dilemmas of dissociative survival

In addition to recovering psychological functioning, dissociative trauma survivors must confront disturbing existential questions and dilemmas. In a poignant inquiry, Davoine and Gaudilliere (2004) ask: What becomes of psyches and lives when all manner of virtue, loyalty, and meaningful language has been destroyed, degraded, or rendered absolutely impotent? Whether their life is normal or eccentric, people who went through hell oscillate between excessive distrust and excessive trust. "They feel they are in exile in the world. They no longer believe in anything. They are outside of time" (p. 115).

Coerced perpetration compounds traumatic damage to the psyche. When trauma includes having been forced to collude in their own oppression or the oppression of others, survivors may feel utterly orphaned from humanity (Grand, 2000). In this abject state, both child soldiers and other dissociative survivors of coerced perpetration may eventually find perverse comfort in the shared alienation with perpetrators. Such traumatic bonding occurs when the state of banishment is reinforced by the ideology of leaders/perpetrators who also provide recognition, validation, outlets for rage, hate, and frustration, a sense of belonging, and soothing master narratives for moderating loneliness and legitimizing perpetration. Dissociative survivors alternate between posttraumatic hypersensitivity and the inability to feel anything, between discursive speech and catatonic trance, hyper-rationality and regressive incoherence, and between affability and contemptuousness. Because of dissociative survival strategies such as memory and identity fragmentation, survivors must recover from a catastrophe they have never been able to completely register. Submerged in the cacophony of chronic posttraumatic symptoms, survivors cloak themselves alternately in amiability and futility while obscuring deeper truths in multiple distractions, addictions, and cover narratives. Dissociative survivors face the apparently insurmountable task of rebuilding a self within a psyche and a world that has completely betrayed them.

The dynamics and structures of internalized perpetration are woven into the classic dissociative response patterns to chronic trauma. Illuminating the core posttraumatic foundations in which internalized perpetration is cultivated, six of seven key dilemmas that face dissociative survivors are reviewed (the seventh – disrupted critical thinking – is the subject of Chapter 4). They include:

- Challenges of living dissociatively
- Confusion of identity
- Dysfunctional aggression
- Disrupted attachment
- Compromised fantasy and imagination
- Compounded shame.

Challenges of living dissociatively

Chronic reliance on dissociative survival solutions attempts to preserve sanity and potential for healing for a future non-trauma based life. However, these adaptations systematically compress the individual's vitality and awareness, leading to a living psychic death under a mask of feigned normalcy. While attempting to maintain control over intrapsychic and interpersonal reality, dissociative survivors feel perpetually out of control, besieged by disorganizing and disturbing experiences that cannot be easily managed or verbalized (flashbacks, rapid self-state changes, catatonic and numbing responses, ego-dystonic ideation, compulsions, and bizarre fantasies).

Narrowing the windows of awareness, dissociative adaptations prevent the updating of survivors' central autobiographical consciousness, which makes guarding against retraumatization the central organizing psychological principle of life (Bromberg, 1993, 1998; Howell, 2011). Since intense experience, regardless of valence, can open floodgates of affect and cognition, the dissociative individual must continually constrict emotional experience to avoid thoughts, feelings, and situations evocative of the original trauma (van der Kolk, 1989). By shutting themselves out and shutting down, survivors expend vital energy by keeping new information out (Alpert, 1995). Old data, often unprocessed and unintegrated, reigns unquestioned. New material, particularly new relational experience, cannot penetrate the dissociative barriers to effectively rearrange traumatic expectations or disrupt pathological belief systems. In severe dissociative adaptations, each self-state or alter personality selectively attends to evidence that reinforces its own insulated version of reality (Bromberg, 1993). In this way, potentially valuable information manifest through obsessions, panic attacks, phobias, psychosomatic complaints, mood disorders, and dysfunctional relational patterns. The traumatic payload pre-empts normal development with survival and camouflage concerns (Grant, 1996). In spite of how hard the dissociative survivor tries to control his or her internal and external worlds, marginalized self-states (which can never be completely negated or anesthetized) inevitably "break out of their dissociative captivity" and create havoc (Bromberg, 2011). The dissociative survivor's present and future are

> plundered by an overly rigid sequestering of "me" and "not-me" self-states that is the legacy of developmental trauma too relationally barren to allow cognitive symbolization and self-reflection [...] the outcome of one's best intentions is most often characterized by unanticipated failures, and destructive patterns of living that feel "sort of" familiar, but are recognized always too late.
>
> Bromberg (2011:5)

The dissociative structure of self is designed to operate outside of cognitive awareness (Bromberg, 1998; Fonagy *et al.*, 2002; Kluft, 1984, 1999; Sullivan, 1956). To be truly effective, dissociative adaptations must eradicate or conceal all evidence or knowledge of dissociation. The dissociatively-organized individual must work overtime "to prepare for almost any conceivable emergency that would startle [some]one into becoming aware of the dissociated system" (Sullivan, 1956:203). The survivor's unconscious motivation to deflect evidence of dissociation is often compounded by the incredulity of society, the lack of training or dismissiveness of the helping professions, and by the manipulations of perpetrators who compound their victims' self-generated camouflage with intimidation, posthypnotic suggestions, and as Miller (2012) reports, programmed resistance and suicidality, and anti-therapy/anti-attachment programming.

Dissociative survivors can present with vague or changeable histories, and can remain willfully confused about their backgrounds, identities, and risk-taking behavior. They can appear unable or unwilling to know their own minds and may seem incapable of thinking their own thoughts. They are often inundated by diverse internal voices so that questions of true identity only arouse deep anxiety and the desire to escape from interpersonal inquiry or contact. Survivors can paradoxically be triggered by seemingly minimal stimuli while remaining oblivious to impending danger. To bind the processes of dissociation and disavowal, survivors can become addicted to many things: sex, drugs, shopping, food, and work; extreme dogmatic, double-binding religions; extremist, righteous politics; obsessive coveting or collecting; prostituting and enslaving relationships.

Survivors can become expert in all forms of collusion and complicity in exploiting themselves or others. These adaptations cement powerful attachments to perpetrators and sustain profound confusion over core issues of identity, responsibility, worth, and personal potential.

Constructing a dissociative system in order to keep toxic emotional states at bay (Briere, 1995), dissociative survivors are held hostage to a protean view of the past. Because the resources of the traumatized self have been devoted to physical and psychological survival, attachment to the sources of trauma has taken precedence over self-awareness and self-actualization. Psychological resources are deployed to avoid painful feelings, memories, and traumatic recurrences, and for maintenance of the stability that has been achieved through identification with the perpetrator's worldview – belief systems, rationalizations, spiritual and political perspectives, and most importantly, the perpetrator(s)' strategic misrepresentations of the victim. The dissociative survivor's inner process includes rehearsal of false historical narratives, cover stories, lies and reiterations of programming which result in the construction of a matrix of elaborate dissociative defenses. Survivors can echo internalized perpetrator messages, accepting them (even arguing for them) as representing the "real me" without any awareness that they are vehicles of an unacknowledged form of posttraumatic ventriloquism. Managing this internal world, sustaining secrets about the self and perpetrators, and preventing traumatic repetitions in the external world is an overwhelming project. These stressed systems exist perpetually on the verge of break down.

Profoundly ambivalent about being known and believed, many survivors are often reticent to listen with curiosity to their own inner voices or to feel entitled to healthy attention. With therapists, the combination of self-generated, post-traumatic and perpetrator-programmed resistances leads to a constant oscillation between presentations of self-states desperate for consolation and validation and those that negate and deride recognition or empathy of any kind. In the unique intrapsychic arrangements that evolve from chronic victimization experiences in pathological families and violent subcultures, protective belief systems usually emerge in treatment as cover stories and confabulations lodged in various alter personalities whose goal is denial and deflection. The discovery of the historic reality of their fractured existence and to really experience the pervasive effects of trauma on their present lives would be such an overwhelming proposition that survivors choose to collude in the silencing and "forgetting" of abuse, perpetrators, and collaborating others.

In these reconfigurations of memory and identity which serve to unconsciously reinforce complicity, false memories (of non-abuse or minimized abuse) co-exist with, but dominate, fragments of disturbing historical truths. Fantasies of invulnerability replace realities of helplessness. Personifications and enactments of self-hate replace healthy assertion, differentiation, and normal fantasies of retaliation. Suicidal fantasies fill the void created by the absence of soothing internal objects and privately become a perverse form of self-mothering and self-love. Fears of intimacy and difficulties with assertiveness supplant a healthy quest for recognition and the capacity for healthy actions. The patient's well-rehearsed narratives of the past (developed with the help of the mainstream culture, his or her perpetrators and collaborators, the limited cognitions from childhood, and needs to pass as normal) are cover stories that obscure other versions of the past's brutality and exploitation. Some of the most common omnipotent solutions to the vulnerability of traumatization which reverse responsibility from perpetrator to victim include: *I made it happen; I made them do this to me; I wanted it; I liked it; I deserved it; The pain makes me stronger; I feel nothing, the abuse happened to her, she is not a part of me; I am impervious to any effects of the abusers then and now; I am secretly in charge of everything and everyone; My anger is dangerous and will annihilate everyone and everything; I am proud of the stress and pain I cause others; I like being evil, I was born to be evil;* and *I choose to be evil.* An abiding sense of futility and condemnation all lie close to the affective epicenter of dissociative self-organization.

The survivor's painful history is buried deep beneath the cacophony of the dissociative diaspora, and because disunity as a survival strategy comes to constitute an independent homeostasis, the survivor initially experiences any breakthrough toward reunification of the self as a serious threat to his or her equilibrium. For example, the survivor may regard relational patterns that hold seeds of integration – insight, empathy, respect, compassion, encouragement to feel and reflect – as so perilous as to merit attack or avoidance; he or she might seek out seemingly protective behaviors that soothe and reduce tension by sustaining psychological disunity through compelling distractions or acting-out.

The constrictive and self-destructive aspects of dissociative survival are most evident when the survivor's attempts to maintain healthy attachments and reclaim some aspect of dignity catalyze an onslaught of self-hatred. Trapped in a dissociative web of internal persecution and unusual displays of pride, indifference, or defensive autonomy, the survivor will often resort to seeking comfort by taking refuge in behaviors and attitudes reinforced in the original abusive developmental context – helplessness, perfectionism, acquiescence, denial, displays of arrogance, righteousness, boundary violations, and provocative sexuality. Anything that jeopardizes the perpetuation of dissociative adaptations, including any threat to survivors' attachments to malevolent but "protective" internal objects, may be perceived as highly threatening. The dissociative survivor's inevitable assaults on the good will of others reinforce the belief that they are contaminated and beyond salvation. The prospect of dismantling their persecutory theater of mind is as hard and terrifying for survivors as sustaining it.

It is not surprising that a psychic death becomes the unconscious goal of chronic dissociative survival. In a way, if you're dead already, no one can hurt or threaten you ever again. If you have no life energy left to sunder, no one take it from you. If your sexual arousal is either frozen or compulsively and promiscuously acted out, no one can co-opt or violate your sexuality again. Repeating disasters, cultivating destructive relationships, and even inflicting pain on one's self to feel alive means that trying to hurt or negate yourself is actually a symbolic form of pre-emptively saving yourself. Hating one's self is saving one's self. If suicidal fantasies are comforting and empowering it's because your being in control of the annihilation is soothing. If perpetrating on others temporarily staves off catastrophic anxieties, then spreading helplessness and dread around the interpersonal world sustains omnipotent control over all vulnerability and death. Hating and harming someone becomes the only relief available to desperate part-selves completely identified with perpetration. If deserving death for wanting life (Grand, 2000) is the solution to the shame of coerced moral transgression, then ongoing punishment and chronic self-hatred become the protective jail in a life sentence without parole.

Adding to the burdens of dissociative survivors is the probability of their role of scapegoat within the family, society, and mental health systems – ironically, this is more likely to occur once effective therapy is underway. The marginalized and the oppressed often recognize the social madness and denial that passes for normalcy, and dissociative trauma survivors have some significant awareness of the patterns of social structure and discourse that keep its citizens in the dark (Grant, 1996), even as they are blinded to their own unconscious perpetrator identifications. Dissociative survivors may become symbols, or unpopular reminders, of the protection failures of society, of the disavowed vulnerability of all people, or of the benefits people receive for colluding in webs of social avoidance and denial. Describing how scapegoats shoulder the sins and darkest truths of their culture only to be driven off into the wilderness rather than embraced as a bearer of unpopular truths, Grant (1996) notes that "scapegoats end up as either overly domesticated citizens who passively accept social denial systems or as wolves who contemptuously observe life from the margins of society" (p. 37). When the severely traumatized are able to enter a deep healing process and finally encounter the sorrow buried beneath the years of dissociative survival, they must face a double grief: what they have lost and what they have never had (a happy, emotionally secure childhood with loving nonabusive parents and siblings, pets who survived unharmed, healthy sexuality, a non-traumatized brain, and untainted spirituality to name a few) (Miller, 2012).

Dissociative trauma survivors often challenge the limitations and rigidities of the mental health care delivery system tasked with treating them. Because of their confusing symptoms and behaviors, many survivors are thwarted (or limited) for reasons they cannot fully understand when they seek to elicit help from various professionals and agencies. Many survivors are treated with ambivalence through a peculiar combination of fear, fascination, and incredulity. When the patient's trauma history includes coerced and internalized perpetration, this ambivalence may be exacerbated by professionals' avoidant and dismissive reactions. When the patient's perpetrator(s) have systematically engineered aspects of the survivor's dissociative self-system beneath the layers of the survivor's own naturally occurring spontaneous dissociative adaptations, then the patient has a triple set of obstacles to overcome: the confusion of living with a dissociative self-organization; the compounding of pain and shame from cultural and professional ambivalence; and the disturbing minefield of perpetrator engineered dissociative states and torture-based mind-control programming. Mental health professionals need to understand the dilemmas and potentials for retraumatization that dissociative survivors of complex trauma face in order to help them disentangle from their confusing webs of mutually reinforcing symptoms.

For dissociative survivors, the psychotherapy process is in part an elaborate series of tests of the therapist. The object of the tests is to determine whether or not the therapist will relate in the familiar terms of the pathological attachment dynamics mastered in the traumatic situations. Tests also represent the survivor's paradoxical wishes to re-enact perpetration (i.e., to do unto others what was done to them), and to have all forms of perpetration prevented, exposed, witnessed, and punished. Highly dissociative patients have a knack for regarding their therapists as simultaneously significant and irrelevant. This replicates the original traumatic-bonding paradox whereby caretaker/perpetrators alternately disparaged and treated them as special. Urgent demands for concrete rescue can coincide with a strident disavowal of the therapist's usefulness – paralleling the patient's internal experience of a deeply conflicted and tormented relationship to him or herself and to the abusers of his or her childhood. In this mix, the inconsistencies of irrational authority had become the seedpearl around which defensive strategies for survival were organized. Behind the survivor's compliant presenting personality's apparent accessibility lie layers upon layers of terror, humiliation, and impotent rage resulting from compounded attachment failures. The therapist must recognize and continuously negotiate with the split-off extremes of traumatic compliance and virulent defiance – accepting both, questioning both, and introducing the patient to the notion of holding these voices in one central consciousness. When dissociative trauma patients can sustain the conflict among polarized parts of the self without resorting to remobilizing their dissociative defenses, they can begin to integrate attachment longings with their attachment fears and develop the capacity to tolerate knowledge of, and feelings about, past betrayals.

Confusion of identity

The most significant transgression perpetrators use against victims of extreme abuse is the systematic confusion of the victim about his or her true identity. Hijacking the victim's sense of his or her own free choice to enact the perpetrator(s)' intentions and ambitions is a key part of all indoctrination practices in most forms of child abuse. The harrowing life and death, double bind, forced-choice traps created in coerced perpetration training represent highly effective methods of seducing the victim into crossing, and then obliterating, moral lines. Initially, states of depletion, apathy, or fury (or alternations between helplessness and blind rage) are generated by perpetrators as essential building blocks to activating (and then internalizing) the capacity for perpetration.

Sexualized violence is almost always a component of this process. Disgust, shame, terror, and learned helplessness are a powerful set of emotional and neurological triggers in the perpetrators' arsenal of identity confusion techniques.

Secondary to coerced perpetration is the embedding of the (false) certainty that breaking free is impossible. This intentional confusion process always includes the eradication of the individual's sense of innocence.[7] Often this negation is followed by the strategic replacement of the victim's identity, or any other potentially autonomous or rebellious strivings, with destructive perpetrator-based perceptions and allegiances. Like many child soldiers, cult survivors undergo a period of initiation. They are given provocative new names; subjected to propaganda; exposed to strategic sexualization of violence; forced to take oaths of loyalty and secrecy; required to witness and participate in murder and the brutal punishment of alleged enemies and traitors; and are continuously infused with a false sense of mastery and power by group leaders. Survivors forget who they used to be, to become who the perpetrator needs them to be.

Forced observation of, and ongoing participation in, torture and murder shatter the victims' innocence, coerce dependence on the group, and cause further deterioration of victims' pre-trauma identity. Compelled by shame and guilt, the survivor (or perpetrator-identified alter personality within a DID patient) feels there is no return to normal life and no escape from the abuser(s). Once the victim (or self-state) has demonstrated a preference for survival at any cost by agreeing to do the perpetrator(s)' bidding, something is forever changed in the psyche and spirit of that survivor. Bound in criminal complicity and forced to identify with perpetrator logic and ideology to manage states of guilt and overwhelm, the victim is impelled to bond with perpetrators for sanity and survival. Victims who are coerced into perpetration are unlikely to ever leave or inform on the abuser or group. If or when such individuals do escape, or get liberated from their abusive groups and find their way to treatment, they will still be bound by traumatic attachments to perpetrator-indoctrinated beliefs. Those attachments and beliefs are the only psychic salve on which these individuals have come to depend.

Because of the problem of identity confusion, effective methods of treatment for all dissociative trauma patients must eventually involve integration of the core internal psychological splits of the classic trauma square – internalized victim, internalized collaborator,[8] internal self-helpers, and the internalized perpetrator identities. Dissociative reconfigurations of identity within the trauma square are survival responses that paradoxically affirm and negate identifications with each of these four roles.[9] Coming to terms with each split-off identity poses unique challenges to the treatment process. The combination of the survivor's own dissociative self-states and the elusive shaping influences of his or her perpetrator(s) creates many obfuscations to the true meanings and history underlying each of the four positions.

For example, many survivors fervently defend against the true realities and experiences of victimization or overdramatize them in a self-discrediting manner in order to disavow their helplessness, suffering, and betrayal by others and for a sense of pseudo-mastery via denial, omnipotent fantasy, or bravado. While the survivor's ambivalent relationship with the victim role is complex, the unconscious renunciation of complicity is even more complicated to work through. This disavowal includes the more ambiguous dynamics of neglect found in the failures of family and social institutions designated to protect children. Dissociation and denial of internalized complicity guard against the painful revelations about sacrifice of the victim's body, mind, and possibly life for the narcissism or predatory self-interest of others. Unconsciously identifying with patterns of passivity, self-betrayal, abdication, self-neglect, obliviousness to danger, the forming of co-dependent relationships with destructive individuals, and collusion with untrustworthy authority are some examples of the victim's unconscious identifications with complicity.[10]

Chronic trauma and perpetrator influences foster deep confusion about the rescue element of the trauma square. Perpetrators convince victims the only way of helping themselves is hurting themselves, harming or betraying others, and by complying with perpetrator(s)' injunctions and belief systems. In general, even without explicit perpetrator influence, trauma survivors exhibit many forms of faulty efforts at self-help; they are often unwilling to recognize the underlying care and self-protection implicit in these behaviors. Instead, they focus on failures and legacies of addictions and self-defeating behavior patterns, confirming their worthless and condemned status. A central task of recovery is reformulating the concept of rescue and self-help to help survivors value the efforts made on their own behalf; and grieve what they could not prevent in spite of their best efforts; and responsibly face the effects of misguided forms of self-protection.

The most potentially problematic of all parts of the trauma square is perpetration. No survivor willingly faces this identity, especially when perpetrator self-states have been camouflaged by torture-based mind control and buried in a field of psychological land mines, "booby traps," and "fail-safes" (Miller, 2012). To significantly transcend the perpetrator-based confusions around identity and culpability, treatment must assist survivors to understand and reconcile their vulnerability and cruelty, their innocence and corruptibility, and their disavowed masochistic and sadistic selves. Guiding the patient toward integrating these apparent opposites, the therapist helps the survivor to foster a new identity based on the survivor's use of compassion and appropriate aggression, to create healthy boundaries and develop self-protective instincts, to assimilate the polarities of their feelings, to cultivate stronger more accurate discernment and critical thinking, and to question and reject allegiances with irrational authority.

Dysfunctional aggression

Individuals subjected to prolonged trauma develop dysfunctional forms of aggression that erode the personality (Eigen, 1992): hyperarousal to emotional and sensory stimuli (Kardiner, 1941; Krystal, 1978; Lindemann, 1944); automatic and repetitive destructive and self-destructive behavior (Grossman, 1991); provocation of attacks on themselves and assaults on others (Galenson, 1986; Glenn, 1978), oscillating between uncontrollable expressions of rage and absolute intolerance of aggression in any form (van der Kolk, 1987). These extremes may be so polarizing that the same individual will have a history of multiple violent enactments against self and others and absolute intolerance for even the fantasied pain of cut vegetables or flowers (H. Schwartz, 1994). In oppressive conditions, survivors omnipotently fantasize everything related to aggression and often misperceive their own and others' aggressive urges and responses.

Winnicott (1971) emphasized that healthy aggression leads to essential developmental achievements in the areas of differentiation and capacity for love, play, mutuality, and fantasy, so accordingly there is no way to avoid fury in childhood; the crucial factor is how this fury is received, and responded to, by others. With no expectation of recognition or dialogue about anger, rage, or individuation strivings, the traumatized withdraw into excessive internalization and re-enactment of abandonment/retaliation scenarios. When all of a victim's self-assertion and efforts at individuation (including thinking one's own thoughts) threaten the omnipotence and narcissistic equilibrium of his or her perpetrators, the perpetrator(s)' retaliation or abandonment foster a developmental "freeze" in crucial areas of self-assertion and individuation. Fears of retaliation or torture by the abuser/caretaker(s) forces abused individuals into states of abject compliance and submission by developmental necessity – but as Freud (1930) so clearly stated, obedience does not exorcise aggression – it directs aggression against the self. In Freud's terms, authoritarian arrangements produce aggression that devolves into forms of self-domination, and the individual's own conscience becomes suffused with the hostility that cannot be directed at the unassailable authority.

When infused with chronic painful bodily and emotional experiences at an early age and isolated from soothing/restorative responses, the traumatized are unable to direct the hyperstimulated arousal of aggression toward the sources of injury. Aggression is dammed up in the internal dissociative matrix with no safe flow to the intersubjective world. The damming up and redirection of aggression happens under the aegis and control of perpetrators who shape dissociative identity states to support criminal or military operations and their camouflage. Elaborate psychic structures based on trigger words, coerced amnesia, and conditioned responses are buried within dissociative survivors' matrices of self-states hidden from themselves and those around them. Some perpetrators have become masterful overseers of this psychological process, turning victims' aggression against themselves (i.e., creating self-states that monitor, spy on, punish, and influence the thinking and communication process of survivors), against those deemed as enemies, or appropriate targets for rage and retaliation. In complex DID survivors of organized child abuse, targets for rage may include other parts of the self, economic or political competitors of the perpetrator(s), or helping professionals. In many perpetrator groups, survivors (particularly perpetrator alters) are taught that they will be killed or reported to the perpetrator or criminally exposed. Many are taught that helping professionals are actually working on behalf of the perpetrator group and thus likely to trick and betray them (Miller, 2012). Hence, perpetrator-identified alters present with a higher degree of paranoia and suspiciousness than is generally the case with self-created hostile, internal abuser personalities.

The dissociative survivor's solution to dilemmas of impotent rage, learned helplessness, and the ongoing need for self-protection is the creation of hostile and abusive self-states that are fearfully compliant, proudly collaborative, or tenderly loving in relation to the psychopathology and tyranny of the caretaker/ abusers. The most commonly found terms in the trauma and dissociation literature referring to aggressive self-states are *abuser, hostile, protector, angry,* and *persecutory alters.* C. Ross *et al.* (1989) found that 84% of DID cases had abusive and persecutory parts. Embodying the patient's and the perpetrator(s)' rage, contempt, and callous indifference, grandiose, hostile self-states commonly found in dissociative survivors are conceived and sustained by the survival capacities of the human nervous system (elements of the "fight" part of the "fight-flight" response) and the activation of potentials inherent in all human psyches under siege (Kalsched, 1996; Van der Kolk, 1987). Early views suggested that the developing child relieves him or her self of rage, and knowledge of betrayal (Freyd, 1996), by placing (and reversing) thoughts and feelings onto other personality segments and then walling them off (Putnam, 1989; C. Ross 1997; C. Ross *et al.*, 1989). Other aggressive alters may be "secretly" constructed around counter-identifications to protect against threatening or dangerous people and eventually impinging memories (and concomitant fantasies). Still other alters are constructed according to elaborate rules of counter-dependence. Once created, persecutor and abuser states become increasingly active in the service of predicting the perpetrator(s)' behavior, pre-empting the perpetrator(s)' violence and threat, and avoiding harm from anyone (Lyons-Ruth, 1999; Howell, 2011).

Since hostile alters come into existence to protect survival, their greatest fear is their own annihilation. This includes fears of being destroyed or literally killed by the therapist or others – often concretizing their anticipation of psychic disintegration in the face of disturbing affects and dependent or vulnerable feelings (C. Ross, 1997; H. Schwartz, 1994). Hostile alter personalities serve as a trauma membrane in the survivor's internal world (Putnam, 1989). Hostile self-states:

- regulate the flow of information and memory (Kluft, 1985; Putnam,1997)
- discharge aggressive and sexual tension states (C. Ross, 1997)
- maintain and protect remnants of healthy self-assertion, self-esteem, boundaries, and self-expression (H. Schwartz, 1994)
- hold rage and contempt so that other socially adept parts of the personality can function (Kluft, 1985; 2000; C. Ross, 1997)

- protect against retraumatization and external danger (Kluft, 1985; C. Ross, 1989)
- serve as an early warning system preventing emotional dysregulation and annihilation anxiety (Bromberg, 1993, 1998; Howell, 1997; 2011)
- defend against the experience of hope, guilt, shame, vulnerability, disappointment (Putnam, 1989; C. Ross, 1989)
- attempt to prevent the repetition of previously shattered fantasies of self in relation to self-objects (H. Schwartz, 1994)
- protect against exposure of criminal actions, sustain and regulate attachment to perpetrators, and prevent exposure of the perpetrators' systems, crimes, and methods (H. Schwartz, 2000).

Although they may appear deformed, the severely dissociative individual's aggressive alter personalities contain much of the life force of the pre-traumatized individual (Kluft, 1985, 1999; Putnam, 1989). This positive potential is less true for highly programmed perpetrator alters whose life force has been systematically regressed toward destructive aims to support perpetrator goals of sustained servitude, potential for lethality, dependency, and loyalty. In spite of this, it is important for therapists to remember that programmed and spontaneously generated perpetrator states often hold much of the survivor's disavowed ambition, ruthlessness, and needs for mastery, all of which must be re-integrated into a central coordinated consciousness and fluid identity for successful healing, and for effectively and creatively meeting life's challenges.

In recent years, the process for best understanding the development of hostile alters is "procedural, enactive identification with the aggressor" (Howell, 2011; Lyons-Ruth, 1999). Invoking research on mirror neurons and imitative/anticipatory procedural enactment, Howell encourages clinicians to consider both imitation and anticipation as part of the relational neurological design that leads to the commonly seen elaborations of "identification with the aggressor" in highly dissociative patients. In traumatic procedural learning, a part of the self disconnected from the hyperarousal response to trauma – a part of the self that can watch from a distance – may automatically anticipate and imitate the abuser's behavior as part of survival, along with maintaining some semblance of self-empowerment. Within these complex identification situations, the perpetrator's omnipotence and hatefulness are uploaded into the patient's trance logic and lead to the perpetrator(s)' arrogance and contempt being later enacted on self and others in response to specific threats or context cues.

Long after the violence has ended, sometimes long after the abusers are dead, the inner world of trauma is laden with persecutory, malevolent figures and the dissociative survivor's outer life experience is often dominated by many patterns of revictimization or enactments of perpetration (lying, stealing, seducing, betraying, manipulating). Through the compounding effects of cumulative trauma, imbalanced energies flood the personality and take up residence. As Kalsched (1996) points out, primitive defenses are not easily educated or updated by life experience. Although protective in origin, when the archetypal traumatogenic agency is set loose within the psyche as a result of psychological trauma, the individual may appear as if he or she were "possessed by some diabolical power or pursued by a malignant fate" (p. 5). Individuals immersed in perpetrator groups are subjected to a fertile ambience in which their fragmented psyches can be subtly or coercively guided to activate (and imitate) extraordinarily malicious personality potentials – potentials one usually only associates with mythology, gruesome war stories, or horror movies.

While serving predictable defensive functions, the hostile alter phenomenon can evolve into diverse forms and disguises. The human aggressive response to trauma can be shaped by self and others to appear as almost any form or structure. When coping with traumatic body-mind invasions via trance logic, dissociative absorption, fight-flight responses, traumatic merger states, implicit procedural learning, imitation, activation of unstable archetypal potentials, are solidified through practice and reinforcement. These protean forms include terrifying mythological creatures, formless blobs of color and energy, dangerous animals, demons, robots, assassins, and duplicates of powerful and successful human beings in film, literature, and the survivor's personal experience. Under the administration of perpetrators, torture and mind control are used to incite rage filled self-states to form the basis of killers, torturers, assassins, warriors, and suicide bombers (Lacter, 2011; Miller, 2012; C. Ross, 2000; H. Schwartz, 2000).

Some hostile and perpetrator alters mutilate the body and set up dangerous situations including rape or other violence. Some sabotage treatment by convincing the patient to miss sessions, distrust the therapist, or drop out of therapy altogether, or by taking over the personality at specific times so the other personalities 'forget' their therapy appointments or forget to take needed medications. Some are specifically programmed to disrupt therapy in various ways (Miller, 2012). Some distract the patient's patterns of thinking and listening with chants, number-counting, headaches, or psychic fog to the point that they can interfere with the person's job and social functioning. Others vacuum out or obliterate unwanted thoughts, feelings, or new information. By transforming themselves from the one threatened to the one making the threat, hostile alters harbor the patient's capacity for healthy protest response, anxiety management, and for separation from attachments to perpetrators. This implicit healthy capacity is not as significantly the case with many programmed perpetrator states whose origins are in torture avoidance and conditioning patterns, and not in secretly protecting the potential of the individual for eventual self-differentiation and autonomy.

Some factors deepen the traumatic response: the evolution of more sophisticated methods of mind control, the need for multiple (and often inconsistent) functions/operations from one psyche, the imperative for camouflage from self and society, and the perpetrator engineering of aggressive states in dissociative survivors often leads to more rigid, hermetically sealed, and hierarchical dissociative self-organizations compared to what clinicians are likely to find in the dissociative adaptations of less severely abused patients and child soldiers.

Perpetrator-engineered violent states are incited to form in desperate forced choice, life and death situations where savage punishments and compelling neuronal reinforcements (i.e., drugs; warmth, food, cessation of torture) forge dissociate splits aimed at harvesting aggression for use on designated targets. Once formed, identifying with righteous violence and enacting loyalty to perpetrator(s) is believed to be the only possible torture-avoidance, sanity-restoring strategy. Distinguishing self-generated aggression from perpetrator-engineered aggressive responses is one of the most challenging (and essential) aspects of working with the various forms of hostility and rage present in dissociative survivor patients. Co-present with most perpetrator-engineered aggression are self-states trained to monitor and report on any deviation the patient might make in terms of revelation, confession, or exposure of the perpetrating or dissociatively engineered system (Miller, 2012).

The "hostility" demonstrated by abuser/persecutory alters and the hostility in perpetrator alters has slightly different qualities. Abusive and persecutory alters are rageful and reactive, but exhibit somewhat more flexibility; they may have access to irony and humor and may be angry at perpetrators. Most perpetrator alters, by contrast, are inflexible, uncritical of perpetrators, contemptuous, take themselves literally, and remain unresponsive to humanizing relationships for long periods of time. Hostile alters implicitly protect the patient's survival, while perpetrator alters are primarily serving and protecting the perpetrating system. For example, hostile alters prevent memories from surfacing in the system in order to avoid pain and maintain the survivor's functioning, while perpetrator-identified states have been trained to interfere with memory access and because such interference serves to camouflage (and thus sustain) the perpetrating system.

In general, it helps to remember that self- and spontaneously-generated angry/protector alter personalities express hostility containing a degree of underlying fear, pain, vulnerability, and vitality along with some remote but discernible evidence of desire for human connection – even if those connections involve only provocative interchange for some period of time. Introjects, implants, and programmed perpetrator alters, on the other hand, generally do not establish (nor respond favorably to) a felt human connection with anyone and often express only scorn for the survivor and profound, unrelenting disdain for the therapist and the values of psychotherapy (Lacter, 2011).

Differences in origin and motivation between self-generated and perpetrator-engineered aggressive states necessarily point to the need for modification in treatment approaches. This distinction can be troublesome for many clinicians accustomed to traditional approaches to trauma and DID patients. Historically, the basic and most effective approach toward abusive/persecutory alters developed out of existing clinical systems presumes aggressive dissociative self-states are organically developed within the survivor's own patterns of posttraumatic adaptation, and not the result of torture based mind control or systematic perpetrator shaping influences. The mode of clinical work with these self-generated hostile alters has been one of inclusion, recognition, and limit-setting. Clinicians have been encouraged to empathize with the suffering and dilemmas hostile alters have faced; validate their importance in the self-system; help them learn to operate in more flexible ways for present life circumstances; facilitate sublimation of rage into creativity, individuation, and healthy self-assertion; help them learn to tolerate vulnerability and ambiguity, and to work through their delusions of separateness (Howell, 2011; Kluft, 1985; 1999; Miller, 2012; Putnam, 1997; C. Ross, 1997; H. Schwartz, 1994; 2000).

Perpetrator states need, first and foremost, to be accessed. They need to be directly engaged in dialogue, helped to tolerate non-violent, non-dominating communication, and the psychological land-mines, booby traps and "fail-safes" comprising their operating system need to be exposed and defused. Confrontation and repudiation of destructiveness, deprogramming, and assistance understanding the perpetrator deceptions involved in their creation are also essential clinical strategies. Confession of criminal actions and exposure of all the patterns of perpetrator influence on the psyche is fundamental to their eventual healing and integration. Because these self-states are frozen in time with limited access to (and minimal interaction) with other parts of the dissociative self-system aside from monitoring, threatening, and distracting, they need assistance to empathically and respectfully link up with the rest of the patient's self-system and reorient to a non-violent world. When, over time, these part selves are understood with compassion and confrontation by the therapist, and helped to unmask the deceptions inherent in their disowned trauma, they can come to terms with two seemingly contradictory elements of their history: their ruthless betrayal by perpetrators and their culpability for violent and duplicitous behavior and its consequences. Here, the treatment of programmed perpetrator alters involves deconstruction of perpetrators' agendas and conditioning paradigms, and not primarily to an understanding of their protective and benevolent functions in the patient's dissociative self-system. Once connected to vulnerability and remorse, awareness of their implicit role in maintenance of survival and functioning can be helpful in their integration.

Self-destructive forms of aggression and their treatment must also be reconsidered from the point of view of differentiating self-generated hostile states from perpetrator-engineered hostile states. Self-injury and suicidal behavior in dissociative survivors have been associated with depression, futility, and the activities of hostile alters that go to any length to prevent retraumatization – even counterintuitively to killing the self to save or protect the self. Perpetrator self-states, on the other hand, threaten to kill the self to save the perpetrators, sustain trauma bonds, or to cover evidence of malfeasance. Systematically trained to distract, punish, confuse, and attack when provoked by any stimuli threatening the perpetrating system's equilibrium or obfuscation, perpetrator-identified alters have no interest in regulating affect, ending the survivor's misery, protesting, passive aggressive acting out, or in establishing boundaries. They are primarily concerned with "doing their jobs," evading torture memories, preventing secrets about criminal activities and perpetrator shaping from being revealed. Suicide and homicide may be interchangeable constructs within their delusive schemas, and automatic, unreflective behavior patterns may require considerable efforts to interrupt. Although discerning the difference between programmed suicidality and naturally occurring posttraumatic suicidality can be difficult, the distinction may have important consequences for stabilization. Empathy and safety contracts alone cannot address the underlying motivational system pressing for self-destruction if it is based on implants, programming, and self-states that have not been accessed and brought into the patient's (or therapist's) overall awareness. For clinicians confronting suicidality in survivors of coerced perpetration and mind control, systematic inquiry may be as important, (if not more important) than empathy. Deprogramming triggers and belief systems may be more important than traditional anxiety, depression, and safety management.

Attachment

Well established in the developmental psychology literature is the notion that the human need for an emotional bond with another person prevails at all costs. Children with histories characterized by violence and forced submission "choose" the pain of contact over the pain of rejection. They develop strange forms of collaboration with their abusers in their own abuse and betrayal. Fear-driven attachment or "trauma bonding" to one's perpetrators is a fundamental *sequelae* of severe abuse (Herman, 1992; Van der Kolk, 1989; 1996) and is foundational to the architecture of dissociative multiplicity (Blizard, 1997, 2003; Kluft, 1985; 2000; Howell, 2011; Liotti, 1999, 2006; Lyons-Ruth, 2003, 2006; Putnam, 1997; C. Ross, 1997, H. Schwartz, 2000). These authors all emphasize that deprivation, violence, and inconsistent relational experiences with the same caretaker/authority not only deeply affects young children's propensity to manifest multiple selves but many of these dissociative adaptations are constructed to solve a maze of complex attachment dilemmas evoked by recurrent relational traumas during critical periods of life.

Perpetrators discerned that the human attachment system is most activated and vulnerable to imprinting when children are in mortal danger. Perpetrators have learned how to manipulate the developmental vulnerabilities of bonding through extreme trauma to foment deeper submission and loyalty to the group and its belief systems. R. Schwartz (2011) points out that perpetrators have discovered attachment becomes desperate and malleable when near-death danger experiences systematically alternate with the intensity of relief during rescue. When the one who is setting you up to be killed is the one who is saving you, or when the person who is drowning you is the person who is resuscitating you, or when the one who is making you harm others in order to save yourself is your primary attachment figure – the one praising and comforting you after the torture or murder of another, the survival neurobiology of the brain and the structural dissociation of the mind overheat and fracture. Higher-order cognitive processing and morality principles are overridden. This mind-shattering set-up works hand in hand to cement indelible bonds with perpetrators and to decimate critical thinking and self-reflective capacities. As Fonagy (2002) notes, the search for alternative ways of mentalization during and after the trauma propels child victims into many pathological solutions for psychological containment including "taking the mind of the other with its distorted, absent or maligned picture of the child as part of the child's own sense of identity [...] this picture becomes the germ of a potentially persecutory voice that is lodged in the self but is alien and unassimilable" (p. 28). When this "germ" of persecutory potential is hijacked and co-opted by mind-control perpetrators, the originally mutated yet self-protective internal persecutor can become an assistant to perpetrator(s) and/or a perpetrator himself or herself. Then, dissociating the meaning, cause, and responsibility for the violence and rearranging all of those constructs according to the perpetrator(s)' psychological, political, spiritual, or even forensic needs, the victim becomes inextricably linked with protecting the perpetrator(s) and/or group myths, ideologies, and delusions.

There is a growing acceptance within the trauma and dissociation field of the notion that a dysfunctional pattern of attachment first noted by Main and Solomon (1986; 1990) called "disorganized/disoriented attachment" – related to patterns arising in response to frightening, inadequate, and inconsistent caretakers – particularly "fright without a solution" (Hesse and Main, 1999:484) may be one of the primary drivers of dissociative self-organization.[11] Some research has indeed linked the development of dissociative symptoms with disorganized attachment (Carlson, 1998; Liotti, 2004; 2006; Lyons-Ruth, 2003, 2006; Ogawa *et al.*, 1997), although the specific developmental conduit or trajectory between disorganized attachment and dissociative symptoms has not yet been fully understood or articulated. Disorganized/disoriented attachment seems to emerge from lack of effective caregiver regulation of fearful arousal as much, if not more than from, explicit fear of the caregiver him or herself (Lyons-Ruth, 2003; 2006). In Lyons-Ruth's analysis, disrupted maternal communication was significantly *more* powerful in predicting dissociative symptoms than maltreatment. Liotti (2011) underscores the implications of parental misattunement in the creation of disorganized/disoriented attachment. She views the combination of childhood helplessness and desperation with adult neglect, indifference, or lack of empathy as emblematic of intrinsic failures in human intersubjectivity.

Expanding upon these concepts, Lyons-Ruth's (1999) update of attachment theory highlights internal working models of human attachment as encoded in implicit memory where they initially operate subsymbolically; as development advances these working models may become encoded verbally and evolve into aspects of autobiographical memory and consciousness. Children develop "unconscious enactive procedural representations of how to do things with others" (p. 385) as the basis for attachment and identification, based on healthy regulation of fearful arousal and distress or on adaptations to caretakers' inadequacies and psychopathology. Her theoretical revision emphasizes that implicitly learned procedural models (i.e., passivity, grandiosity, compliance, duplicity) of how to be in a relationship becomes automatic, and unlinked, and therefore unavailable for reflection, so it arises as procedural, imitative dyadic enactments. When faced with contradictory internal working models or when confronted with inconsistencies between implicit knowledge and explicit information, these contradictions pave the way for segregation or compartmentalization of internal working attachment models – precursors to both dissociative structuralization of self as well as other problematic psychological adaptations.

In order for severely dissociative individuals to maintain their trauma models, they must systematically misperceive discrepant aspects of their current reality; they must continually ignore evidence of, and continue to forget, their abuse and exploitation and they must drive away (or keep testing) those who might support their individuation and emancipation from destructive patterns of relationship. These avoidance processes are naturally occurring. Yet when effectively harnessed and co-opted by perpetrators, these traumatic attachment "accommodations" can be shaped and structured into habitual dissociative reactivity and trigger responses without the survivor (or the therapist) having any idea these relationship patterns were not the result of the survivor's own independent posttraumatic adaptations. Within self-protecting malevolent systems, the trauma bonds are such that the perpetrator(s)' agenda becomes the victim's. Survivors may eventually cover more effectively for perpetrators than they can for themselves. Self- and trauma-containment solutions evolve into perpetrator adhesive identifications and perpetrator protection machinations. If all else fails, perpetrators can rely upon their victims to be assaulted by incredulity, skepticism, and doubt – undone by perpetrator(s)' threats and confused by professionals – hereby perpetrator(s)' omnipotence is easily protected and potentiated.

Independent of the burgeoning clinical literature on attachment and trauma, perpetrators have figured out that intentional assaults on the human attachment system constitute an extremely efficacious strategy for personality destruction, traumatic bonding, and receptivity to programming. In cruel attachment dilemmas, victims are left with the inability to rely on their own reality-testing for soothing and security: only the perpetrator is left to guide bonding, belief systems, and personality development. As a consequence of the child-victim's chronic enmeshment in double binds or mind control – with counterintuitive circumstances like the child's feeling safe only when the perpetrator is nearby (C. Ross, 1997) – the survivor's attachment circuitry becomes re-wired in a way that adhesively coheres bonds with perpetrators (in psychoanalytic terms, malevolent introjects). After these psychobiological patterns are set, nondominating, nonbetraying, and nonhumiliating relationships may simply make little sense and bring on great anxiety for the survivor. Healthier relationships, while longed for, are so disruptive to survivors' pseudoequilibrium that survivors may repeatedly retreat from contact with the therapist to return symbolically (or actually) to the bond with the abuser(s). This may happen many times before any durable and therapeutic attachment is established.

In the interpersonal and therapeutic mine fields that emerge out of attachment trauma during therapy, the dissociative survivor's suspiciousness alternates with naivety; impenetrability with porosity; and defiance with compliance. Desperate clinging to, and contempt for, the therapist can ricochet so fast in one session (or over many weeks and months) and can disorient the therapist. Brilliant insights about the corruption and chicanery of perpetrators that activate separation anxieties or programmed responses can also precipitate rabid denial and recanting of traumatic experience (and memories), while sponsoring startling surges of idealized abuser representations. Clinicians unfamiliar with these potentials or with the dangers to dissociative survivors of positive attachment experiences may easily become confused, overwhelmed, or intolerant of the relational shifts between the patient's neediness, indifference, urgency, and contempt. Thus, reworking attachment issues and the concomitant identifications with abusers is elemental to successful treatment of severely dissociative patients. This reworking is also fundamental to reclaiming critical thinking abilities because the fracturing and segmenting of awareness about attachment by extension leads to a fragmenting and de-linking of the self-states' views of (and capacities for reflection upon) the hypocrisies and duplicities occurring in interpersonal reality. Because survivors have been wounded and betrayed by caregivers or authority figures, they commonly develop simultaneous phobias of attachment and of fear attachment loss. These opposites are located in different segments of the personality that incite each other in vicious cycles of aggression and withdrawal when the survivor experiences perceived or actual changes in closeness/distance in a relationship (Van der Hart et al., 2006). As Howell (1997) states, many trauma survivors experience interpersonal danger as unavoidable, and as much as they work hard to avoid retraumatization, they are "quite susceptible to declarations [...] of love [...] by unsavory types of people [....] They often cannot tell the difference between the fools' gold of false promises and the real gold of sincere caring" (p. 243).

For survivors, attachment has been based not on mutuality but on camouflage and servitude. The recognition failures, boundary violations, and chronic exposure to the vagaries of irrational authority establish in the minds of survivors that only through their withdrawal and deference (including performances pleasing to the perpetrator) could they feel a right to exist. To be found is to be humiliated, devoured or destroyed by the perpetrator/caregivers' consumption-based narcissistic needs. The mere act of self-exposure is fraught with terror and annihilation anxieties, hence the therapist's search for the patient's self (and selves), and most difficult of all, the perpetrator-programmed self-states may be construed by the patient (or alter) as a mission of destruction (or seduction). Ultimately this brings the therapist into the quadruple transferential role of seeker-destroyer, seeker-seducer, seeker-betrayer, and seeker-rescuer. Merely sharing knowledge about the self/selves with the therapist (especially revelations of organized, hierarchically structured perpetrator states, or criminal activity) – indeed any intersubjective discourse where pain and vulnerability are revealed – can precipitate acute dread as the perceived demand for relinquishment of ties to one's internal objects or actual perpetrators arouses destabilizing anxiety.

Compromised fantasy and imagination

Repeated confrontation with trauma and mortality (Janoff-Bulman, 1992) results in a disintegration of the symbolic world of the dissociative trauma survivor. Coerced perpetration redoubles trauma's destructive effect on imaginal and symbolizing capacities, stretching survivors' dissociative adaptations to their limits. Traumatologists describe how chronic reliance on dissociation interferes with symbolization, keeping memory locked in iconic and somatosensory levels of experiencing (Van der Kolk and Van der Hart, 1989). Dissociative adaptation to chronic trauma leads to severe compromises in reflectivity, metacognitive processes, and linking functions (Fonagy *et al.*, 2002). Adapting to chronic abuse, victims minimize contact with the external world in an effort to nullify the ideational, affective, and interpersonal effect (and meanings) of the posttraumatic deterioration. In the psyches of highly dissociative individuals, the distinctions between reality and fantasy, remembering and reliving, and past and present, are blurred or lost altogether. The survivor's innate capacities for self-observation and tolerance for ambiguity are overwhelmed by intrusions of traumatic material and within therapy by powerful aggressive or sexualized transferences (Levine, 1990).

Thus chronic trauma can be said to constrain symbolic elaboration and to sponsor a suppression or repetition of what limited symbolic functioning exists (Bollas, 1992). The disturbance in symbolizing capacity among survivors of complex trauma can severely constrict the ego's ability to represent elements of the trauma and its aftermath or to develop affective associative connections between the traumatic experiences and other sectors of the mind. By segregating feeling states and self-other perceptions, dissociation freezes and compartmentalizes experiences, making them inaccessible to the dynamic restorative workings of the creative unconscious (Peoples, 1992). The resulting internal fixity and defensive commitment to the non-restitutive deployment of fantasy severely challenges treatment for reactivating developmental strivings or stymies clinical interventions aimed at cultivating transitional/potential space and re-engaging critical thinking.

In Bion's (1963; 1965; 1967) and Ferro's (2005) terms, the transformational and container functions of human psyches (and their environments) can be ineffectual, fragile, or overwhelmed by trauma. Then, vast quantities of unmetabolized sensory and emotional stimulation can only be dealt with through disavowal, evacuation, acting out, psychosomatic disorders, hallucinations, perversions, psychic dismantling, or narcissistic operations: "...we devise strategies to evacuate, split-off, hyper control or phobicize the quantities of proto-emotions and the proto-sense impressions we are unable to transform into 'poetry of mind – i.e., into thoughts, emotions, and affects" (Ferro, 2005:3).

Chronic trauma severely compromises survivors' recuperative psychological capacities for fantasy, reflection, dreams, creativity, and play. In addition, dissociative survivors lose the capacity for wish-organized symbolic functioning (Auerhahn and Laub, 1987) and often fail because of traumatic impairment of the capacity for fantasy (Fish-Murray et al., 1987), or to use mental activity to transform traumatic experience. Fantasy becomes conservative and preservative rather than mastery-oriented and progressively constructive. Where trauma cannot be transformed through fantasy operations, the survivor will resort to repetitive behavior and intrusive imagery in an effort to repeat or undo it. The world feels so fundamentally insecure that omnipotent fantasy solutions are not gradually relinquished but tenaciously retained.

In severe dissociative conditions, the collapse of subjectivity and intersubjectivity is intertwined with the developmental arrest in transitional experiencing (Winnicott, 1971). Neglect from caretakers and bodily violence severely disrupt developmental achievements that foster mind–body integration from infancy onward, causing a split that disables the individual from accepting the separation of inner and outer reality. This impairs the capacities to tolerate psychic pain and to experience the other as an independent object. The transitional space is an "intermediate area" between the infant or child's illusion of omnipotence and objective perception based on reality testing – a sort of third world that is neither wholly subjective nor wholly objective, neither purely inner nor purely outer. Winnicott describes transitional phenomena as permanent facets of our mental lives that are made possible when bridging the gaps between self and other, and internal and external reality is supported/facilitated by caregivers. Transitional experiencing is, among other things a child's way of handling the shock that results from the loss of omnipotence. In normal development, this intermediate zone of experiencing continues to grow in complexity and richness and supports the development of capacities for play and the process of symbolization associated with human culture.

Although complete mastery of intense pain and prolonged trauma may be too much to expect from any individual or any psyche, Eigen (1996) reminds us of the hope that rests in the primary processing capacity of the human mind. The reworking of psychic injury in the primary process may always be only partial and fragmented. By biting off bits of painful experiences and reworking savage wounds a little bit at a time, within transitional experiencing, the psyche can grow its digestive capacity – absorbing terrifying impacts, shrinking masses of unmetabolized pain, and reworking states of shock and paralysis. When traumatic experiences (and/or biological predisposition, destructive drugs and chemicals) completely overwhelm, or damage the primary processor, the psyche's inablility to metabolize catastrophe inevitably becomes part of the catastrophe, and the primary process itself can be wounded. The frozen states and chronic repetitions of posttraumatic conditions reveal a psyche that cannot develop images, fantasies, narratives, or dreams capable of effectively breaking up and reworking psychic damage. For relational theorists, treatment is more than making the unconscious conscious – it involves helping unconscious processing (of affects, ideas, and experiences) reset itself so that it can work effectively (Eigen, 1993).

Providing us with a model of mind that is always capable of, or susceptible to, continuous expansion, Bion (1967; 1970) underscores the value of "reverie." In the shared reverie of psychotherapy, proto-emotions and proto-sensations ("Beta elements") are evacuated and received by the mind of a therapist capable of transforming and returning to the patient these previously unmetabolized elements in elaborated form, along with the "method" of performing this operation (Ferro, 2005). Ferro's stress on transforming content and imprinting process (i.e., "transmission of the method") is essential to appreciating the role of the therapist in the healing of traumatically disrupted container, fantasy, and transitional experiencing capacities. In Ferro's view, the therapist provides previously unavailable functions (through mirroring, interpretation, reverie, improvisation, or implicit procedural identification), and he or she provides the patient with the opportunity to upload the therapist's creative and mutative mental operations.

Compounded shame

Among the most potent elements driving dissociative adaptation is compounded shame. Dissociative survivors, particularly those with coerced perpetration trauma in their histories, are vulnerable to multiple vectors of mutually reinforcing shame so it is essential for clinicians and policy makers to understand the pernicious effects of shame in the lives of trauma survivors. Shame, particularly sudden shame, is a threat to the self similar to intense fear, signalling the self that violation is imminent. This often ignites the mind's dissociative process geared to prevent a recurrence of the original violation (and its related overwhelming affects) (Bromberg, 2011). The shame of the dissociative trauma survivors is based on:

- Pain, humiliation, betrayal, and degradation endured during and after the trauma
- Helplessness and the inability to have stopped the traumatic event(s) from taking place or to have prevented their impact
- The inability to have pre-empted or stopped the abuse of others
- Humiliated and impotent rage
- Lost and/or desecrated innocence
- Humiliation and loss of control via posttraumatic intrusive and numbing symptoms, along with the constant need to cover these up to the self and others
- Recognition of what has been lost, what has never been, and what can never be recovered

- Societal response to posttraumatic symptoms including denial, fascination, fear, pity, avoidance, incredulity, and misdiagnosis
- Fragmentation and inconsistency of memories, and the constant challenge to reality-testing and critical thinking from internal discrediting and external skepticism
- Chronic medical problems resulting from violations of the body (and mind)
- Coerced violation of one's own ethics or moral principles in order to survive; betrayal/violation of others in order to survive
- Learned helplessness, passivity, and a legacy of profound self-sabotage
- Vulnerability of reliving unprocessed traumatic affect with the therapist
- Social marginalization for being a symbol of social madness, loss of control, loss of dignity, and abandonment
- Misrepresentations of trauma, trauma survivors, dissociation, and therapy in the media
- Deep alienation, not belonging, and the loss of a sense of kinship with humanity
- Excessive dependency on therapist or other professionals due to the lack of a supportive family and the lack of healthy childhood dependency experiences
- Feeling marked, damaged, or "branded" with the feeling that others can see right through you and know what you have done or what has been done to you
- The social stigma of being an abuse survivor and the internalization of society's impatience with the vicissitudes of recovery ("*get over it already, move on*"), and the dismissal of your therapist (perhaps the only person you trust with this material) as a quack
- The internalization and constant reiteration of hateful, degrading messages from the perpetrator(s)
- Harboring of "dirty secrets" of participation in criminal activities including transgressions that occurred while not directly under the aegis of the perpetrators
- Harboring of hateful, vengeful, destructive, or murderous thoughts (and/or part-selves) and the memories of actualized violence and emotional violation of others
- The residue of bizarre sexual compulsions or utterly absent sexual needs and desires
- Knowledge that you welcomed or could not resist feelings of specialness or actual comforts, rewards or privileges conferred by perpetrator(s)
- Realization that mind, body, and spirit have all been invaded, co-opted, and defiled
- Inability to forgive perpetrators in a culture that insists on the romanticization of forgiveness
- Vulnerability to experiencing certain normal activities as triggers (e.g., films, holidays, gatherings, sensuality, intimacy, sexuality, contact with children and animals), such that they can no longer be enjoyed

- The effects of a history of self-destructive acting-out, and the accrued losses from trauma in terms of vocational, financial, medical, and interpersonal functioning
- The psychological and physiological damage that will not heal in spite of your own (and others') best efforts.

Bromberg (1998; 2009) views shame as central to the enactments that take place in psychotherapy when trauma and dissociative experience are involved. The patient is shamed by the original event from the past and by the strong need to be understood about the event in the present. These shame-based events arise most often as disruptions in the therapeutic alliance, perceived hurts, misunderstandings, unconscious tests, or empathic failures. "As with the original trauma, the patient desperately needs recognition of the pain from the person [...] who is least likely to offer it (in this case, the therapist) [...] because [this] is also the person who is causing the pain (in this case, inadvertently)" (Bromberg, 2009:648). Bromberg (2011) describes the dilemma of the dissociative survivor whose chronic shame has de legitimized his/her very personhood while also negating the specific realities of his or her internal experience. Living in a kind of tortured isolation where language and communication appear to be only empty lies or tricks, the patient's longing to communicate dissociative self-experience precipitates internal shaming of this longing by other parts of the self. These collisions leave the patient in a protracted dual state of frustrated desire to be known, yet besieged by chronic feelings of worthlessness – undeserving of any consolation or solace (Bromberg, 1998; 2011). For effective treatment, therapists must not only systematically attend to this dilemma but must help patients feel that they understand the heart of the patients' shame predicament. This allows the patient to feel less confused and alienated, and perhaps less likely to be re-victimized by manifestations of these daunting posttraumatic patterns.

In the case of survivors of coerced perpetration, the dissociated experience of shame, and their defenses against that shame (often in the form of haughtiness, contempt, and malice toward the therapist and other parts of the patient's self-system) represent crucial elements of what needs to be resolved in treatment. Some of the most valuable and efficacious elements in the transmutation of shame are the therapist's capacities: to empathize with the patient's multiple and conflicting perspectives on reality, regardless of how distorted they may seem; to authentically own his or her own contributions to treatment impasses and disruptions; to engage his own and the patient's curiosity and vulnerability about the deeper meanings within disruptive interpersonal events; to authentically apologize; and, to model and appropriately use his or her sense of humor.

Chapter 4

Mind control

> I've been given the choice of joining the Sybionese Liberation Army.
> I've chosen to stay and fight. Try to understand the changes I've been
> through [...] I have been given the name Tania. There is no victory in
> half-assed attempts at revolution [...] Death to the fascist insect that
> preys upon the life of the people.
>
> Patty Hearst

Destruction of critical thinking

Variously known as brainwashing, coercive persuasion, thought reform, or
thought control, the term mind control refers to processes or dynamics in which
an individual or group systematically deploys manipulative methods to persuade,
influence, or coerce others to conform to the manipulator's wishes and ideologies. The term mind control has been applied through many tactics – psychological or physical torture – which subverts an individual's sense of control
over his or her own thinking, behavior, emotions, actions, or decision-making
functions (Hassan, 1990; Lacter, 2011; Miller, 2012; H. Schwartz, 2000). The
shaping of a captive's thought patterns and belief system – called *brainwashing*
in reference to the Chinese indoctrination techniques discovered in the 1950s
– leads to some of the most pervasive and devastating consequences of child
abuse. Long before *The Manchurian Candidate* – Richard Condon's 1959 novel
of an American army sergeant captured during the Korean War and programmed
as an assassin – brought mind control to the attention of the American public,
the psychological techniques it describes had been used by various groups as the
blueprint for the creation of an army of programmed individuals, some of whom
were assassins prepared to kill on cue, informers hypnotized to remember minute
details of events and conversations, and couriers carrying messages outside
the chain of command, their secrets securely hidden behind posthypnotic
blocks (Bowart, 1994; Marks, 1979; C. Ross, 2000; Weinstein, 1990). Bowart
impels us to remember that only failures of mind control survived to tell us their
stories. When mind control is successful, there is no memory left and no story
to tell.

Articulating a methodology that cuts across incestuous families, ritual abuse cults, and military mind-control programs, Nachmani (1997), describes the basic scenario for eviscerating the capacities for self-witnessing, memory, critical thinking, and narrativity in interpersonal trauma. First, victims are isolated, their credibility and judgment are destroyed, and their shame at their own helplessness is exploited. Then victims' humiliation and degradation are intensified as they inevitably find themselves powerless to make any choice other than colluding in their own captivity and subjugation, and unwittingly consolidating their loss of will and agency through identifying with their aggressors. Next, victims are deprived of what they care most about. Abusers then create double binds around pain-avoidance and attachment-needs to cultivate dependency and engender betrayals of self and others. In the final step, victims are deliberately confused, forced to re-assign responsibility for all violations according to the perpetrator(s) meaning system, and to subscribe to a new worldview in which pain is pleasure and pleasure is pain; feelings are bad, numbness is good; vulnerability and resistance are bad, power and compliance are good; keeping secrets is praiseworthy, speaking openly is dangerous.

Most forms of child abuse result in the destruction of the victim's capacity for critical thinking and psychological reflection. Traumatized children unconsciously adapt their attributions of traumatic situations in ways that enable them to reduce the stress of life-threatening situations, and in order to stave off psychological annihilation (Vogt, 2012). Intense abuse and/or prolonged captivity (which isolate the child from other sources of attachment and information), can seriously damage the survivor's essential psychological functions that promote and sustain a sense of agency and independence. Depending on the perpetrator's goals, the perpetrator's assaults may consist primarily of double binds, suggestion, and threats. Less subtle domination may be achieved when perpetrators coercively manipulate victims' perceptions, memories, and beliefs. Vogt (2012) notes that perpetrators use the vulnerability and openness of the traumatic situation to imprint specific instructions for repression and misattribution in children's internal systems. In more extreme cases, perpetrators use torture and mind control techniques to create psychic slaves to support criminal, political, paramilitary, and spiritual cults and perpetrator-subcultures.

Abused and neglected children are easy to manipulate, as predators can easily exploit children's basic survival needs. Children's undeveloped sexuality can also be shaped to match a perpetrator's appetites. Traumatized children's innate needs for affection, recognition, comfort and protection can be sexualized or conditioned to violence (including violence against the self). Their sense of innocence and self-worth can be completely undermined and replaced with perpetrator(s)' perceptions and opinions. Psychological usurpation can be so thorough that the perpetrator's agenda can be substituted for the child-victim's spontaneous desire, initiative, and worldview to foster a complete eradication of the child's sense of self and invalidation of the child's sense of reality. Overwhelming and intolerable shame can dominate every waking moment of victims' lives when chronically abused children are coerced into having sex with, or harming other children (or animals or other adults), for the entertainment or economic profit of the perpetrators, or are forced into kidnapping or otherwise seducing other children into the hands of perpetrators.

Many children find ways to tolerate immersion in evil subcultures by identifying with evil to maintain their psychological equilibrium. Malevolent authority has succeeded in creating the developmental conditions where the perpetrator(s)' inflexible, automatic psychological organizing principles (Stolorow *et al.*, 1987) govern the child's inferences, convictions, behaviors and sense of future possibility. Perpetrators' exploitation of shame, self-hatred, and disgust can "destroy self esteem with a ferocity unequaled in human experience" (Nathanson, 1992:463). When a child's sense of self has been undermined to this extent, all forms of mind control are possible.

The combination of brutality, sadistic sexuality, inconsistency, and fear-based ideologies or religious practices can devastate any child's self-esteem and create perpetual insecurity and shame. This template makes for a commonly found type of double-speak in many pathological family systems and perpetrator groups: the child develops a socially acceptable personality whose normalcy masks the perpetrator-identified sub-system. With or without programming, traumatized children make enormous efforts to camouflage their confusion, despair, and psychic injuries such that even in our putatively enlightened era many children's real torment goes unnoticed by community members and trained professionals. Adult survivors of abuse consistently report a startling lack of interest or investigation from the medical professionals who treated their physical injuries over the years.[1] Many adult survivors of severe abuse describe childhoods where they moved among sadistic family systems, criminal cults, public schools, neighbors' houses, and religious institutions without activating even the slightest awareness that anything in their lives or families was awry. New perpetrators, on the other hand, seemed to possess the uncanny ability to spot and stalk them as children and adult survivors.

Even traumatized, dissociative children, malleable as they might be, must be intensively conditioned and trained to handle the complex demands of perpetrators – especially when basic survival needs or spiritual belief systems are at stake. Several patients who were trained for long-term participation in sex/death cults and criminal groups making snuff films report undergoing forms of classical and operant conditioning to help them learn how to tolerate witnessing animals, children, and adults being tortured, raped, and killed, and/or how to become sexually aroused by these stimuli. By the time they were responding automatically (against their own moral imperatives) to the torture with sexual arousal, their memories of having been conditioned had disappeared; they knew only that they were filled with a confusing mix of shame, specialness, and relief at the discharge of tensions. Some survivors' beliefs in their new identities, allegiances, and meaning structures are consolidated by perpetrators recounting their victims' involvement (and "choice") or by replaying the victim's perpetrator activities recorded on film or video. Many survivors report that while their own or others' torture was occurring (or immediately after) they were given specific instructions on how to behave outside the group: who to associate with, who to avoid, and the consequences for talking about the group activities with outsiders. Programming in these cult-like contexts indoctrinates children with beliefs in their superiority over others, further isolating them from potential identification with healthy human beings and narcissistically bonding them through a distorted but compelling sense of specialness and omnipotence. For many organized child abuse survivors, the fruits of this bonding were the only possible forms of recognition or validation available, and pride of membership in the elite group was the only allowable form of belonging (Miller, 2012; Noblitt and Noblitt, 2008; Sinason, 1994; M. Smith, 1993).

In these destructive conditions, the survivor will virulently hate himself or herself and not the perpetrator(s), and will become highly invested in concealing his or her destructive or violent activities, with or without programming, all the while believing that he or she is, and has always been, evil. Later, obfuscation in therapy will be partly motivated by the survivor's fear that exposure of his or her "true evil self" will drive the therapist away, along with the remaining hope for themselves through dissociative purification (i.e., eradication of all memories and links to their perpetrator sub-selves) that these aspects of self, history, and human life can be perpetually avoided.

When murderous rage emerges, it will likely be the survivor's self that is the subject of the rage and not the perpetrator(s). When memories of perpetration emerge, it will be the survivor's culpability and not the perpetrator(s)' training or criminality that will be recalled. When programmed states are exposed, it will be the survivor's self that deserves to be extinguished and not the perpetrating system that warrants exposure and prosecution. When a therapist initially uncovers such an elaborate perpetrator-identified dissociative matrix in a patient, the therapist is likely to be disparaged, and emotionally assaulted in a variety of ways, analogous to the retaliation responses of an exposed perpetrator. Or the patient him or herself, can be subjected to derision, doubting, and urges toward violence to the self and others through perpetrator-shaped alters whose job it is to sabotage revelations and the survivor's independence of thought and action. This defense system has been specifically trained via torture-based mind control, anti-therapy, and anti-attachment programming, and perpetrator-loyal self-states.

Case example: Sonja

While being repeatedly raped and sodomized by a group of men from a satanic/Aryan cult in the basement of a local church, Sonja was told that she was satan's child, whose special position in the cult hierarchy made her worthy of privileged treatment, and simultaneously that she was a worthless whore who was good for nothing except being excreted upon. Following torture sessions, Sonja was repeatedly indoctrinated with beliefs that God hated her and had rejected and abandoned her (how else could such satanic abuse be taking place?), that satan would protect her from future harm, and that whenever she entered a church she would be reminded of her torture and would not hear (or remember) anything being said during church services. Not surprisingly, Sonja developed a complex set of phobias and traumatic reactions to churches, clergy members, and crucifixes. Sonja's embedded beliefs in her abandonment by a benevolent deity were highly resistant to change. Only direct access to the alters containing torture memories and programming allowed the tentative emergence of critical thinking abilities. Sonja's evolving and maturing reflective capacities enabled her to cultivate an understanding of victimization that gradually replaced compulsive and relentless self-hatred and rejection of others' affection and goodwill.

Case example: Fran

For many years, Fran had been sexually victimized by her father and older brother and viciously emotionally abused and poisoned by her mother before her father introduced her to a group of pedophiles, then eventually to sex-death cult gatherings. Early group initiations involved gang rape, isolation (mock burials), electric shock torture, and the creation of two systems of personalities assigned to occupy the left and right side of her body. As her involvement with the sex-death cult increased, Fran was brought before an altar and following the administration of drugs and ritualized sexual abuse with several high ranking members of the group and administration of drugs, she was ordered ("offered the privilege") to sacrifice an infant using a special ceremonial knife placed in her hand by the group leader. Her father stood in the circle of men around her, glaring.

When Fran refused to kill, she was humiliated and beaten. When her refusals continued, she was subjected to genital shock treatments. She curled up into a ball, rocking, and continued to refuse. There was a short waiting period in which she was left alone, naked on a cold basement floor. Following an unknown period of time, Fran's mother suddenly appeared on the scene with her toddler brother in hand (the mother had never before appeared in group events, at least as far as Fran could remember). With Fran's mother and father's full cooperation, the group leader took Fran's beloved brother out of her mother's arms, placed him on another altar and made Fran choose which child would die. The group leader assured Fran that no one was leaving the ritual until one of the children was killed. Fran was desperate, almost unable to move or walk, the group leader held the ceremonial knife over the body of her baby brother who was by this point naked and ferociously screaming. Fran remembered her parents being expressionless.

The exploiting of Fran's protectiveness and empathy in a classic forced choice paradigm that is deployed in the mechanics of coerced perpetration throughout the world. Fran was assisted by the group leader to hold the knife and stab the unknown infant to the applause of the cheering crowd. This stabbing event was filmed, and Fran was forced to watch the film whenever she hesitated to participate in subsequent violent activities. Fran was also told the film would be sent to her teachers and to the police if she did not continue to comply with perpetrator directives. Fran became convinced that she was truly evil and that she had made the choice to kill of her own free will. With repetition, Fran's recalcitrant but inevitably cooperative perpetrator alter was conditioned, structured into her dissociative system, and hidden behind numerous amnesia barriers. Her young brother (who she allegedly "saved") grew up to perpetrate sexual violence and torture on Fran and was later convicted of molesting his own children and step-children. As an adult, Fran had a brilliant career helping emotionally disturbed children in the school system who were beyond the reach of other helpers. Fran struggled with disabling guilt and self-hatred and avoided and sabotaged intimate relationships for most of her life.

Case example: Lina

Lina was considered a valuable child/teenage prostitute, pornography "star," and drug runner in her criminal intergenerational family and their cult. Much effort was put into silencing Lina, sabotaging her future potential, and keeping her within the confines of the perpetrating system. Painful genital torture was administered in conjunction with hypnotic messages impressing upon Lina that she was being filled with literal poison. These destructive chemicals, she was told, would infect anyone she would ever get close to (outside of cult/family members) or love (and indeed it affected all her intimate relationships). She was programmed to believe her entire life would be a failure regardless of any efforts she made to achieve anything outside of the criminal organization.

When repeated therapies were focused on intimacy issues (but did not address trauma or programming), they failed. Lina became increasingly depressed and suicidal, feeling impotent and helpless to change her life in any significant way. Learned helplessness had been an essential part of the programmed breakdown of her personality. Lina had been repeatedly hypnotized to imprint an inexplicable urge to find a razor blade and cut herself whenever she was about to reveal anything about her trauma In addition, Lina was programmed with training to make her appear psychotic or delusional[2] if she were ever to disclose anything about her trauma history. False and improbable narratives about abuse (alien abduction, kidnapped by covens of witches) and training to act like an animal (i.e., animal alters triggered to respond to disclosures with bizarre and primitive behavior that would likely get Lina classified as psychotic) were all aspects of her programming. The ongoing interplay between the unconscious narratives inculcated during torture and the naturally occurring re-enactments of trauma in everyday life created a psychic prison for Lina. She was helped to disentangle the complicated overlapping domains of self-generated and perpetrator-generated dissociative states and eventually found meaningful work, intimate relationships, and a satisfying spiritual tradition.

The dissociation of meaning

The mechanisms of thought reform and mind control operate on a continuum whose points include subtle influence, coercive persuasion, systematic thought reform, and torture-based indoctrination. From television advertising exploiting people's fears to Stockholm Syndrome situations, or from incestuous families to fundamentalist religions, or from military and paramilitary training to the criminal abuse of children in cults, the distance on the continuum between the myth making and denial characteristic of the enmeshed, secretive incest family system and the orchestrated tactics of most child soldiers or cults is a matter of degree more than of kind. If the former kind embodies attachment to the abuser and the disruption of critical thinking, the latter can involve greater dissociative compartmentalization, absolute identification with perpetration, collapse of critical thinking, and the encapsulation of a destructive belief system in a complex psychic organization that can take years to dismantle.

The meaning structures derived from perpetrator propaganda can be extraordinarily difficult to access, and quite challenging to disrupt and resolve in therapy. Reality defined by perpetrators and collaborators, imposed on a child victim's natural strivings to make sense out of abusive incidents (and their after effects), disrupts healthy observing ego and critical thinking capacities. Survivors' memories of the ways their perpetrators used language often reveals how perpetrator(s) sought to influence the intrapsychic relationship between memories and identities (in terms of what survivors are allowed to remember, how to discuss those memories, and who to discuss them with). The natural unconscious process of linking goals, perceptions, evaluations, memories, and self-regulating activities that function to help people behave in consistent ways and effectively pursue their objectives (Bargh and Chartrand, 1999) can be corrupted in environments where volition and perception are systematically undermined. Because the relationship between autobiographical memory and sense-of-self is a dynamic interactive process, self-concepts are inevitably tentative and never final. Internal and external realities are interpreted according to current organizations of self, and an individual's identity is based not solely on images or concepts but rather on embodied systems of meaning that are held together by learned behaviors, temperament, genetics, personal history, and vast networks of relationships and influences (Grant, 1996). When the family or subculture is extremely sadistic, cult-like, and/or part of a criminal or paramilitary organization, the subtle power of meta-communications (Bateson, 1972) to silence and to shape personality and behavior may eventually have effects as powerful as the use of torture.

Waites (1997) describes the many ways in which, throughout a lifetime, external or internalized authority figures serve gatekeeping, reminding, or censoring functions. Extremely powerful others, when they are excessively rigid and absolute, may govern all narratives that shape memory in a child's life; these others may also implicitly and explicitly forbid questioning and impair development of critical thinking. In traumatic contexts, an external orientation is forced upon the will of the child as the only chance to survive the cruelty of the perpetrator (Vogt, 2012). In these hypervigilant moments, Vogt explains, the brain computer is frantically copying without any observing-ego or critical thinking functions; survival is secured by speed analyzing what the perpetrator wants and by aligning with the perpetrators' objectives and interpretations of the situation. Perpetrators manipulate malleable posttraumatic psyches and the dependency of the children they abuse, encouraging the rapid internalization of false beliefs that will reliably regulate victims' identities and camouflage the perpetrators' crimes.[3] By silencing protests, labeling actual experiences as dreams or fantasies, orchestrating elaborate cover stories, dismissing accusations as products of wild imaginations, or insisting that the victims are guilty and will be punished for disclosing anything to anyone, perpetrators manipulate malleable posttraumatic psyches and the dependency of the children they abuse; this encourages the rapid internalization of false beliefs that will reliably regulate victims' identities and camouflage the perpetrators' crimes.

Vulnerability to undesirable suggestion and an over-reliance on external authority as arbiters of truth and reality are consequences of a reduced capacity for critical analysis, and these consequences culminate in excessive self-censorship, over-compliance, and failures to discriminate between appropriate and inappropriate demands. As Waites (1997) points out, "Instituting the self as a distinct authority who can override other authorities is a complex aspect of individuation that is typically not fully achieved until adulthood and, in some individuals, never achieved at all" (p. 81). Chronic trauma seriously hinders this developmental achievement, but mind control trauma renders this developmental potential almost impossible.

Describing the defensive encapsulation of mental life in the service of sustaining primitive ties to malevolent caretakers, Brandchaft and Stolorow (1990:108) state: "Developmental traumata derive their lasting significance from the establishment of invariant and relentless principles of organization that remain beyond the accommodative influence of reflective self-awareness or of subsequent experience." Similarly, Stolorow and Atwood (1994) describe the primary developmental motivation of the self to be maintaining the organization of experience by consolidating pathological structures that rigidly restrict the individual's subjective field. These inflexible structures allow traumatized individuals to predictably order their experiences to prevent the emergence of emotional conflict and subjective feelings of danger. In the case of extensive thought reform and coerced attachments to violent perpetrators, the constriction exists to prevent any free thought and feeling that can disrupt the rigid belief system internalized during the prolonged immersion in the abusive relationship or pathological system. In cases of torture-based mind control, these constrictions and the self-states that oversee the restrictive process exist to prevent a psychic free fall into re-activated, unbearable torture/annihilation memories.

When traumatized individuals develop cohesive psychological structures whose primary goal is to prevent the consolidation of new structures, the thus-enfeebled core self is as trapped intrapsychically as the captive child was in the malevolent family or perpetrating system. So when highly dissociative patients begin in therapy to demonstrate increased self-reflection and observing ego functions, powerful internal voices emerge almost immediately to sow profound doubt and confusion. Now fears of repeating traumatic childhood experiences consolidate unconscious defensive resistances to change. These fears arise unpredictably in the transference as the process of therapeutic inquiry illuminates and therefore threatens "the matrix of emotionally enslaving early ties" (Brandchaft, 1994:67). When these natural processes intersect with perpetrator implants, "fail-safes," and programmed alter personalities, sophisticated assaults on the reality testing and critical thinking of both the patient and therapist may ensue. When protection of the historic truth – against its emergence in memory or discourse – have been conditioned with torture, the pursuit of truth comes to beassociated with agony. In treatment, within the transference-countertransference matrix, the truth-seeker and the cause of agonies are one and the same: the therapist. The therapist's dual role of liberator/destroyer is unavoidable in the psychotherapeutic extrication of dissociative survivors from the effects of mind control.

When psychotherapy fulfills its mandate to support the individuation process, the patient's emerging capacities for critical thinking may coincide with access to previously unavailable knowledge about traumatic personal history – both in its details and in its meanings. When psychotherapy betrays its essential functions, it can leave the patient's dissociative matrix unexplored or it can suppress the patient's autonomy and critical thinking and train the patient to inappropriately lean on the therapist's power and perspective.

The following beliefs and messages, internalized by victims, can lead to predictably rigid cognitive schemas, and accumulate in proportion to the frequency and intensity of abuse, or the number of perpetrators, or the degree of organized cult or criminal involvement[4]:

- You (victim) deserve punishment and condemnation (God has abandoned you)
- Resistance is futile; worse – it will lead to your annihilation
- If you disclose anything about your history or us to anyone we will know about it and either you will die or the people you disclosed to will be injured or die
- There is no escape and no hope, and hoping will cause you more pain
- No one can hear you scream, no one cares; faith in any person or in God is useless, and continued screaming or struggling will elicit more torture (for yourself and others)
- No one will believe anything you say no matter what you tell them; people will think you are crazy and will lock you up in a mental institution
- Feelings are dangerous; stay away from them or you will be destroyed
- Weakness and vulnerability are despicable; they merit punishment and humiliation

- You will do, think, and say exactly what you are told, but you will think you are doing as you freely choose
- Your choices have made all this happen – your choices, not our actions
- It is honorable to die for us (perpetrators), but not for yourself unless we tell you to kill yourself which is to die for us
- Power is everything, and love is a lie
- You will have no memories but the memories I/we (your abusers) authorize
- We are always watching you; we know your every thought, feeling, and action; if you betray us we will know immediately; our spies are everywhere, even in the places where you might go to get help
- You can hate, be angry, and express your rage, but only at yourself or those we direct you to hate and harm
- Something is deeply wrong with you and you must constantly hide it from others, but your only hope of "belonging" is with us
- You must always act normal and fit in as though nothing out of the ordinary has ever happened to you
- If you get close to other people outside of the group you will poison or harm them, or they will reject and despise you
- You belong only with us, and to us; we are your safety net and we will protect you but your life is not your own – you gave it to us and we can do what we want with it
- You will die if you tell anyone or if you try and leave us; if you die in that way you will be trapped in Hell forever; the only real freedom is our freedom to do what we want to whomever we want, whenever we want to, and to get away with all of it

Mind control

The basic methods[5] for developing dependency on, and obedience to, the captors have been known for more than 45 years (Bowart, 1994; Hassan, 1990; Lifton, 1961; M. Singer, 1995); these are the same methods described by people who have been indoctrinated into cults, gangs, paramilitary groups, or underground criminal cartels, including satanic groups:

- Isolation
- Monopolization of perception (sensory deprivation and prevention of access and exposure to alternative perspectives)
- Induced debilitation and exhaustion
- Threats to self and family
- Strategic indulgences
- Demonstrations of omniscience or omnipotence (complete knowledge of victims' activities, control over their fates)
- Degradation (reinforced helplessness, violations of privacy, insults, coerced incontinence, disregard for human dignity)

- Programming ideas, beliefs, and behaviors into victims during or immediately after torture sessions, or during periods of shock, and/or following periods of sensory isolation and incited terror
- Enforcement of trivial demands (obedience to detailed rules governing all aspects of daily living)
- Establishment of "special" relationship between perpetrator (or group) and victim, promising power, relief, and protection

Case example: Robyn

Robyn had been hypnotically trained to open her front door when she heard a specific sequence of footsteps, by means of commands implanted during and after torture sessions, when Robyn was in robotic self-states of whose existence she had little or no awareness for most of her life. After she let the cult-operative into her home they often transported her to rituals where she was retraumatized and reprogrammed. This continued while Robyn was in her first stages of contact with the mental health system. At that time, and prior to her being diagnosed with DID, she was almost completely dysfunctional and unable to communicate about most of her experiences. When she tried to tell her psychiatrist and the staff at the mental health center about people entering her home at night and her agitation about sequences of footsteps, they told her she was paranoid and administered antipsychotic medications. Because her perpetrator group knew Robyn was in treatment, they initiated intense supplementary silencing programming. Caught between two subcultures, each abusing and betraying her for different (justifiable) reasons, Robyn repeatedly attempted suicide. For many years, her repeated suicide attempts and misdiagnosis obscured the true nature of her psychological distress and caused both cult leaders and mental health staff to be chronically frustrated and enraged with her – further exacerbating her psychiatric symptoms.

Case example: Veronica

Among Veronica's many tortures and trainings in her childhood, "spinning" was used to split her personalities and to attain compliance and obedience. With a burlap bag over her head, Veronica was hung by a rope from a hook in a barn and mercilessly twirled. As Miller (2012) notes, spinning programming teaches children that they have no control over their bodies. Their wrists and ankles are usually tied, but their heads are free to flop and great pressure is exerted on the spine and neck. Spinning makes children physical ill and sick to their stomachs and typically they are spun until their screaming stops. Spinning programming evokes anger, excitement, and numbness. In Veronica's case, her perpetrators used sticks and paddles to poke at her while she was spinning and screaming.

When she achieved complete stillness, Veronica was allowed out of the torture, and the dissociative self-state that successfully split off the event and achieved compliant neutrality was given instructions and training. As soon as any – even minor – inattention or disobedience was noted, Veronica was either placed back up into the suspended situation or threats to return her to spinning were made. A huge split developed between aspects of Veronica's self-system that contained the fragmentation and sensory overload of the spinning experience and aspects of herself that had mastered this. Perpetrator and masochistic alters were cultivated by the perpetrator group from this torture-induced dissociative adaptation. Long before her treatment started, Veronica used to spend hours at amusement parks repeatedly riding the most frightening roller coasters. During group therapy sessions that became particularly intense in the early days of her inpatient treatment, Veronica would become completely unresponsive and enter catatonic and tonic immobility states that were so severe in some instances that emergency medical intervention (tranquilizers) had to be ordered to help her body relax and return to normal functioning.

Case example: Keith

Keith was a mild-mannered man who initially presented with a history of depression, chronic fatigue, intermittent and strange somatic pains (particularly in joints), and periodic rage outbursts at strangers who encroached on his boundaries or who did not respond favorably to his requests for fairness, politeness, or compromise. After years of relatively successful non-trauma focused treatment, explorations of recurrent medical impasses eventually led to hidden layers of traumatic experience.

It was never clear how involved Keith's parents were with the group of mind-control perpetrator(s) to which they had allowed him to become prey. Clearly many cult systems are intergenerational in nature while other self-sustaining malevolent groups (gangs, or systems) make use of the children of unwitting outsiders or people who have been implicitly or explicitly bribed to bring their children for "special testing" or "special training." In some cases, it is the parent's narcissism and insecurities that are being exploited. Other times, the parents exchange the child for drugs or sexual privileges without actually knowing that their children are being subjected to great harm. Instead, the parents choose to benefit from the exchange and self-soothe with the orchestrated cover-up narratives supplied by the perpetrator/experimenters. Keith's mother periodically took him to a medical-like office and told him that he would be having fun, taking tests, doing puzzles, and if he performed well, would be rewarded with ice cream or other treats. Keith believes that his mother received drugs during these visits in exchange for his participation in a "special program for gifted children."

At first Keith was presented with normal games and puzzles to relax his defenses. Following this, he was drugged through a sweet drink offered by the perpetrators. The challenges of the games and tests soon escalated to variations on forced-choice situations. At times there were two different voices coming from headphones each recommending a different option, but neither option was actually the accurate choice for solving the problem. The dichotic listening and forced choice set-ups were being used solely to depattern his mind and prepare it for cultivation of encapsulated dissociative states and later perpetrator-programming.

After Keith was reduced to a state of absolute fragmentation through very painful punishments and learned helplessness training, the perpetrators escalated the electric shocks he received for incorrect answers until he was nearly unconscious and no longer struggling or reacting. Apparently this state was the goal of the entire project. At that point, the perpetrators repeated the statement emphatically and with great authority, "you are not who you thought you are; you are who we tell you you are." Following this preparatory phase various definitions, ideologies, and shaping of dissociative self-states took place. At the end of these sessions, memory-loss conditioning was layered on top of the torture-based training to reduce the likelihood of reflection or disclosure. When Keith awoke with a bad headache some time later, with his mother now at his side, he began to utter fragments of memories of the terrifying experiences. His mother and the presiding "doctor" repeatedly told him he had fallen asleep during the testing and that he was "having a bad dream, just a dream," that he was safe and had been safe the entire time. The cover dialogue was followed by ice-cream which Keith hungrily devoured as comfort and escape from his pain and disorientation. All of the Keith's mind-control traumas were psychologically sandwiched between layers of seductions, cover-ups, memory scrambling, drug states, rewards, and denial training. It took many years of wading through complex patterns of symptoms to identify the actual nature of Keith's childhood trauma and the real meanings and implications of his recurrent somatic and emotional problems.

From mind control to programming

Foa and Kozak (1986) note that pathological fear structures, including unrealistic elements that may become associated with states of absorption and heightened arousal often attendant with extreme stress, are extremely reisistant to modification. Hence, the power of all statements made during and immediately after abusive episodes while the victim is in an altered state will be enhanced by the absence of an operative critical consciousness (Conway, 1994), and by the indelible connection with intolerable terror or dread. Psychologically sophisticated abusers who have mastered the methods of mind control know how to induce psychobiological state changes, how to elaborate and encapsulate them, how to provide the cues to trigger them, how to tap into and alter the victim's motivational and belief systems, and how to layer amnesias within a personality. In this way a polyfragmented dissociative individual can appear to lead the life of a normal hardworking citizen, yet can function undetected (by himself or by others) as a mind- controlled operative and remain available for service to individual perpetrators or groups.

Defining the programming tactics used in cult contexts, M. Singer (1995) identifies three staged preconditions for thought-control: (1) *destabilization* of the victim's sense of self; (2) *indoctrination* into the leader's re-vision of reality; and (3) *dependency* on the group. Hassan (1990) labels the same phases (1) *unfreezing* – by means of drugs, hypnosis, torture, shock, or trauma (which can be accomplished in children through seduction, shaming, or sexual arousal alone); (2) *change* – commonly registered with the deliberate inculcation in the victim of a special belief; and (3) *refreezing*. Perpetrators program the minds of victims by accessing the deep unconscious through near-death torture, creating a complete breach in self-agency. Torture procedures are performed until all of the victim's

> self-states have been taxed beyond endurance, before the victim can create another self-state, before the victim loses physical consciousness, or occasionally in the moments between two pre-existing states taking executive control[...] Survivors report that, once accessed, the mind is 'laid bare' and records information with no ability to process, question, or reject input. It has no self-awareness, no emotion, no ability to act on its own behalf. It 'believes' or more accurately, 'takes in whole,' what it is told or shown. This is when programmers reportedly 'install' much foundational programming, especially structures to organize the system of self states.
>
> Lacter (2011:84–85)

This is most often accomplished using commands and illusions. When these commands and illusions are reinforced with torture, as Lacter explains, they can be perceived by survivors to be as real as the torture itself. Programming installed in the unconscious mind – placed between self-states and never consciously registered by any part of the self – is almost impossible to access without knowledge of mind control methodology. Such programming operates as if the programmer/perpetrators used victims' unconscious minds as "writable memory chip[s] to store information, and use blank slate mental states to develop self-states that can take executive control to serve abuser functions (p. 85). If the survivor is finally able to transcend the pseudo-safety of "betrayal blindness" (Freyd, 1996), to surmount the anxiety involved in breaking the unconscious contract with the perpetrator(s), or to access and undermine the perpetrator-engineered system of self-states, the patient should be on guard against the still active perpetrator(s)' attempt to reinstate the original subjugation by means of a letter, a phone call, a look across a courtroom, a hypnotic pre-programmed trigger word or signal, or a direct threat. If these methods fail, the still active perpetrator might switch to disparaging the victim's narrative. And if that fails, the perpetrator will shift gears again and try to make the victim look like the victimizer.[6]

Basic types of mind control programming[7]

Although not exhaustive, the following typology is based on almost three decades of reports of patients, colleagues, supervisees and other clinicians/authors treating mind control survivors. This typology represents a schema of basic categories of programming used across diverse perpetrator situations. These basic programming templates are the foundation of other more complex combinations and sophisticated elaborations of indoctrinations and perpetrator-structuralized dissociative states. Aside from updating clinical knowledge and refining clinicians' awareness, it is essential to demystify the programming aspect of psychological trauma to help therapists and professionals from other disciplines to become more cognizant of the precise elements of psychological abuse. By knowing what specific tracks and patterns have been laid down in our patients' psyches and dissociative structures, we may be able to help them make some sense out of their most confusing, disturbing, and intractable post-traumatic symptoms. The eight major types of programming are: memory loss, camouflage, task, suicide, hostage, failure/futility, ideology, and resistance programming.

Memory loss programming

A primary imperative of a perpetrator is to maintain the secrecy of the perpetration to insure the ongoing viability and sustainability of the abusive situation. From the single molester of a child to multi-member cults and government-sanctioned operations, they all use amnesia techniques (hypnotic suggestions, threats, shaming, drugs, classical conditioning, dissociation-training) to erase victims' memories of incidents, names and faces. Many confusion and amnesia-inducing techniques are used to establish memory loss and self-doubt, and to instill in the survivor a fear of his or her own mind and reflective capacities. The most common version of memory loss programming (used especially in drug-induced training situations) consists of the simple statement, "it was only a dream; you were just having a bad dream. Nothing happened." Drugs and torture are also frequently deployed to create states of amnesia, and to inculcate self-doubting, memory-avoiding, memory-negating dissociative responses. More disturbing injunctions include: "If you ever begin remembering you will fall asleep, immediately think of something else, take a drink, go shopping, call the handler, cut yourself, drive your car off the road, or walk into traffic."

Some training emphasizes to the child victim that if he or she remembers the abuse, or talks to anyone else about, it he or she will immediately re-experience the worst of the traumatic events as if they were happening all over again – including the intense pain, terror, and neurological overload. Self-states implanted by perpetrators as "fail-safes" or booby traps operate to support this agenda. Other survivors have reported the creation of alter personalities that they experience as immediately vacuuming out of them any memory of having told about the abuse, or any material in books, the media, or experience in the mental health system that might activate remembering trauma or disclosing perpetrator activities. Over the years, many dissociative survivor patients have reported the use of dichotic listening, forced choice, and aversive conditioning methods for eviscerating memory. For example, the truth of a given event is presented, followed by a falsification (either acoustically, visually, or in both modalities). When the survivor chooses or attends to the truth, in some versions of this set-up, he or she is brutally shocked. When siding with the falsification, the victim is either not punished, or rewarded. This is repeated. Sometimes in trainings of this sort the victim is shocked randomly to program and establish a complete panic or dread of remembering and revealing under conditions of inquiry.

Supporting memory loss programming are generalized denial training, injunctions discouraging truth-telling, and continuous messages to victims suggesting that people outside of the perpetrating system – law enforcement, medical, and mental health professionals, school teachers and officials, and clergy – are not likely to believe anything the survivor has to say; or worse, anyone to whom the survivor discloses will either immediately reject, hate, imprison or hospitalize the survivor. Even more inhibiting are injunctions suggesting that the listener will be forever endangered and poisoned by the survivor's disclosure. Unconscious fears of harming the therapist through the potentially (i.e., programmed) destructive effects of the patient's revelations on others may be an invisible yet powerful unconscious force obstructing many treatment situations. Memory loss can be motivated by multiple perpetrator interventions but these are unfortunately always built upon the natural posttraumatic memory difficulties inherent in the naturally occurring human response to severe chronic trauma.

Camouflage programming (confusion, deception, and cover dialogue)

While the ostensible purpose of this category of programming is also the containment of perpetrator identity and protection (masquerade) of the perpetrating system, the methods do not merely obliterate actual memory, but in fact involve implantation of bogus memories, fallacious symptoms, and compelling distractions. At its most basic, camouflage programming exploits the natural posttraumatic avoidance and denial tendencies of dissociative trauma survivors. Camouflage programming is constructed with the perpetrator(s)' confidence that most of society will unwittingly collude with the alternative narratives presented by dissociative survivors for most people to preserve their own sense of safety and sanity, and/or benign beliefs about humanity. In the extreme, as Miller (2012) describes, survivors are programmed to display psychotic-like symptoms, to act like an animal, and to reveal, recant and create conditions where their credulity will be permanently suspect.

Camouflage programming is built upon trauma survivors' compelling needs for distraction, deflection, and evasion of traumatic memories, feelings, and meanings. This type of programming runs rampant in the early stages of psychotherapy, leading therapist and patient on "wild goose chases" after ever-changing and cascading symptom patterns. Survivors often change the topic or abruptly focus on here-and-now life events whenever a revelation or recollection seems about to take place. Or these victims, without apparent provocation, may become suddenly self-abusive or contemptuous toward the therapist. Such responses may arise from natural dissociative survival adaptations (e.g., hostile/protector alters, perpetrator-identified states, or from programmed alters). It is challenging for a therapist to simultaneously honor a patient's deflection or "choice" to focus on a present day life stressor while retaining the right to inquire into the possibility that this "choice" is an attempt to evade critical issues or that such a "choice" reinforces perpetrator(s)' injunctions or programming. In an unenlightened mental health arena, the accumulated effects of this type of programming can lead to multiple treatment failures, retraumatization, and wasting of precious resources. If clinicians become frustrated with patients because they are failing to make progress, remaining symptomatic, or getting worse in spite of their best efforts, it is likely that the patient will end up feeling deeply misunderstood, rejected, or abandoned – an outcome that would facilitate and/or enable most perpetrators.

In the simplest cover-story situation, the child is programmed to recall incidents that never happened or to recount them differently when asked by outsiders for explanations. Fresh bruises, for instance might be described as caused by a fall on the ball field. In cults, the cover-programming is far more complex: children are often trained to dissociate and/or feign ignorance on hearing such trigger words as "child abuse," "multiple personality," "satan," "sacrifice," "rape" "feelings," "cult," or "torture"; or the demeanor of abject confusion itself operates as the cover. Many survivors are taught the mantra that they are "crazy," "damaged," or "awful" whenever traumatic memories emerge; the shame of exposing their defective self becomes the motivation to guard secrecy while offering up a plausible (and ego-syntonic) narrative for deflecting further introspection. If anyone gets close enough to become acquainted with the survivor's internal process, these negative self-affirmations will seem part and parcel of a problem in self-esteem and will more than likely be accepted as neurotic symptoms rather than suspected to be the posttraumatic tip of a brainwashing iceberg. Or the naturally occurring shame conflicts of the posttraumatic dissociative self (discussed in Chapter 3) may substitute for or obfuscate (in both patient and therapist's mind) the presence of camouflage programming.

In other situations, a child is taken to a local pick-up point, say a shopping mall or theme park, and used for hours in prostitution, pornography, and rituals, and then programmed to tell about his or her day at the cover location when anyone asks where they have spent their time. When one survivor patient I treated was sent away for entire summers to earn large sums of money for her perpetrators through prostitution and child pornography, the cover story that she spent her summer with her "uncle" in the country was implanted and trained into her mind, and told by all of her family members. On the first day of school when all of the children gave reports on their summer vacations, this highly dissociative patient performed superbly, giving a compelling scripted portrait of a pleasant vacation in the countryside.

In long-term abuse, cover dialogue and camouflage programming becomes an intricate and well-developed part of the child's identity and worldview. The programming can be so extensive that nothing of the original child's personality remains, instead an outer shell[8] is built that functions in the victim's day-to-day life. This pseudo-identity can eventually become (and indeed is intended to become) more real than the child's personality. With time, the innocence of the original child is stored in a sub-child alter personality. Like a prisoner who has been kept in isolation for most of his life, this personality often remains autistic and unable to function without the help of its guard: the hostile alter. However, it is important to note that the innocent alter is a source of hope for successful treatment – evidence that return to innocence and integration may in fact be possible.

Most cover narratives that surface during therapy have a repetitive and affect-less quality (or at times are overly dramatized). Cover stories begin to unravel under scrutiny as factual improbabilities, insufficient detail, the therapist's lack of (or discordant) emotional responses to the cover story, and as false meanings become clear. The mere revelation of ill-fitting pieces of a cover story may lead to a breakthrough. Often, the cover story emerges simultaneously with other traumatic memories and competes for attention and allegiance within the mind of the patient. While listening to patients' stories and revelations, therapists can use their reactions (or lack of them) to inquire and disrupt the fixity of camouflage programming. Unfortunately, many therapists prefer to believe innocuous stories over trauma memories, or fail to delve beneath the initial presentations of patients' narrative content and affective presentations, and are inadvertently seduced by the many variations of cover dialogue and camouflage programming.

Task programming

Training and programming children to perform specific tasks – everything from stealing money to delivering messages or drugs to committing criminal acts that include kidnapping, torture, or murder – requires an extensive period (or frequency) of abuse to insure compliance and to highly develop dissociative adaptation. That is, the child is repeatedly victimized in specific ways that will break him or her to do whatever he or she is asked to do; eventually the victim is rendered not just malleable to the perpetrator but actually a "willing" collaborator and a co-conspirator. Terrors, threats, and rewards are used, specific to the personality of the victim, along with promises of escape from stress, pain, isolation, or starvation. Promises of protection of beloved others (animal or human) may be used to seduce the child's cooperation in learning skills important for the perpetrator(s). Once the victim has been shaped for complicity and successful performance behavior, the person or animal that had been promised protection might then be killed in order to begin the training of a co-perpetrator or assassin self-state.

A typical way this seduction process occurs is by forcing a child to choose between being tortured again or the child torturing someone else. Once the child "chooses" to harm another, he or she becomes ensnared in guilt and shame and "willing" to do whatever the perpetrator asks. When victims accept rewards following perpetration (rewards they have no choice but to accept due to the stronger authority of the perpetrators), victims unwittingly reinforce the connections in their own brains and personalities that will enable themselves to successfully engage in tasks to ensure their personal survival and support and to strengthen the perpetrating system. Many child victims are also trained to recruit and initiate other child victims.

Following the breakdown of the child's personality through spinning or electric shock torture, opiates are given with hypnotic commands so that post-torture pain relief becomes conditional on compliance with specific tasks and functions. Some perpetrators are trained in torture and personality re-structuring. They monitor the breakdown and reconstruction process through measuring levels of arousal, dissociation, breathing, heart rates, and brain waves.

In sophisticated child prostitution rings, victims are trained and conditioned under threat of pain, terror, and death, to fulfill the fantasies of different types of child molesters. Many who treat ritual abuse survivors note how alters are trained to perform a variety of functions – masochistic and sadistic sexual performances, watching and "snitching" on the victim, abusive child care, igniting dissociative processes in other child victims, courier duties, performances in rituals, torture and programming of others, and homicide. In her review of programming in ritual abuse, Miller (2012) was among the first to document specific pedophilia and necrophilia training.

Task training may coincide with espionage training, foreign language learning for purposes of the perpetrator group, and psychic training. Many patients have reported being evaluated for their potential psychic abilities and intuitive gifts; when their demonstrated capacities prove useful to the perpetrator group, many survivors are then referred to others for further training in activities such as remote viewing, psychic sabotage, energetic violence, and other intuitive skills one usually only associates with "dark shamanism" and "black magic."

One DID patient explained how she was trained to stalk and lure children to waiting cars with the promise of candy or a toy. In parks, playgrounds, theme parks, and beaches, she was taught to detect parents who let their children wander or children who seemed lost. She was instructed in how to approach the potential kidnap victim and begin to play with him or her to gain the child's trust. Once in the car, where a perpetrator would immediately drug the kidnapped child, she was trained to contain the kidnapped victim on the floor of the back seat until the vehicle arrived at a transfer point. She was told that if she did not comply she would end up as one of the "van children." Some undocumented children (i.e., cult-born, or kidnapped infants and young children) exist who never went to school, have no records, and have no life outside of the perpetrator group, and who were shuttled about in trucks to be repeatedly prostituted, raped, used in pornography, and eventually murdered in a ritual or used in snuff film.[9] Another patient described intensive psychic training where methods of long-distance psychic tracking, interfering, and poisoning of enemies of the group were taught. Believing that she had harmed large numbers of people in this way, this survivor lived with intolerable guilt and was fearful of anything related to intuition, mysticism, or science fiction.

Miller (2012) points out that three basic categories of "jobs" are commonly assigned to implanted or cultivated alters by perpetrators using mind control: (1) internal organizers to keep track of memories, alters, to monitor switch controls for turning programs on and off, to recycle and sequester memories; (2) internal enforcers to make threats, sound alarms, punish transgressions, scramble, distract, upset the person, make them feel crazy, spin internally, harm the body; and (3) navigators of contact with perpetrators for memorizing and responding to triggers, reporting on disobedience, returning to the abusers, observing calendar rules and obligations, engaging in trained sexual behaviors, killing, cutting, sacrificing, fighting, spying, and other military-type activities.

Suicide programming

In some cases where an abuse survivor has witnessed the victimization of others, or where he or she has been privy to illegal actions of other kinds, suicide is encoded into the child's programming as a mind control "safety net" for the perpetrator(s). This is accomplished through a variety of self-injury, suicide-attempt training, "fail-safes," internal homicide training, booby traps, and overseer alters implanted within a hierarchy of perpetrator-engineered self-states to oversee maintenance of the survivor's loyalty, secrecy, and undetected movements in the world (Miller, 2012; H. Schwartz, 2000). A very specific lifelong suicide program, often designed to pass as something else, can entail becoming dissociative and walking in front of a moving bus, steering into oncoming traffic, having accidents, or "falling" out of a window. In cult or governmental/military assassination programming, the individual is programmed to kill himself after killing the assigned subject(s); in some apocalyptic cult groups the individual is programmed to commit random acts of violence prior to self-destruction.

Ideology programming (to be discussed below) overlaps with suicide programming in the case of suicide bombers or others raised to believe that dying for the righteous cause is not only noble and validating, but is guaranteed to win reward and redemption in the after-life or another lifetime. The subject of suicide programming is complex and operates at numerous levels, not the least of which is the natural suicidal posttraumatic response to cognitive and somatic intrusions, pain, and overwhelm from the past or its lingering and deteriorative effects in the present. One point underscored by Miller (2012) needs to be made clear: the dynamics and behaviors related to self-harm and self-injury programming are not the same thing as suicidality. Self-mutilation and self-destructive behavior in DID patients with organized child abuse and coerced perpetration backgrounds must be evaluated for self-generated versus perpetratror-implanted suicidal and self-injury states.

Many survivors are programmed to cut themselves with razor blades, to drive off the road, or to overdose with drugs and alcohol, or to stop taking needed medications when they are about to remember and/or reveal the traumas or group secrets. Very urgent, peculiar, and often ego-dystonic thoughts, disconnected from major life concerns – an impulse to slash one's wrists, for example, in the middle of washing the dishes – may be the result of suicide/self-injury programming. Some survivors have described being cut with knives or razor blades by their perpetrators following rape or torture as a "demonstration" accompanying hypnotic suicide programming. The combination of hypnosis and cutting creates repetitive, powerful state-dependent imitations that are very difficult to undo even when the survivor becomes aware that the operative thoughts, intentions, and actions are not his or own. Ritual abuse victims report implanted commands to enact suicide on birthdays, anniversaries, and special perpetrator-defined "holidays."

It may be difficult for clinicians to discern the varieties of suicidality and programming present in a single survivor's DID system. However, I have found that when a therapist is aware of the multiple influences and motivations behind dissociative survivors' self-injurious and self-destructive behavior, and when the therapist raises various possibilities in the spirit of inquiry, informed consent, and psycho-education, a patient usually begins to develop the ability for introspection and discernment. After finding some initial relief and upset at the disturbing possibilities raised by mind control suicide programming, and often obtaining some validation from internal self-helper figures within the dissociative self-system, some patients can make great progress in regaining control over their own minds and behavior. This affectively-charged combination of relief and upset can be an important type of benevolent disruption, interfering with automatic, unconscious, and mind-controlled states of imperative or impulsive self-destructive actions.

Hostage programming

Intended to keep the victim bonded to the perpetrator and thereby insulating the individual or group's inner spheres, hostage programming inculcates a false form of loyalty. This dynamic is similar to when an incesting parent convinces the child (using threats, physical abuse, manipulations, seduction, authoritative/authoritarian influence), that disobedience, disloyalty, or displays of anger or disagreement, indeed any expressions of independent thought which are part of all children's normal development, would victimize or endanger the perpetrator, or remove the child from the perpetrator. Thus, a father abusing his son might explain in an elementary version of hostage programming that he has every right to touch and even hurt him, that all adults have the same right, and that telling anyone will be bring more pain on the child victim and will be tantamount to harming the victim's entire family.

In its most extreme form, hostage programming becomes a vehicle of personality fragmentation. The victim is programmed to feel no anger or thoughts of revenge toward the perpetrator. Normal, healthy self-protective reactions are obliterated; what is left to the victim is only an empty shell, a compliant sub-self with little substance and great potential for the creation of robotic self-states. The victim is taught that separation from the perpetrator is impossible and undesirable, and attempts to escape will either cause more torment to the victim or will be futile. Unconscious memories of painful coerced drug withdrawal imprint anxiety on the victim when any thoughts of loss of or separation from the perpetrator emerge (or are mentioned intentionally or accidentally by others, including therapists).

If the victim with hostage programming enters therapy, he or she will find therapy useless: after assembling shattered memories, the patient will find it difficult to do anything with them, or will re-dissociate them as soon as possible. When hostage programming is activated, the patient usually becomes highly resistant to the therapist he or she may have previously learned to trust and may "decide" to quit treatment or create a compelling, legitimate excuse for a break from therapy or termination. The patient will probably become agitated, resentful, depressed and/or suicidal, convinced that there is no existence from an allegiance to which he or she was long ago internally programmed for life. When the survivor undergoing therapy is also still in contact with his/her perpetrators, either consciously and/or unconsciously through alters created behind amnesia barriers, advances in therapy will remain problematic. According to Miller (2012) some alters sustain information exchange and contact with the survivor's perpetrator(s), unbeknownst to significant sectors of the (mainstream) individual's personality.

Some patients have described set-ups in their early childhood where they had imagined escape was possible, when the perpetrators were allegedly "not watching." However, whenever the child tried to leave the perpetrator(s)' arena, alarms were sounded or other adults in hiding pounced on and brutalized the child. Watching the torture and murder of alleged traitors of the group also solidifies the commitment to find safety in the group by remaining silent and obedient. In trafficking situations, hostage programming is easily achieved by taking the victim to another country where he or she does not speak the language and confiscating his or her identity documents. In sex-death cults, children are deprived of contact with anyone, left temporarily buried, cold, hungry, and isolated for long periods of time. Through these actions a bond with a particular group member or handler is activated through the contrast between isolation and the resumed contact (which often involves sadistic sex). Hostage programming operates powerfully in the lives of child soldiers when their military leaders replace the village authority and elders that had previously protected the village. Drugs, violence, conditional protection, food, sex, and the right to harm others are the local currencies for child soldiers; child soldiers have little choice but to accept and use the available currency.

A particularly disturbing subset of hostage programming can be termed "spiritual hostage programming." In this variation, the goal of the perpetrator(s) is to sabotage the individual's potential for redemptive interpersonal relationships and his or her potential for redemptive personal spirituality. This is achieved through severing the connections with the victim's internal guidance system or through interference in the survivor's belief and faith in, or perceived contact with, external benevolent spiritual resources. Explicit messages about being doomed, damned, condemned, spiritually outcast, and eternally unlovable are often features of ritual abuse and other sex-death or diabolical perpetrator systems. The victim is subjected to repeated tests/inquests to ascertain whether during rituals or traumas the victim experiences any contact with angels, demons, protective mythological figures, or any internal sources of comfort, guidance, or support. If a child reveals such experiences, which many do, the perpetrator(s) then builds in conditioned aversions to these spiritual resources while substituting perpetrator-preferred icons, deities, and guidance figures (often including images of the leaders of the perpetrator group or familiar demonic figures from mythology or literature).

Lacter (2011) explains how many survivors describe torture and rituals in which diabolical perpetrators placed parts of their "spirits" inside of them, usually in specific self-states designed for holding such information, through the transfer of body fluids, other substances, and/or incantations. "Attached spirits" may be experienced by the survivor in both childhood and adulthood, as repeating the controlling messages, commands, and injunctions that were first spoken in the indoctrination rituals. Self-states most deeply affected by these experiences may also believe, from having been told or programmed, that "the abusers captured parts of their own spirit to hold captive within themselves" (p. 83). Lacter calls this type of programming "anti-God programming" (p. 101). Many survivors describe a mix of torture and verbal programming used by their perpetrators to instill a fear of God; many are programmed to invert all Judeo-Christian terms such as reversing God and satan, love and hate, and reversing directions and intentions of prayers. Often the child victim is shown evidence that he or she is as evil as the perpetrators, through choices allegedly made of the trainee's own free will. Such identification with evil is then used by perpetrators as proof of the victim's eternal rejection, damnation, and condemnation by God. As Lacter attests, many mind control survivors consistently report that "their will and spirit were the most sought after prizes of their abusers" (p. 100) and that their perpetrators sought absolute sovereignty over their entire psychological, spiritual, and aspirational inner world. In shamanic and indigenous systems of healing, resolution of spiritual hostage programming is often referred to as "soul retrieval" (Eliade, 1964; Harner, 1980). Interventions often involve returning to the scene of traumatic rupture with the self's relationship with soul, Divinity, and community, accompanied by a spiritual protector/warrior in order to reclaim aspects of the self/soul that had been "stolen" or "abandoned" in desperate circumstances.

An even more bizarre derivative of spiritual hostage programming is "after-death programming." In this conditioning paradigm, instructions are given to the victim when he or she is either in a hypnotized, de-patterned (post-electric shock), perpetrator-loyal, or otherwise receptive state about how to exit the body and avoid contact with benevolent spiritual beings in the death and dying process. The victim is told that versions of the perpetrator group are waiting to receive him or her on "the other side"; specific instructions are given on making these connections, evading "light beings," and remaining loyal to and part of the group even after death. However, unlike religions that emphasize graceful stewarding of a person through the death and dying process in order to ease the soul out of the body and into the next world, this type of programming aims for the victim to experience maximum terror, mayhem, isolation and chaos in his or her death transition. Regardless of whether a survivor (or therapist) consciously believes in life after death, toxic ideas and beliefs left un-neutralized in the survivor's unconscious mind keep the survivors linked to their perpetrator(s) and separated from the natural development of their own unique spiritual idioms, identities, and destinies.

Failure/futility programming

An important subset of programming not extensively discussed in the literature is what I refer to as "failure/futility programming." This programming is easily disguised or misrecognized as low-self-esteem, self-defeating thinking, or depressive cognitions. The goal of failure programming is to specifically booby trap the survivor's field of potential individuation and self-actualization. Failure programming carries the perpetrator message of, *if we can't have you, then you can't have you either; if you can't help us sustain our omnipotence and operations, then we want to make sure you can't sustain any of your own dreams or plans.* Common in many dysfunctional and abusive family systems are variations on futility programming relating to attitudes and injunctions geared to thwart the individual's capacity for independent functioning, or to destroy his or her belief in the capacity for self-sufficiency and success. Whether these dynamics are enacted because of envy, spite, family or sub-cultural programming, possessiveness, or other nefarious familial/perpetrator motivations, the goal is always the same: to make sure the victim (or family/group member) either completely serves and protects the perpetrator/system or is significantly disabled. One of the most common and unfortunate forms of this programming occurs via the transgenerational transmission of beliefs in scarcity and limitation among colonlized, enslaved, and oppressed groups.

As with all programming, normal human traumatic responses of self-limiting, dysphoric or fatalistic thinking can co-exist with failure training. To ascertain the presence of failure/futility programming it is important to review the survivor's trauma history for episodes of breakdown in functioning and performance, and for their exit story from victimization and perpetrator contacts (if there is one). Once a mind-control operative or cult victim is no longer of use or no longer performing what is required, torture is unleashed on the individual within which an entire catechism of self-sabotaging, self-defeating, and self-interfering beliefs, mantras, injunctions are laid down. Each time the survivor makes a developmental leap forward in therapy (or personal or professional life), a strange, persistent, and lingering self-defeating litany is trailing them in spite of progress made in therapy and in spite of real life improvements in self-esteem, vocational and interpersonal functioning.

Uncovering failure/futility programming is enormously helpful to the observing ego and critical thinking functions of the survivor as well as to his or her overall sense of well-being, mastery, and reality-testing. Dissociative survivors are being dynamically returned to the psychological ambience of the perpetrator group whenever a doomed feeling persists that regardless of whatever they do, or whatever progress they think they might make, they will fail due to an inherent (and non-remediable) defect in their make-up. Irrational as it may first appear, unconscious shame and guilt for not performing to the standards of perpetrators (e.g., for not being wicked enough) sometimes looms in the survivor's unconscious as a magnet for inchoate feelings of inferiority, incompetence, and hopelessness.

Ideology/propaganda programming

Ideology/propaganda programming is pan-cultural. It is used as a psychological leverage in every arena such as advertising, intergenerational transmission of family and sub-cultural values and traditions, standard religious, military, or political training and extreme cults by indoctrination and mind control techniques. It is in use to some degree in all educational and sub-cultural systems throughout the world, from the most benign to the most totalitarian, and ideology programming is elemental in establishing group loyalties based on shared logic, goals, and motivations. Ideology programming depends on coerced receptivity and inculcation of belief systems.

What is common in all methods of ideology programming is that the essential controlling messages are suggested or forcibly implanted, after the victim's receptivity has been demonstrably established. In family systems, intergenerational transmission – for example storytelling about morality – may come at meal times, during festivities, or in other periods of high emotional valence. Transmission is probably most potent in family and other systems when delivered implicitly or by innuendo (including knowing glances and dissociative absences). In cults and socially accepted religions, the transmission of doctrine happens after periods of chanting, meditation, enactments of rituals, or expostulations of emotion. In violent perpetrator groups that eroticize power based on malevolent hierarchy, sadistic sex, torture, or painful death, the receptivity and indoctrination is accomplished in a variety ways:

• casual conversations at the dinner table with parents who are members of the group
• simple repeated exposure to the perpetrator/group and the natural seeking of approval and security from this individual or group
• hypnosis
• classes for training children to tolerate participation in rituals, sexual trauma, violence, and torture
• edicts and declarations following group events such as executions, rituals, or orgiastic sex
• torture-based mind control using electricity or other pain-inducing devices to break down the body and mind's defenses and resistances
• the deliberate creation of dissociative states to hold and contain programmed beliefs, guidance systems, and policies of punishment and control

Beyond its coercive aspect, the main difference between dissociatively-internalized indoctrinations and more mainstream versions of ingesting spiritual or political ideology (either wholesale-as-received or through self-paced study and inquiry) is that the dissociative individual's reflective and critical thinking abilities are absent from the process or rendered ineffectual. Ideologies buried in encapsulated states surrounded by fear, desire, or omnipotent fantasies are difficult to access, and certainly challenging to disrupt.

Effective programming encapsulates information in ways that insulate it from conflicting information, and from self-reflection. Discussion, doubt, or disagreement are virtually impossible and dissociative survivors fervently defend against the internal (or interpersonal) collision of ideas or thought systems. In many cases, survivors may or may not know that they tenaciously hold and obey certain beliefs because in their conscious, and primary functioning personalities, their attitudes and commitments are contrary to what has been implanted. When the first collisions occur between the survivor's two contradictory thought systems, the perpetrator-implanted system will inevitably attempt to seduce the survivor into believing that his or her more compassionate beliefs are incorrect and fraudulent, and that they (perpetrator-programmed states) represent what the patient really feels, and who he or she really is. Few dissociative survivors can withstand the early onslaught of re-activated ideology programming without sinking into a period of deep doubt and despair as to the true nature, identity, and allegiance of their "real" self. Effective therapy helps the patient understand the differences between ideology, identity, and intention – domains that became entangled and undecipherable during the years of trauma. What is most challenging about treating ideology programming is identifying its subtle and scattered remains – implications and inferences in the survivor's psyche based on programmed beliefs that have permeated the self-system in ways that are not easily discernible. Once critical thinking and observing ego functions are re-engaged, most survivors can diligently apply themselves to the deprogramming task, and eventually find comfort in their abilities to think their own thoughts and ally with principles, meanings, and values of their own choosing.

Resistance programming

Resistance programming is aimed at establishing a protective psychological moat around the survivor's perpetrator-engineered dissociative fortress. Many examples of this type of programming are explained and illustrated in Miller's (2012) thorough treatise on types of programming commonly found among survivors of ritual abuse. These include:

- silence and compliance training
- recantation training
- internal hierarchies of overseers, torturers, and gatekeepers
- anti-attachment training
- anti-therapy training
- anti-expression training (i.e., verbal, artistic, affective)
- access programming (trained to be hypnotically accessible to handlers or perpetrator(s) using codes, signals, hidden messages, etc.)
- self-report programming (i.e., self-monitoring and "snitching" on the self for the perpetrators)
- return programming (i.e., instilled obedience for returning to the perpetrator(s) for specific holidays, required tasks/missions, or to be re-programmed if the survivor enters treatment or begins to remember and reveal)
- booby-traps, land-mines, and fail-safes (i.e., triggers to be activated to interfere with the patient's independence, autonomy, disclosure, rebelliousness, or self-respect)

At first it may be challenging, for therapists to discern for themselves, and to help their patients learn to discern the differences between the naturally occurring posttraumatic avoidances and therapy resistances from those obstructions to communication and therapy that are based on resistance programming. The latter tend to have an inflexible, non-negotiable, automatic, unreflective quality and can only be accessed by inquiring into the ways in which the particular reactions (to certain types of inquiry or feeling words or moments of intimacy and breakthrough in treatment) have played out in the survivor's life and in previous therapy relationships or earlier stages of the current therapy relationship. Extending Lacter's (2011) observation, a key difference between self-created and perpetrator-installed dissociative states is that even in the realm of defiance and non-cooperation, from self-created states there appears to be a desire for some bonding or relatedness with the therapist. Perpetrator-engineered resistances are indifferent to, and inexorably contemptuous toward, reflective dialogue. Working with this type of obstructionism, it is best for the therapist and patient to have achieved some accrued successful experiences in negotiating the ordinary variety of posttraumatic, dissociative avoidance and triggers, and for both the patient and the therapist to have acknowledged the existence of two overlapping but distinct sets of resistance.

Chapter 5

Perpetration and perpetrator states

Hell is empty and all the devils are here.

William Shakespeare

Perpetration

The icy core of perpetration is the nullification of the subjectivity of the other. Fairy tales and science fiction often portray the consuming, mechanical *entrapment-betrayal-evacuation-colonization-annihilation* aspects of evil, invariably cloaked in disarming or compelling disguise, or in scenario of seduction. In C.S. Lewis's (1963) classic satirical novel on evil, *The Screwtape Letters*, the senior demon Screwtape explains his diabolism to his trainee in this way: "To us a human is primarily food; our aim is the absorption of its will into ours, the increase of our own area of selfhood at its expense" (p. 38). In George Orwell's (1949) classic novel *1984*, the mind manipulator O'Brian says to his victim Winston: "Things will happen to you from which you could not recover, if you lived a thousand years never again will you be capable of love or friendship, or joy of living, or laughter or curiosity or courage or integrity. You will be hollow. You will be squeezed empty and then we shall fill you with ourselves" (p. 211).

The term perpetration, like the term evil, can be difficult to define. Beyond denoting acts of performing, carrying out, and executing, the word "perpetration" derives from the Latin *patrare* which means to bring about or to "father into existence." Interestingly, a betrayal guised in patriarchal authority is often a driving force in perpetration. In the literature on abuse and criminality, the term perpetrator refers to those who commit (and benefit from) violence against others. The scope of perpetration has been revealed in recent years to be so vast and diverse that taxonomies for types of perpetration have been developed in order to help patients (and therapists treating those patients) to come to terms with the specifics of their experiences (Salter, 1995; H. Schwartz, 2000).

Acts of perpetration are, by nature, opportunistic. Exploitation and/or annihilation of the subjectivity of the victim is most often the goal. Violence may or may not be involved but violation always is. What is violated, or undermined, are the victim's innocence, freedom, vulnerability, and spirit. Perpetration is invariably predatory and it triggers the victim's instinctive survival mechanisms. For perpetrators, predation operates through primitive, reptilian behaviors (and brain functions) in concert with higher order cognitive processes involving real and symbolic pleasure, triumph, retaliation, and/or delight in power over others. The exploitative and scapegoating devices characterizing perpetration are usually masked by narratives of paranoia or righteous indignation, and driven by political or religious/philosophical agendas.

The essence of perpetration is objectification and the systematic undermining of the victim's sense of agency. With the victim's innocence, and obedience at the perpetrator(s)' disposal, the perpetrator(s) finds diverse uses for the victim's mind, body, and spirit: to fuel the perpetrator's sense of omnipotence; to supply gratification for sexual and sadistic urges; to support the perpetrator's economic and status advancement; and to augment the perpetrator's psychological self-regulation. Relief of the perpetrator's tension states is attained through the victim's re-enactment of the perpetrator's dread and inner torment. In other words, the perpetrator evacuates intolerable feelings into the victim's mind and body. Then when the victim is fully objectified, he or she is psychologically colonized to serve as a receptacle or slave. As Grand (2000) points out, perpetrators require endless repetitions of their destructive acts because the relief from displacing their own agonies onto their victims is always temporary. The unending cycle of perpetration requires a constant supply of victims, collaborators, and thwarted rescuers.

The destructive interpersonal processes typical of perpetration in general and evil in particular include: envious attacks on goodness; the malignant armor of narcissism; the evacuative management of the dread of extinction (Alford, 1997); fractured or impaired psychological containers (Bion, 1965; Ferro, 2005); malignant greed and retaliation; and failed attempts at coping with catastrophic loneliness (Grand, 2000). As an archetypal force in human life, the patterns of evil are familiar, even if evil itself defies easy definition. Evil and perpetration flourish under the pressures of scarcity, chronic fear, and futility. Evil is essentially an anti-creative (undoing) force, dependent upon hierarchy, divisiveness, intimidation, contagion, and coerced complicity; it always seeks expansion and replication. The prodigious, homogenizing, and cruel intelligence of evil is often successful in instilling confusion, fear, and a sense of futility in professionals tasked with recognizing and treating evil's effect on individuals and communities.

> We define evil because it scares us, because we do not know where it starts or stops, so we try to confine it with a definition. We define [in order] to confine, to keep evil from becoming a precategorical blur. We define evil so that it is something rather than no-thing. It is precisely the no-thing quality of evil that is so disturbing. [...] The need for a definition is itself a reflection of precategorical dread, an attempt to give shape and boundaries to an experience that we fear possesses neither. Perhaps this is the most terrifying aspect of evil, its unbounded quality, neither inside nor

outside, but both, passing through us possessing us in ways we hardly know but deeply fear.

Alford (1997:117)

The systematic corruption of children for the purposes of slavery and exploitation in sex and violent subcultures, depraved religions, or civil wars by way of coerced perpetration exemplifies the relentless replicating nature of evil more than almost any other form of perpetration. Physical torture and mind control become hallmarks of a person's history with coerced perpetration and result in encapsulated states of destructive characterological patterns that co-exist with more mature modes of interpersonal functioning. The simultaneous presence of these destructive and healthy aspects of the victim's psychological make-up serves two purposes. First, it is evidence of the victim's attempts to dissociate destructiveness, camouflage his or her dissociation, appear normal, and preserve a capacity for a healthy quality of life and mental development. Second, it serves perpetrators by exploiting the mind's abilities of dissociating to conceal and protect the perpetrators and their activities. Nothing serves a perpetrator's agenda as effectively as victims whose apparent normalcy allows their perpetrator to re-victimize them at will, while simultaneously camouflaging the process from the victim, from helping professionals, and from society in general.

Acts of perpetration extend from the perpetrator's diminished capacity to empathize, to grieve, to share, and to evolve (Grant, 1996). Based on a mentality of negation and a commitment to undermining intrapsychic and social cohesion, accumulated or ongoing acts of perpetration lead to impairments in the perpetrator's ability to recognize his or her own humanity in others. The perpetrator's subtle or violent projections and evacuations of shame, dread, terror, annihilation or apocalyptic anxieties are the most common forms of psychological exploitation. Retaliation and traumatic re-enactment are also common motivations for perpetration. The potential for perpetration festers in any environment rife with petty behavior, lies, gossip, objectification or demonization of others, self-absorption, greed, competition, and personal betrayal. Another breeding ground of perpetration is within a person struggling to manage more than he or she can bear, morally compromising him- or herself at varying levels of selfishness or malice, in order to survive or prosper. Well-coordinated coerced perpetration in tandem with coerced social complicity can wreak havoc on an entire society, crippling in months traditions and institutions that may have taken centuries to develop (e.g., the societies of Rwanda or Cambodia).

The Neo-Kleinian psychoanalytic literature on destructiveness is invaluable for illuminating the underlying nature of perpetration. For Bion (1965; 1967) and Ferro (2005), perpetration is inherently related to an excess of what Bion calls Beta elements in the psyche and breakdowns in Alpha functioning.[1] Beta elements are, among many aspects of unformulated experience, trauma fragments bearing traces of anxiety, terror, and dread – having the feel of undigested facts or shards of feeling unlinked to experience. Beta elements are inherently toxic, unstable, inchoate, potentially explosive, and cannot be usably linked in the process of generating thoughts to be stored in memory or used for generative fantasy or productive action. When inadequately metabolized by overwhelmed higher order psychological processes (Alpha functions), Beta elements can only be managed through evacuation, projective identification, addictive behaviors, or acting out (Ferro, 2005). In this view, the residue of unmetabolized trauma (in both victims and perpetrators) accumulates due to limitations or breakdowns in intrapsychic functioning and to some extent interpersonal functioning. Because of developmental failures in thinking-feeling-dreaming functions, the recurrent floods of primitive agonies (unprocessed, overwhelming experience) within the mind of the perpetrator generate pressures for discharge in violent or bizarre forms.

According to Ferro (2005), violence and antisocial behavior result from specific failures in the maturational (containment, detoxification, reflection) functions of the perpetrator's mind. The minds of violent criminals are ultimately cannibalized by their own Beta elements, and their destructiveness toward others derives not from an instinct but from a failure of containment and transformative mental functions. In Ferro's analysis, what underlies perpetration are defective efforts at mastering trauma and faulty reparation of broken or absent psychological containers for coping with trauma. Perpetrators' own childhood histories of helplessness or communicative isolation may predispose them to a lifetime of acting out, evacuation, hallucination, and addiction. Human history and patients' trauma narratives have demonstrated that perpetrators misappropriate the minds, bodies, and spirits of other human beings for containment, "communication," and re-enactment.

When survivors of traumatic victimization become perpetrators, they "share" their annihilation trauma with his or her own victim "at the pinnacle of loneliness and at the precipice of death" (Grand, 2000:6). This doomed search for redemption through the scripted annihilation of an other sets up perpetual loops of destruction. In these shared encounters with the moment of execution/extinction, a dance between the violated self of victim and the no-self of the perpetrator takes place. The survivor-perpetrator strives to master obliteration or obliterate their unbearable self-judgment through his or her desperate evacuation of shame and dread into an "other" victim.

Evacuative processes are graphically illustrated by a variety of well publicized phenomena: the brutal assaults by child soldiers on innocent fellow-villagers; the repeated sexual violation of (usually female) child soldiers or prisoners tied to trees for weeks or months at a time; child participants in the torture and humiliation of scapegoats born from the loss of familial and communal bonds; self-appointed or indoctrinated suicide bombers; alienated high school students using guns to unleash torrents of rage and terror on their classmates; returning war veterans evacuating posttraumatic aggression and unmetabolized grief by murdering or attempting to murder their family members. Less violent examples of perpetration/evacuation include using hateful (racist, homophobic, anti-Islamic, or anti-Semitic) graffiti to deface sacred spaces; and various forms of internet seductions and/or stalking. Less violent, but perhaps more consequential, perpetration occurs when selfish economic behavior by individuals, groups, or institutions exploits the financial vulnerability of others and redistributes power and money into the hands of financial perpetrators (predation). Sowing the destructive seeds of poverty and desperation (the evacuation of dread and helplessness) into victims and communities, these economic deceptions represent a significant (and currently rampant) form of perpetration that has dire personal and social effects – including serious mental health consequences for the impoverished, shocked, and humiliated survivors of unethical economic opportunism.

In therapy, some survivor-perpetrators upload their dread and apocalyptic anxieties into the transference-countertransference dynamic by confusing the therapist, and rendering the therapist helpless, with threatening, provocative, or "gaslighting" behaviors. For example, a dissociative survivor might recount gruesome traumatic experiences not for any sort of cathartic relief, but purely to exploit the therapist's psyche as dumping ground, to retaliate for real or perceived hurts and disappointments, or as an attempt to feed off the therapist's emotional/intimacy experience. These enactments may occur while the patient is pretending to him or herself (and the therapist) that therapeutic progress is being made. While a therapist's discomfort with difficult trauma material can be a natural response as a component of compassionate witnessing, a provoking of the therapist's emotional disequilibrium may also be a perpetrator-victim enactment; this possibility requires inquiry, illumination, and confrontation.

Clinical example: Irene

Following an apparent breakthrough in therapy, Irene, a female DID patient with a history that included multiple perpetrators parked her car in front of her therapist's home one night (many miles from the therapist's office where the treatment takes place). She fell asleep with her head on the steering wheel. At first the therapist was not sure who the "stranger" was parked in front of her house. Uneasily, the therapist and her husband approached the car to determine whether the car's occupant was sleeping or dead. When the therapist finally recognized her patient, she was shocked and exasperated as she dialed 911. Hearing voices calling her name, the patient was roused from her sleep. She was dazed, confused, shocked, and could not explain to the therapist how or why she had arrived there, or how she had found out where the therapist lived. Irene appeared to be communicating, not communicating, and having internal interference with communicating on many levels all at the same time. In Irene's psyche, attachment longings, destructive urges, and states of oblivion had become fused. The therapist was eventually able to use her own experience of fear, uncertainty, dread, shock, and helplessness to assist Irene to connect with, and decipher, her own unarticulated tangle of feeling states and the perpetrator dynamics this morass of feelings obscured.

Clinical example: Mira

Mira, a dissociative trauma survivor, systematically cut the eyes out of the faces of people in magazine images in the shared waiting room of her therapist's suite. This was unbeknownst to her therapist and to many parts of her complex dissociative self-system. Because there were six therapists in the suite – some who did custody evaluations and some who treated families and children – it remained unclear for a long period of time whose patient (if it was a patient at all) was mutilating the magazines. The awkwardness and ambiguity of the situation – including the potential risk of false accusations against a patient if he or she were innocent – seemed to mirror and re-enact elements of the patient's pathological family environment where perpetrator, victim, and collaborator roles were constantly in flux and violence and sexual abuse were rampant. In her early family system, malice and malevolence prevailed, hypocrisy and betrayal were ever present, and this was skillfully masked by a façade of middle-class normalcy, Christian morality, self-righteousness, and conservative and racist ideologies. The patient's relief at finally being "discovered" came quickly on the heels of her initial fragile defensive evasion. Mutilating faces in the magazines served a variety of functions: it re-enacted family dynamics and ambience; it unconsciously communicated about trauma, programming, and perpetration history; it concretized old threats to breaches of secrecy; it indirectly expressed rage at the therapist; it tested the therapist's boundaries and capacities for tolerating destructiveness; it represented an attempt to intimidate the therapist; it undermined the patient's credibility and integrity; and it precipitated a disruption that might have ended treatment while potentially supporting perpetrator alters' efforts to undermine therapy. Most importantly, the enactment contained a veiled cry for help and rescue that replicated all the hidden ways Mira as a child had tried to signal to the the world to take notice of her desperate situation. By eventually taking the risk to confront Mira, the therapist passed a significant unconscious test. This successful therapeutic negotiation created a sense of safety that allowed Mira to make great strides in revealing to her therapist the extent and nature of her internal world, and the depths of the depravity and criminality to which she had been exposed as a child.

Clinical example: Steve

Steve, a male DID patient presented with a confusing profile of sexual promiscuity, HIV infection, a high functioning professional life, and severe depression. Steve's description of his family ranged from exaggerated claims about the family's benign, run-of-the-mill narcissism to a fragmented portrait of a radically evil family system that included involvement in secret, underground sex-death cult activities in which the patient's physician father played a prominent role. Steve's mother was also purportedly in periodic attendance. Steve alternated between long periods of celibacy and dangerous, degrading sexual acting out in group situations, during which he would secretly fantasize his mastery and superiority over the men who he had allowed to "use" him sexually.

At first subtly, then in increasingly more overt ways (but always veiled in the ambiguity of sadistic play), Steve threatened to report me, his therapist, to the state licensing authority and to the False Memory Foundation for my willingness to believe his trauma narratives. He made vague references to spying on my private life and to the possibilities of my being tracked by members of his family and perpetrator group. When I was unwilling to answer certain provocative personal questions I saw as re-enactment attempts, Steve found duplicitous ways to solicit or uncover the information he had been seeking. Some of Steve's alter personalities supported, reassured, and pleaded with the aggressive/perpetrator-identified alters on my behalf, perceiving me as rescuer and potential liberator because of my understanding of perpetrator group behavior, while other of the patient's more perpetrator-like alters continued to threaten and deride me for my willingness to consider any possible truth in his clinical material. Following every incremental step forward that established trust and a consistent narrative thread, there was an "undoing."

What remained for some time unclear was whether Steve's dissociative system contained implanted/conditioned resistance-to-discovery programming or whether these persistent and extreme discrepancies in presentation were the result of the patient's own self-constructed struggle with memory, identity, trauma, and dissociative organization. Additional possibilities that were also investigated included Steve's potential responses to my empathic failures, re-enactments of family dynamics, or other elusive attempts at communication about our relationship and/or Steve's traumatic past. All of these options provided opportunities for Steve to displace his dread, confusion, and helplessness onto me, while crying out (and pretending not to be crying out) for help and recognition. The lingering ambiguity about Steve's continued involvement with his perpetrators and their possible role in the therapy impasse cycles were particularly unsettling because the dynamics of gaslighting, coerced confusion and paranoia threatened to turn the entire therapy enterprise into a theater so thick with enactments that it could eventually suffocate every potential pathway to reparation.

Clinical example: Maureen

An extremely fragmented DID patient, Maureen, with a history of child prostitution, pornography, ritual abuse, and mind control acted out in a most unusual way while she was hospitalized on an inpatient treatment unit I coordinated many years ago. My contacts with this patient included twice-daily community meetings and daily group psychotherapy. In the community room of the unit, I had set up an aquarium for the patients as a relaxation device and a reminder of natural beauty. I often joked with the patients that they might be able to take fewer anxiety medications if they spent 15 minutes once or twice a day focusing on the living world inside the fish tank. The patients loved the fish and took turns volunteering for weekly fish feeding, cleaning, and management tasks, which I supervised. Sharing the fish tank with the patients was especially meaningful for me since aquariums had been a positive element in my childhood experiences. I had to go to considerable lengths to get the administrative staff of the hospital to agree to my experiment in "pet therapy." The aquarium allowed the patients and staff to exchange relaxed communication around something other than personal problems or unit business. Many of the traumatized patients were devoted caretakers of the fish and alerted me to any slight disruption in the aqueous community – often when nothing was actually wrong – enacting dynamics related to overprotection, failed protection, traumatic anticipation, and fears of loss.

During a week when Maureen was responsible for the care of the fish tank something strange occurred. Most of the fish seemed to be ill or dying. At the same time, Maureen began to rage at the staff, (following a confrontation of her destructive communication patterns in group therapy earlier in the week) and particularly at me for not "doing anything to help the fish." In the community meeting the following day, Maureen had fomented a small uprising among the more passive patients, claiming that the staff and director of the milieu program (me) were neglecting their duties, not intervening quickly enough, and that this was tantamount to "murdering the fish."

We attempted to deal with the incident as a community. However, we were missing one important piece of information which was supplied within 24 hours by Carrie, another DID patient, who in general seemed to operate with a higher level of personal integrity, and who was not then working out any particular upset with the staff or myself. Carrie revealed that she had seen Maureen sneak into the dayroom when she thought no one was watching and took several fish out of the tank, held them in her hands until they were almost dead, and then returned them to the tank. The possibility arose in my mind that Carrie could be lying and that the drama could be escalating, that Carrie could be re-enacting complex betrayal dynamics of her own. I had the uneasy gut feeling that Carrie was telling the truth. These events occurred in a community context, and because the second patient was willing to confront the alleged perpetrator patient in the unit's morning community meeting where all versions of events could be heard and potentially worked through, a different process took place than if this event had been enacted and treated within the dyad of psychotherapy. After vehemently denying the allegations in front of the community, confusing and dividing the community even further, Maureen eventually confessed the truth to her individual therapist. Maureen admitted she had been harming the fish and inciting a civil war on the unit. She followed her confession with an act of serious self-destructive behavior, resulting in a two-week stint in the locked unit of the hospital.

The web of complicity

Both Grand (2000) and H. Schwartz (2000) emphasize that perpetration cannot exist without a web of complicity, collusion, and collaboration. "It is through denial that evil consolidates its power [...] evil seems to be everywhere. And even as it is everywhere, it is everywhere denied; perpetrator and bystander collude in its obfuscation" (Grand, 2000:10). The primitive, opportunistic intelligence behind perpetration is adept at enforcing complicity and incredulity through seduction, blackmail, intimidation, obfuscation, bribery, and deception. The negating of history, discrediting testimony, and devaluing the witnessing process are typical strategies of deft perpetrators. The goal is to generate a perpetual haze of confusion about responsibility, veracity, and accountability that precedes and follows the perpetrator(s)' deeds. Perpetrators rely on bystanders' incapacity to imagine the darker regions of human possibility, or our desire to disavow them and/or bystanders' own desire to profit from the spoils of perpetration.

Perpetrators are enabled by numerous aspects of our society's characteristic reactions to potential evidence of perpetration:

- Widespread inability to understand perpetration's cues, meanings, and implications
- Allowing one's children to be left in the care of suspect or dangerous individuals due to ignorance, convenience, urgency, re-enactment, or vicarious sadism
- Selective inattention
- Turning a deaf ear to the protests of victims
- Refusal to confront explicit acts of domination and perpetration
- Denying the extent, the intent, the consequences, or the meaning of various abusive behaviors toward women and children
- Ignoring the connections among prostitution, trafficking, child abuse, child sexual slavery and economic slavery, and child soldiering
- Ignoring or distorting statistical data on child abuse
- Uncritical idealization of existing family and social institutions, arrangements, and customs
- Publicly declaring an accused perpetrator innocent (after ignoring or hiding evidence); protecting an institution (e.g., church, school, or government) through cover-ups at the expense of victims
- Refusing to confront the realities (or include in one's worldview) of organized child abuse, sex-slavery, and mind control trauma
- Using simplistic notions about trauma, children's suggestibility, children's resiliency, memory problems, or tendencies to lie in order to discredit them
- Diagnosing and pathologizing the sequelae of child abuse without linking to the external events that precipitated the need for extreme psychological adaptation
- Valuing personal anxiety reduction above all other ethical or moral principles
- Punishing children or adults for exposing perpetrators or for revealing sex crimes
- Failing to adequately investigate child abuse charges
- Mistakenly invoking the notions of choice and free will for women and children caught in forced choice dilemmas

- Continuing the social acceptability of using other people for psychological, spiritual, or economic benefit
- Blaming the victim and/or minimizing (or contemptuously mocking the extent or persistence of) his or her pain
- Not investing in reparation efforts
- Profiteering from the remains or after effects of perpetration
- Pressuring victims to give premature forgiveness to their perpetrators

Perpetration and evil

The destruction of a victim's autonomy and the replacement of a victim's identity with a perpetrator-induced identity is a key element of perpetration in child abuse, cults, mind control trauma, and the training of child soldiers. When coerced perpetration is essential to the perpetrator's practices, as Grand (2000:93) articulates: "It is a tribute to the perpetrator's brilliance that the survivor's coerced transgression obscures questions of agency and responsibility, guilt and innocence. In the survivor's breach of his own moral integrity, the perpetrator locates a mirror for his own disavowed culpability." When a system like this involves large numbers of victims and collaborators, Alford's (1997) concepts of "moral autism," "self-serving morality," and "cultivated malevolence" describe the dynamics of perpetration.

Perpetration reaches its apotheosis whenever four conditions are simultaneously present: (1) survivors want to die or be killed (for wanting life [Grand, 2000]), for surviving the torture or killing of others, and/or from their indelible conviction they are damned or unredeemable; (2) collaborators and bystanders refuse culpability, and escalate their justifications, victim-blaming, and denial, while continuing to reap the benefits of perpetration and victimization of others; (3) perpetrators become immune to constraints, exposure, or prosecution; and (4) interveners find themselves chronically confused, intimidated, and divided: warring among themselves about what is actually happening and who can be trusted.

Grand (2000) writes about "the reproduction of evil." The "replication of evil" is a more accurate description of its process of contagion – especially since evil appears to prefer homogeneity to multiplicity. The propagation of evil always seems to direct itself against diversity,[2] human potentiality, and, most of all innocence. For those identified with the archetype of evil, it is innocence – a particular transpersonal aspect of goodness – that activates evil's deepest envy, and its most violent rage. It is innocence that incites the desire for consumption or defilement. One of my patients told me that as a young child she was trained to torment other child victims in front of her gloating perpetrators "until the light went out of their eyes. I was taught how to take the light out of them and they praised me and rewarded me for doing it quickly – when they wanted it done quickly, that is." The eradication of luminosity in the quality of eye contact of the child victim was considered a sign of great success in her perpetrator group, and the process eventually became a mechanical undertaking for trainees.

Melanie Klein's (1975) belief that envy is the deadliest of sins and is the root of all evil can help clinicians understand the relationship between perpetration, human destructiveness, and evil. In her view, primitive envy is the desire to destroy what is good because one cannot have it or be it. The evidence or mere existence of goodness outside the self generates a destructive narcissistic rage that demands eradication of all signs of innocence. Moreover, while most sins are in opposition to a specific virtue, envy simultaneously is opposed to all virtue and all goodness. Regarding evil as a defect of the will (or willfulness run amok), Klein believes evil is more than the mere negation of good, it is a destruction/corruption of the good *because* it is good. Evil is not the devaluation of others because they are threatening and dangerous (although ideology masking evil's true nature may use this motivation to justify complicity), it is the destruction/corruption of the other because the other is good (Alford, 1997).

Innocence is a transpersonal back-up or a fail-safe mechanism underlying human goodness, generosity, and benevolence. Although its psychological form can be devastated, camouflaged behind profound delusion, or deeply confused, there remains a nagging presence of an indestructible core of innocence in all human beings, regardless of the extent of victimization or degree of corruption. It is this unassailable element of goodness that most deeply disturbs practitioners of evil's methodologies. (Evil is truly befuddled and disrupted – as demonstrated by escalations of derision and mockery – by the presence of human generosity, non-defensive vulnerability, mutuality, random acts of kindness, devotion, love, and compassion.) It is this indestructible element in the human spirit that clinicians treating survivors (and perpetrators) of the most heinous crimes against humanity must hold faith with, and understand, in order to guide the treatment process in its passages through domains of futility, impenetrability, and despair.

Children are the archetypal containers of innocence, and as such they are the most valuable target/commodity for abusers and traffickers throughout the world. Perpetrators mine the innocence of children and its potential for use in the perpetrator(s)' psychological, economic, military, and spiritual agendas. Although the specific details of the exploitation will be based on the perpetrator's psychological vulnerabilities, torments, and ambitions, the perpetration will almost always be embedded in a paradoxical relationship with the victim's innocence (and the perpetrator's own lost and abandoned innocence) – coveting and despising it, fearing and violating it, attempting to obliterate, torment, or consume it. The construct of innocence contains the elements of goodness and virtue alluded to by Klein, but it also represents something more – that which is pure, devotional, loving, and unspoiled; a quality of being, not of behavior or action. It is this specific quality of goodness that evil is addictively compelled to mock, destroy, devour, or in its most triumphant stance, to seduce into self-betrayal and self-destruction. When innocents can be trained to "choose" to repeatedly betray themselves and betray other innocents without overt signals from the perpetrator(s), the hand of evil is off the wheel and the machinery of destructiveness becomes self-perpetuating and self-sustaining. Such a malignant arrangement exponentiates "duping delight" (Salter, 1995) and maniacally inflates the omnipotence of diabolical perpetrators who may then experience uncontrollable fantasies of limitless power.

The 20th century is replete with examples of the cascading effects of coerced complicity and perpetration. Pol Pot's regime in Cambodia was one of many haunting post-Holocaust dramas of evil's rapid, virulent proliferation in what was previously a relatively peaceful, Buddhist society. Turning young children into ruthless disciplinarians and mass murderers of their own families and communities in support of Pol Pot's megalomaniacal fantasy is a chilling portrait of coerced perpetration, child soldiering, and social disintegration. The legacies of predation upon the innocence of children are a major element of the collective human shadow that haunts individuals and societies. Clinicians must remember survivor-perpetrator patients are characters in psychotic passion plays whose narratives display the repertoire of evil's replication strategies and whose plots are always the same: the systematic eradication and self immolation of innocence.

Because of evil's fundamental dynamics, therapists treating survivors of extreme human malevolence and perpetration trauma will certainly experience an assault on their own innocence and their belief in a meaningful and redemptive universe. Describing and confronting the myriad manifestations of this battle over innocence can be a vehicle for illuminating traumatic injury and its legacies. Whether or not there is an indestructible core of innocence in all beings, whether even the most mindless perpetrators of evil still retain a potentially contactable core of innocence, whether all traces of innocence can ever really be completely eradicated – and/or whether these questions must remain unanswerable – should all become part of the therapy dialogues. Therapists must make sure that a new discourse about this complex subject replaces – and is not merely co-opted by – indoctrinated beliefs about the power of evil.

Clinical perspectives on the nature of evil

Two theoretical perspectives on human destructiveness that underlie evil and perpetration appear in the neo-Kleinian and relational psychoanalytic literature. Hate, greed, and envy are instinctually-based forces of pure negation, pulling the individual away from meaning and human contact into the void (Bion, 1965; Freud, 1930; Grotstein, 1990; M. Klein, 1975). Or, the combined force of extinction, dread, and nothingness is actually a perverse reaction to the "object-lessness of annihilation" as Greenberg and Mitchell (1983)[3] – presaging the relational turn in psychoanalysis – have suggested. Bridging these positions, Grand (2000) proposes that perpetration is a paradoxical flight from dread and a desperate attempt to recreate annihilation in an other: a form of existential confirmation over the self's extinction.

A relational approach to therapy for trauma survivors presupposes that a remote longing for healthy human connection – however veiled, distorted, and suppressed – does indeed exist for the survivor and for the perpetrator. Beyond Grand's (2000) elegant analysis of "no-self" evacuations and communions of annihilation, underlying even the most cunning, diabolical evil is a submerged yearning for reunification with the innocence that galls evil the most. The therapist clears a clinical space for the beleaguered and tormented desire of perpetrators (including perpetrator self-states in DID patients) to restore a relationship with their own (and by implication a portion of humanity's) lost and desecrated innocence. Although clinicians (and society) may be forced to describe some individuals (or situations) as untreatable and unredeemable by the limitations of our current methods and understanding, holding this potential in our minds may be our only foothold in what may otherwise feel like psychic quicksand.

When the therapy relationship can illuminate the consciousness that underlies evil and perpetration with personal and archetypal benevolence, significant and beneficial shifts in perpetrator identifications can occur. When contained, witnessed, and exposed, the structures of evil and perpetration fragment, because these structures can only thrive in an ambience of obscurity and divisiveness. This potential can only be activated when the dynamics of complicity, avoidance, seduction, polarization, or intimidation are fully understood and prevented from undermining the relational-communicative field. When therapist and patient are able to hold the tensions between intrapsychic, interpersonal and archetypal opposites, without collapsing any of them, rare and important opportunities for deep transformation of the individual shadow appears. As almost all non-dualistic spiritual traditions remind us, the shadow obscures a hidden radiance.[4]

We can track human evolution by its maturing relationship to preventing (and not denying or colluding in) perpetration and by its commitments to developing sophisticated approaches for reparations at the individual and societal levels. We can construe perpetration as a dissociated element of the human psyche that needs containment, integration, and transformation. Because perpetration is enabled by conditions of scarcity, terror, failed witnessing, and divided consciousness, it can be confronted and contained, and, in some cases, transmuted, by the power of shared human vulnerability, compassion, repudiation of destructiveness, and courageous witnessing.

Perpetrator states[5]

Although no taxonomical system can fully capture something as complex as internalized perpetration, in my clinical experience most dissociative psychological symptoms manifest – at least initially – in three basic categories:

- Hostile-depressive
- Grandiose-contemptuous
- Robotic-vacant

Hostile-depressive type

In Kleinian terms, hostile-depressive perpetrator alters operate from a predominant paranoid-schizoid mode of experience but have some limited access to the depressive mode. Although initially posturing with a disdainful attitude, hateful-depressive alters' protective shields do not involve manic glee at destruction, memories, fantasies, or behavior and these alters tend not to be traumatically loyal to perpetrator(s). They are more animated by the goal of avoiding excruciating torment (including memories) than in gaining approval from perpetrators. This type of personified self-state "went along" with perpetration yet took no great pride or pleasure in doing so. In spite of their initially stubborn misanthropic presentations, hostile-depressives are ultimately the most susceptible to treatment. They are the most likely to reveal traumatic material and the most likely to become (or cause the self-system as a whole to become) mired in intractable depression, and shame shortly after introductory interviews. These parts of the personality seem to have a relatively superficial identification with the abusive group and its ideologies, thereby enabling them to enter treatment with somewhat less resistance than their more thoroughly brainwashed self-state counterparts. Their existence as separate entities within the personality system seems to have arisen from the instinct to survive, the desire to minimize perpetrated torture, and the capacity to "get the job done" with minimal feeling and maximal precision. In addition, their dynamic function in the DID self-system may also operate to help other pro-social, conflict-avoidant personalities stay clear of facing both traumatic and psychological conflictual material. Through binding nihilism and distrust, their presence in the dissociative system may allow other self-states to engage in productive work and meaningful relationships.

Hostile depressives have rationalized their actions, and may initially present with numbness or cavalier attitudes about perpetration, but their psychological connection to the larger self becomes more concrete as they reveal more of their histories. Their emotional vulnerability lies close to the surface and can be accessed once several interviews have been conducted and a functional clinical relationship has been established. They are able to face the inevitable revelations of perpetrators' deceptions and set-ups, which are essential to deprogramming and integration processes. More challenging, however, is the process of helping them take responsibility for whatever "positive" feelings and rewards they might have gained from participating in perpetration. These alters' disavowed needs for mastery, perpetrator-approval, status, states of oblivion, or vengeance may ultimately have to be faced as part of the integration process.

Since these hostile-depressives never expect to meet anyone who can accept their cynical nihilism, merely maintaining ongoing clinical dialogues becomes a form of creative interference that defeats their anticipated rejection or counterattack. A mere five or ten minutes of sustained, uninterrupted dialogue with these alters can disrupt traumatic fixity. Continuous discourse about the patient's feelings of contempt, indifference, and meaninglessness serves to lubricate the participation of the patients' alters in therapy at a deeper level. The self-protective function of these internalized perpetrator states may become readily apparent. As one alter poignantly stated: "I did what no one else was willing to do." Stated another, "I don't care, I never did care and never will and that's what it took to do the job so I did it, so don't make me start feeling or caring now or this whole thing will go up in smoke."

This type of alter personality typically has some minimal conscious awareness of the exploitation that took place during childhood. A few may actually reveal to the therapist full knowledge of the corruption and deceptions of their perpetrators. Yet, unlike other perpetrator-identified states, they tend not to have idealized their experiences of indoctrination and initiation: they still remember the pain of torture and the horror of violence against others, even if these feelings have been sequestered and relocated elsewhere in the psyche. Opiate addiction is often part of these patients' histories, with violent, sometimes homicidal behavior reinforced with cessation of (purposely-induced) withdrawal symptoms.[6] Most child soldiers who make it to treatment probably have variations of this type of perpetrator-identified state, molded by addictions, within a mild to moderate dissociative self-organization.

Hostile-depressive alters are loyal to no one, including perpetrators. All forms of benevolent attachment have been aversively conditioned, often through coerced perpetration against beloved pets or other innocents. For hostile-depressives, emotional bonding causes nothing but pain and vulnerability to suffering, and possibly traumatic re-experiencing or reactivation of programmed torture memories. Their first significant relationship outside of the abuse context may be with the therapist. Since their trust and loyalty have been manipulated by perpetrators, these alters are hesitant to commit themselves to psychotherapy. Likely to begin treatment with a high degree of narcissistic investment in separateness (Kluft, 1984; Putnam, 1989), hostile-depressives maintain an unwavering belief in their own autonomy and distinctness from the rest of the patient's personality. Following establishment of basic trust, the next steps of clinical work involve: orienting them to the rules and methods of therapy; helping them understand the nature of their DID system; validating and examining the alter's role in the patient's survival of trauma; helping the patient to take responsibility for what is appropriate and to release guilt which the patient has falsely assumed; and unmasking the perpetrators' indoctrination methods.

Like individual DID patients, alters vary widely in their general knowledge about dissociative multiplicity and in their awareness about this aspect of themselves. Sometimes a hostile-depressive alter possesses a sort of sardonic savvy about the destructive aspects of human nature that can be useful in the later stages of treatment. The alter's firsthand knowledge of victim, collaborator, and perpetrator behavior can guide the patient toward integration once the nihilistic defensive style is worked through and a solid attachment process is underway. After most of the trauma memories and feelings have been processed, and after the therapist co-creates a relational alliance with the rest of the patient's personality system, these hostile-depressive states can become the vehicle for accessing and working with malignant aspects of the psyche's most dissociated perpetrator-allegiant parts.

In order for hostile-depressives to become true collaborators in therapy, they must process and integrate the memories directly related to their traumatic origins (Lacter, 2011; Miller, 2012). This work often makes dissociative barriers porous and facilitates a reduction in defense-motivated anxiety. Hostile-depressives seem to derive particular benefit from contextualizing their experience within the wider scope of the history of man's (and woman's) inhumanity to men (and women), creating new broader contexts of meaning, capable of containing the complex mix of horror, absences, and fragmentation inherent in perpetration memories. Courage and cowardice are dangerously fused in the history of these patients (and alters). They must be helped to embrace both of these facets of their experience. As these alters' cynicism and bravado dissipate allowing affectively-charged experiences of intrapsychic conflict about their pasts to be felt for the first time, they are also able to accept kindness and other forms of benevolence as real. Hardest of all is their struggle to hold onto a sense of self-deservedness and the possibility of self-forgiveness. Periodic cathartic break-throughs of profound sobbing or screaming help dissolve the patient's emotional-muscular rigidities and character armor, and the therapeutic "holding environment" may at times include safe, humanizing, physical contact. Even a brief respectful handshake with one of these alters can gently undermine patho-logical perpetrator attachments and beliefs.

Therapists must however remember to refrain from any subtle misuses of their power (including failures or fears to appropriately and effectively use their author-ity). The therapy discourse should include specific conversations about how power is operating in the therapy dyad as well as among alter personalities in the DID system. When the therapist acknowledges his or her own empathic failures or misinterpretations and demonstrates thinking about power and mutuality openly and sincerely, hostile-depressives are better able to learn intimacy and vulnerability in a way that moves them closer to integration. Because hostile-depressives are likely to be the parts of the dissociative self-system that have been most adversely affected by having reality systematically denied and distorted, therapists unwilling to own and discuss their countertransference feelings may be less able to help these alters (and dissociative patients in general) learn to develop faith in their own emotional perception when it is accurate, including differentiat-ing projected from actual emotional experiences (Dalenberg, 2000). Therapist transparency may be particularly important for hostile, mistrustful alters who likely pick up on whatever vulnerabilities the therapist has (and expect therapist to deny or deflect), and these alters may benefit, at times, from having their perceptions and awareness validated. In some instances, a therapist's sharing with the patient some of the therapist's internal process about the course of treat-ment – the pressures, strange sensations, vulnerabilities, double binds, frustra-tions, and some of the mistakes the therapist may have made (always inviting the patient's comments and perspectives) has the potential to significantly undermine programming, emotional detachment, and rigid identifications with irrational authority.

Unlike other internalized perpetrator states, hostile-depressives maintain a fear of re-perpetration and therefore a fear of their own primitive impulses and potential for violence. They are initially hesitant to describe fantasies of wanting to attack the therapist, fearing that articulating these impulses and thoughts will result in actual violent behavior. The therapist must engage and re-orient previously destructive aggression for the sake of helping to reveal and liberate other constituents of the patient's personality system. It is essential that therapists acknowledge these hostile-depressives' anxieties. The goal is a shift toward an enlivening and playful rebelliousness of the alters against their abusers and the perpetrating system they are struggling to escape. When able to find safety in verbal and artistic expressive modalities, fearful and impulsive manifestations of violent aggression can be replaced by a more relaxed and accepting approach to these emotions. Assisting these alters to play with anger in fantasy is an essential element of healing, since the normal development of restorative fantasy involving themes of destructiveness has been derailed by involvement in criminal actions and by patients' fears of reawakening their own violent potential. As healing progresses, treatment will involve these alters and the patient as a whole to investigate the underlying fragility and vulnerability, memories of deprivation and abandonment, and understandable rage at the perpetrators and the individuals and the social systems that passively colluded with the trauma. Once perpetrator defensive patterns are shed, a hostile-depressive self-state can be extremely resolute in its quest for truth, justice, reconciliation, as well as freedom for, and service to, others.

Grandiose-contemptuous type

Grandiose-contemptuous perpetrator alters operate from a mix of paranoid-schizoid and autistic-contiguous modes of experience. These defiant, arrogant, dissociative personifications of malice are easily enraged and tend to retreat when confronted with dialogues in which they cannot immediately gain the upper hand. Before an event is fully processed they "hit and run" by flaring up with threats, intimidation, or accusations, or by fleeing from the relational field by terminating therapy or postponing appointments. These types of perpetrator state are cunning and masterful in deploying the psychological defense of undoing; they use deception and undermining with astounding alacrity.

Perpetrator-engineered versions of this type of alter threaten, punish, deride, humiliate, distract, and lie to the patient (and therapist) within a fusion of past and present dangers. Like actual perpetrators who hide behind the vulnerability and protection exacted from their child victims, grandiose-contemptuous perpetrator states often practice another "hit-and-run" tactic by striking out at the therapist or patient (distinct easily abused alters) and immediately flood the patient's system with a traumatic memory or command to self-injure. Not uncommonly, a frightened and confused child alter will appear in the wake of one of these sudden "departures." These alters become enraged and haughty when disrupted in any way. Grandiose-contemptuous types can use language in evasive and provocative ways to re-establish their omnipotence with disdainful and omnipotent assertions following even minor affronts to their sense of power or ideology. They avoid intrapsychic conflict so that feelings or information at odds with their authoritarian belief system (or inflated self-concept) can be deflected. Some of these alters represent the far end of the continuum of self-generated identifications with the aggressor, and many more represent perpetrator-engineered states borne from torture based mind control. Although these tactics are sometimes "successful," their omnipotent defensive ploys and underlying structure are also decidedly fragile. To some extent, this type of alter also holds ruthlessness and vindictiveness for the rest of the patient's self, and may also embody the dissociated and extremely shameful childhood desires for omnipotent power over others (and for love and recognition by perpetrators), all of which other aspects of the patient's dissociative self-system wish to disavow.

Grandiose-contemptuous alters, steeped in catechisms of the particular group, can also at times be crafty participants in debates about morals, history, and ideology. People raised in satanic cults may perform compelling theatrical displays of a demonic character. Intimidating eye contact, hypnotic speech, and chilling presentations can, at times, obscure the differences between the psychological, the paranormal, and the performance dimensions of human experience. These alters are organized around power, loyalty, and securing the approval of the perpetrators rather than pain relief. They have split off the fact that their origins lay in torture and extreme coercion and brutalization. The part of the psyche holding those memories has been convincingly declared dead by the perpetrators (after debilitating torment), disorientated by drugs, and walled off from other alters by death threats. Opiates for relief from torture, as well as amphetamine-enhanced training to maim and kill, are often instrumental in the creation of these grandiose-contemptuous alters. They may have exalted their own suffering – or their mastery of it – for self-aggrandizement, reinforcing their narcissism with sadomasochistic beliefs about power and prestige. This use of ideology to consolidate omnipotent fantasies is similar to the deployment of blood sacrifices in training child soldiers to enable them to overcome their fear of killing to gain fantasized strength and imperviousness, and to imbibe the group ideology by directly participating in one of its most adhesive rituals.

The presentation of grandiose-contemptuous perpetrator states in a DID patient reflects their strikingly restricted range of expression and cognition, and their negligible to non-existent connection to healthy guilt or shame. These cold and supercilious part-selves recall and represent their history in full accordance with the script fashioned by perpetrators. These self-states embody many of the features set forth in Rosenfeld's (1971) concept of destructive narcissism and Goldberg's (2000) psychodynamic formulation of evil, discussed in Chapter 1.

These alters adamantly negate and punish others within the DID patient's self-system for every "heretical" viewpoint, disclosures of perpetration or group secrets, or fantasy of escape. Their knee-jerk regurgitations of their own "stories," when presented with any alternative perspective, are emblematic of their entrapment in a paranoid and solipsistic cognitive system. These alters almost invariably begin therapy by claiming to take full responsibility for, and delight in, the perpetration activities (following periods of complete denial and negation of all trauma and criminal behavior). Pompous and haughty, they tend to be either endlessly argumentative or provocative, self-consciously evasive, and are driven to escalating displays of power and one-upmanship. They exist in seemingly impenetrable encapsulated states, enclosed in layers of dissociation, episodes of linked drug abuse and torture, ideology programming, psychotic denial, and superiority.

Grandiose-contemptuous alters mirror the malignancy of their perpetrators with chilling precision. Fortunately, perpetrators are not the sole authors of the patient's history, however anathema that fact may be to these alters and perpetrators. Looking for weaknesses in the therapist and in other aspects of the patient's personality system, they will strike at the heart of the mutual regard, good intentions, and accrued positive attachment between patient and therapist. Their assault on the accumulating store of goodwill achieved in therapy represents a re-enactment of the brutal betrayals of childhood and a paradoxical attempt to experience human warmth and empathy. At the extreme end of posttraumatic shattering, these alters may play out the dynamics of evil with a full and righteous assault on meaning, goodness, and faith as a testament to, and transfer of, annihilating experiences that can never reach the level of conscious awareness, articulation, and interpersonal reflection. Continuously operating behind the scenes of whatever is happening in therapy, they insist to themselves, to the patient's other self-states and to the therapist that they are indeed the only real and authentic personality; that the others are merely fabrications and covers for their truly malevolent core.

Because they have been in (and indoctrinated within) relationships with criminals in the world, many of these arrogant alter personalities have an acute understanding of human vulnerability and are likely to regard any hint of uncertainty or any questionable decisions on the part of the therapist as an opening for exploitation. Like brilliant religious or political zealots endowed with mesmerizing rhetorical gifts, some deploy a form of seamless intelligence along with ideological ratiocination to fend off feelings, and to prevent exposure to any new experience that contravenes the perpetrator or group's belief system. These internalized perpetrator states operate most powerfully when maneuvering independently and unobserved by other aspects of the patient's self. They are therefore successfully undermined – over time – by the willingness of the whole patient (or his or her most mature part-selves) to engage in inquiry and dialogue without giving in to the voices of intimidation or to impulses of reactive self-injury. One of the most promising milestones in the recovery of a grandiose-contemptuous type is reached when confusion emerges to displace indignant self-righteousness.

Small openings of reflectivity can pave the way for their eventual confrontation with the perpetrator trickery, betrayal, and deception that lies just beyond the reach of their dissociative consciousness. Since their conscious presentation is organized around how much they benefited from, and enjoyed participation in, perpetration, their eventual healing lies in expressing their hidden ego-dystonic thoughts and feelings about their own and the perpetrators' cruelty.

Clinicians must be prepared to respond to insidious challenges from these grandiose alters. By interrupting the patient's abusive rhetoric and the interject-ing inquiry and interpretive efforts, the therapist can illuminate the underlying motivational system from which these challenges emanate. "Hit-and-run" tactics, threats, or blackmail styles of relatedness are best named, linked to perpe-trator culture, and actively countered. Destructiveness can be met in a variety of ways, but it must be met and repudiated as it is identified and empathically understood. Sometimes, effective interventions with grandiose-contemptuous alters depend less on interpreting perpetrator dynamics and more on "benevo-lent disruption" of traumatic relational fixity. After a few rounds of the perpetra-tor alter's hateful rhetoric and mind-numbing negations and deflections of therapeutic contact and inquiry, the therapist might playfully ask the alter to "try something – anything – new! Play with diversity. Say the same thing in a different way." The therapist's respectful use of comedy or light-hearted commentary in the face of doom, gloom, and dread can be gently disarming. Sensitive timing when introducing humor, recontextualization, and improvisation with these alters is essential to avoid paranoid reactions and activation of humiliated rage. These tools in the therapeutic arsenal cannot be underestimated for their power to gently pierce encapsulated states and undermine rigid perpetrator thinking and identifications.

After a patient's prolonged demonic diatribe, the therapist can continue to encourage inquiry, reflection, and risk-taking in expression and communication. Over time, these unanticipated and unfamiliar communication processes gently disarm the fixity of grandiose alters' posturing and bravado. Even the therapist's encouragement of new, safe ways to express or play with feelings of contempt and destructiveness (e.g., with art, writing, verbalizing fantasies) can have a lubricat-ing effect on these alters' rigidity of cognition and communication. Inquiring about the alter's somatic responses (and the patient's as a whole) to various expressions can also disrupt the mind–body disconnections that fuel their defen-sive ploys while offering them an opportunity to more authentically relate to themselves and the therapist. Sometimes, the therapist's sharing of his or her own somatic and emotional reactions to the therapy material and interaction, as a way of facilitating non-rational relating in the immediacy of the moment, can be valu-able to the therapy process. Witnessing the therapist speak vulnerably from his or her own experience of numbness, dread, and horror, without backing away from, or becoming intimidated by, the alter can be an important healing experience for these seemingly impermeable, invulnerable aspects of the self. These clinical interventions may eventually facilitate contact between the patient's states of aliveness and underlying deadness and brokenness. This can restore linkages that, if left unhealed, perpetuate the divisions within the self-system that have allowed perpetrator states to operate unimpeded.

While accepting, or even facilitating, the grandiose-contemptuous alter's expression of negative transference and antagonistic feelings toward therapy and the therapist can be a useful starting point, waiting too long to confront and interpret the perpetration inherent in repetitive disparaging or threatening behavior runs the risk of unconsciously abandoning the patient as a whole. Grand (2000), for example, cautions therapists against inadvertently reinforcing the catastrophic loneliness and isolation of perpetration through failure to appropriately repudiate destructive behavior and deceptive relational dynamics. Although convincing to the inexperienced clinician, arrogance is often a brittle mask for profound insecurity and extreme narcissistic vulnerability as well as a manifestation of perpetrator identification. The protective carapace surrounded perpetration must be systematically understood and creatively challenged, establishing an alternate, interpersonal form of holding and containment that eventually allows extreme dissociative polarizations to negotiate and relax. Therapists must continue to explain the dynamics (and deceptions) of perpetrating systems to all parts of the patient's personality, and remain steadfast in exploring grandiose-contemptuous alters' disagreements in the analysis of these systems. Although the process is challenging, therapists must help these alters understand the difference between expressing feelings and evacuating feelings, between power and destructiveness, and between self-protection and self-betrayal. Therapists must consistently challenge and reroute the therapy process from perpetrator re-enactments toward mutual reflection, enhanced tolerance of unsettling emotions, and restoration of a full range affectivity.

These intensely perpetrator-loyal self-states are uncomfortable with the admixture of knowledge, vulnerability, and authority of the therapist. When these grandiose-contemptuous parts witness the therapist's ability to simultaneously repudiate destructiveness and work with his or her own vulnerability and limitations in a non-defensive manner, it can beneficially destabilize the alters' rigid beliefs about human nature. Witnessing the therapist's reflections on his or her response to the patient's criticisms, to empathic/interpretive errors, and to the therapist's unavoidable expressions of frustration and irritation humanizes the therapy process for these alters in significant ways. Similarly, the continued experiencing of the therapist's strength and benevolent use of authority has an osmotic effect over time that erodes the alters' entrenched commitment to domination-based interpersonal dynamics and motivations.

Contemptuous perpetrator-loyal self-states tend, initially, to strongly dis-identify with other facets of the patient's personality, to the point of flatly denying their existence. Some maintain a belief that they (or the perpetrators) have succeeded in killing off the others. Indoctrinations and spiritual rebirthing rituals that are staged in some destructive perpetrator groups create traumas in which the part-self being cultivated to master the intimidating challenges of violent group life is taught that the "other" previously whole personality is dead. Understandably, the reality-testing of some dissociative identities thus spawned seems psychotic, delusional, or paranoid. Accordingly, these alters' narcissistic investment in separateness (Kluft, 1984) can create much more formidable perpetrator states of the hostile-depressive type. The therapist needs to examine, with these alters, the methods of indoctrination (i.e., including the use of drugs to construct encapsulation) to cultivate new and more-mature critical thinking. Grandiose alters' ability to face their own shame at being deceived must come to replace their propensity for humiliating others. Awareness of their own violation must come to replace propensities for violating others. Waxing and waning resistance should be expected. These grandiose-contemptuous part-selves experience vulnerability as annihilating, and thus will go to absurd lengths to avoid facing the reality of them being merely a splintered part of a larger whole, and the reality that they were merely pawns in a maniacal perpetrator(s)' game.

Helping these grandiose-contemptuous part-selves to tolerate conflict, negotiation, and differences of perspective is a long and arduous socialization process as they do not easily tolerate collision with other constituents of the DID patient's personality system (except on their own terms of domination and intimidation). When the most obdurate righteousness begins to dissipate, many of these patients will develop intense fears about death and other forms of personal dissolution. Sometimes they have been programmed with terrifying imagery about death and dying. Naturally, anything resembling a change of internal boundaries or dispersal of established identity elicits intense posttraumatic feeling states. These symptoms result from confronting the conditions of their "birth" within the DID system by means of mind-bending torture – torture they had previously disowned, negated, or valorized.

Joining with the therapist in new understandings, these grandiose-contemptuous self-states can be gently guided toward integration through cultivation of the presence and tolerance for intrapsychic conflict and intense affect states. This can be done at first through intellectual means and eventually through empathic resonance with other aspects of the self. Encouraging these perpetrator alters to remain co-present with other parts of the patient's DID system – once all the alter personalities have agreed to use relatively non-dominating forms of relatedness – facilitates the gradual dissolution of dissociative barriers. Experiencing the therapist's compassionate authority and fearless inquiry into all aspects of destructiveness slowly erodes the alters' commitments to malevolent hierarchy and perpetrating systems' ideologies. When grandiose alters experience other parts of the patient's self (to which they have always belonged but toward which they have enacted with cruelty) "holding" and supporting them through painful memory work, a profound previously unimaginable experience of generosity and compassion breaks down the defensive barriers previously sustained by iterations of cynicism and contempt.

Exposing the weaknesses and manipulations of grandiose-contemptuous self-systems may precipitate both disappointment and relief. Facing the truth about their own acts of deception and betrayal (and self-deceptions and self-betrayals) demands considerable courage since feelings of this kind may destabilize their rigid identities. Such exposure can lead to periods of heightened (and potentially productive) anxiety and possibly useful states of confusion (about meanings, allegiances, and beliefs). Since these extremely polarized alters may experience both confusion and anxiety as demoralizing, disempowering, and at times, potentially life-threatening, empathic commentary and attention to anxiety management techniques – including breathing, movement, vocalizations, journaling, art and adjunctive therapies – may facilitate these alters' persistence through the vicissitudes of the transition process. As these alters progress in treatment from rigid and repetitive deflections of any alternative to the logic of the internalized perpetrating system, through states of confusion and affective and somatic dysregulation, they can slowly gain greater tolerance for affect, ambiguity, emotional contact, and human tenderness.

A therapist's non-judgmental encounter with extreme perpetrator-loyal and perpetrator-identified alter personalities requires meeting them with a combination of receptivity, compassion, and steadfastness. This systematically disrupts old traumatic attachments and worldviews, and replaces them with a new relational experience co-created with the therapist in contravention of perpetrator values. For steady progress to be maintained with particularly obstinate states, the patient must relinquish some automatic habits of dissociative retreat. These adjustments require resisting both the reflexive collapse into passivity when intimidated, and returning to related forms of over-learned complicity manifested by other parts of the patient's personality.

Goldberg (2000) makes several valuable recommendations relating to the treatment of extreme states of destructive regression and identification with evil. He posits that when the world of meaning has been completely dismantled and the trauma of annihilation remains unknowable and unintegrated, the psyche of the patient may not be accessible through the usual associative channels. A patient who has endured obliteration of all belief and meaning may simply be unable to tolerate the therapist's faith in emotional linkages and meaning-making functions. The therapist's attachments to a preferred mode of clinical relating may therefore alienate the patient and may also trigger further dissociation. Although at first these alters appear lacking in imagination, multidimensional thinking, affect, or memory, the therapeutic encounter may, through attention to shifting mental and bodily states in the clinical field, slowly become the vehicle for the regeneration of vital, previously undeveloped or atrophied psychological functions. For this reparative process to proceed, the therapist must disclaim any sovereign knowledge. He or she must vulnerably enter an experiential field laden with environmental failure and psychic collapse (Goldberg, 2000). Only then can the therapist slowly begin to represent (and help the patient to symbolize) the conditions of the previously unthought, unmetabolized emotional and psychological devastation.

Some grandiose-contemptuous alters will eventually be enlisted to support the liberation project of treatment. A small number may defy integration efforts and persist unintegrated, and remain essentially non-threatening, defused, and contained, as the rest of the patient's personality moves forward toward a more unified and coherent whole. A few internalized perpetrator states may not be open to re-education and redirection of skills and abilities toward more pro-social, pro-integration goals. For some grossly mutated aspects of the self, grieving and mourning are impossible tasks and full participation in the project of therapy can only be experienced as submission and defeat – or, annihilation. Thus recovery from complex dissociative disorders does not always result in a completely unified fully integrated self. Some dissociated remnants may endure however earnest the treatment. A small number of the most damaged grandiose-contemptuous alters maintain a lifelong (though impotent) perpetrator loyalty. This unfortunate outcome is more likely when the patient has some ongoing contact with, or continues to receive tangible threats from, one or more representatives of the original perpetrating system.

Robotic-vacant type

Of the three broad types of perpetrator-identified alters, robotic-vacant states are the least personified and the most impervious to the dynamic interplay of the therapeutic relationship since their capacity for reflection, dialogue, or critical thinking is minimal. They are most clearly distinguished by an incongruous combination of vacant affect with violent (or disruptive) perpetrator-programmed activity. Like psychic zombies, they exist primarily for the completion of specific tasks, and the compartmentalization of secret instructions for other personalities to carry out. Robotic-vacant states provide unimpeded access to the patient (and his or her dissociated self-system) for actual perpetrators and can provide "reinforcements" for other internalized perpetrator states. Robotic states are sometimes constructed behind hypnosis-created one-way mirrors so they cannot be witnessed by other parts of the patient's DID system; yet they can react to, and report on, the patient's thoughts and behaviors. They can also function as psychological land mines invested with suicidal or homicidal intent, for example, set up to be tripped by revelations of abusive group information specifically commanded to be concealed.

Patients with perpetrator-generated robotic-states report feeling dead inside, remote-controlled, empty, their motivation becomes a moot point. Nothingness dominates their internal landscape. Robotic-vacant types fade in and out during treatment as if in a dream state because they were sculpted in a field of coerced amnesia and forced dissociation (usually through electric shock treatment, torture and/or drugs) and respond best when collaborating with other self-states that have developed stronger alliances to the goals of treatment. The therapist's alertness to countertransference feelings of severe coldness, deadness, alien-ness, of themselves being rendered into a passive, helpless, dehumanized "thing," coercive self-doubting, or having one's mind taken over, dulled, or neutralized, can help the therapist understand both the internal experience of the robotic-vacancy and the feelings of other alter personalities when that state is operating.

The treatment goal for robotic-vacant types is their deactivation and assimilation into the rest of the personality. This often involves other alters remembering (and re-experiencing at least some of the feelings of the torture/trauma) the traumatic conditions in which these states were formed. Once the process of demobilizing robotic-vacant self-states is underway, it requires commitment by the whole patient to know, feel, and transfer disturbing information (often about crimes perpetrated) from robotic self-states to more developed and individuated components of the patient's personality. This transfer can be somatically challenging for the patient as it often engenders flu-like symptoms or other forms of transient physical distress lasting anywhere from minutes to days that coincide with the erosion of dissociative barriers between the robotic and other self-states.

Creative use of fantasy by the patient's other alters may serve as an important antidote to the extremely mechanical and scripted discourse and behavior of robotic self-states. Ego-states of this type may be impervious to the process and effects of linear logic-driven therapeutic dialogue but they are defenseless against plays of the imagination for affect discharge by other parts of the personality (provided this capacity is operative in other parts of the patient's personality). These alters have little recourse against the patient's reparative fantasies, such as visualizing wrapping the alters in bubble wrap and/or sealing off their functions in safe houses to disarm them. Other patients have used sequences of colors or sound healing or songs to dissolve barriers between states, and dissolve previously deformed aspects of themselves back into their primary identities and consciousnesses.

With patients severely deficient in fantasy functions, it may be necessary to jump-start the imagination process with images, suggestions, or healing rituals provided by the therapist. Making use of tools such as storytelling, nature imagery, color, music or spiritual parables, the therapist facilitates the patient's mastery over dissociative barriers and helps to subdue feelings of intimidation and dread. Creative imagery-based alternative narratives or spiritual healing rituals can disrupt a robotic-vacant alter's limited cognitive-affective repertoire in part because the actual perpetrators have likely not prepared them for being challenged this way. In the end, robotic states are dissolved counterintuitively in a field of gratitude offered to them by the rest of the patient's self for whom they have served an invaluable survival function. True to their original affect, the integration of robotic states happens without much hype, fanfare or "personality." Nonetheless, integration results in a substantial reduction in the patient's anxiety and hypervigilance.

As robotic-vacant states dissipate, patients may experience transient somatic distress, brief blackouts, and similar side effects that periodically interfere with higher order cognitive functions. The complete integration of these self-states is often followed by a sense of depression (not usually a major clinical depression), then deep relief coupled with heightened vulnerability stemming from a newly emergent capacity for feelings by the patient's entire self. These changes, however, are not without complications. Such progress has its ups and downs. Patients may be elated to experience a fuller spectrum of feelings and a sense of self-direction to replace their psychic numbing and chronic helplessness. At the same time, they are fully entering the human world for the first time and will need guidance in learning to manage "normal" human affairs with equanimity – the frustrations, disappointments, betrayals and reversals of fortune that are part of everyday life.

Integrating perpetrator states

Patients, as well as clinicians, may be lulled into thinking that the only way to defuse or deprogram dense and non-responsive internalized perpetrator states is to use hypnosis or to gain access to some secret programming code around which this system of intrapsychic land mines and psychological zombies were set up. Of course some alter personalities will claim to hold the key to deciphering these complex and esoteric situations and may be useful in the therapy process. Miller's (2012) valuable work on deprogramming ritual abuse survivors strongly recommends working one's way up the perpetrator-installed hierarchies, and systematically gaining access to the triggers and codes that sustain resistance programming and perpetrator identities. At the same time, several survivors whose testimony is cited in Miller's work emphasize how, at the end of the day, it was the combination of "I've had enough," curiosity, and a committed refusal to not act on programming (thereby weakening it through non-reinforcement) that has most effectively undermined perpetrator-based automaticities. Some survivors feel that using the perpetrator's framework to deprogram the psyche is tantamount to buying into the perpetrator thought system, while others view subverting perpetrators' patterning from within the framework in which it was laid down as equivalent to taking the proverbial puppet strings out of the abuser's hands. Miller (2012) reminds us that love, respect, and friendship are the most powerful elements in undermining programming, and that we must remember when dealing with programmed states, we are dealing with frag-mented human beings and not just "programs."

In treating survivors of torture-based mind control, Lacter (2011) reports that patients have used a combination of defiance and restorative fantasy to defuse and heal destructive and perpetrator self-states. The same illusions deployed and installed by perpetrators can be used (and reversed) to the advantage of survivors as they experience a level of mastery in the use of their own integrated creative and aggressive energies. Once these modifications are made in the survivor's inner world, Lacter found they tend to remain, and do not usually require ongoing conscious effort or continued re-modification. Turning the tables on their perpetrators by undoing learned helplessness in the same domain where it was developed is a significant, gratifying experience of healthy, non-violent retaliation. "What programmers initially established in the inner world through torture, illusion, and hypno-suggestion the survivor now re-sculpts in ways that [are directed by the self and] serve the self" (p. 109).

In other words, the good news about programming and deprogramming is the leash pulls in both directions. Programming works best when it remains out of awareness, undisturbed, intact in dissociated self-states and in the unconscious mind (Lacter, 2011; Miller, 2012; H. Schwartz, 2000). Conversely, when the history and the mechanics of programming become conscious, programming is disabled, and then, as Lacter (2011) states, it can be defied or changed. Lacter (2011:108–109) uses the term defiance

> to refer to the assertion of one's will against doing or believing as one's abusers and programmers directed, trained, conditioned, hypno-suggested [or] claimed [...The term] "change" [...] refers to making modifications in the [patient's] unconscious mind, inner world, or self-states [...] Programmed directives can be changed to self-affirming statements [...] Toxins, explosive substances, and drugs can be removed in prayer by a spiritual source or 'beamed [up]" as per *Star Trek*. Program removal codes can "erase" programmed structures form the internal landscape [...] program reset codes can be changed to impossible stimuli [...] Perceived malevolent human spirits and entities can be expelled by assertion of will or prayer.

Some patients have created spiritual rituals of healing and purification based on their own belief systems that have remarkable similarity to shamanic practices employed in the treatment of child soldiers in Africa. Other patients ask for the assistance or guidance of the therapist in re-working issues of psychological and spiritual contamination. Lacter (2011) and T. Ball (2008) document the effective use of prayer and imagery (including the patient's use of his or her imagination to concoct implausible scenarios that perpetrators would have never considered using in order) to remove toxins and explosive substances, to erase codes, to expel unwanted foreign objects, beings, thought forms, and energies the patient once believed were indelibly imprinted on his or her psyche and soul. One patient who loved dolphins called upon these creatures to assist in her imaginative purification and healing ritual. Another patient invoked benevolent divinities from a little-known religion to engulf and then dissolve perpetrator implants and programs after they had been made conscious. Yet another patient used walls of sound and light to burn and dissolve remnants of toxins, booby traps, and negative "entities" that had been implanted during rituals and were supposedly linked to supporting perpetration directives. When the power of imagination and non-violence trumps the power of traumatic abuse and mind control, survivors feel empowered and safe in their own skin.

Different therapists approach the spiritual needs of Western dissociative trauma survivors from varying perspectives depending on their own training, belief systems, and scope of practice. Some clinicians treat survivors with predominantly spiritually-based approaches (T. Ball, 2008), some reframe everything in psychological terms while still making room for the patient's experience (Miller, 2012). Some, like Lacter (2011) and myself, integrate working with the belief systems and specific histories of patients, including both psychological and spiritual interpretations and interventions while still honoring the primary psychotherapy goals of autonomy, free will, critical thinking, and healthy spirituality. For example, if the host personality (or the therapist for that matter), views the idea of being inhabited by "attaching spirits" or "evil forces" as impossible, it must be remembered that for the self-states – formed and indoctrinated in the theology of many perpetrators – these phenomenon are perceived as real, and their impact can be devastating (Lacter, 2011). On the other hand, Miller (2012) believes that it is simply the act of making the trauma conscious along with strengthening the use of the patient's free will that creates the deepest healing of the patient's struggles with negative spiritual attachments. Miller is concerned about the possibility of inadvertently reinforcing patients' pathological and perpetrator-based beliefs and delusions through adopting their vocabulary and by clinicians straying from the scope of their clinical, ethical and legal training. While specific practices of deprogramming and spiritual healing remain the subject of clinical inquiry and debate, most clinicians agree on benevolent disruption of all perpetrator-indoctrinated beliefs, exposure of alters to alternative information and viewpoints, empathic interpretation of the victim's trauma experiences during mind control and spiritual abuse episodes, and engaging the survivor's will and healthy self-assertion against all forms of domination and oppression.

Chapter 6

Transforming perpetration

Science without conscience is but the death of the soul.
Michel de Montaigne

Regardless of the form, the emergence of perpetration dynamics and enactments significantly challenges the therapeutic alliance and disturbs any equilibrium which had been achieved in treatment. Perpetrator identifications and behaviors in treatment often function to reinforce the survivor's false beliefs that he or she does not deserve compassion or redemption – this includes some survivors who feel they have lost their right to membership in the human community altogether. Many therapists lack the training to handle the demands of confronting and treating internalized perpetration when it is exposed. This chapter focuses on witnessing as the essential process for understanding and engaging the dynamic of perpetration as it enters the therapy relationship. Each of the three ways perpetration emerges in psychotherapy – direct revelation, enactments, and perpetrator states – present unique obstacles and opportunities, and require specific clinical perspectives.

Forms and presentations of perpetration[1]

How internalized perpetration presents itself in treatment can be parsed into three categories which overlap and intersect to some extent. It helps to view the three clinical presentations as corners of a triangle rather than as three mutually exclusive groupings:

- Direct revelation and confession – as the patient's conscious but carefully guarded secrets;
- Analysis of transference/countertransference – only partially accessible to the patient's awareness; and
- Perpetrator-loyal states and alter personalities – emerging from behind layers of obfuscating symptoms.

Direct revelation and confession case examples

- A female DID patient revealed (with little affect), after many years of treatment for complex trauma, including coerced perpetration, that as a teenager she had molested several children while babysitting. In her mind, these molestations occurred completely independently of any perpetrator direction or influence and stood as proof to her of her underlying true evil nature. This is a view of herself that her perpetrators had strongly reinforced. The babysitting story reappeared without full integration throughout several years of therapy, sometimes feeling like more of a testing of the psychotherapy relationship than a revelation of emotional significance to the patient. Persistent therapeutic inquiry and confrontation led to the accessing of more deeply dissociated perpetrator self-states. Eventually, this led to expressions of profound guilt and shame, catharsis, and in time to a reduction in symptoms – particularly self-hatred and intimacy avoidance.

- A male patient who initially presented without any trauma history, and in fact persistently and aggressively denied any possibility of his own child abuse, confessed he had molested his younger brother for two years during childhood. He said he had made amends with the brother who purportedly had no memory of the events. Years of inquiry and analysis revealed the patient to be a survivor of child pornography, child prostitution, and intergenerational cult abuse. The true sibling abuse narrative had served as a cover story for more complex trauma, sustained denial, and served as a vehicle for self-hate and self-condemnation which also operated to obscure the dissociated memories, camouflaged self-states, and perpetrator shaped psychological strucutres and patterns.

- A polyfragmented female DID patient (following years of treatment for her complex trauma including sadistic sexual abuse, ritual abuse, and child prostitution and pornography) began to have memories of luring and kidnapping children from public parks into the waiting cars of her perpetrators. As the specific details became clearer of her "procurer training" under the direction of perpetrators from age 5 to 9, the patient also remembered having to participate in gruesome rituals in which she proved her loyalty to the group by participating in the killing of one of the children she had helped kidnap. These revelations, fueled by unbridled shame and guilt, activated self-destructive programming, precipitating a dangerous suicidal crisis. Following successful resolution of the crisis, the therapy dyad gained access to layers of dissociated perpetrator states and eventually reduced the patient's previously intractable posttraumatic symptoms in a way that may not have been possible prior to the revelations.

Many dissociative survivors have consciously kept silent on longstanding secrets of their sexual or violent or criminal actions committed against animals, other children, and adults. Revelations of perpetration presented in relatively linear narratives usually emerge only after much testing of the therapeutic bond and boundaries of the therapist's emotional sturdiness. A patient's confession of consciously remembered perpetration can represent a leap forward in trust. However, it may also represent a test of the therapist's loyalty, capacities, and integrity. This category of clinical presentation is by far the most complex of the three because confessed revelations can also be part of an enactment, and may also relate to the accessing and early integration of previously untreated dissociated self-states. Further diagnostic and treatment complications include the possibilities that patients' confessions are actually screen memories camouflaging other traumas and/or intrpsychic conflicts, or that confessions are manifestations of confabulations, deceptions, or psychotic processes.

Initial accounts of perpetrator activities must be revisited several times to access all of the details, feelings, and fantasies, along with the multiple perspectives the patient holds on this history in different self-states. The patient's first version of moral transgressions is often lacking the still-buried feeling states or the specifics of events around which most of the guilt and shame is organized. The most effective starting point is to listen quietly and non-judgmentally through the first rendition of this historical material, while honoring the significance of the revelation itself within the therapy relationship. An important aspect of the integration process will be tracking the patient's underlying feelings and responses to his or her own experience (and the victims' experiences) during the acts of coerced (or self-initiated) perpetration.

It is essential that clinical interviewing not be limited because of the therapist's disgust and unconscious avoidance, or through a self-satisfied, shared relief that the difficult material is finally on the table. After tracking the patient's initial reactions to the revelation experience including his or her perceptions of the therapist's responses, the therapist can openly acknowledge to the patient the viscerally disturbing nature of the material and the breakthrough represented by the act of breaking the silence and sharing. Fostering reflection on the precursors in the therapy process which allowed the revelation to come forward helps the patient to become aware of the motivations at work in the decision to share this aspect of his or her history. This process should include reviewing the patient's attendant fears and expectations of the therapy process and therapist's reactions. At this point, the therapist's diagnostic doubts and countertransference responses guide the direction the inquiry might take in order to evaluate whether the patient's revelation represents an authentic confession or is part of an evasion or enactment (i.e., potentially involving fantasies of rescue, redemption, condemnation, or seduction).

Seeking permission to inquire more fully into the unsettling and painful details, the therapist can clarify how the perpetration events and dynamics reside in the patient's internal world. Throughout the process, therapists should closely monitor their own feelings and their patients' feeling (including lack of feelings). If the revelation process seemed to involve a destructive, seductive, or complicity enactment, a delicate juggling of the content with the inquiry and interpretive process is needed. If the revelation seems straightforward, the therapist could simply affirm the patient's courage and share his or her feelings of relief at finally hearing about long-held secrets about victimizing others while interpretively linking the confession to dynamic themes, and patterns already in play within the patient's treatment. Depending on the severity of the transgression and the patient's behavior during the session, the therapist can foreshadow the psychological and somatic distress that might come from further exploring the issues. Then, honoring informed consent as a dynamic process, it is best for clinicians to follow with unambiguous questions designed to track the patient's entire experience through the minutiae of the event(s), including how their thoughts, feelings, and beliefs prior to perpetrating may have changed during and/or after the perpetration event(s).

A common mistake therapists make when facing narratives of historic perpetration is being overly timid or passive in the inquiry phase for fear of making the patient feel humiliated or rejected. Instead, the clinician must err on the side of displaying courage in pursuit of emotional and historic truth. Here the therapist needs to model unflinching courage as a core virtue; this will help buoy the shared vessel of therapy as it moves, inevitably, into deeper and more turbulent waters. For example, prematurely accepting the patient's initial presentation of superficial guilt and remorse (or indifference) may later impede the healing process. When therapists press forward with the inquiry process, systematically investigating the details of patients' thoughts and actions related to specific acts of perpetration, patients will often report that they had experienced a mixture of shame, compulsion, relief, mastery, and a temporary sense of omnipotent ego-inflation during the peak of their acts of perpetration when their victim was made to feel helpless or degraded. Their transient relief from re-enactment, evacuation, and omnipotence is often reported to have been followed by paralyzing remorse (or hollow remorse), self-hatred, and/or dissociation immediately after these vainglorious moments within their episodes. Sometimes powerful urges to re-offend as a way of managing the anxiety of moral transgression are reported. The therapist's acceptance and comfort with discussing the full range of the patient's experience is an essential moderator of the patient's shame and represents an important example of "surviving destruction" (Winnicott 1971) as a transformational vehicle of treatment. By contrast, the protracted absence of understandable details and expectable feelings from patients during in depth inquiry may reveal the confession to be a confabulation or part of an enactment. Depending on the case and level of trust established, therapists' "surviving destruction" may need to focus interventions primarily on the transference-countertransference dynamic and less on stewarding and witnessing process.

Following a sequence of authentic confession and successful inquiry, the destabilized patient may defensively take too much, or too little, responsibility for his or her actions. Survivors may initially minimize, or overly dramatize, their pasts to compensate for guilt or shame, to deflect "outsider" probing, to placate the therapist, or to cope with disorganizing feeling states. Professed delight in perpetrator activities may represent absolute honesty, a sidestepping of culpability, or provocation-style testing of the therapist's capacity for non-judgmental listening and acceptance. It may take time before the patient fully opens to examining the nature of his or her actual states of mind during the perpetrating events. The therapist's empathic access to the patient's non-evasive, non-self-serving representations of experiences may take longer to achieve but is an essential aspect of integration. When the patient hears the therapist put into non-judgmental language what the therapist has come to understand of the patient's transgressions and serious reflections on these events, an important rupture in the patient's lifelong psychological isolation and alienation is underway.

The daunting process of "a searching and fearless moral inventory," a term used in 12-step programs, holds an even greater challenge where revelations of perpetration are concerned. Previously unknown levels of courage and trust are required for a patient to take this leap in the therapy process. Along with the patient's eventual ability to fearlessly describe the details of what took place, the beginning of a restoration of the patient's dignity and self-respect is fostered by the capacity to "own" and take responsibility for his or her destructiveness. In this process, the patient deconstructs the self-generated or perpetrator-implanted confusions about the true meanings and motives behind victimizing others, along with the attendant sadistic drives, thirst for power, pain relief, revenge, prestige, and perpetrator (or group) "love" and acceptance. Successful focused interviewing with a balanced combination of therapeutic compassion and confrontation can lead to a key transformative sequence in psychotherapy: catharsis, contrition, and mourning. This process involves walking a thin line not-easily drawn by conventionally held views of morality – it is a nuanced dialectical examination of the distinctions contrasting accountability and condemnation where the patient can take ownership of inhumane acts while mindfully pardoning them.

Following revelations of perpetration, the patient often experiences an initial feeling of relief along with a fear of disruption in the therapy based on presumed disgust from the therapist. Intense feelings of worthlessness collide with the appearance of tentative hope for self-forgiveness and redemption. The release of secrets often leads to transient states of identity disorganization when the experience of confession – met with compassion, honesty, and acceptance from the therapist – intrinsically disrupts the fixity of perpetrator identifications and pathological attachments. After confessing past crimes, many patients draw on their urges to self-harm as a tactic to cope with overwhelming shame or as a misguided method of repentance. The therapist's expressed comfort in discussing any and all aspects of the patient's revelations will, in itself, help to destigmatize the patient's history. This helps the patient to avoid collapsing into self-pity, contracting in self-hatred, or shutting down through various other escapist forms of self-soothing. When both partners in the therapeutic dyad learn to sit with the moral ambiguity of what has been revealed and share an understanding that there are no simple solutions to lived histories of perpetration, then a healthy grieving process can follow.

As the previously impenetrable self-damnation begins to ease, isolation and alienation can be replaced by a new human connection and contextualization. The therapist adds a compassionate human voice to the solitary interpretation that had played in the patient's head for years. The patient's fear of his or her own potential dangerousness can then be encountered and eventually ameliorated by a willingness to accept and grieve what has been lost through his or her violent actions in the past. Mixed with this grief is the patient's new appreciation for the healthy use of aggression in service to protection and defense of self-directed individuality. As the patient comes to understand that all perpetration is simultaneously an assault on both the self and the victim, he or she can come to see that all past actions, however distasteful, can be subjected to compassionate inquiry and dialogue with a caring, non-judgmental witness.

The simple act of "airing out" deeply held secrets of perpetrator activity can prompt disruption and potential reorganization of rigidly held self-defeating beliefs – beliefs that may have motivated misguided actions. The disgrace of past perpetration can begin to be apprehended as a part of one's life story, instead of one's undifferentiated identity. Progressive empathic dialogues help the patient to develop the maturity to live courageously and non-dissociatively within moral ambiguities of the past.

Analysis of transference/countertransference case examples

- Following a disruption with her therapist involving a narcissistic injury and feelings of competition with another patient, a volatile female dissociative survivor snuck/broke into her therapist's office after hours and read her own and other patients' records, specifically the records of the patient who she believed had been receiving preferential treatment from the therapist. After several weeks of not mentioning this to her therapist, the patient confessed about the event. The therapist was initially unsure whether the perpetration was a fabrication meant to test, or intimidate, or a true boundary violation. Further explorations led to analysis of the precursors of the enactment (a perceived empathic failure of the therapist), revelations of previously hidden perpetrator alter personalities, and a reconfiguration of the therapy contract with the therapist, mandating complete cessation of all boundary violations for the protection of the continued treatment.

- A depressed male patient who alternated between presentation of florid DID symptoms and vehement denial of all trauma history and posttraumatic behaviors repeatedly revealed and recanted a terrifying memory of dogs being tortured in an organized multiple-child abuse scenario. Again and again, as the memory surfaced and was then denied, the therapist's empathy was alternately appreciated and despised/humiliated by various alters within the patient's system until a new version of the story emerged. This one involved children instead of dogs being harmed by other children and adults. The revised version brought elements of the patient's self-generated and perpetrator-engineered dissociative systems into direct collision for the first time, leading to a suicidal crises and efforts to drop out of treatment. Further investigation revealed the patient's intense fears of harming the therapist and destroying the accrued beneficial experiences of the therapy relationship. Explorations eventually to the exposure of several layers of the patient's perpetrator-identified and violent, indoctrinated self-states.

- Following a period of apparent progress, a female DID patient revealed that she had brought a gun to session in her purse and that some of her alters found great comfort in carrying around the weapon. She wanted the therapist not to worry about, or intrude on, this form of self-soothing and self-protection. As the many elements and meanings of the enactment were analyzed, it was eventually revealed that the patient had been sadistically sexually abused with guns by perpetrators. These explorations led to accessing previously obscured perpetrator identified states within the patient and to the many meanings of guns in her intrapsychic and interpersonal life. In addition, these explorations made it possible to access and interpret the patient's wishes for rescue, and her intense shame and self-hatred for her needs for protection, and her complex ambivalence towards the therapist (and dangerous attachment figures from the past).

Beyond simple revelation and confession, patterns of perpetration visible to the therapist yet invisible to the patient (or invisible to both) may reveal themselves in subtle or symbolic forms. In the relational treatment of trauma and dissociation, interpretations move back and forth between descriptions of the patient's internal world and the interpersonal dynamics produced by the intersection of the separate yet now interdependent worldviews of the therapist and patient. In various contemporary relational schools of psychoanalytic theory and practice, concepts such as "turning passive into active" (Foreman, 1996; J. Weiss, 1993) and "enactment" (Aron, 1996; Ehrenberg, 1992, 1996; Maroda, 1991, 1999) are used to describe the complex system of unconscious communication between therapist and patient that can support potential revelation. Clinicians can expect to encounter classic perpetration patterns occurring within the therapy relationship in both concrete and indirect expressions such as: silencing; double-binding, "gaslighting," boundary encroachment; challenges to the therapist's reality-testing; forced choices; seduction; rejection or abandonment; "duping delight"[2]; abiding hatred; coerced disgust; coerced helplessness and dread; emotional sadism; betrayal of trust; blackmail; threats of legal actions; threats against the life of the patient's family, the therapist's family, or both; stalking; hostage-taking; and other life and death confrontations. When patients are still actively involved with perpetrator(s), these dynamics can greatly intensify and complicate these dynamics. It is important to note that therapists can unconsciously engender, even enact, some of these dynamics. Efficacy of treatment is enhanced when each of these patterns can be illuminated with cautious inquiry and improvisational dialogue.

The perpetrator's use of the relational dynamics of subjugation and obfuscation are often internalized by their victims. Therapeutic progress is most effectively maintained by way of the therapist's immediacy in confronting destructiveness in response to the patient's provocations and avoidance maneuvers (Ehrenberg, 1992, 1996; Grand, 2000; Maroda, 1991, 1999; H. Schwartz, 2000). The ultimate goal of this aspect of the therapy, of course, is more than a simple halting of the original malevolent relational patterns through the therapist's modeling of empathy, kindness, and compassion. The opportunity in this genre of "emotionally corrective experience" (Alexander and French, 1946) is the full exposure of the trauma-based pathological–relational dynamics to the light of day so they can, in turn, be undone. Exploration of enactments within the psychotherapy relationship sets the stage for the systematic disconfirmation of the core set of expectations (false beliefs) indoctrinated into the mind of the patient by the pathological and abusive systems. Undoing previously fixed unconscious perpetrator-identifications through the patient's conscious choices (in direct contrast to the forced choice scenarios of child abuse and indoctrination) can lead the patient to own and reject perpetrator patterns of identity and behavior.

Disconfirmation of pathogenic beliefs, benevolent disruption, and creative interference are essential tools for resetting psychological structures that have been warped by coerced perpetration and complicity. A therapist must attempt to avoid repeating (consciously or unconsciously) the pathological dynamics of the past. A commitment to honesty, empathy, and respect sustains the disconfirmation process. The process of undermining pathogenic beliefs disrupts embedded expectations and reflexes to help the patient to feel secure in pursuing his or her healthy developmental strivings (J. Weiss, 1993). As relational psychoanalytic perspectives on trauma treatment increasingly recognize, it is not the complete avoidance of re-enactment on either the patient's or the therapist's part that holds the key to transformative awareness and successful treatment outcomes; rather, it is the willingness and capacities of both parties to recognize when these pathological dynamics are at play (Ehrenberg, 1992; Hoppenwasser, 2008; Howell, 2011; Maroda, 1999). It is the humility to acknowledge how easily anyone can be pulled into the enactment maelstrom, and how we are able to simultaneously use our sensitivity to toxic relational patterns as a guidance device to move through dangerous territories.

Some patients eventually confess to participating in particularly guileful enactments where they had enjoyed disturbing or frightening the therapist while simultaneously disavowing any knowledge of or agency in their provocations. This dynamic is related to what Bollas (1992) has termed "violent innocence" in which the patient (sometimes by way of an alter) sponsors affective ideational confusion in the therapist (or others), knowledge of which they deny. When this occurs, the disavowal is the higher violation. The unconscious aim of repetitions of violent innocence is the coercion of the therapist into a position whereby the process of self-other relating is rendered impossible. This dynamic is co-present in almost all cases where dissociative perpetrator identifications are operative.

This form of transference/countertransference experience is also consistent with Goldberg's (2000) psychoanalytic definition of evil, in which an assault on meaning-making functions and containers – indeed on the value of any meaning itself – is played out within the therapy relationship. Other related, nefarious enactments associated with the most severe emanations of torturers and psycho-pathic sadists involve the eroticized exploitation of basic trust and the need to merge sex and death (Bollas, 1995). In these extreme cases, the tormented soul of the perpetrator is manifest in what Bollas describes as "an envious hatred of life mutating into an envious identification with the anti-life [...] to work his trauma upon the human race, trying to bring others to an equivalent fall" (p. 189). The therapist and patient will likely have urges to collude in distractions, avoidances, or benevolent but false reframing in the face of grotesque inhumanity.

Contemporary relational psychoanalytic theories posit that psychological transformation occurs not via interpretation and insight alone, but through new relational experiences. In an updated relational context, innovative representa-tions of self and others, and a restructured understanding of human relationships categorically, can be developed and internalized (Greenberg and Mitchell, 1983; Levenson, 1972). Thus, no true healing can occur without some of the patho-logical dynamics of the abusive system being played out within the therapy dyad (Aron, 1996; Maroda, 1999). From the relational perspective the recreation of disturbing interpersonal perpetrator-initiated dynamics are not to be avoided or prohibited. Instead, it is the shared witnessing of the old patterns and their containment within the healthy boundaries (including limit-setting and repudiat-ing destructiveness) of the co-created relational context of benevolence and mutual respect that fosters reparative outcomes. Immersion in such a process of compassionate inquiry and object-related hatred (Grand, 2000) systematically offsets the dominating responses that were created by the original trauma, along with their underlying set of internalized expectations.

Balancing recognition of the patient's core innocence while repudiating destructiveness in the analysis of enactments can be quite challenging. Dangers inherent in confronting the patient with their own accountability and culpability involve the risk of inciting or aggravating the patient's propensity for shame, retaliation, and withdrawal. Helping the patient understand his or her own inno-cence may be even more difficult since self-condemnation and indifference often alternate in the psyche of dissociative survivors. To pursue the goal of "reestab-lishing innocence," within the matrix of malevolent transference, five key clinical postures must be simultaneously maintained.

1   Recognizing perpetrator re-enactments as essentially communicative in nature. There is an effort by the patient's unconscious to express historical,

relational dynamics in the only way possible at that particular juncture of treatment.

2   Holding the patient accountable for his or her behavior and its effects while maintaining the basic agreements of the therapy contract.

3   Maintaining the view – and assisting the patient to maintain the view – that all encounters and re-enactments with internalized perpetration are opportunities for re-education, reparation, and redemption.

4   Repudiating and confronting destructiveness (Grand's [2000] non-condemning, non-retaliatory object-related hatred) while supporting vulnerability and self-awareness.

5   Understanding that the therapist's conscious and unconscious role and participation in the enactment is essential to the process, regardless of how minimal or obscured, and that the therapist's timely and appropriate sharing of this part of the process may be highly beneficial to positive therapeutic outcome.

The eventual reparation process for perpetration enactments may begin through a variety of means: disruption of the patient's rigidly-held beliefs about the self or perpetrators; new experiences of self-reflection; being empathically heard, accepted, and respected; detoxification of unmanageable feeling states; ruptures of states of isolation and alienation; disconfirmation of pathological expectations; and abreaction. Healthy metabolization of perpetration dynamics could likewise be advanced when the patient's traumatic expectations are met with non-traumatizing responses, thereby creating safety and space for emotional development. Similarly, the patient's experiences of passionate but peaceful argument and internal and interpersonal discord, combined with the therapist's demarcation and observance of healthy boundaries, disrupt old object-relations while new relational patterns are imprinted.

These clinical postures support the patient's underlying innocence and form the foundation of the aspect of psychoanalytic treatment that Winnicott (1971) termed "surviving destruction."[3] Winnicott's original formulation speaks to the patient's need to test the realness and reliability of "the other" by seeing if the relationship survives efforts to destroy it. It is the therapist's responsibility to meet destructive engagement without withdrawing or retaliating against the patient – regardless of what is taking place in the treatment process. Nowhere is the posture of "surviving destruction" more germane than in work with perpetrator states of mind that can wheedle and likely incite the therapist to act out dismissively or caustically. Invitations to engage in aggressive, polarized, or abandoning countertransference behaviors must be met by the therapist with compassionate confrontation – linking the behavior back to its origins in the patient's perpetrating system (and upon reflection and consultation, to the therapist's own psychological process). If available, and appropriate, humor can be a very powerful disarming clinical tool at these treatment junctures. The therapist's inevitable slips into angry, frustrated, overprotective, or overwhelmed states of mind can be strategically acknowledged as grist for the mill. Such expression can be utilized for clarifying various roles in the enactment process as well as in modeling vulnerability and humility as an alternative to shame and isolation. All re-enactments present the opportunity to reveal the psychological dynamics of the past and play them out in a different, more honest, self-respecting, and mutuality-based manner. Over time, the therapist's systematic creative interference in unconscious repetitions of perpetrator identifications displaces the destructive programming embedded in unhealed traumatic injuries.

Perpetrator-loyal states and alter personalities case examples

- In response to the emergence of new traumatic material in the treatment of an extremely passive-compliant female DID patient, a brooding, frightening, demonic male alter personality arose in the patient's mind and in the therapy relationship to threaten and humiliate the patient and the therapist. The patient's first reaction was to crawl under the desk of the therapist's office and regress to a quivering child alter while the therapist looked for a way to contain the perpetrator alter and disrupt the complicity and avoidance maneuvers of the patient's self-system. Eventually, the therapist found a neutral way to dialogue with the alter and to propel previously intimidated aspects of the patient's DID system into communicating, arguing, and eventually integrating this hateful, perpetrator-identified state. The therapist's fostering understanding and acceptance (including confrontation) by the patient's other, nonviolent, pro-social self-states, of their "use" of the perpetrator self-states to contain disowned feelings and avoid conflicts, was also essential to the integration process.

- A virulent perpetrator state of a high-functioning female DID patient had been precipitating head-banging, face slapping, and other bodily contortions in response to therapy-compliant alter personalities' increased trauma revelations and deepening attachment to the therapist. After passing some unconscious testing of the therapist, following months of efforts to create the conditions for dialogue, the perpetrator state emerged to finally tell the story of its creation in the system for the purpose of getting the therapist to "leave them all alone." Reflecting back to the past when a moment of childhood peace in a neighbor's yard was brutally interrupted, the alter explained how "they" were taken by surprise when the perpetrator (a friend of the family who had been sadistically sexually abusing her for years) unexpectedly appeared. While raping her in a storage shed in the yard, the patient grabbed a pair of pliers off of the perpetrator's belt (he was a contractor) and attempted to hit him. This was the first time she had ever had the wherewithal to attempt resistance. When the perpetrator anally raped her with the pliers down her throat, the perpetrator-alter "took what was left of her spirit and ran away with it." Following this, the perpetrator-identified alter re-enacted violence on the self whenever "he" felt there was any danger of the patient attaching to anyone in a way that might endanger the last bit of self that was left. In his system, intimacy and violation and annihilation were significantly linked. Emergence of this narrative and its deconstruction in treatment led to a cessation of self-injury and the beginning of dialogues among previously segregated aspects of the patient's self-system.

The first encounter with sequestered, personified perpetrator states does not usually take place until psychotherapy has been well underway. If the therapist is not aware of the possible existence of these personified perpetrator states (both self-created and perpetrator-engineered), it is unlikely such encounters will occur at all. In the contemporary psychoanalytic understanding of unconscious therapist–patient communication, it is generally assumed that patients are able to sense what the therapist can or cannot handle and what the therapist is or is not open to hearing, feeling, or tolerating (Aron, 1996; Greenberg and Mitchell, 1983). As a result, if the therapist does not want to know what the patient is experiencing then the patient will contain or deflect this psychological material in directions that thwart the revelation and hence the possibility of substantive analytic work.[4]

Ideally prior to the emergence of perpetrator-states, there has been a fair amount of trust developed in the therapy relationship by way of a number of successful experiences working through trauma memories, affects, and the aftermath. In spite of how thorough the preparation, when hateful, arrogant, or robotic perpetrator alters emerge, in the background or foreground, to sabotage treatment, they wreak havoc in the therapeutic space. Perpetrator-loyal alters, who may or may not be organized in a hierarchy with levels, "fail-safes," and trap doors (Miller, 2012), may come out for committed, acrimonious verbal assaults on the patient's other alters, the therapist, and the treatment process. When perpetrator states boldly come forth to profess a satanic, racist, or nihilistic ideology, an entirely new set of treatment challenges results. Some of these alters re-enact experiences that lead patients to self-injure, attempt suicide, return to perpetrators, or cross into the personal life of the therapist.

When an otherwise gentle patient, with whom the therapist has nurtured a productive and caring therapeutic alliance, makes bizarre self-righteous pronouncements reflecting an intent to carry out violent and malevolent acts, it is naturally unnerving. When the patient first experiences the conduct of a perpetrator alter or expresses himself or herself through the personality of a specific alter for the first time, he or she usually wishes to run away, suffer punishment, or die immediately. Herein exists a doubly bound suicidality: the innocent victim-identified part-self wants to die from "irredeemable" guilt and shame, while the perpetrator-loyal part-self wants to kill the others as the ultimate damnation or to keep the secrets of the abuse forever hidden. Threats to drop out of treatment tend to run high at this point. Normal posttraumatic avoidance to being seen is likely to kick into high gear if "resistance programming" or ideologies are threatened.

The initial encounter with one's own perpetrator alter is inevitably quite stressful and changes the patient's sense of history and identity forever. It is one thing to have a metaphorical shadow one is attempting to integrate; it is quite another to realize one has an "independent" self-state cultivated and controlled by the purveyors of childhood terror. Even worse for the patient is hearing the braggadocio and disturbing content that parts of themselves proudly claim to have enjoyed while participating in heinous acts. Some of these arrogant perpetrator self-states convey a genuine sense of confidence, power, and danger while others appear fragile behind the façade of sadistic reverie. Dissociative survivors, who are quite intimidated upon initial contact with these haunting aspects of themselves, often fail to differentiate between self-generated dissociative adaptations to attachment dilemmas and perpetrator-engineered states. The most common "gut reaction" of survivors is to massively re-dissociate the experience, obfuscate it, or run. Unfortunately this reaction serves to reinforce unconscious patterns of collusion with perpetrator-camouflage and silencing programming.

Sophisticated camouflage, cloaking devices,[5] and subterfuge strategies are common challenges to the therapy process when attempting to directly dialogue with perpetrator-identified states. These "tricks" are used by perpetrator self-states to avoid detection by staying in the background of the patient's psyche. They have been useful in maintaining control of other parts of the patient's personality through intimidation, promoting confusion, and pulling emotional triggers. Such tactics help preserve the silence about the specific mechanics deployed by the abuses in the patient's childhood – in some cases through adulthood. Some patients have such an elaborate matrix of perpetrator-trained self-states that it is often impossible to keep track of all the moving parts. These intricate self-systems often contain an array of booby traps and set-ups for sabotage of self and treatment. There can be numerous alter personalities nesting within one another other like Russian dolls charged with suicidality, self-doubt, and homicidal programming.

Any therapist confronted with these challenges is likely to become understandably overwhelmed by the seemingly unmanageable volume of details. Therapists may feel so daunted that terminating treatment altogether may be seriously considered. To move forward, the therapist must communicate the expectation of help from the rest of the dissociative patient's non-perpetrator-identified personality system, regardless of how overwhelmed or intimidated the patient may feel at this time. A new and deeper therapeutic alliance must be built upon the foundation established during the earlier period of psychotherapy when coming to terms with basic aspects of victimization was the focus. The patient as a whole, and particularly conflict-avoidant, helplessness-enacting aspects of the patient's dissociative self-system, must become willing to own (and eventually embody) the disturbing feelings states, and evasions of psychological conflicts, that all perpetrator aters and introjects represent (i.e., ruthlessness, vengeance, needs for mastery, ambition, power, and needs for approval and recognition by perpetrators, and grief and empathy avoidance).

Psycho-educational and psychodynamic therapeutic interventions can operate in mutually beneficial ways to advance the clinical process. The therapist can illuminate and illustrate patterns of internal and external perpetration using movies, literature, and historical events in order to demystify some of these experiences and create a broad platform upon which the mutual reflection and integration processes can take place. Having some distance from the chaos and confusion of the personal through other mediums of representation can help a patient return to the interpersonal and the intrapsychic challenges empowered by information from outside the realms of perpetrator conditioning and logic. This work cannot proceed without the informed consent of the patient (by way of the majority of his or her alter personalities). Therapists must explicitly contract with the aspects of the patient's self-system that have sustained the strongest therapeutic alliance over time and that understand the basics of the therapy process. Specific cautions about navigating perpetrator self-states and dynamics can be offered by therapists without contaminating or unduly influencing the natural unfolding of the patient's struggles with the roughest edges of his or her history and identity. Not only is the process of ongoing informed consent an ethical and legal imperative of clinical practice, it is a central relational tool for treating patients whose wills and identities have been damaged.

There can be a subset of extremely intractable, hostile perpetrator-identified states that may severely impede treatment, sometimes permanently. Self-states reflecting personifications of what Rosenfeld (1971) has called "destructive narcissism," may find the therapist's efforts to unmask their underlying worth or goodness absolutely intolerable. This impenetrability may be due to a combination of several factors: massive early deprivation and traumatization; deep commitments to a criminal way of life; commitments to corrupt political or spiritual ideologies; adhesive enmeshment in perpetrator systems; limited or no access to vulnerability, creativity, or capacities for sublimation; and/or inadequate dissociative defenses. These self-states (or individuals in the case of a less fractured personality organization) experience shame for not being cruel or malevolent enough. Some child soldiers in the field find solace and power in ceaseless random brutality, "Rambo" identifications, and menacing nicknames that ward off pain and fear. In early demobilization treatment, former child soldiers find civilian comments on their innocence intolerable. In this peculiar reversal, a therapist may be construed as a perpetrator, not for hurting or failing the patient, but for indicating that the patient or alter personality is not all bad.

When such strong identifications with criminality or evil are present, any sign of therapeutic progress is seen as weakening the patient's strength, thereby anathema to the sense of superiority on which the righteousness is based. Guilt, shame, and vulnerability have been so effectively bypassed by these strange personality machinations that any contact with genuine kindness or compassion is experienced as a devaluation. With some of the most florid perpetrator states, the level of identification with malevolence is so severe that assaulting the treatment, the therapist, and the self provides an endless source of pleasure. Sometimes, after years of confrontations and strengthening alliances with other sectors of the self, these perverse psychological predispositions can be systematically undermined and gradually eroded. In such cases the treatment is like a slow titration of light into the darkness in the heart and mind of the patient. (H. Schwartz, 2000).

Case example: Anna

Anna was a DID patient from the East Coast, raised in a family system involved in drug trafficking, prostitution, pornography, and ritual abuse that included the making and distributing of snuff films. With a combination of sexual abuse, torture, and familial loyalty programming, her personality was split by her family system into mainstream and criminal segments. This split enabled her to attend school and appear normal during the day and to participate in criminal activities in the evenings and on weekends. Anna's clandestine activates included acting as a procurer, courier, and trainer of other children for exploitation; at times she also participated in extreme violence, even murder. In second grade, Anna was coerced into luring her best friend from school to her home where the friend was then subjected to abuse while she watched. This ended any future bonding with other children. Anna developed an aversion to intimacy and behaved in ways that discouraged her peers from forming attachments with her. These and other events cultivated in Anna a "preference" for procuring and harming "unfamiliar" as opposed to familiar children and adults. Extensive programming insured that Anna deeply believed she freely chose to participate in all of these activities. Extreme social isolation was a major feature of her long-term patterns of posttraumatic stress and dissociation. It is important to note that Anna's social isolation was concurrently an artifact of abuse, a self-perpetuating coping mechanism, and a perpetrator protection system.

Before beginning treatment with me, Anna had three problematic therapies that severely compounded her posttraumatic injuries. The first therapist, a staunchly traditional psychoanalyst, completely missed her trauma history and tried to help her learn to socialize without an appreciation of the layers of trauma giving rise to her symptoms. The second therapist was a young trauma-focused therapist who had a psychotic break in a session in Anna's home where gruesome material was revealed. The therapist was psychiatrically hospitalized within 24 hours of the session and abandoned the patient not long after her release. Anna's third treatment was with an inexperienced male therapist claiming to specialize in trauma and DID. The therapist was going through a complicated divorce and somehow became sexually involved with Anna. Memories or revelations of the sexual involvement did not surface in her therapy with me until after many tests of trust were passed and many provocations were survived.

Anna was engaged for many years in a profound hostile-dependency in our therapy relationship and she refused meaningful involvement with other people outside of 12-step and survivor recovery groups where she often had inter-personal struggles and disappointments. Her difficulties with intimacy and nego-tiating interpersonal relations made Anna feel safer alternating between clinging to me and hating me. She drove away several therapists who covered for me while I was on vacation and for years sabotaged prospective intimate relationships. Together we struggled with numerous issues related to her health, poor hygiene, disorganization, and avoidance of developmental challenges. We also worked on her malevolent perpetrator states, some of which claimed to relish violation and violence toward others. Anna had diabetes, obesity, and other health-related problems throughout her life. When memories about her participation in her family's depraved activities began to emerge in treatment, hostile perpetrator-loyal alters, which had been implanted to sustain amnesia barriers, began to subvert her self-control. In calculated actions to keep her memories hidden from other mainstream parts of the personality, these alters would "forget" to take their insulin, precipitating recurrent medical crises.

Anna had been programmed by her perpetrators to indefatigably believe in her capacity to destroy anyone who got close to her. Her three prior failed therapies were reinforcements of her programmed belief in her destructive powers over others. My early countertransference fantasies fluctuated between states of help-lessness, hope, frustration, and dread. I had considerable affection for Anna, and faith in her capacity to heal, but for a long time her primary bond with me was based on doubting and rejecting my benevolence and interpretations. At times I felt angry at having to bear the brunt of her rage at the professionals of her prior therapy failures, and at other times I feared Anna might hold me hostage indefi-nitely with her self-righteous retreat from life. I would endeavor to try multiple modes of intervention while Anna would ritually respond, "Is this therapy. Are we doing therapy yet?" Anna simply could not let herself bond with another therapist and risk more failure, yet she could not let go of treatment or consider other alternatives for healing. At several points in the treatment when I felt almost no progress was being made and when Anna escalated her professed unhappiness with the therapy, I raised the possibility of our having hit a possible limit in my ability to help her and discussed her finding a new therapist. We discussed this potential solution with the shared awareness of the multiple accrued identification with my authority and meanings, pressures, and influences, based on what we were each experiencing – particularly enactments of abandon-ment, rejection, impotent rage, and helplessness. My own issues of professional ethics, limits, and secondary traumatic stress became part of the therapy discourse. We also discussed our dilemma about continuing treatment from the perspectives of our therapeutic compatibility and from what her prior failed therapies might have caused her to believe about the process and prospects of treatment.

For conscious and unconscious reasons, several close calls at the precipice of termination seemed to be an essential part of Anna's healing process. Her free-dom to repeatedly choose to stay in therapy in a field of hostility and open inquiry was a crucial ingredient in the treatment. Another facilitating factor was her direct experience of my generosity and frustration. This humanized me as her therapist and the therapy relationship itself, and slowly over time disarmed some of her previously intractable hatred and avoidance. Underscoring her freedom in the recurring therapy impasses, along with acknowledging my own limits, proved to be a beneficial contrast to the prior therapies. This had a disarming effect on much of her programming and perpetrator-identifications. Anna's dissociative system began to relax in my presence and reveal itself to me in a more vulnerable manner. Her trauma history was extraordinarily brutal and we began to mutually reflect on it instead of re-enact it. Eventually steady significant developmental advancement unfolded out of the long tumultuous incubation period. Anna's opening to her own role in healing came forth incrementally on the stepping stones of humor, patience, creative dialogue, contained disagreement, a shared love of literature and poetry, and my occasional direct request to tackle specific health, weight, and hygiene problems as an "offering" to the therapy process (markedly in counterpoint to the vile "offerings" to her childhood cult).

Prior to the completion of therapy, a pattern of petty lying reappeared at a time when she and I were accessing some of her most deeply sequestered torture-based mind-controlled perpetrator states. Her history of lying had periodically become the subject of treatment. Her propensity to justify anything to herself seemed to have been residue from her traumatic childhood: bending reality to make it more bearable. Anna's petty and pointless lying about weight management and diet ultimately became an entry point into deeply hidden perpetrator states, yet the experience felt like a renewed assault on the therapy. As the revelations of electrocution-based torture and trauma induced self-states came into focus, Anna and I analyzed the lying experience to include as many potential meanings as possible including: bringing my attention to the hidden levels of unmetabolized wrongdoing; a re-enactment of some of the subtle betrayals and "surprise attack" traumas of her childhood; last ditch efforts to hold on to a degraded, self-hating, and worthless identity at a time when major progress was being made across many areas of her life; and an assault on my faith in her at the eleventh-hour by way of an alter that said it "hated that I could love and accept all of her" when she still felt wretched and beyond redemption. The petty lies covered up significant damage, but the small lies brought the damage that needed therapeutic attention into the foreground. Anna took a significant step forward in treatment by revealing she had been presenting an extended lie over several months (again on the subject of her health and weight). Anna's authenticity in handling her remorse in facing the violation of a trust that had become sacred between us eventually led to the unraveling of her most remote and intractable perpetrator states. In a note to me near the end of this episode, Anna wrote:

> [...] in the wake of my recent desecration of your trust and the sacred space between us, the experience of your forgiveness is shatteringly deeply resoundingly beautiful, one of the greatest sweetnesses I have ever

experienced, as is the depth of your willingness and ability to remain open to me. So incredibly reparative. Nourishing. Whole. And holy, and in the process, I think you know but I need to say this, you have opened the door of my prison cell more fully than I could ever imagine [...] I used to say is this therapy, well, your Herculean efforts have not gone unnoticed. Yes, indeed, this is therapy.

Anna went on to complete a successful long-term treatment. A key feature of Anna's final integration involved her decision to consciously reclaim and repurpose her ruthlessness – previously disavowed or placed in the service of perpetrators – and use these feelings in the service of healthy ambition, perseverance, and self-direction. She gradually cultivated the ability to build and sustain social relationships – and to enjoy sharing them with me. The development of healthy, safe attachments within a progressive, compassion-based spiritual community was a cornerstone to her ability to recover her trust of others and her trust of herself. Toward the end of therapy, her creativity and spirituality blossomed in some surprising and moving ways. Most strikingly, she evinced a deep capacity for love and intimacy and was able to express these feelings to others and to me in a variety of verbal and artistic ways.

Case example: Jack

Jack was an extremely bright, high-functioning DID patient who initially presented with self-destructive sexual-acting-out and substance-abuse behavior that disguised his underlying personality fragmentation. After sustaining recovery from his addictions and on the heels of revelations of his family's involvement in a violent criminal cult, Jack began to remember having been trained to kill others. Victims of his perpetrator group were exposed to assassin training along with child prostitution, child pornography, and bizarre sadistic rituals not linked to any particular religious tradition. The initial training used implosion methodologies[6] to coerce violence as part of a group initiation.

At the age of five, following the forced ingestion of psychoactive drugs and multiple-perpetrator sexual abuse, Jack was transported by car from his home – naked and cold in a wooden box – by his father and a "friend" of the family. When he arrived at the second location he was removed from the box, kept naked, and placed in a circle of waiting adults. He was then directed to a central station or alter within the circle and invited to fatally stab an infant that had been strapped down on a surgical-style metal table. His efforts to avoid looking were met with insistent pressures not to turn away. Various torture and group-pressure practices were used to urge him on. Threats of sadistic rape, which he had already experienced prior to this, were also used to promote the "choice" to murder the victim. When he caught sight of his mother in the circle of adults his heart went numb. Following what he recalls as a knowing nod from his mother, Jack was somehow finally able to make use of his numbness and stab the infant. The group shouted their approval then celebrated with a big feast. Consumption of the sacrificed infant was an essential part of the gruesome festivities. Jack's assassin training continued, but by early adolescence he showed signs of "leakage" through creative writing projects during junior high school in which he exhibited unusually morbid and macabre preoccupations. When attempts to strengthen his commitment to violence and contain his unconscious leaking of cult secrets were unsuccessful, Jack was dropped from the grooming program and amnesia programming for his cult experience commenced.

Jack made great strides in treatment but could not commit to working through all of his traumatic experiences. He would drop out of therapy for extended periods of time to pursue foreign travel or employment in other cities. Some of his perpetrator alters professed that they were doing all they could to keep him from going any further in treatment. His other personalities were convinced they were trying to have the happy life for which they had always hoped. At times it felt as if Jack teased me with the possibility of tremendous breakthroughs, only to fall back into dangerous sexual behavior or another set of distractions. This seduction-disappointment-betrayal pattern paralleled his methods of gaining power over his perpetrators in fantasy as a child, and were re-enacted as an adult in his sexual encounters. I used my experience in the transference/countertransference to reflect on seduction–betrayal dynamics that lay at the core of his relationship with his parents who brought him into the perpetrator group and who tried to use him to attain status within the group. Jack could discuss these dynamics with incredible insights that were promising and compelling. It seemed as if layers of secrets and horrors would come briefly into focus and then recede from view. For a while, some of his alters made good use of the false-memory controversy to bog down the therapy, while other alters gave me their brilliant analysis of the fallacies within this same cultural backlash. Jack saw his relationship with me as inspiring and frustrating. It held potential for the freedom and clarity he longed for but was unable to actualize. Eventually Jack took a job in a city on the opposite side of the country. Some of his perpetrator alters claimed this relocation as a triumph, and as having been part of their plan all along, to prevent any further disclosures in treatment. At the same time, they vociferously declared that there was nothing to disclose because nothing traumatic had ever happened to him. Other alters saw this relocation as just another delay before an eventual healing. Yet other personalities felt grateful that the therapy had enabled him to make the move and find the best job of his life. And for them, just having survived and arrived at a new beginning was sufficient.

Case example: Tomas

Tomas was a high functioning DID male with a fragile and vulnerable demeanor. His mother was a US citizen; his father was a World War II refugee who had been confined in Nazi forced labor camps following the invasion of his country. Thomas was raised alternately in the USA and South Asia where multi-national corporations employed his father as an engineer. Tomas was placed in a "special school" where numerous adults engaged children in sadistic sexual abuse and training in pain infliction and tolerance. Eventually it became clear to Tomas that his mother and father were somehow involved with this criminal group that maintained links in drug and weapons trafficking, child prostitution and pornography, and illicit paramilitary operations.

Tomas's initial coerced perpetration experience occurred in a classroom setting where a slightly older female student was being used in what at first seemed like an innocuous demonstration. However, the scene quickly shifted as the young girl role model stabbed herself with pins and proudly showed no pain. Her mastery over physical pain was highly revered by the instructors through verbal approbation. Each child was then asked to stab the girl with pins to prove his or her own bravery. Children who resisted were subjected to group intimidation and humiliation that included urination and defecation. When each child successfully completed the task, they were praised for their courage and given sweets. Although Tomas was subjected to long periods of training for perpetrating violence against others, the leaders of the group deemed his behavior too inconsistent and unpredictable. He was then used as a training target for the other children, and eventually he was made the victim of intense amnesia programming meant to prevent future revelations of the group's secrets.

Tomas also underwent "failure programming" to sabotage his own potential for self-esteem and healthy development. The attitude of the group was, "if we can't have you, then you can't have you either." For me, the greatest challenge of the transference–countertransference dynamics with Tomas was to tolerate his cyclical pattern of revelations followed by reflexive doubting and recanting. When shared openly, my experiences of shifting states – including between patience and frustration, deadness and overstimulation – seemed to help Tomas move forward in his own relationship with ambiguity and oscillating subjectivities.

In our work, shifting feeling states – pleasant and unpleasant – came to be differentiated from trauma-based shifts in states of mind functioning to sustain amnesia, incredulity, and unconscious identifications with perpetrators. Occasionally, sharing my own visceral sensations, for example my brain being turned upside down and inside out, or strange unexpected sensations of numbness and coldness, helped Tomas feel understood at the deepest level while he struggled to arrive at a stable and truthful rendition of his history. Although I did not pursue this course with a specific objective in mind, relating some of the intense somatic sensations I experienced during the treatment, without interpretive overlay, enhanced Tomas' capacity to access bits and pieces of the torture and mind control he had endured. The intimacy of our relationship seemed to help Tomas redefine what power could mean to him. The echoes from these exchanges helped him to disengage from conscious and unconscious bonds with perpetrators and to challenge his habitual self-devaluation. Through years of therapeutic collisions and negotiations (Bromberg, 2011), Tomas' accrued identification with my authority and perseverance allowed him to claim ownership of his own ambition and ruthlessness – feelings sequestered in partially formed perpetrator states, previously too threatening to embody. He went from being a ghostly, ephemeral interpersonal presence at the beginning of treatment to exhibiting a more solid and inhabited physicality, a wider range of affect, with an increased capacity for humor and play by its conclusion. Tomas completed a successful psychotherapy, integrated the disparate parts of his personality, and entered into a loving secure long-term partnership for the first time in his life.

Case example: Stacey

I was the consultant on the case of Stacey, a 38 year-old DID female patient raised in a child pornography and child prostitution ring. She was brought up in California not far from where the therapy was taking place. Her training in perpe-tration involved a slow systematic desensitization to violence and death in a mock classroom setting. Following exposure to eerie songs imbued with satanic-type messages, a small group of children was asked to crush chicken eggs in front of the class. They were then instructed to crush eggs containing nearly full-term baby birds. Signs of upset or disturbance were actively discouraged while the "courage to kill" without blinking prompted consistent praise. Continuing in this vein over time, the children were coerced and rewarded for each successive act of violence, progressing from small mice to cats and dogs. All expressions of hesitation and resistances from the children were punished with administration of physical punishment, peer pressure, and humiliation (verbal and forced nudity). Children's games such as Musical Chairs were played with violent conse-quences visited upon the loser. Violent perversions of the innocent diversions of childhood were integrated into their training for participation in a variety of underworld activities.

At a certain point in the training, each child was forced to "choose" whether or not to commit a given act and inflict pain on the other children, or become the tortured object for target practice in the training. Once again, using system-atic desensitization principles, the perpetrators administered pain, from mild slapping to stabbing, and finally to placing the "loser" child in confinement or other frightening situations such as hanging, spinning, or being confined with insects. Sometimes disorienting drugs were added to the mix to further the chil-dren's inculcation. Coerced perpetration events were often filmed. These movies were used to prove to the children that they had freely "chosen" to commit the crimes and used as evidence to convince the children of their "true" character. These films were also used as threats of exposure. If children misbehaved or showed evidence of breaking the code of silence, the leaders told them the films would be broadcast on television, given to their teachers, or to the police. Throughout this training their non-violent selves were disparaged as inferior, untrustworthy, and illegitimate.

After about a year of psychotherapy, Stacey revealed that she was still active in her family's intergenerational perpetrator group and that one of her mind-controlled "informer" alter personalities had been reporting the disclosures going on in her therapy back to the group. Stacey eventually declared that the group had been monitoring the movements of the therapist and the therapist's family members, and had in fact situated people to "watch" the therapist's children at their school. Her hostile perpetrator-loyal alters announced that the perpetrator group was considering kidnapping one of her children to be used in a ritual sacrifice.

It was impossible to discern if what Stacey was presenting was actually going on, a transference test, a re-enactment, sadomasochistic enactment, or an artifact of intense programming aimed at shutting down the therapy progress. Against my advice, the therapist who was in consultation with me gave Stacey my name, phone number, and office address when she called the therapist in an upset state about her treatment and was demanding to know the name of her consultant. For a brief period of time prior to this event, the therapist was able to explore various alternative meanings and perspectives involving reality, fantasy, re-enactment, perpetrator alters, and unconscious testing of the therapist–patient relationship. However, the stakes eventually became too high for both the therapist and patient to feel they could safely continue in treatment. Meanwhile, although the therapist was able to understand the parallel process and her own acting out, she had now theoretically put my patients and me at risk. In consultation with police around issues of security and protection for the therapist's family, Stacey and the therapist came to a mutually agreed upon termination. Stacey was provided support in relocation, making the decision to leave her perpetrator group and find a safe house. Following intense and productive processing sessions I also terminated my professional relationship with this consultee. The therapist eventually gave up her practice and moved out of the state, uncertain if she would ever continue doing psychotherapy.

Witnessing

Approaching traumatically sequestered aspects of self is a daunting task. Even when therapy is conducted in a thoughtful way by a skilled clinician, severely dissociative patients will experience aspects of the therapy process as similar to his or her abuse, leading perhaps to forms of unconscious opposition resembling what was felt toward the perpetrator during the original trauma. Bromberg (1991) posed the question of how psychotherapy can enable someone who has fought all his or her life to keep traumatic aspects of self-experience from being thought or exposed to find a voice and enter dialogue. How can a patient who has learned to defensively sustain a fragmented sense of self in the face of chronic catastrophic anxieties learn to experience disorganization and chaos as generative and healing? How can the perpetrators internalized within a dissociative survivor come to trust that they will not be destroyed by revealing their actions to another human being? How can pro-social aspects of the survivor's self-system come to accept their own disavowed ambition, vindictivenes, ruthlessness, and recognition needs personified and exaggerated in disturbing perpetrator identities?

In the treatment of trauma, the need for witnessing collides with the inevitable obscuring patterns of the victim's testimony – absences, fragmentation, and the difficulties of narrating what can never-fully be known. One of the enigmas of survival and recovery from trauma involves gaining access to – re-entering – a life story that the survivor has never fully known. Trauma is often a story from which the survivor has been ejected prior to building a coherent narrative: a narrative that might have effectively contained, detoxified, and managed the incomprehensible and the disastrous. In spite of the difficulties of narrating one's survival (to a witness), when a voice is given to their trauma – answering absences with words, if only to protest and moderate the absences – survivors may be externalizing, in the only way possible, that which would destroy them if it remained internal. Caruth (1995) describes one of many clinical and moral dilemmas at the heart of the difficult task of recognition and healing of trauma survivors.

> How do we help relieve the suffering of victims, and learn to understand the nature of suffering, without eliminating the force and truth of the reality that trauma survivors face and quite often try to transmit to us? […] The difficulty of listening and responding to traumatic stories in a way that does not lose their impact, that does not reduce them to cliches or turn them all into versions of the same story, is a problem that remains central to the task of therapists, literary critics, neurobiologists, and filmmakers alike.
>
> (p. vii)

Compassionate witnessing is unarguably essential to any healing process from trauma (Gerson, 2009). Much has been written about the cognitive restructuring and emotionally corrective experience of working with traumatic re-enactments and transference analysis; however clinicians and theorists can easily forget that listening to, and witnessing the testimony of, survivors is fundamental to the reparative process. As psychotherapists, we often take for granted that we know how to listen and hear people in their pain. Dissociative survivors' expression of their suffering – and the complex maneuvers to minimize the suffering with fractured and internally inconsistent narratives – needs to be empathically witnessed. The therapist's desire to look away as well as the therapist's voyeurism are essential to be aware of, and called into service to relationally work through first-person histories of trauma.

Sachs (2008) highlights what she refers to as the "rather obvious fact that therapists, while aiming to help, are aided by – and hampered by – their own emotional and mental scope, not least by their capacity to hear evil" (p. 3). Underscoring challenges to witnessing, Sachs explains that sooner or later most dissociative survivors will begin to talk about horrendous crimes – crimes committed against them, crimes they have witnessed, crimes they have been forced to commit, or crimes they have intentionally committed. Bearing witness to crimes that are shocking and appalling, crimes that often sound unimaginable is extraordinarily difficult on many levels, not the least of which is that these criminal activities are almost always unproven or contain many missing pieces of information, so that "one can hardly think how they can ever be proven – or, for that matter, proven wrong" (p. 3). The mix of horror, incredulity, helplessness, assault on the therapist's imagination and worldview, and irresolvable ambiguity all underscore the challenges of witnessing trauma testimony.

The emphasis on a therapist's function as a witness to the patient's traumatic experiences was elevated to a central position in theories of trauma treatment that began emerging decades ago (Briere, 1996; Freyd, 1996; Herman, 1992; Laub and Auerhahn, 1989, 1993). Clinician-theorists who have spent a great deal of time in the presence of enormous suffering have attempted to organize theoretical concepts around the processes of witnessing and testimonials. Laub (1995) distinguishes three levels to witnessing: (1) being a witness to oneself, (2) being witness to the testimony of others, and (3) being a witness to the process of witnessing itself. Standing in all these places at once is a key to avoiding collapse into an anxiety-relieving comfort of either arrogant and premature belief or disbelief. Hearing people through their pain is described by Egendorf (1995) as consisting of four distinct but overlapping registers: *decoding* ordinary meanings, *resonating* with the significance for another's life, *awakening* to the reality of one's experience and identity in the presence of a witnessing other, and *communing* with the other through the dialogues that occur between the witness and the witnessed. Egendorf likens this form of listening to meditation and mindfulness.

The exacting process of attending thoughtfully mandates us to rescue ourselves from distraction and preconception. "What hits in the moment of confronting trauma is ultimately nothing we can name. [...not] some speculative category in a philosophical system, but a life-sucking void that takes our breath away." (Egendorf, 1995:20). Egendorf encourages us to remain in a constant state of readiness to be surprised, to discover hidden meanings not immediately apparent, and also to realize that pain and illumination are so intricately intertwined that we must direct the search for understanding into the heart of human agony. This is at the core of the reparative process of psychotherapy. When patients are ready, healing dialogues can lead them through the confrontations with symbolic death to accept what is given and what is taken away.

> By inviting them to speak into being the great absence in their lives. And as they do, and grow willing to turn from their reflexive turning away, we may guide them further – to verify for themselves that they, as the ones who are raised up in wakefulness to meet trauma's demand, do not perish, not even in the face of nothingness.
>
> (p. 21)

A non-judgmental atmosphere combining safety and risk-taking is a precondition for hearing trauma testimonies and for gently but continuously steering traumatized people toward and through their pain. Through testimony, the narrator reverses the process of objectification and loss of identity: "to testify is to engage precisely in the process of re-finding one's own proper name, one's signature" (Felman, 1995:53). Through testimony and witnessing, the legacy of annihilation inherent in trauma is subjected to the reparative processes of making a difference on another human being. The patient's awareness of his or her traumatization cannot be presupposed. Knowledge about trauma "can only happen through testimony: it cannot be separated from it. It can only unfold itself in the process of testifying, but it can never become a substance that can be possessed by either speaker or listener outside of this dialogic process" (Felman, 1995:53).

Testimony as a process refers to the healing and empowerment aspect of language itself and reverses the obliteration of language and connection that took place in trauma. Using language and receptive silence to penetrate to the wounded and helpless state of being is to enter the state of paralysis imposed by trauma and frozen in dissociative states to foster motion from that psychic inertia. Testimony also provides a link between the psychological and the political, between the private and the public, and its power can help to restore affective ties and integrate fragmented experience. Without avoiding the transference and countertransference enactments, and without ignoring the issue of unconscious conflict, psychodynamic clinicians have to work from a non-neutral commitment to help patients convert a sociopolitical crime from an individual illness into something amenable to cultural elaboration (Becker, 1996). With the passage of time and the deepening of the therapy process, the reconstruction of gaps in the patient's own history is catalyzed (Kornfeld, 1996). The re-possession of the past by a self in dialogue with itself and a reliable witness supplants the possession and fragmentation of the self by the perpetrators.

Witnessing undertaken in an empathic manner is indispensable in facilitating patients' evolution past their isolation, perceived incredulity, and shame. Laub (1992; 2005) observes that the presence of another human being, who can witness what a victim has been previously unable to share, can help provide a more neutral or positive meaning to terrifying experiences. Empathic witnessing has the capacity to mitigate the damage sustained both through neglect and abandonment by non-offending, yet often tacitly colluding, family members, along with the tacit collusion of the passive bystander, or society as a whole. A secondary harmful consequence of traumatic events comes from the invalidation of a victim's experiences resulting from insensitive responses in personal and professional relationships; this can compound some of the most destructive effects of the trauma, leaving a devastating and enduring sense of abandonment in the trauma survivor's psyche. Misrecognition, blaming the victim, or urging the victim to move on and stop focusing on his or her pain and trauma are more insidious forms of failed witnessing.

The relationship between the internalization of traumatic events and the presence, or absence, of a humanizing observe powerfully affects a victim's interpretation, context framing, and potential for recovery from traumatic injuries. As Gerson (2009) describes, it is not in recognizing and metabolizing trauma that witnessing is so fundamental, but also in undermining the internalization of absence, of failed caretakers and authority figures, and of what he calls "the dead third" (p. 1341).

> What then can exist between the scream and the silence? We hope first that there is an engaged witness – an other that stands beside the event and the self and who cares to listen; an other who is able to contain that which is heard and is capable of imagining the unbearable; an other who is in a position to confirm both our external and our psychic realities and, thereby, to help us integrate and live within all realms of our experience. This is [...] the witnessing other that constitutes a "live third."
>
> (p. 1342)

Witnessing can never be solely an intellectual exercise. Bromberg's (1980) dual emphasis on empathy and anxiety, and the equilibrium needed between attunement and confrontation underscored his conviction that there is no method for a patient's personal narrative to be transformed through a cognitive editing process alone (Bromberg, 1996). Only a dynamic which arises out of witnessing and testifying from the direct experience of the dissociated self-states involved in the traumatic experience can make momentous alterations in the patient's internal object world. Such a transformative dialogue differs radically from "neutral" narration and listening, and brings deeper meaning to the term witnessing. Now an interactive process, it introduces a new relationship, and a shared consciousness, into the dissociative psyche's splits, blank spots, and points of traumatic overwhelm. Based on mutuality and power-sharing, the new relationship constitutes a bridge through the terror, anxiety, and pain that have existed previously in isolation, a trustworthy easement that the patient can choose to use or not. The challenge for the interactive witness is to tolerate confusion, ambiguity, and contradictory realities without prematurely foreclosing meaning.

Among the most beneficial therapeutic aspects of witnessing-relationships is the cultivation within the patient of his or her own consistent witnessing self. Important observing ego capacities, healthy detachment, and vital critical thinking abilities are strengthened as the witnessing aspect of the patient's self becomes institutionalized in the psyche. This maturation includes the patient's ability to navigate both traumatic and characterological issues revealed in the treatment situation, and, at times, the courage and discernment to know when one of these sets of issues or patterns is serving to obscure or evade the other. Reflectivity and awareness then supplant reactivity and psychic servitude to perpetrators. Knee-jerk dissociation of disturbing feelings and intrapsychic conflicts into passive or cruel aspects of the self is replaced by an integrated, reflective mind capable of responsible "ownership" of all aspects of human experience.

"Mindfulness" is a potent alternative to the classic posttraumatic adaptations of indifference, learned helplessness, dissociative management of the self and others, and unconscious re-enactment of destructive relational paradigms. Mindfulness resulting from effective witnessing prepares anxiety to be tolerated and penetrated. This, in turn, pre-empts circular repetitions and offers the patient a flexible response under the guidance of self-control. Effective witnessing helps cultivate a mindful self-awareness that can disentangle itself from false beliefs. The spacious awareness that results from mindfulness makes room for new conceptual and relationship experiences. When two minds are joined in a fierce commitment to awareness and mutuality, many self-defeating dynamics of internalized perpetration can be systematically undermined.

Witnessing and neutrality

As psychoanalytic theory matured, it was influenced by trauma theory, feminism, intersubjective theory, and the relational movement. This shift assisted in the development of analytic humility, and an appreciation for ambiguity and paradox that gradually replaced the misleading notions of analytic objectivity and neutrality (including beliefs in the therapist's impermeability and superiority). The nature of the psychotherapy relationship, the psychoanalytic process, and witnessing itself changed profoundly when clinicians began to define themselves as a "collaborators in developing a personal narrative rather than as scientists uncovering facts" (Mitchell, 1993:74). Expanding on the definition of "neutrality" in the interpersonal processes, relational theorists do not exclude the importance of interpretation and the role of fantasy. The goal of treatment is to co-create an interpersonal therapeutic ambience where meanings can be creatively mined beyond the threshold of "objective" truth and consensual reality. For Spezzano (1993), because there is "always more to be said. The point, as a matter of fact, is to keep talking" (p. 179); truth emerges out of therapeutic conversations and confrontations.

Witnessing is an inherently relational process. Pizer (1998) identifies the importance of "neutrality" as the therapist's responsibility to maintain an area for illusion to be negotiated within the psychotherapy relationship. This position ensures preservation of the interplay between reality and fantasy. It helps sustain long periods of "not knowing" and support for the patient's capacity to face previously unassimilable traumatic realities. The intersubjective critique of the illusory and defensive aspects of "the doctrine of neutrality" of classical psychoanalysis (Orange, Atwood, and Stolorow, 1997) has catalyzed appreciation of the reciprocally influencing, co-determining nature of psychotherapy interactions: the therapist's perceptions and perspectives can never be viewed as intrinsically more real or true than the patient's. From a relational perspective, the role of the therapist is not that of neutral purveyor of expert knowledge. Rather, the therapist is a facilitator of transformative conversations, a moderator of benevolent disruptions, a co-processor of unmetabolized pain, helplessness, and terror, and a navigator of creative and disturbing dialogues that assist traumatized patients to expand their imaginations and their repertoire of relatedness to self and others. At the core of this process is an equal honoring of multiple narratives, multiple meanings, and multiple identities (H. Schwartz, 2000). Relationally reformulated neutrality by its very nature disrupts the authoritarian paradigm internalized by dissociative trauma survivors and offers them an opportunity to experience benevolent authority, power-sharing, and mutual respect.

It is impossible to treat survivors of severe childhood trauma and remain morally neutral. Because rape, child abuse, coerced perpetration, and mind control take place in the spheres of sexual, gender, familial, interpersonal, religious and tribal politics, they may be viewed as pathologies of power relations. Consequently, the posture of "neutrality" for clinicians is erroneous when it comes to child abuse, torture, child soldiering, and organized violence against innocents and can be considered a variety of denial (Simpson, 1996). Behaving as if nothing has happened or failing to contextualize it in its largest psychosocial and historical context is not neutrality – neutralizing is not neutrality. Not only is this type of neutralizing a pathological form of denial, these types of omissions enable perpetrators. Simpson states: "No doctor feels bound to be neutral toward cancer. Why should we treat torture, the cancer of freedom, any differently?" (1996:209). Becker's (1996) position supports Simpson's: apolitical treatment of trauma, including the use of some clinical language and attitudes that excessively pathologize and decontexutalize victims' responses and posttraumatic symptoms can mirror the self-justifying attitudes of victimizers.

Challenges to witnessing

From a relational perspective, the therapist witnesses experientially through empathic resonance, dissociative attunement (Hoppenwasser, 2008), projective identifications (Bion, 1965) and through his or her participation in enactments (Aron, 1996; Bromberg, 1994; 1998). Listening to trauma narratives, the therapist's bodily sensations of nausea and pain may alternate with numbing and distraction. The therapist's rage at the patient's perpetrators may be difficult to contain while the patient is rarely even close to anger in his or her initial presentations. Sometimes, during the patient's memory recovery or recounting of traumatic events, the therapist may feel as though he or she is lowering the patient into a dark well and straining to prevent the connecting rope from breaking. When to tug the patient back into the present and when to allow a plummeting fall into the traumatic material is the constant dilemma for clinicians trying to balance dosing, pacing, and containing with the ultimate goal of gently advancing into the pain that the patient has spent his or her entire life trying to avoid. For DID patients the witnessing process is always a double-edged sword, as returning to the scenes and affects of the trauma carries the dual potential for protracted retraumatization as well as the hoped-for transformation.

Witnessing trauma narratives laced with criminality, the roles of victim, perpetrator and collaborator are ambiguous and hard to define. While not taking a morally "neutral" position on criminality per se, clinicians engaged in witnessing complex, polyfragmented narratives that strain credulity can help themselves and their patients by slowing down the process and subjecting the credulity–incredulity dynamic to a sophisticated level of inquiry and observation alongside inquiry into the narrative content itself. In general, the process of ongoing informed consent should include information on memory research concerning the nature and validity of traumatic and other memories, including the effect of torture and mind control on dissociative organization and memory recovering. With sensitivity to the posttraumatic dynamics of shame, therapists also need to understand and help patients' understand, the personified inner conflicts concerning patients' longings to be seen and known, their anticipated negations and humiliations of these longings, and the highly structured regulation of these fears and conflicts built into the dissociative self-system.

All therapists treating severe, complex trauma survivors need to be well-versed in the history of torture and perpetration worldwide so they have a broad context within which to hold and contain the patient's traumatic narratives. In the witnessing process, therapists must be careful not to prematurely foreclose the nature or meaning of any given traumatic event or revelation. They must also be mindful not to avoid inquiry or doubting for fear of alienating, retraumatizing, or abandoning the patient. Both Lacter (2011) and Miller (2012) question the potential pitfalls of therapist abdication under the guise of neutrality, such as telling patients whatever the patient concludes to be true is "entirely up to them." Therapists should let patients know they are prepared to hear and believe whatever the patient tells them but that independence of thought and response are necessary preconditions for dialogue.

When positioning witnessing as a central element of treatment, it is important to remember that retraumatization can take place in any therapy situation. For patients with dissociated injuries, confused histories, mind control, and fragmented memories, the trap of collusion with a therapist's misrecognition or narcissistic needs is a possibility. When a therapeutic posture permits repetition of traumatic non-recognition experiences (non-recognition itself is a form of clinical abandonment according to Bromberg, 1995), it reinforces the patient's false belief that others do not want to know who he or she really is. Ironically the therapist's misrecognition may be felt as a relief since most trauma survivors are ambivalent about being known because of the painful challenge to their identities, bonds, and belief systems. Additionally, based on programmed messages from perpetrator(s), there may be a heightened sense of the danger of approaching intimacy outside of the trauma bonding system. At a deeper level, the failure misrecognition signals drive a wedge of despair into an already despondent and cynical psyche, confirming the abandonment and lack of concern on the part of the adult world that created the traumatic childhood experiences in the first place.

The processes of witnessing and testifying with severely dissociative patients differ from the processes with survivors of collectively experienced adult trauma (e.g., the Holocaust). During psychotherapy, witnessing itself is fragmented, sporadic, and often interspersed with re-enactments and alternate versions of events. The narrative process may be the nonlinear outgrowth of screen memories made up of fragmented images, which themselves can be fragments of memories representing preliminary attempts to historicize (Kornfeld, 1996), all punctuated with revelations of omnipotent fantasies organized by a child-victim struggling to make a less disturbing, less overwhelming meaning of what he or she was experiencing. Sometimes, with DID patients, segments of traumatic experience appear as partial constructions of what may have happened, but the mechanisms adopted by the dissociative survivor patient for psychic survival may mask his or her recognition of them as elements of his or her experience. Sometimes the patient's narcissistic needs and dynamics and developmental conflicts can be obscured behind the drama and fragmentation of memory recovery processes. Other times, segments of memories and testimony may represent perpetrator-implanted beliefs and strategies of obfuscation more than actual history. Only awareness of these potentials, careful scrutiny, and persistent inquiry can reveal the actual torture and mind control events (or other psychological subterfuge) that systematically structuralized false beliefs, or counterfeit meaning, into the survivor's dissociative matrix.

One of the primary challenges for the therapist working with internalized perpetrator identifications is the seemingly paradoxical healing and disruptive aspects of witnessing. The clinician's witnessing can lead to significant progress advances in tandem with the patient's disclosure. It can also lead to dangerous regressions. Polarized aspects of a dissociative self that is further complicated with perpetrator introjects and implants may have different responses to seemingly innocuous clinical interventions involving empathy, witnessing, and compassion. For example, graphic details of abuse can be presented by a patient as a step forward in trust or as a way of seducing, testing, or traumatizing the therapist. Furthermore, graphic aspects of abuse can be withheld as a way of protecting the therapist (and the patient) from the in-depth exploration of what really took place. Implants and obstructive alters can be activated to disrupt therapy in the presence of extremely effective witnessing processes. Dissociative survivors may test therapists to see if therapists can handle their traumatic material by demanding the therapist's immediate and total belief in a given narrative, and/or by doubting and recanting their testimony immediately following disclosure.

Validation and recognition – implicit core aspects of witnessing – are anathema to perpetrator-loyal states, yet life-saving for other constituents of the self. In the cases of patients with complex DID, the vulnerable aspects of the victim's self are longing to accept validation for the suffering they experienced. As validation is accepted, retaliation and shutdown mechanisms may be activated in other perpetrator-identified self-states that are often described as watching over the patient's shoulder in an Orwellian manner, poised to block any opportunity for betrayal of perpetrator mandates. By negating any revelations of victimization and vulnerability, perpetrator-identified states adamantly deny the culpability of the abusers, often blaming other aspects of the patient's self with which they have completely disidentified. These perpetrator states see the other sub-personalities as "not me" and as deserving all the violations that took place.

There are states of mind seeking only conflict-avoidance and anxiety-reduction that do not wish to engage in any discourse that "rocks the boat." These conflict-avoidant, collusive states of mind have little integrity or independent will, and are easily available for activation by both perpetrator-states and victim-states seeking relief from the disruptions of the dissociative status quo. Their ready stockpile of distractions and addictions is impressive. Witnessing can cause victim-states to withdraw in shame. It can cause complicity-states to devalue and distract, and cause perpetrator-states to threaten safety and promote incredulity. An informed and empathic witness becomes a dangerous and subversive "other" to be warded off at any cost.

The dual roles of agent-of-disruption and agent-of-containment challenge the therapist's ability to sustain the patient's faith and trust throughout the process. The task of witnessing should not be abandoned or lost in the chaos of competing psychological interests (e.g., stabilization, present-day life stressors, interpretation of non-traumatic dynamics). However, the paradoxical effects of witnessing can be explained to the patient as a natural aspect of the recovery process that is indispensable to the maturation of observing ego functions and critical thinking skills. Beyond its contradictions, and to its highest aim, effective witnessing shifts the nature of "collaboration" from an unholy secret alliance with perpetrators to a healthy partnership with the therapist.

Chapter 7

Treatment concepts and trajectories

> Life is a process of becoming, a combination of states we have to go through. Where people fail is that they wish to elect a state and remain in it. This is a kind of death.
>
> Anais Nin

The egalitarian, and democratic ethics inherent in the relational tradition stand as an essential contrast to dissociative adaptation and to the ethos of perpetration. Relational modifications to psychoanalytic theory have been shaped in part by the constructivist influences of postmodern philosophy, science and hermeneutics and above all, by the principle of "embeddedness" (Benjamin, 1988; Mitchell, 1995; Rorty, 1989; Spezzano, 1995). Embeddedness regards all observations and understandings as contextual, based on the interpreters' values, assumptions, and concepts of experience. Along with empathic introspection/attunement and an emphasis on the restoration of the patient's affectivity, relational theories propose deconstructing the inevitable enactments that take place between therapist and patient as a primary vehicle for identifying and working through posttraumatic and dissociative patterning. Clinical progress and identity transformation is to a great extent seen as dependent upon the spontaneous emergence of dissociated memories and identities rather than orchestrated memory work or hypnosis-based facilitation; progress follows negotiation of interpersonal and intrapsychic conflict and not on sidestepping or working around transference-countertransference entanglements.

Relational perspectives

Relational psychoanalysis contributes at least six significant dimensions for effectively treating dissociative multiplicity and internalized perpetration.

1. *The relational model of mind views personality as a system of selves in relationship – the unconscious and psychopathology are defined by lack of intactness of self-state linkages*[1] (Aron, 1996; Bromberg, 1998; 2011; Howell, 2011). A major therapeutic commitment involves providing bridging/linking functions so that various

aspects of the patient's psyche, self, history, and identity can be reconfigured without the patient's over-reliance on dissociative solutions and unconscious traumatic re-enactments. Helping the patient co-construct a richer subjective world, the therapist provides a scaffold for the patient's subjective experiencing through reflective listening, improvisational communication, and analysis of enactments. The therapist not only embraces the client's subjectivity but actually deepens the patient's experience of him or herself by giving voice to aspects of the patient's experience, which for numerous reasons (dissociation, programming, denial), are not being felt or represented.

2. *No one set of ideas, feelings, or beliefs should dominate therapeutic interactions.* This ethical and humanistic, philosophical commitment echoes the clinical postures of recognition, inclusion, and mutuality. These postures are absolute essentials for healing psyches ravaged by trauma. The implicit element of inclusion also facilitates integrating diverse theoretical contributions from fields of knowledge outside of psychology and psychiatry.

3. *The therapist and the patient must learn to identify and comment on shifting self-states and disturbing unwelcome experiences in themselves and in the relationship.* Aspects of dissociated enactments occurring within the transference and countertransference matrix are regarded as a product of the patient's psychopathology, and also as reverberations between the therapist and the patient's dissociated self-states (Bromberg, 2009; 2011). The therapist's increased awareness of his or her own denial, dissociation, and avoidance is viewed as essential to treatment progress and for modeling observing ego and critical thinking functions for the patient. Therapists working relationally are encouraged to be as attuned to the subtleties and nuances of their own emotional and visceral responses as they are to tracking the patient's state changes. Clinicians are obliged to create an environment of shared inquiry, shared authority, and eventually mutual recognition and influence without negating the fundamental asymmetrical aspects of the therapy relationship (Aron, 1996). The commitment to humanizing and democratizing the therapy relationship, instead of encumbering it with the unnecessary trappings of a fundamentally patriarchal hierarchy based upon professional expertise (Hedges, 1994) does not preclude the therapist's interpreting and confronting. Therapists should not underestimate the reparative potentials inherent in a relational theoretical posture for the respectful and transformative treatment of dissociative trauma survivors, who have been subjected to extremely malevolent forms of hierarchically-arranged abuse.

4. *Therapists should keep their focus on the patient's subjective experience and question the patient's and their own presumption that the therapist has superior knowledge of the patient's psychodynamics* (Aron, 1996; Orange *et al.*, 1997; Rabin, 1995; Stolorow and Atwood, 1992). This stance invites the patient to become a co-constructor of interpretations and of the therapy process itself and it creates a new context for the negotiation of power dynamics and conflicts in the therapy relationship. Accordingly, surprise, curiosity, improvisation, creativity, and humility become central elements of the treatment process.

5. *Dissociative adaptations to trauma should be compassionately viewed as organizing the individual to prevent further traumatization while maintaining potential for growth and development beyond coping with trauma and its effects* (Bromberg, 1993; Kluft, 1985, 1999; Putnam, 1997; C. Ross, 1997). This reconceptualization of psychopathology helps the survivor to restore his or her dignity while taking responsibility for the unconscious reverberating effects of trauma.

6. *The essence of successful treatment lies in the transformative shift between therapist and patient from "doing to" to "doing with."* Echoing the work of Hoppenwasser (2008) and her concept of "dissociative attunement," and Maroda (1991; 1999) and Ehrenberg (1992) on the creative use of countertransference, successful treatment interrupts and compassionately disrupts (Nachmani, 1995) dissociative automaticity, emotional isolation, and destructive enactments. Encapsulated states and repetitively enacted sequences of domination, complicity, perpetration, and isolation are confronted and identified as such for the purpose of developing a productive form of discourse, and a deeper level of witnessing. In other words, revisioning the meaning of repetitive dissociative enactments replete with fantasies of heroes, villains, torment and retaliation, rescue, betrayal, and alternating feelings of helplessness and entitlement, can lead both therapist and patient to new awareness, to improved interpretive abilities, and to greater emotional attunement.

This group of clinical postures and intentions acknowledges the paradoxical nature of dissociative multiplicity while urging the patient to move beyond a balkanization of his or her mind with its polarized, mutually deceiving factions that attempt to dominate or eradicate each another. Relational treatment challenges forms of internalized irresponsibility and authoritarianism, engaging the patient's development of an internal social "democracy of self" organized around tolerance of internal diversity and intrapsychic conflict. Therapists must help dissociative survivors explore alternatives to their expert avoidance, camouflage, and polarizing skills. Therapists should inspire patients to observe and resolve their perpetrator programming and mind control as well as help patients understand and take ownership of their own disturbing needs and motivations (e.g., power, ambition, mastery, recognition) split off and disavowed within programmed and perpetrator-identified states of mind. In effective relational treatment, containment becomes as important as risk-taking, reflection and improvisation are regarded as equally valuable, and empathic successes should be valued and investigated along with whatever disruptions or "microfractures in communication" (Ferro, 2005) are encountered.[2]

Working relationally

Relational theorists (Aron, 1996; Bromberg, 1994; 1998; Ehrenberg, 1992; Maroda, 1991; 1999) have proposed innovative ways to conceptualize and use the countertransference experience. When urging the therapist to rely on authenticity, and emotional involvement, these theorists recommend working within the re-enactment process rather than pathologizing it, "translating" or interpreting it through the lens of a priori assumptions, or discounting its existence and multiple meanings. The relational theoretical modifications of classical psychoanalytic approaches to trauma address patients in ways that avoid retraumatizing survivors through "experience-distant" interpretation (Kohut, 1971), misunderstanding the nature of resistances, incredulity, or inadvertently compounding the patient's shame and self-blame. Maroda (1991; 1999) believes that in conditions of disruption or impasse, it is important for the therapist to take into account his or her side of the emotional interactions with the patient and to provide a clear experience of mutuality as an alternative to the domination/subjugation paradigm so often characteristic of the patient's family of origin. This clinical posture models a responsible self-observational stance that promotes risk-taking and inquiry.

Relational theorists view the objective of therapy to be the establishment of an interpretive dialogue that can regulate and contain the emotions (and restore affectivity) being defended against by the patient. This simple reformulation places greater responsibility for the quality and freedom of therapeutic discourse on the therapist's emotional availability, and cognitive flexibility, and less emphasis on the patient's overt compliance and communication skills.

Therapy patients want to be known and are always trying to communicate something – even when obfuscating, dissimulating, or enacting programming to avoid revelations. Spezzano (1995) posits that patients specifically want their disturbing affects and representations placed "first in a mind that can manage them" (1995:24). The efficacy of treatment depends on the therapist's ability to create an atmosphere where all of the patient's material and enactments can be welcomed, contained, and explored. Subtle domination or abdication by the therapist is therefore countertherapeutic. The therapist's assertions of unquestionable knowledge and authority along with reluctance to use his or her authority, and minimizing contact with the patient's destructive self-states should be avoided. In addition to cultivating the patient's self-awareness and self-respect, effective treatment involves helping the trauma survivor to experience and understand non-exploitative, mutual, mature – and imperfect – intimate relationships.

The reintegration of basic attachment patterns is essential to recovery from perpetration-induced trauma. Despite differences in clinical orientation, therapists reworking traumatic attachment patterns should consider the dissociative patient's simultaneous and conflicting desires to be witnessed along with the patient's fear or resistance to being known (Bromberg, 1994; H. Schwartz, 1994). When treatment respects this seemingly intractable double bind, it is better positioned to recognize resistance without pathologizing it. The survivor's loyalties to omnipotence-claiming authority figures function as a surrogate for self-cohesion; the necessary disruptions of their ties to bad objects are exceedingly upsetting. The therapist must carefully balance the imperative to challenge a patient's illusions with accepting them and to some degree participating in them (Mitchell, 1993). The therapist must learn to discern, and to help the patient learn to discern resistances which are self-generated (based on natural responses to trauma) apart from those resistances perpetrators have cultivated and implanted. While both types of challenges to treatment are to be interpreted and understood from within the subjective experience of the presenting self-state, perpetrator-implanted resistances need to be approached through specific strategies of deprogramming and not through negotiation and empathic commentary alone.

To help the dissociative survivor, the therapist must adopt a posture that consistently opens up avenues for restorative fantasy and play, especially with themes of destruction, protection, and dependency. The therapist should resist a tendency toward concretization, particularly when the dissociative survivor unconsciously strives for a fantasy-less theater of concrete self- destructive re-enactments or when the patient threatens to drop out of treatment, demands concrete re-parenting, makes an excessive amount of phone calls and/or appointment cancellations, makes demands for prescription drugs, admissions to hospitals, or for other inappropriate special treatment measures. Inexperienced therapists, or those intimidated by the patient may (with the best of intentions) unwittingly participate in perpetuating the defining patterns of pathological multiplicity: intimidation, domination, divided loyalties, perpetrator-victim-complicity re-enactments, inability to surpass concretized thoughts, power imbalances, and false-self construction. Psychotherapy should help the patient develop the capacity to bear and integrate anxiety and psychological conflict by co-creating a space that allows some measure of illusion – an intermediate space – to support the loosening of the binds/identifications with perpetrators and collaborators sustained by rigid defenses and beliefs, drug addictions, psychic numbing, and concrete non-critical thinking. Fostering this intermediate zone, where curiosity about ambiguous identities can take place leads to a synthesis of new meanings built from the patient's expanded awareness of his or her personal history (H. Schwartz, 1994).

How the therapist tolerates painful affect states and remains in contact with both the patient and him or herself will be fundamental to the patient's inter-nalization of new attachment experience. The patient's collisions with the thera-pist's subjectivity, including the therapist's limits and protests about actions and ideologies of hate, self-abuse, and other forms of destructiveness are important to reworking deficits in posttraumatic attachment, aggression, and imaginal capacities. In line with Grand's (2000) views on treatment, the therapist's repu-diation of the patient's destructiveness may be as important, if not more impor-tant, than empathy to the establishment of safety, tolerance for internal diversity, and disruption of domination patterning. Direct experience of the therapist's imperfect human responses of frustration, anger, helplessness, and personal and professional limits, can be a humanizing effect in treatment, even if these encounters sometimes create empathic disruptions requiring subsequent mending (or enactments requiring interpretation) and reworking of trust and attachment conflicts.

The early phases of treating severely dissociative patients can require urgent reactions to the patient's rush to the precipice of self-destruction or violence toward others. During this time, both therapist and patient will be forced to reconsider their identities and worldviews. Because of the ubiquity of abusive power dynamics in survivors' lives, the clinician needs to be adept at attending to the potential replication and unconscious re-enactment of the relational themes of coerced dread, complicity, and helplessness. In this struggle between the paradigms of domination and mutuality, the therapist's defenses will be consistently assaulted. There is no way to shortcut or bypass painful mergers and collisions with the patient's traumatic affects and memories or direct encounters with the cruel and cunning split-off aspects of the patient's self. For the deepest growth to take place, a patient needs to allow him or her self to be a mess within the therapy relationship; and, in order to truly know the patient, the therapist needs to become part of the mess in a way that the therapist can experience internally and viscerally (Chefetz and Bromberg, 2004). Clinicians who are inexperienced in treating victims of evil may have their worldviews and spiritual systems challenged in disturbing, unforeseen ways. Rivera (1996) contended that a commitment to scrupulous personal honesty is the best insurance that therapists will neither burn out or act out toward their tortured and terrorized patients. She identified the need for in-depth consultation and treatment for clinicians whose defenses have never been significantly confronted. As the therapist negotiates the assault on his or her professional competence and most cherished beliefs, he or she can guide the patient to tolerate ambiguity and reconfigure new meaning systems.

Principle of inclusivity

Healthy development involves equal opportunity for all facets of a personality to be recognized and to evolve, regardless of the patient's initial presentation or level of functioning. The principle of inclusivity in the treatment of dissociative trauma survivors is based on the sociological principle of an "inclusive value system" (Miller and Katz, 2002) where diversity is celebrated, and a sense of belonging, respect, and being valued for who one is and what one contributes to the organization of the whole self are established through equal and non-exclusive treatment of all constituents (regardless of background). A posture of inclusivity implies operating through recognition and opposition to dynamics of exclusion and domination. As such, inclusivity represents a significant undermining strategy for the pathological forms of relatedness internalized from one or more perpetrators.

Only direct contact with dissociative self-states, with their alterations in perception, identity, and memory, has the therapeutic power to change the survivor's rigid internal worlds and belief systems. The negotiation of any new sense of identity can occur only when there is creative participation of all of the patient's selves as well as participation of the therapist in the entirety of the patient's dissociative self-system (Bromberg, 1993, 1994; H. Schwartz, 1994), including all perpetrator-engineered states (Miller, 2012). Multiple self-states must be listened to, and negotiated with, and brought into relationship with one another and with the patient's here-and-now reality (Kluft, 1985, 2000; Putnam, 1989; C. Ross, 1997; H. Schwartz, 1994). Direct contact with the affective and perceptual substrate of dissociative part-selves allows the therapist to penetrate the trance logic or rigidified belief system contained in that self-state, to ascertain the historical events, perpetrator messages, and fantasies that have consolidated the cognitions and motivations of that state, and to gently disrupt the rigidities within the patient's entire self-system. Honoring diversity, this inclusive approach to the psyche respects the balance in psychological life of unity and multiplicity and of the literal and the metaphorical. In contrast to other treatment approaches, relational models emphasize a nonlinear progression of healing, along with the increasing ability for patients to function comfortably and creatively with internal conflicts and psychological diversity. Therapeutic success is reflected in patients' increased tolerance for the ambiguous and the unresolvable.

The therapist must support the patient's efforts to sustain the struggle between (and dialogues among) divergent aspects of the self to help start the shift away from dissociation to a non-pathological capacity to sustain the tensions inherent in intrapsychic conflict (Bromberg, 1993). This process requires not only confrontations with the patient's dissociative habits of mind and relatedness but also acknowledges the patient's fears about surrendering them (Bromberg, 1994). Initially intimidating collisions between opposing or previously negating self-states can eventuate into true conversation, and, sometimes, cooperation. This process will likely be fraught with enactments and power struggles based on the dissociative self-system's intricate self-reinforcing tendencies, especially when programming is involved.

Helping the dissociative survivor renegotiate his or her internal world requires the therapist to urge the patient's alter personalities who were intimidated, and reflexively collusive to negotiate with alters who have been cruel, and obstructionistic. The vulnerable alters must connect with their underlying aggression and moral outrage, while the cruel and malevolent self-states must eventually connect to their own fragility, grief, and regret for exploitation and deception. These goals, like those of all relationally-oriented treatments, are accomplished through immersion in, and survival of, the transference-countertransference matrix of feelings, fantasies, enactments, and memories and the patterns and insights they reveal. In this "forum of healing," stewarding the dissociative survivor's reconciliation of internal opposites can lead to mutual reflection and depolarization, fostering true self-direction and freedom of mind.

Successful treatment of internalized perpetration inevitably involves substantial engagement with hostile (and perpetrator-identified) aspects of the patient where an invitation into the intersubjective dialogue can be experienced as safe and containing for all aspects of the patient's self. In this protected field, extremes of the patient's aggression (and aggression-avoidance) can be renegotiated through recognition, and limit-setting. The accumulation of such engagements (where anger is observed in dialogue rather than acted out, where fighting is safe, where creative expression replaces robotic or repetitive hostile displays), gently disrupts the sense of omnipotence that organizes and orchestrates dissociative life. Aggressive alter personalities who boast about their sense of power will begin to accept feelings of vulnerability; compliant part-selves cowering before conflict or any revelation of their own sadism will become acquainted with the creative processes of diplomacy, assertion, resistance, and confrontation. The diverse array of aggressive responses, from the most benign passive-aggressive coping mechanisms to the most vicious and calculating actions, eventually must come to be owned by all of the part-selves as "ours" instead of being denied, justified, or bandied about among alters like a hot potato. Within this transformative container, multiple realities held by different self-states can find opportunities for linkage (Bromberg, 1994; 1998). Through the quality of language that emerges from participation in, and mutual reflection on, the patient's enactments, cognitive symbolization actually supplants the dissociative language often used by the patient to manage his or her self (selves) to avert the danger at once denied and anticipated.

Two important commitments a therapist can consistently offer a dissociative patient are an understanding of the patient's impact on the therapist, and an unyielding stance against all forms of domination, coercion, and destructiveness. The most valuable commitment a survivor can offer the therapist and the therapy project is a deep and unremitting interest and curiosity about the truth – even when the truth is hard to establish and/or painful. The dissociative survivor of coerced perpetration trauma will be making huge strides when he or she exchanges all forms of intimidation and collusion with a consistent, rebellious stand against all forms of deception and irresponsibility by the self-system, perpetrators, and society. Identification with the therapist's power (to access feelings, subvert denial, contain destructiveness, disrupt collusion, unmask deception, value differences, support vulnerability) and identification with the benevolent use of that power, constitutes a central intrapsychic and relational shift that contrasts with the patient's compulsive use of automatized, dissociative solutions to anticipated retraumatization. Difficult as it may seem at first, the survivor must come to believe that the therapist/therapy relationship could actually be as powerful as the perpetrators, or more so – and that the therapist's power is accessible and shareable, and not aligned with subjugation or sacrifice.

The therapist may be the first individual with whom all parts of the dissociative patient experience a relationship, the first to sustain a current and ongoing reality for all the self-states. The therapist may become the first transitional object (Winnicott, 1971) the dissociative patient has ever experienced – "the first constant object ... the first lighthouse, first North Star" (Marmer, 1996:201). In Marmer's analysis, the fulfillment of relational needs can activate transitional fantasy functions that may allow the patient to reorganize him or herself in a more integrated fashion for the first time. The therapist may be the first person to enter the mind of the survivor with permission and respect. As each alter internalizes the therapist's attitudes of inclusion and acceptance, along with the therapist's challenges to dissociative relatedness, the therapist eventually can be experienced as a unified transitional object instead of a collection of partial transitional objects mirroring the patient's inner fragmentation and dividedness.

Essential therapeutic postures

More than any array of therapeutic techniques, it is the therapist's direct or indirect transmission of the therapist's own values that holds the greatest potential to transform the patient's rigid dissociative matrix. This view is in line with Ferro's (2005) reconceptualization of the therapeutic process – "to transmit the method" – wherein the therapist helps patients develop an alternate apparatus for thinking, allowing them to be in a better position to process their emotional experience on their own. The therapist

> thus presents him or herself as a person capable of listening, understanding, grasping and describing the emotions of the field and as a catalyst of further transformations – on the basis that there is not *an unconscious to be revealed*, but a capacity for thinking to be developed, and that the development of the capacity for thinking allows closer and closer contact with previouslynonnegotiable areas. [...T]he analyst does not decode the unconscious but brings about a development of the conscious mind and a gradual broadening of the unconscious [...] as a probe that broadens the field it is exploring.
>
> (p. 102)

These key relational-based therapeutic postures and clinical commitments include:

- Fostering mutuality, inclusivity, and interconnectedness (restoring linking functions)
- Supporting the dismantling of internalized patterns of domination and complicity
- Articulating and embracing all of the patient's dissociative states (in recognition and dialogue), regardless of the degree of concretization, primitivity, or apparent threat
- Encouraging restorative fantasy and development of transitional experiencing/potential space over repetitive and concrete self-defeating solutions
- Fostering the patient's use of aggression in the service of the self rather than against the self or in service to perpetrator(s)

- Supporting the patient's questioning of the therapist's authority and understanding the patient's challenges to societal failures, hypocrisies, and betrayals
- Helping the patient to better tolerate ambiguity and paradox
- Restoring the patient's capacity for healthy self-assertion, self-protection, and discernment (including ownership of ruthlessness and ambition and needs for recognition encapsulated in perpetrator states)
- Supporting the patient in identifying and metabolizing fragments of helplessness, pain, dread, and terror
- Expanding the patient's capacity for freedom of association and freedom of thought (restoring critical thinking and capacity for imagination and improvisation)
- Reconciling the patient's original innocence and guilt, with perpetrator-created culpability
- Encouraging the grieving and mourning of lost life experience, past crimes against others, and the cumulative effects of self-destructive behavior
- Helping the patient to discern the difference between self-generated dissociative identities, and belief systems and those which have been implanted or conditioned by perpetrators through torture and mind control technologies
- Developing more flexible psychological organizing principles, expanding and enriching the repertoire of relatedness to self and others
- Developing a unified observing ego, balancing internalized limits with internalized compassion
- Undoing patterns of learned helplessness, unconscious complicity, and abdication
- Working through programming
- Assisting the patient in restoring narrativity, historicity, affectivity
- Helping the patient to obtain a meta-cognitive perspective on the trauma history and construction of the dissociative self-system
- Facing existential and spiritual issues regarding the self and human nature; restoring healthy spirituality
- Rejuvenating the patient's mythopoetic imagination
- Helping patients to learn to live in the present: finding, creating, and tolerating joy, meaningful work, and interrelatedness in a life that is governed neither by posttraumatic symptoms nor the injunctions of perpetrators nor the negations of collaborators

Treatment trajectory

The flow of relational psychotherapy for complex trauma survivors is a nonlinear road with peaks and valleys, plateaus, switchbacks, and unexpected changes in climate. When successful, the therapy dyad moves from initial states of isolation and confusion through an uneasy détente between hope and dread, and eventually into a sphere of genuine intimacy and mutual respect. Some patients never develop past the preliminary steps and make only modest headway before losing momentum and sliding backwards. Others persevere through long-term treatment, make noticeable progress, and yet never reach higher levels of integration. A small number of survivors, exemplified by Ishmael Beah (2007), transcend their bondage and achieve full actualization; in the most exceptional cases, their triumphs gain popular notice through their ascendance as masterful advocates, educators, artists, or healers.

The treatment trajectory for internalized perpetrator self-states includes three basic phases,[3] each of which is examined in rough chronological order in the pages that follow:

- Restabilization and Informed Consent
- Deprogramming and Restoration of Critical Thinking
- Integration

Restabilization and informed consent

It is important for the therapist to clearly introduce new expectations for the patient's therapy, once perpetration dynamics have become apparent. The patient must make a commitment to help the therapist access and negotiate with perpetrator states in order to supplant longstanding patterns of default to dissociative flight or conditioned collapse into inaction. The revelations and processing of internalized perpetration may prompt a return to previous dysfunctional coping mechanisms – substance addictions, shoplifting, workaholism, self-injury, threatening termination, or dangerous sexual acting-out – that had ostensibly been "laid to rest" by earlier therapy. The therapist and patient can reactivate previous safety contracts or create new ones containing constructive alternatives for self-harm if patients feel too endangered, with a hierarchy of actions to be pursued before emergency actions are invoked (Howell, 2011). Helping patients learn to discern the different meanings (and origins) of states of self-destructive impulses and feelings (or lack of feeling as the case may be) and understanding the distinction between self-generated versus perpetrator-conditioned self-states are essential at this juncture. The essence of all re-negotiations of safety (or safety contracts), as Courtois (1999) explains, is to help the patient assume control of, and to take responsibility for, his or her own safety while taking the therapist out of the role of reparenting or rescuing agent.

Informed consent involves helping the patient cope with the stress following abreactions, and discussing what to expect from accessing and working through perpetrator-engineered self-states, and how this work may differ from previous treatment dynamics involving memory, attachment, and aggression. Specifically, patients need to be prepared for potential encounters with extreme robotic and malevolent states. Anticipating the emergence within the patient of intense shame, alienation, arrogance, and disconnection from attachments to the therapist can help mitigate some of the compelling power of these states. The therapist's holding and containing functions are strengthened when the patient and therapist work cooperatively within established frameworks used by clinicians confronting internalized perpetration and mind control, including accessing hierarchies of alter personalities, "fail-safes," and deconstructing perpetrator deceptions (Lacter, 2011; Miller, 2012). Patients are often comforted by clinicians' demonstrating knowledge of perpetrator patterns. Although the therapist's knowledge might arouse conditioned paranoia in some patients, the demystification and normalization of programming and traumatic bonding can ease the survivor's sense of intimidation and isolation and make difficult revelations easier to bear.

Informed consent at this point has psycho-educational benefits and, more importantly, it protects the rights of the patient. Deliberate renewals of informed consent create a scaffolding of mutual respect and trust between patient and clinician. As an example, repeatedly attaining explicit permission from the patient for the therapist's inquiry to progress into shame-based psychological zones that are encapsulated by conditioned avoidance or mind-control is an important respectful practice. Preparing the patient for possible aversive or resistant reactions prior to such inquiry can also be quite useful in facilitating the patient's anxiety management and observing ego functions; this practice supports the therapeutic alliance by avoiding an unconscious repetition of the overstimulation, intrusion, or domination-compliance dynamics of the original traumatic conditioning. The clinician's knowledge about perpetrators' impact on victims' psyches will help advance the patient's self-investigation, as will an examination of the legacy of the abuser's methods of ensuring compliance. Focused attention must be brought to bear on cultivating critical thinking skills to enable the patient to take a higher vantage point from which his or her own behaviors and habits of mind may be more clearly assessed and modified. Informed consent always involves negotiations with the patient as to what the various parts of the self are ready to, or able to, handle, including unpacking the patient's deeper conflicts about sharing information (Howell, 2011), exposing vulnerability, and facing demonized aspects of the self.

Deep memory work and catharsis are unadvisable during this preliminary recognition and orientation phase. It is crucial to make initial inquiries into the nature and location of psychological landmines in the form of suicidal, homicidal, "return," and informer programming (or more subtle adhesive attachment to perpetrator feelings and beliefs). The therapist should help the patient observe and deactivate "cloaking" devices that have been implanted to protect loyalty to perpetrator secrets. The therapist should begin to introduce alternatives to dissociative compartmentalization as more "lateral internal dialogues" slowly unseat dysfunctional hierarchies fashioned by the abuser(s). Such an emphasis can disrupt tendencies to forget sessions or re-dissociate important material or breakthroughs.

The dissociative web redistributes traumatic anxieties, annihilation fears and fantasies, and unbearable meanings to contain that which might otherwise have led to a breakdown or to stop movement toward a more dysfunctional mental state. If the patient's dissociative geometry is exposed prematurely, that is before enough capacity is developed to handle the psychic earthquakes attendant on the deconstruction process, the patient will likely take flight, generate a series of crises, or find other ways to stalemate the treatment. Yet as the therapist is drawn deeper into the patient's world of disabling relational patterns, the therapist might be seduced to prematurely act or "cure" the patient of his or her unrelatedness as quickly as possible (Bromberg, 1995). Foisting too much reality on the patient too soon is, in fact, a survival strategy for therapists who feel they are losing their own minds in the turbulent, fragmented treatment process.

Deprogramming and restoration of critical thinking

The processes of deprogramming (including abreaction, identity reconfiguration, discernment, boundary reconfiguration, accessing perpetrator injunctions, implants, and engineered states) defines the middle phase of treatment for internalized perpetration. Integrating relational approaches with deprogramming strategies can seem theoretically and technically confusing to clinicians because the two approaches may at first appear contradictory: relational therapy embraces ambiguity, nonlinearity, and improvisation while deprogramming recommends the use of some structured/guided interventions. Although each therapist will likely find his or her own unique way of handling the challenges of deprogramming, success will inevitably involve finding the balance (and appropriate pacing and timing) in the use of psycho-education, recontextualization, abreaction, interpretation, analyzing enactments, active imagination, and accessing perpetrator-implants.

Deprogramming involves reconfiguring the patient's false sense of omnipotence and unworthiness; restoring affectivity; activating the patient's critical thinking abilities; remembering and systematically analyzing the perpetrator's inculcated messages, identities, behavioral chains, secrets, tactics, obfuscations, mystifications, and values; and cultivating an informed protest response. Effective deprogramming also assists other, prosocial aspects of the patient's self to accept and own their rejected feelings and motivations (i.e., power, ruthlessness, recognition) contained in perpetrator-identified and programmed states. During this phase, the patient's blind acceptance of the perpetrator's definition of his or her identity gradually shifts to embrace the therapist's compassionate alternative perspectives. Lively disagreement about many philosophical issues, and confrontation of ideologies of destructiveness and hate (as well as acting out and threatening behavior) may become important aspects of the deprogramming process.

During the "conversion" process, the therapist helps the patient to hold contradictory identities and histories in his or her mind without polarizing, foreclosing, or dissociating. Therapists must maintain a parallel process of patiently maintaining space for the experiences of confusion and ambiguity that result. The therapy dyad should take care not to foreclose on the discourse prematurely, nor offer superficial praise of the patient's efforts, simplistic explanations, or facile absolution. This extension of inquiry allows the patient to reach a still more expansive position where deeper resolution may be attained. A great deal of perseverance is required on the part of the therapist to wrestle with the patient's self-damnation and attendant rejection of his or her core innocence.

Many mind-control survivors report that their will and spirit were the most sought-after prizes of their abusers (Lacter, 2011). To obtain these victories, perpetrators mystify and manipulate victims using a variety of programming tactics to foster their victims defining themselves as evil or unworthy of belonging anywhere else but with their perpetrators. Lacter maintains that newly formed, highly vulnerable and receptive *tabula rasa* self-states emerging from conditions of severe torture "naturally" attach to perpetrators. The perpetrator is their significant other, and sometimes their only significant other. "Good-cop/bad-cop" set-ups and intermittent reinforcement schedules are deliberately used by perpetrators to fortify attachment bonds; "child victims excuse and dissociate massive amounts of abuse in order to earn a pittance of highly conditioned love" (p. 96). Because programmers understand that genuine loving bonds are a significant threat to ongoing control of the victim, they seek to extinguish all hope for, or sense of deserving, love. In these compelling confabulated scenarios, protectors may be made to appear as abusers and vice versa. Numerous set-ups are created to destroy the victim's trust in (or belief in the potential of) protective, redemptive, or benevolent authority. Anti-God injunctions, possession states, spirit entrapment, and torture blamed on, or connected to, God and satan are common features of this kind of programming reported by survivors around the world (Noblitt and Perskin, 2000; C. Ross, 1995; H. Schwartz, 2000; Sinason, 1994, 2011a; M. Smith, 1993). Anti-attachment and "resistance programming" are used to squelch all loving bonds, to firmly establish chaotic and anxious attachment patterns, and to create a world limited to hate, sadism, and persecution. Combined, these methods facilitate the construction of an anti-social psychic structure and a willing perpetrator (Lacter, 2011). Accessing and then undoing behavioral and ideological programs, which have been traumatically installed into the psyche of the victim, becomes a primary goal for the intermediate phase of treatment of internalized perpetration.

During deprogramming, the therapy dyad accesses overwhelming memories and affect states which have been induced under the stress of double-bind "choices" and violent initiation experiences. Memory work of this kind is the most daunting challenge of trauma treatment. Patients must confront perilous – sometimes nearly lethal – ordeals from their pasts where extraordinary physical and emotional torment annihilated the self's prior integration. Unearthing and revisiting the annihilation experience is tantamount to psychic death; successful negotiation of this passage will require considerable stamina, trust, and commitment. Chefetz (1997) underscores the central role in treatment of the re-accessing affect: without re-experiencing through remembering the emotional aspect of abusive events and pathological communications, the survivor's history remains incoherent and bereft of meaning. Yet avoiding all traumatic affects and reminders of the trauma are what the entire shame-avoidant, dissociative self-system has been constructed to accomplish. Thus the patient's fears (and programming about) of the destructive power of feelings and vulnerability must be deeply understood and effectively analyzed. Memory, affect, and meaning must all be part of the reconfiguration of traumatic experience during and after abreaction. Along these lines, Howell (2011) reminds clinicians that abreactions should be relational, not merely cathartic. That is, what is most essential about abreactions is the communication of emotions, memory, meaning, and distress to another human being, and not just affective discharge. With the integration of each memory, the patient's sense of individuation is strengthened, advancing the restoration of self-esteem, empowerment, and dignity.

This demanding aspect of treatment helps the patient face the complex dynamics involved in exploring previous claims of having enjoyed participating in acts of perpetration. Clinicians should pay close attention to the delivery of such declarations which may have as many as five functions:

- a defense against shame and guilt;
- magical thinking that violence can be exchanged for power or other rewards;
- a self-hypnotic device to ward-off weakness when perpetrating;
- fabricating a sense of strength and mastery through aggressive hardening; and,
- "liking violence" can actually mean "liking it" for its own sake.

Self-states of DID patients that have been significantly organized around sadistic behavior or gestated in the field of torture-based mind control may demonstrate a profound and relentless craving for violent fantasies, verbalizations, and behavior.[4] Relating the experience of glorifying perpetration to a kind of sexualized pleasure, Straker (2007) calls the excitement experienced in the annihilation of a human being and the raging, unchecked expression of primitive impulses, "an awful *jouissance*" (p. 155).[5] For uninitiated clinicians who have not treated war veterans or survivors of torture and collective violence, it is difficult to accept the truth of a human being's potential for addiction to the adrenaline "rush" of bloodlust, torture, and murder. When any of these aspects of "liking violence" are found inside the psyches of survivors of coerced perpetration they must be normalized, contextualized, demystified, and integrated. This work provides the thin edge of the wedge for advancing the treatment of perpetrator-induced cognitive distortions.

Deprogramming perpetrator injunctions

The essential process of deprogramming involves inquiry into the injunctions and indoctrination practices used during and immediately after traumatization by abusers. Ideological motivations, deceptions, and perpetrator footprints laid down in the survivor's psyche must be reviewed and demystified. The therapist's open-ended inquiry concerning perpetrator alters' specific jobs and roles within the self-system, including wondering what might happen if the specific role or function were unfulfilled or changed, is useful in cultivating critical thinking (Miller, 2012). Similarly, gentle but probing questions and comments about the perpetrator state's values and beliefs related to topics such as slavery, child abuse, obedience, freedom, power, and integrity may eventually disrupt their cognitive rigidities and introduce healthy doubt and inspire individuation from adhesive authoritarian identifications. It is essential to abreact specific memories, unfreeze affects, and foster catharsis in order to gain access to, and deactivate, implanted programming; this process facilitates the dissolution of barriers separating disso-ciated alter identities. The many self-deceptions that mask the inculcated beliefs implanted by the perpetrator(s) must be made transparent to allow deconstruc-tive reflection and dialogue. Clinicians must become skilled interviewers to disen-tangle the specific conflations and reversals that have undermined a victim's autonomy.[6]

Some conflated themes requiring analysis and deprogramming that therapists are likely to encounter are:

- Humility and humiliation
- Identity and actions
- Truth and propaganda
- Guilt and blame
- Self-directed action and coerced action
- Strength and force
- Punishment and justice
- Hedonism and satisfaction
- Independence and self-indulgence
- Vulnerability and disgrace
- Intimacy and violation
- Independence and betrayal
- Freedom and death
- Freedom and terror
- Autonomy and abandonment
- Loyalty and servitude
- Healing and death
- Love and disgust
- Loyalty and self-punishment
- Failure and death
- Valuing lives and controlling lives

Getting to the root of patients' ideological, spiritual, and psychological misun-derstandings is essential to the psychic extrication process that ultimately liberates patients from the totalitarian gulag in which they were imprisoned in childhood.

Blind obedience and dissociative surrender to perpetrator dogma are subverted by emancipatory dialogue and healthy intrapsychic conflict. The patient's experience of safe (nonviolent, nonretaliatory) arguments and disagreements with the therapist is essential to the establishment of a transformative container for deprogramming, and for transmision of new relationship patterns. The clinician should not aim to replace one set of doctrines with another but rather to create an unbounded psychological space where multiple points of view may be impartially (and mutually) evaluated. When rigid dissociative interpretations of traumatic events (especially coerced perpetration), which were previously held in stagnant isolation, are reevaluated and redefined, the deconstruction of malevolent programming begins and psychological space is made for a healthier reconstruction of identity. Successful deprogramming culminates in a celebration of the spontaneous and improvised elements of life.

Goals and challenges of deprogramming

Where mind control and malignant attachments are concerned, the goal of therapy is to enable the state-bound commands, beliefs, identifications, and automatized mind/body reactions to be accessed, deconditioned (unlearned), demystified, and integrated (Conway, 1994). Whether referred to as deprogramming, correcting cognitive errors, breaking trauma bonds, illuminating unconscious organizing principles, or reversing brainwashing, Brandchaft (1994: 57) felicitously calls the process "freeing the spirit from its cell." By whatever name, it presupposes belief in the fundamental importance of individual autonomy, including a subjective sense of agency, critical thinking, and the capacity for protest. To accomplish this, all manner of perpetrator(s) deceptions and methodologies must be unmasked and deconstructed. This is difficult and laborious because the abusers usually layer mind-control programming with suicidal and homicidal thought-behavior patterns. Perpetrators also encapsulate dissociative states in drugged conditions that block access in the therapy setting, program memory loss, and this often leaves the patient terrified of recalling the points where splits under torture were created.

The goal of thought reform, whether in the incest family or in the criminal or military cartel, is the same: gaining control over the individual and his or her identity and dissociative states to establish the greatest degree of compliance and the greatest degree of silence. The more complex the actions expected of the victim, the more elaborate is the shaping and structuring of the dissociative system. To counteract these effects, the therapist must create an atmosphere of safety so that the patient can choose to begin crossing the amnestic barriers constructed by the perpetrating agent(s) and the colluding social systems. Survivors' relationships with themselves must come to be regarded as more important than those with family or any other group or religious system (including the theoretical system of the therapist). Unless the therapist understands and repeatedly contextualizes the patient's unavoidable shame over his or her victimization and loss of free will, the working-through process will be stymied and the reciprocally reinforcing unconscious protection system between victim and perpetrator will not be exposed and undermined. The therapist must apprehend, and help the patient to apprehend, the reversals of trust/distrust and safety/danger produced when perpetrator-manipulated shame is at the root of dissociative identities. The therapist must help the patient value feelings at least as much as thoughts; doctrine and logic must be circumvented by exposing double binds and the explicitly deceptive practices of the perpetrator(s). The therapy relationship itself must be simultaneously exposed to the same scrutiny. Any doubts or fears the patient has about the therapist or the clinical practices must be immediately and sensitively addressed, and when possible, the patient's perceptions must be validated. When extremely negative or distorted, perpetrator alters' perceptions of the therapist must be investigated with curiosity and neutrality. This posture promotes tolerance of ambiguity, demonstrates flexible authority, and allows the patient's healthy (versus conditioned) doubt and internal attachment conflicts to emerge naturally.

Until all destructive messages are verbalized and the context of their inculcation recalled (when possible), unprocessed injunctions from the perpetrator continue to control the victim-survivor's identity and self-esteem and to some extent his or her behavior. Beyond the restoration of affectivity – the capacity to sob, to rage, to feel gratitude and hope, and to tolerate helplessness and despair – the essence of "deprogramming" involves accessing perpetrator-shaped dissociative identities and belief systems and linking their existence to the observing ego capacities of an integrated self. The therapist and patient should maintain a reflective focus on the patient's (and therapist's) automatic (and somatic) state changes, extreme shifts between feeling and deadness or between terror and blankness, and the patient's rapid changes in feelings toward the therapist and vice versa. Specifically, a patient's sudden, intense and unexpected or intrusive homicidal and suicidal feelings, or uncanny flight reactions may, if reflected on and not acted upon, reveal perpetrator-implanted thought patterning. This is not, however, to suggest that patient and therapist avoid intense rage and hate emerging in the transference by gratuitously labeling these emotions "programming."

The cognitive dissonances stimulated by therapy dialogues inevitably lead to great anxiety and turmoil in the survivor which, when navigated ineffectively, may propel the patient into a speedy retreat to the security of the old belief systems, regardless of how absurd or destructive the beliefs might be (Brandchaft, 1994). Hence, this reparative discourse must take place in a relationship ambience where the therapist consistently communicates that the individual's free will and free choice will be respected at all times. Even the freedom to return to his or her abusive original group/family or to sustain a particular belief system must remain a free choice. The therapist and patient must empathically understand and disrupt cognitive distortions, mutually reflect on the methods and intentions of the captors/perpetrators, and help the survivor understand his or her adaptations to authoritarian arrangements. They also must learn to tolerate the ambiguity whereby the therapist is regarded as simultaneously or alternatingly a potential liberator and a new form of captor/perpetrator/torturer. Similarly, the therapist will have to tolerate the patient's shifts among moments of self-liberation and threatening and intimidating behavior, or both overt and subtle efforts to make the therapist the object of thought reform and mind control.

Attempts to integrate the effects of mind control programming will require the patient (and therapist) to face disturbing realities about the existence and nature of evil, raising intense anxiety and unsettling fears about the fragilities of selfhood and the illusory nature of security in the self and society. Most difficult to confront is the deep shame that surfaces when the patient becomes fully aware someone has stolen his or her mind (sometimes subjectively experienced as something he or she has given away, sold out, or "sold to the devil"). The realization that one has been completely deceived and subjugated leaves in its wake a haunting recognition of the self's vulnerability. Struggling with this unbearable awareness, survivors of mind control tend to be more angry at the absence of something in themselves (something they imagine should have been there to protect them), than at their families or at society for perpetrating or colluding in child exploitation. Sometimes, their anger is at God for not intervening or for allowing such atrocities to go on in the world; however, this can be a potential precursor to a beneficial reconfiguring point formed with abandonment rage and a re-allocation of responsibility – to willingly include an other in the narrative. This anger at various divinities can only become useful if it is encouraged to enter prolonged dialogue and not if it is a knee-jerk response or part of spiritual programming. Because mind control programming happens under rigid conditions and in absolute isolation, the intrusion of otherness (or the fantasy of otherness) – from the therapist and/or spirit world – can be a very powerful antidote that arouses dormant critical thinking. Awakening from delusion and deception is never an easy task. For many, feeling the pain of catastrophic disappointment with betraying authorities is regarded by the patient as worth avoiding at any cost because that disappointment is associated with feelings of collapse and annihilation.

The treatment of thought reform and traumatic bonding cannot take place simply on the insight or psychoeducational levels, important as they are. Essential for providing the framework of a powerful "new object" or "emotionally corrective experience" are the therapist's consistent disarming of the dissociative self-protective system through: empathic resonance and empathic introspection; authentic and spontaneous use of emotional presence and authenticity; a sense of humor; persistent challenges to the automaticity of both patient and therapist's response patterns; repudiation of destructiveness and sadistic ideologies; use of language that enlivens rather than deadens therapy dialogues; and maintaining a therapeutic posture that welcomes protest, disagreement, and discourse about the patient's experience of the therapist.

Therapists unfamiliar with the dynamics of perpetrators, sadistic groups and subcultures, or authoritarian systems may be at a disadvantage in understanding the thinking and relationship dynamics of survivors of coerced perpetration. They may misrecognize the common patterns of impermeability and they may misunderstand the layering phenomenon whereby self-generated dissociative identities strategically mask the existence of perpetrator-structured dissociative states. They may directly or indirectly disparage (or submit to) the patient. Comfort and collusion may unwittingly replace inquiry and negotiation as urgent anxiety management stalemates the treatment process. Therapists may become so frustrated at the other end of dialogues with dissociative mind control victims who do not know they are mind control victims that the inevitable trans-ferential assaults on the therapist's hope, faith, and capacity for critical thinking become unbearable. Therapists may find it difficult to avoid chronic worry, irritabilty, and the impulse to encourage the patient to restore observing ego functions too rapidly when states of mindlessness and robotism emerge in an otherwise responsive and/or intelligent individual. DID patients working through complex mind control programming need to pass in and out of the states of mindlessness and deadness (that originated as a result of the original trauma and mind control) in order to link up all of the previously separated self-states. However, mind control survivor patients desperately fear that re-experiencing these extreme states will entrap them forever in destructive urges and beliefs, and therapists' reassurances to the contrary may not always feel reliable and trustworthy.

To be effective in disrupting mind control, the therapist must begin relation-ships with, and facilitate dialogues with, these unfeeling unreflective parts of the self (including the "cult alters" and "perpetrator alters") and help the patient (as a whole person) to own these mentally impoverished and thoroughly indoctri-nated self-states. The patient should not be encouraged to avoid or disavow self-states in fear of losing the therapist's respect by revealing part-selves who are automatons, prostitutes, couriers, kidnappers, mind-controllers, torturers, or kill-ers. Many dissociative patients are afraid to think out loud or mention the cues, triggers, trainings, directives, and specifics of their mind control programs, for fear doing so could lead to their acting on suicidal or homicidal feelings or to their regressing to mindlessly enacting the structured identities or behavior patterns. Dissociative survivors are also afraid that the therapist will abandon them after the horrors (and identities) are revealed. It is only by directly facing these fears that a patient and therapist can co-create a safe environment of suffi-cient trust and shared power to overcome the real and imagined dominion of the perpetrators in the patient's mind and their coercive influence on the patient's emotional and spiritual life.

Therapists who treat severely dissociative patients equipped solely with fanta-sies of restoration and reparenting may be forgetting survivors have experienced repeated failures of attachment and a lack of meaningful, protective, well-bound-aried relationships. Because, survivors suffered explicit torture aimed at altering their psyches and souls to the core, avoiding the individual's distrust and rage with reparenting strategies is only a temporary and, in fact, doomed effort.

Overnurturing and overdirection can reinforce counterproductive compliance, eclipse paradoxical experiencing, collapse intersubjectivity, subvert mutuality, and perpetuate embedded sadomasochistic relationship patterns. These countertransference enactments implicitly foreclose sitting with the patient's despair and helplessness.

Deprogramming should not be considered something outside of, or adjunctive to, psychotherapy or psychoanalysis, nor should it be mystified or associated solely with cult-related phenomena. Critical thinking, healthy assertion and agency, and the capacity to belong to, and relate to, others out of choice and not out of desperation (or command injunctions) are goals of therapy that cut across all modalities and all symptomatology (or diagnoses). The patient needs to establish a strong empathic bond and a relatively stable trust (where distrust can be safely discussed) with a therapist who is seen as both powerful and compassionate. Indeed, the power of a healthy therapeutic relationship is usually underestimated by those who program children and by the survivor as well.

New forms of grieving and mourning will inevitably follow as the dissociative survivor recovers memories of myriad betrayals and manipulations that had co-opted his or her will. Survivors need an enormous amount of patience and understanding from therapists for working through the intense shame that accompanies recognition of mind control subjugation. While taking responsibility (without guilt, blame, or judgment) for the co-creation of traumatic bonding as a survival solution with its resulting vulnerability to thought reform, the survivor must come to accept the truth of his or her helplessness and powerlessness in the authoritarian or abusing system. This acceptance applies especially to the alter personalities within the system who are most identified with power, omnipotence, and privilege. Ultimately, all patients must be helped to realize recovery from mind control and separation/individuation from the traumatic matrix is a potent form of self-love that is also the most constructive, permanent form of retaliation against one's abusers (H. Schwartz, 2000).

As destructive attachments are slowly released and risk is taken informing new kinds of relationships, the cast of characters in the dissociative patient's subjective world changes, and the possibility of a new life emerges. The patient will experience a new sense of connectedness with others but also, paradoxically, he or she will experience a new type of non-traumatic aloneness. This positive but disorienting aloneness is related to having autonomy, boundaries, responsibilities, and freedom for the first time. Critical thinking replaces betrayal blindness, dissociative flight. When human malevolence and evil is faced consciously for the first time by the patient – including in the presence of someone willing to witness atrocity without turning away – a form of human benevolence is experienced by the patient, and the necessary inner strength is created to face his or her history. Rigid thought reform and beliefs based on viewing the self through the eyes of the perpetrator or through the collaborating family members and society, or the misrecognitions of the unenlightened mental health system, can be replaced by an ability to more accurately detect deception and betrayal in interpersonal affairs, and most of all by an ability to consider multiple perspectives. This includes tolerating the anxiety of "not knowing" without collapsing into rigid, arrogant, and other defensive postures learned in the context of traumatic captivity.

The fundamental transformation of severe dissociative disorders and most traumatically bonded individuals takes place when the mystification of the omnipotent is replaced by a healthy respect for, and valorization of, the more mundane yet enormously powerful forces involved in human compassion and mutual respect. More than any technical procedure or therapeutic stance, the enduring power of a compassionate human bond that can survive the vicissitudes of traumatic transference/countertransference enactments and polarizations leads to the disempowerment of the internalized traumatic bonding and to the disarming of mind control programming. It is the therapy relationship, not a theory or a series of techniques, that results in the trauma victim's empowerment as a thinking, feeling, protesting, witnessing, working, remembering agent.

Integration

Integration is a subtle ongoing process where new experiences of empathy and mutuality restructure a personality previously organized around separation consciousness and malevolent hierarchy. Integration engages the survivor's developing capacities to tolerate ambiguity, paradox, and inner conflict (H. Schwartz, 1994). Whatever form it takes, integration – a unique path based on each individual's emergent needs, capacities and "destiny drive" (Bollas, 1989:3) – is a by-product of the core treatment processes of recognition and internal cooperation. When identity is constructed on the basis of inclusivity, instead of isolation and alienation, psychological health is demonstrated by the ability to think one's own thoughts and to independently evaluate thoughts expressed by others and the ability to discern and extricate oneself from any relationship or context (including work, communities, belief systems) that feels destructive or invalidating.

Integration is well underway when the patient begins to understand the power dynamics underlying victimization. This occurs when a patient is able to contemplate or speculate without becoming terrified, to examine perpetrators' scripts without becoming entranced by them, and when he or she can evaluate the therapist's suggestions without reflexively complying with, or defying, them. Integration should never mean complete adaptation to the prevailing social or clinical value systems. Nor should integration mandate the creation of (or belief in) a unified self (Rivera, 1989). Coherence of self is one thing; conformity of self is quite another. Rather than being dictated by some abstract ideal of what posttraumatic mental health or identity is supposed to look like, concepts and practices related to integration must be uniquely negotiated by the therapy dyad to respect the patient's subjectivity and emerging autonomy.

Integration for victims of coerced perpetration must involve the reinstitution of previously derailed and deformed protest responses so that the once traumatized and fragmented patient can assertively, not violently or timidly, respond on his or her own behalf. From here, the therapy can lead the patient to deconstruct the duplicity and double binds of the abusive social matrix, and sublimate aggression into a fierce self-advocacy and a committed respect for the rights of one's self and others. With the invitation to learn how to challenge (and enjoy) the authority/ leadership of others on equal terms, integration represents the return of innate dominion of the self to the self.

> Integration means the patient no longer avoids his or her suffering but allows it to exist in an internal place from which it can inform other aspects of life. Integration means that intrapsychic experience no longer bypasses the mind, language, symbolization, and relationship on its way to the body. Integration means that the patient knows a lot of what happened to him or her as a child and does not let those violent and violating experiences define his or her essence.
>
> H. Schwartz (2000:206)

Beyond integration: individual, community, and society

In the rehabilitation of individuals and societies in the wake of trauma, the integration process can be described as intricate, murky, and arduous. At its psychosocial roots, the term "integration" refers to a central component of healing: the multifaceted process of coordinating separate personality elements into a balanced whole, and harmonizing the integrating individual within an optimally accepting environment. From the widest angle of vision, integration comprehends the dynamics of internal (intrapsychic) and external (interpersonal) forces that are themselves mutually constituted and refined. Successful approaches to clinical and social integration require cross-fertilization among professional cohorts – psychologists, psychoanalysts, anthropologists, physicians, lawyers, international policy makers, politicians, social workers, sociologists, and others – to develop thoughtful and efficacious solutions to the psychic disruption of individuals and communities following exposure to, and participation in, violence and social upheaval. Child soldiers and other survivors of coerced perpetration trauma represent a unique population. Survivors of coerced perpetration embody the extremes of innocence and corruption, segregated in disparate psychological states of victimization, complicity, and perpetration – operating within the same mind, body, and life; they encompass in microcosm the enduring problems of humanity. Since psychological schisms can sometimes be traced to fractures and malfunctions in the social and political systems from which they emerged, creative solutions developed to illuminate paths of healing for these trauma survivors may contain the keys to responding to some of humanity's longstanding and perplexing psychosocial challenges.

Most psychotherapeutic traditions treating trauma have matured in a manner that parallels the evolution of organizations responsible for administering international justice and developing innovative humanitarian solutions to the problems that emerge in the aftermath of war, genocide, and the decimation of indigenous communities. While avoiding facile and formulaic prescriptions, Drumbl's (2012) call for widespread application of transitional/restorative justice practices to address the socio-cultural and legal challenges of former child soldiers offers valuable insights for clinicians managing the psychological integration of survivors of internalized perpetration across diverse cultures and contexts. Emphasizing relationship-building instead of punishment, witnessing instead of denial, communality instead of isolation, confession instead of blaming, deterrence instead of revenge, and developing life/vocational skills and spiritual healing instead of simple military demobilization, the transitional justice model[7] (Minow, 1998; Parmar, 2010; A. Smith, 2010; Teitel, 2000) Drumbl's (2012) perspective affords a sophisticated means of reckoning with the ambiguities of good and evil in post-traumatized psyches and societies.

Transitional/restorative justice as a template for psychological integration

Certain themes of the transitional/restorative justice movement offer clinicians a useful vantage point on intrapsychic integration for healing coerced perpetration survivors' relationships with society. The practices of restorative justice approach the individual's psychological integration within the cognate processes of community re-integration and social reparations. Respecting, but reaching beyond, criminal law, transitional/restorative justice is primarily concerned with redress of grievances (compensation, institutional reform, symbolic reparations), historical clarification, and reconciliation rather than with punishment and prevention. Transitional justice[8] pursues social repair based on a conviction that durable stability – individual, communal, national, and international – is only possible when human rights violations and related injustices are thoroughly acknowledged, and when the pain and destruction wrought by these transgressions are redressed through non-violent, non-retributive means. Accordingly, restorative justice seeks to: establish an accurate record of the past; prevent denial of crimes and human rights violations; prevent the exacting of revenge; seek funding or prevent the withdrawal of funding for rehabilitation programs; remove human rights violators from state institutions and prevent their re-election; and reform health care and education systems (International Center for Transitional Justice, 2009; Parmar, 2010; Teitel, 2000). Because they refuse to ignore evidence of collusion and complicity in the analysis of perpetration, transitional/restorative justice mechanisms may serve a vital transformative function, replacing an ethics of victimization with an ethics of responsibility and engagement.

From the perspective of transitional justice,[9] demobilized child soldiers should neither be criminally prosecuted for suspected violations of international criminal law nor yet completely absolved of responsibility for their wartime behaviors.

They should be viewed simultaneously as victims and witnesses. Their perpetration activities are not overlooked, yet neither are they are elevated to the status of full criminal liability. As an advanced model for individual and group healing and holistic restoration in the wake of pervasive destruction and traumatization, the transitional justice template creatively negotiates the ambiguities and paradoxes inherent in the lives of victims of coerced perpetration trauma across diverse interpersonal and sociopolitical contexts.

Because punitive practices such as imprisonment, shunning, and financial penalties may potentially compound posttraumatic suffering in a way that can further devastate afflicted individuals and communities, the restorative justice alternative relies on witnessing, testifying, community reintegration, and practical rehabilitation. This transitional justice approach seeks psychological healing and social integration beyond ethical categories of accountability and responsibility. For instance, many child soldiers harbor resentment toward their communities for failed protection and for the mounting consequences of their lost childhoods. They may feel victimized by scapegoating, shunning, and glaring misrepresentations of their war experiences. As previously noted, many child soldiers feel spiritually tainted and fearful of retaliation from members of their communities as well as from former military officers. Transitional justice mechanisms specifically target the psychological burdens of guilt, shame, and social alienation, developing methods capable of alleviating former soldiers' sense of indignity and injustice (Drumbl, 2012; Parmar, 2010).

By encouraging public witnessing of all aspects of their wartime experiences, transitional/restorative justice provides opportunities for history gathering, forgiveness, authentication of claims of resistance to inhumane orders or protests against atrocities, and for identification of non-combatants who may nonetheless have aided and abetted unscrupulous warlords or other primary perpetrators (Drumbl, 2012). Education, economic rehabilitation, and spiritual healing according to the traditional practices of the soldiers' specific culture are regarded as invaluable elements of individual and community integration. Further, within the practices (and intentions) established by restorative justice, each individual's journey toward healing and repair is treated with dignity and respect for the specific individual's journey.

Practices of transitional/restorative justice are invaluable for clinicians studying psychological integration. Cultivating authentic integration in the wake of chronic trauma and realizing restorative justice in response to human rights violations necessitate development of innovative interventions. The understandable wish for short-cuts and quick solutions are relinquished in favor of sitting with ambiguity and the problems of lost faith. For a sustainable integration, the fragmented and the intractable are contained with patience and compassionate understanding. Helplessness and mastery, the messy and the sublime, the warped and the untainted, the coerced and the chosen must all have their place at the integration table. Uncertainty and unpredictability are honored rather than avoided. Grief and gratitude work together to gradually dissolve psychic numbness and detachment as previously sequestered states of being emerge with newfound purpose, inspiration, and healing solutions for self, local community, and nation.

The value of transitional/restorative justice for speaking to psychological integration with all trauma survivors struggling with the legacy of coerced and voluntary perpetration lies in, among other things, its non-binary approach to individual and group reconciliation. The objective is a unique, depolarized vision of justice, ethical sensibility, and communal and intrapsychic repair. Dualities, such as guilt and innocence, victim and perpetrator, redemption and retaliation, prevention and punishment, accountability and compassion, are held in a frame that ultimately aims at a transcendence of their polarities in service to psychic and social resolution.

Integration of psyche, community, and spirit

Whatever its particular contours, authentic, durable healing is always intricately embedded within shared humanity with other imperfect, worthwhile, struggling beings. In such humanized arrangements, the victim-in-you is the potential victim-in-me, the collaborator-in-you is the potential collaborator-in-me, the killer-in-you is the potential killer-in-me – no one is considered outside the human family completely and everyone recognizes that under the right circumstances we are all capable of all deeds – good and evil. Everyone assumes responsibility for resolving the effects of (and preventing future) trauma. If individuals and communities cannot apprehend a spectrum of good and evil within themselves without indulgent polarization, then the perpetrators will have triumphed. At its root, successful individual and collective integration following massive trauma must inspire a feeling of connection to a universe that celebrates life, and an identification with (and acceptance of) a flawed humanity struggling together. Stressing the way coherence, continuity, and cohesiveness are brought about through human relatedness, Bromberg's (2003) important articulation of unity captures the essence of successful integration:

> Unity is a shorthand term for the experience of feeling fully in life, and "life" is our experience of connection with the rest of humanity. That is, unity is the connection to mankind and other people [...] When the therapist is able to relate to each aspect of the patient's self through its own subjectivity, each part of the self becomes increasingly able to co-exist with the rest, and in that sense is linked to others.
>
> (p. 704)

At the deepest level, psychological and social integration for individuals and communities in the wake of encounters with violence and massive trauma must involve a "return of the good" – individual, collective, and spiritual – rather than simply an interruption or an eradication of "the bad." Regressions resulting from chronic trauma stir primitive and polarized psychological responses when previously balanced individuals and groups fracture into paranoid-schizoid modes of relatedness. Latent human potentials for unimaginable cruelty and "orgies of death" are activated and played out. Facilitated by paranoid-schizoid thinking, retaliatory narcissism, disinhibited by an immersion in hatred that is often exacerbated by psychoactive drugs and manipulated by malevolent idealized leaders, individuals and groups commit heinous acts. These ongoing violations of self and others weaken the psyche and spirit, paving the way for downward spirals into complete, contemptuous abandonment of one's humanity and reverence for life. In treatment, as in social policy, the achievement of an enduring, mature transformation of traumatization requires more than a dynamic reworking of good and bad object splits with their concomitant developmental regressions.

Stable integration requires one's relationship with "good and evil" to be reconfigured to advance to a higher perspective. The care and compassion that seemed absent or effectively obliterated by traumatizing agents can begin to manifest as a subtle, yet indefatigable force. The survivor will naturally continue to question the reliability of the good after experiencing the extremes of trauma and perpetration, but the felt existence of goodness can be reconstituted through deep introspection and the accrual of redemptive interpersonal experiences. Complicity, collusion, and collaboration may come to be recognized as a greater problem in the proliferation of evil than perpetration itself (H. Schwartz, 2000), so that responsibility for violence and its aftermath is reconceptualized as belonging to everyone. The compelling and seemingly all-pervasive wickedness that distinguishes the trauma zone can come to be understood as an aspect of a profound woundedness. When the survivor becomes capable of examining this woundedness without intimidation, and eventually with equanimity and compassion, liberation is at hand.

Through integration, the good comes to be understood not as diametrically opposed to evil, but rather as capable of limiting it. Identification with the phantasmagorical glories of violence is replaced by a healthy, humbling fear of humanity's capacities for destruction – including an appreciation for an inexhaustible potential for destructiveness (and for the limits in our capacities to fully understand it) (Bion, 1965). The survivor's relationship with personal and archetypal goodness can come to be seen as both an inexorable reality and a latent potential – a position that is always optional and never attainable through guilt or coercion. The sense (or fantasy) of the good being greater, immanently more powerful than evil, and faith that the containment of destructiveness is possible within a larger sphere of benevolence, can arise in the individual and communal psyche because of the experience of redemptive, healing relational processes. Yet the integrating patient (and community) may eventually recognize that despite all appearances, goodness has been mysteriously operative all along. The presence of perpetrator patterns in the self, the other, and the culture can be fully recognized as potentials in all human beings – potentials that are particularly inflammable, and generative under conditions of chronic stress, torture, and real or imagined abandonment. Through new loving relationships, collective awareness, and compassionate witnessing, integrating patients begin to imagine the possibility of containing and disempowering destructiveness.

Within the mystery of evil, the therapist and integrating patient must inevitably make room to grapple with an aspect of human behavior that is beyond conceivable redemption – an impenetrable malignant sociopathy. Although both good and evil are often supported by legitimizing virtue and compelling ideology, for some seriously impaired individuals, self-righteously inflicting (and relishing) torment becomes an end unto itself. The last vestiges of humanity in these personalities seem to have been eclipsed, if not entirely erased.[10]

There may not be a psychic state composed purely of destruction (Bion, 1965). However, there is ample evidence of the existence of personalities that have merged almost completely with the archetype of evil. In such psyches, unresolved primitive agonies persist with "searing contempt and uncompromising self-hatred" (Eigen, 1993:202), completely subjugating the life force. Primal apocalyptic anxieties such as M. Klein's (1946:297) fear of "being annihilated by a destructive force within" appear to bypass all vulnerability and reparative mental or interpersonal operations, morphing these psyches into "a cynical and diabolic consciousness set against the genuine possibility of experiencing saving meaning" (Eigen, 1993:202). Compelled to evacuate instead of express their anguish, these individuals have become relentless purveyors of the very annihilation to which they have felt helplessly subjected. An individual's mind (by way of an immoral conscience) and life may become so permeated by an inflexibly rampaging destructive force (Bion, 1965) that the psyche of the individual becomes completely usurped by a predatory compulsion to "spread" annihilation (Eigen, 1996). Such deformed psyches, as Eigen explains, provide an inviting habitat for archetypally destructive forces that infiltrate into "existence in order to proliferate and annex all of it and turn it into nonexistence" (Eigen, 1996:64). Such a deteriorated personality, organized with rapacious determination – an obdurate will intolerant of limits or resistance (Bion, 1965) – may degenerate to the point where "nothing outside of it balances its determination to reduce life to a single purpose, to food for itself" (Eigen, 1996:65). Through the process of integration, troubling paradoxes regarding the origins and limits of evil must be factored into our understanding of humanity. The capacity for evil does indeed exist in us all, whether the seemingly "inhuman" or "other" has a distinct and eventually discernible psychopathology or psycho-spiritual phenomenology.

As the journey of integration proceeds, the spectacles of evil and perpetration are witnessed rather than judged, illuminated rather than eliminated, confronted but not necessarily vanquished. The dance between catastrophe and faith (Eigen, 1992; 1993) that had previously collapsed into states of dissociated dread and defensive futility, paves the way for grief, vulnerability, self-awareness, and embodied aliveness. The culminating forces of recovered innocence and manifest benevolence activated in the psyche of the survivor (or community) – lived out in the therapeutic and communal relational fields – steadily disrupt and finally undermine the egoic (and social) structures that had previously assimilated and identified with evil. Uncertainties and fragilities will remain in the psyches of all survivors of perpetration trauma. Yet, psychotherapeutic integration helps these individuals go on to experience contact with something sacred, inviolable, and sustaining in themselves and in the world.

> While it was force and threat that drove us away from our original inno-cence, it is free choice that enables us to find it again. Through having abandoned our true self to languish in an inner prison, we awaken one day to recognize that we may return […] We realize that fear and doubt have kept us from seeing that the prison door has never been locked, and that we could leave at any time. We even see that having betrayed ourselves was somehow necessary for our learning, and for the development of our humil-ity. We are able to see that this is a life for learning, and for understanding ourselves and the Cosmos in which we live; the light and the dark are there to enable us to see with greater vision" (Anthony, 1998, p. 35).

Chapter 8

Using archetypal concepts as a vehicle of integration

> For those who immerse themselves in what the fairy tale has to communicate, it becomes a deep, quiet pool which at first seems to reflect only our own image; but behind it we soon discover the inner turmoil of our soul – its depth, and ways to gain peace within ourselves and with the world, which is the reward of our struggles.
>
> Bruno Bettelheim

Introduction

In the final stage of the healing journey, the trauma patient has the opportunity to enter a prospective field of archetypal potentials. An archetypal wide-angle-lens recontextualizes trauma and recovery to hold the promise of promoting wisdom and inspiration. However, this part of the treatment can take place only after patients have rigorously processed their history of perpetration, including the distinctive operation of their perpetrator identification, and after the internalized "rules" of power and control, intimidation, domination and submission, cease to determine their sense of self. Patients should no longer be at the mercy of self-sabotaging emotional triggers and now should be able to sustain a connection to their core innocence. At this juncture, the therapy's scope has expanded to include the capacity for archetypal potentials as Joseph Campbell quintessentially defines them in his seminal book "*The Hero With A Thousand Faces*" (Campbell, 1949). As the patient's identity moves from the fragmented and conflicted roles of victim, collaborator, and perpetrator to a more integrated, self-respecting, and self-defining being, the therapist can encourage the patient to embrace contradictions inherent in the Kabalistic phrase "descent for the sake of the ascent" (Sholem, 1974). This idea of sacred return is probably best known by the alchemical imagery of the phoenix rising in flight from the ashes, after all hope has been destroyed by an all-consuming fire.

Alchemists symbolized the process of rebirth by way of total destruction with the *Ouroboros*: the circular symbol of a snake eating its own tail. This primordial image not only embodies the concept of devouring oneself for the purpose of nourishment and re-creation, but most importantly it signifies the interdependence of both processes. For clinical purposes, the *Ouroboros* represents the striving toward wholeness through the integration of opposites: the fragments of the shadow self assimilated into the now-ascendant ego self. At the same time, the image of a loop is a reminder of the never-ending quality of the infinite. Representing rebirth, the *Ouroboros* slays itself then brings itself to life again (Jung, 1958).[1]

These archetypal concepts contain valuable meaning and models to assist patients to better understand their own potential to alchemically convert unimaginable suffering into accessible forms of redemption. For trauma survivors who are able to make a sustainable return from perpetrator-identification and misdirected loyalty to abusers to a fidelity to self and community, the mythic tales of rebirth and assimilation of opposites become the transformative actions of their own heroic journeys. "The hero's journey" can supply a stark contrast to the self-defeating narratives which pre-empt the potentials for hope or recovery. As in heroic legends, the patient adopting such a narrative for himself or herself must courageously and compassionately face humanity's wickedness as it appears within the self. The patient must also look for themselves in the many stages of the hero's journey: corrupted innocence, struggle, failure, suffering, hopelessness, unexpected opportunities, hope, awakening, and redemption. From an archetypal perspective, each step in a patient's recovery re-enacts the universal process of human maturation and liberation. Because our culture lacks the notion of communal healing found in indigenous societies, survivors' meaningful connections between their own healing and potential participation in, and contributions to, the collective represent a powerful antidote to the isolation and futility of their trauma years. Community connections may also help temper the challenges to the endurance required by the patient during the long, arduous healing journey of later-stage psychotherapy.

Archetypal constructs in treatment provide an informal invitation to the patient to re-enter the community of humankind from which he or she has felt exiled. The therapy relationship dyad models the possibility of co-creating deeper intimacy and partnership. With the patient's growing capacity for relationship and learning to regard his or her own journey as the foundation for developing more flexible ways to process conflict, the patient may also find greater comfort "sitting with" ambiguity and contradictions. Suicide as the ever-present option for the cessation of pain recedes as an option, as the certainty of an eventual natural death now becomes a compelling frame for the opportunity to attempt to live a redemptive fulfilling life. With resolute investigation, patients may come to see their inner conflicts in another light: as part of their dues for membership in humanity's collective history of self-inquiry. Thus, a private unshared hell has the potential to be converted into a starting point for previously unknown feelings of kinship and compassion. Solipsistic confusion can be elevated into philosophical contemplations of the sort that have sustained fellowships of sentient beings throughout the ages.

Integrating relational and archetypal perspectives

In the crucible of trauma therapy as the survivor's belief in a benevolent universe is reconstructed, the therapist and patient will threaten each other's worldviews, belief systems, and personal mythologies. If all goes relatively well, therapist and patient can move beyond a series of painful enactments and disturbing merger states into a different kind of consensus. This new communion fostered via individuation and mutual respect emerges only after the patient and the therapist earn a sense of having survived each other and the shared experience of an encounter with archetypal darkness. Actually and symbolically, they will have "come through the whirlwind" (Eigen, 1992), and moved "from catastrophe to faith" (Eigen, 1993).

From the perspective of archetypal psychology, the survivor-perpetrator gains a unique vantage point on life. The devastation of the patient's early life is juxtaposed with possession of a rare possibility of transforming his or her relationship to self, spirituality, and the human community in a way that non-traumatized individuals may never attain. Since survivor-perpetrator patients contain within themselves the numinous opposites of disowned innocence and cultivated corruption, their internal healing processes can inspire other kinds of healing journeys. These processes also throw light on some of the most entrenched social and political problems plaguing humankind.

Coerced perpetration is a direct assault on the individual's psyche and spirit. The survivor-perpetrator patient's return to humanity and psychological re-integration requires a deep anchoring in a set of new meanings powerful enough to provide an alternative to the archetypal demonic belief system inculcated within the traumatizing relationships. If one major conundrum of traumatic experience is the problem of decontextualization – stories consuming stories, fragmenting some, secreting away others – then one paradox of survival involves opening up foreclosed and fragmented narratives to new territories and a larger framework within which to contextualize. Archetypal psychology and transpersonal psychology, with their connections to sacred, universal wisdom traditions, offer invaluable guidance for therapists and patients trying to understand the breadth and depth of traumatic injury. These perspectives also stress the need for the holistic healing of the survivor to reverse the damage inflicted by perpetrators and malevolent systems. In the archetypal vision of healing, heroic myths are not viewed simply as interesting fables, or therapeutic maneuvers, but as condensed dramatizations of what all seekers, traumatized or not, tend to encounter on their way toward integration and wholeness (Grant, 1996).

Archetypal psychology cautions against a premature return to functionality by medicating survivors' pain and suffering. Instead, archetypal approaches view the struggles of trauma survivors and treating professionals as requiring investigations deep into the symbolic phenomenology of the human soul (Kalsched, 1996). Within archetypal perspectives, trauma and transcendence are regarded as parts of a dialectical relationship. Echoing the wisdom of shamanism

(Eliade, 1964; Harner, 1980) and other mystical traditions, psychological injury and suffering are viewed as potentially valuable ingredients on a redemptive journey toward wholeness and enlightenment. As Kalsched points out, not everyone is helped by an understanding of the parallels between the struggles of a trauma survivor and his or her therapist, with ancient religious notions and a system of the soul's symbolic phenomenology. In my 30 years of practice, this perspective has sometimes been the only lifeboat available at a crucial impasse or during protracted treatment.

Kalsched's (1996) Jungian approach to treating trauma underscores how the specific psychological mechanisms designed to protect the self – the self care system – can become malevolent and destructive. The inherently explosive, aggressive nature of dissociative self-organization in response to trauma undermines the normal integrative tendencies of the psyche, activating complexes (and splits in complexes) that end up functioning with excessive autonomy. Diverging somewhat from psychoanalysis and trauma/dissociation theorists views of psychic splits, Kalsched emphasizes that internal attacking and persecutory figures of the traumatized psyche are not simply internalized versions of the abusers. Rather, these psychological forms represent traumatically-activated psychological potentials inherent in all human beings. These dormant potentials, which can be set loose in the psyche in the aftermath of violence, neglect, betrayal and abandonment, can take on particular forms. Though influenced by specific local culture and traditions, these manifestations reveal uncanny cross-cultural consistency and uniformity. Further, as Kalsched illuminates, this universal, traumatogenic agency within the psyche functions at an unconscious (and metaphysical) level and may not be responsive to logical therapy discourse. Storytelling, myths, artistic expressions, humor, paradox, and metaphor may be the only ways to reach and negotiate with the calcified, dissociative aspects of some patients.

Integrating psychoanalytic and archetypal perspectives in therapy can be challenging because most therapists are strongly bound to theoretical allegiances and biases. Using an archetypal perspective in healing does not indicate the therapist should spiritualize, legitimize, or license patients' suffering or destructive behavior. Clinicians treating trauma should understand that exploring archetypal realms or to the opposite-end steadfastly avoiding discussing anything existential, mystical, or religious can cause short-circuiting in the therapy and individuation processes. A therapist could misappropriate the use of spiritual material and archetypal viewpoints to avoid direct confrontation with the traumatic, the conflictual and/or the characterological. Likewise, a strictly traditional psychoanalytic approach could be used to invalidate the patient's legitimate spiritual fears, conflicts, and longings, or worse, attempt to reduce them to legacies of the patient's sense of infantile omnipotence. As clinicians working in transitional psychological spaces, we must be careful not to pathologize or psychologize spirituality; we must be similarly vigilant not to use (or collude in the patient's use of) spiritual narratives to avoid acknowledging traumatic injury or to avoid the difficult task of learning to resolve psychological conflicts.

The use of archetypal perspectives to complement the primarily relational approach is not meant to propose another system of intervention techniques but rather as an essential philosophical frame for the therapeutic project. The inherent redemptive potential of archetypal perspectives lies in its expectation that the therapist can help the patient broaden his or her understanding of woundedness, freedom, and responsibility. When a dissociative survivor makes a natural, spontaneous connection to something larger than the self, deeper than the trauma, greater than the pain and torment, a potentially beneficial therapeutic plateau has been attained. Cultivating the patient's awareness of the connections between the interpersonal and the transpersonal can lead to new redemptive meaning structures where the patient can begin to construct an identity distinct from the one fashioned by the imperatives of the perpetrators. Archetypal treatment perspectives may also diminish trauma survivors' sense of isolation from humankind and human history as they come to learn to see themselves in a new context informed from history, literature, and mythology about others' journeys out of hell and escapes from psychic captivity.

Working with a combination of the psychological and archetypal therapeutic paradigms can be a tricky task for the patient and therapist. Each perspective can potentially enhance or disrupt progress. For example, the therapist can misread perpetrator states or mind-control experiences as paranoia or psychosis, or reductively pathologize the patient's mystical experiences. On the other hand, compelling spiritual narratives can serve to obscure deep character pathology, seduce and charm both therapist and patient, and interfere with the goal of confronting painful memories and disturbing meanings. The healthy mindfulness and detachment characterizing spiritual maturity may be difficult to distinguish from symptoms of depersonalization, depression, or ego-inflation. Patients may try to dilute or delay the inroads of psychotherapy by defending particular belief systems or attachments to spiritual leaders and traditions. Adding to these areas of potential confusion is the belief among many clinicians that discourse about spiritual or transpersonal matters lies outside of the purview of their scope of practice. When a clinician proceeds with caution and openness the challenges of including archetypal and transpersonal perspectives in the treatment of trauma outweigh the risks of leaving them out of the process.

In any genuine psychological and spiritual integration, both mastery and humility must be present and mutually informing. The mysterious must be integrated with the mundane. Clinicians must appreciate what many spiritual teachers (particularly from the Zen Buddhist and Taoist traditions) have always stressed: in the archetypal journey, the individual must accept the sorrows and joys, along with the banalities and noisy obscenities of life (Campbell, 1949). Even after significant progress, the survivor and therapist must accept living with the possibilities of residual destructiveness that may never be completely transmuted or integrated, and must simply be contained. The perspicacious archetypal viewpoint can never totally eclipse the humbling process of learning to live with the killer within which, once activated and materialized, remains a potential for violence in spite of the most successful healing processes. Potentials for the emergence of delusional omnipotence and hypocrisy must be repeatedly acknowledged. As C.S. Lewis (1963:209) aptly cautions, "the finest flowers of unholiness can grow only in the close neighborhood of the Holy." As the wisdom of the Kaballah (see Sholem, 1974) tells us, the most powerful faith of all is faith that is lost and found again after a journey through profound darkness, despair, and cosmic abandonment.

Case example: Jenny

Presenting initially with chronic depression and intractable somatic/medical anxieties, Jenny's history soon revealed that she served as the psychological scapegoat for her upper middle-class family. She supported the official portrait of the perfect family by showing nothing of her pain to the outside world or to herself. Jenny's unusual sensitivity and capacity for compassion became a receptacle for her family members' evacuation of hatred, dread, frustrations, humiliations, and thwarted ambitions. Jenny's mother idealized Jenny's older sister, yet her mother routinely projected negative aspects of herself into Jenny with protracted monologues involving disparagement, ridicule, and endless complaints. Attentive listening to these diatribes was Jenny's only hope for maternal attention. Most painful were the ways in which Jenny's separate identity (apart from her container functions) was neglected, and opportunities for the expression and validation of her innocence, achievement, joy, or delight were ironically denied. The impenetrably cruel, united front of disturbed, vicious mother and ruthlessly narcissistic older sister coupled with an alternately seductive and betraying father overwhelmed and fragmented Jenny's young psyche.

"Betrayal blindness" (Freyd, 1996), self-negating loyalty, and subtle but pervasive patterns of internalized perpetration became deeply imprinted into Jenny's psyche; she survived emotionally by dissociating the meaning and implications of her emotionally toxic family system. For many years, Jenny rarely strayed from the family to make new friends, somehow believing that her family was actually her best friends – this was one of many maternal indoctrinations. Although physical violence or coerced violent perpetration was not part of her trauma history, emotional treachery, viciousness, and collusion was enacted within her family, particularly dynamics of lethal competition, "gaslighting," primitive envy, degradation, and threats of ex-communication. From immersion in (and dissociative adaptation to) this destructive system, Jenny's keen intelligence and perceptive abilities had become entwined in the unconscious web of perpetration identifications instead of serving her development of compassion, self-protection, or self-love. Internalized patterns of perpetration were unwittingly enacted by Jenny on herself, close friends, romantic partners, and in therapy relationships – often with extreme righteousness and intransigence. There was confusion on Jenny's part as to why her interpersonal situations invariably deteriorated and about her role in these downward spirals. In complex interpersonal situations, the schism between Jenny's provocative, perpetrator and victim selves was amplified and extended with self-righteous justifications that often, and ironically, derived from accurate observations of the disowned shadow elements of others.

For people whose self-concepts lack a developed concept of responsibility, or for whom an understanding of the limits of their personal accountability for their circumstances have been disrupted, various types of felt innocence are inevitable. As Grand (2000) has observed, the innocence of the victim and guilt of perpetration may be "located and confounded in the same sequestered wordless self" (p. 73). Jenny's true self was experienced as authentically innocent of her actions while "enactments of ghost selves [were operating] in a theater where they may speak without being known" (p. 69). Unbeknownst to Jenny, when behaving righteously in social situations, she was enacting both victim and perpetrator roles at the same time, one covering for the other. In some of these interpersonal conflicts, Jenny was misunderstood, abandoned, rejected, and isolated – precisely re-enacting the conditions her family had set up for her to occupy. Just as her family had taught her to feel, it was "all her fault," Jenny seemed doomed to unconsciously replay the worst feature of her childhood – a scenario of emotional execution where the death blow was always struck when she was most vulnerable.

Following a reasonably good start with deep empathic resonance operating between us, and in spite of my intuitive faith in Jenny's relational and reflective capacities, inevitable emotional collisions in therapy took place. Her perpetration patterns often manifested in her exploiting my availability to her and my benevolence for her. Her uncanny openness to my feedback when I confronted her about these abuses, especially in view of her usual defensiveness about her conflicts with others, slowed down the speeding train of unconscious re-enactments. My attempts to acknowledge my own role in some of these incidents probably helped Jenny experience a new kind of intimacy and mutuality. However, even with a growing attachment and trust, whenever I pointed out instances of Jenny's self-righteousness, excesses, or perpetration patterns, Jenny would usually withdraw from our bond, and engage in fantasies that I loathed and despised her. This happened regardless of how empathic or gently I pointed out her perpetrator re-enactment patterns. Numerous rounds of this cycle eventually led to shorter cycles, and eventually resulted in our spending more time in neutral reflectivity and creative dialogue and discovery. Slowly, more trust and mutual respect developed between us. Jenny's self-lacerating shame and temporary regressions continued to erupt, but less often, and subsided more quickly. As Jenny became more interested in what she and I were actually experiencing, she developed a deeper interest in how others might be experiencing their interactions with her, and less of an interest in her own woundedness and victimization experiences.

For example, learning how to distinguish the difference between being right and feeling self-righteous became an important theme of her healing. Eventually, Jenny was able to understand and internalize my message that self-righteousness always undermined truth, and that self-righteousness – regardless of how justified it might be – always contains a disowned (often trauma-related) shadow element. My respect and support for Jenny's astuteness about other peoples' behavior, along with my encouragement for her to put those insights to a different use, eventually helped Jenny discover something deeper within herself – a benign inner form of guidance that had emerged to replace the litany of self-hate and chronic disgust with the shortcomings of humanity.

The archetypal aspect of Jenny's journey began with her relationship with nature. During times of stress or joy, Jenny talked to the trees and the trees answered her; she spoke to the wind and the wind responded; she observed some ducklings being hatched and communed with them as if they were part of a sacred family she was stewarding. During one extremely rough period in her integration process, Jenny took to intensive daily observation (via a computer camera) of an eagle's nest, watching three baby bald eagles being devotedly parented and nurtured. Her weekly description of her encounters with the mystery of the natural world brought us into a different type of communion. My deep respect for her psychological process and the reawakening of wonder allowed her to experience sharing joy and awe with a benevolent collaborator and fellow celebrant – the same domain of innocence that had been ravaged by her pathological family system, and themes of violation and exploitation enacted with me in the transference-countertransference matrix. Jenny's capacity for wonder deepened under these conditions and a profound appetite for life emerged after years of depression and futility. Relatively freed from posttraumatic excess and perpetrator identifications, Jenny's intuition and inner guide began to ripen.

As she became more aware of and responsible for her own behavior, Jenny also struggled with certain intolerances and hypersensitivities to the everyday hypoc-risy and dishonesty operating in the world. Many forms of insensitive and selfish human social behavior became more difficult for her to tolerate. Nature was her refuge and link to hope and innocence. For a time, nature was her only place of respite outside of work, therapy, and one extremely devoted friend. The holding environments of therapy and the natural world allowed Jenny's heightened awareness of human cruelty to be processed without perpetrator re-enactments or regressions to positions of self-righteous victimization. Through these mutu-ally reinforcing twains, Jenny began to metabolize the stagnant toxicity of her early family environment.

In addition to Jenny's connections with the natural world, my introduction of shamanism, Buddhism, film, literature, and historic and current events with relevant themes to our work became important parts of the therapy discourse. Jenny's interest in some of these topics pre-dated therapy; other topics were introduced by me, based on my own hunches about what larger narratives might help Jenny de-center from the remnants of self-absorption and biases imprinted by her pathological family. Jenny allowed me to "jumpstart" her spiritual journey but eventually on her own she began to seek written material and spiritual teachers who spoke to her growing love of nature, and who supported her newly-emerging compassionate wider-angle perspectives on life. She became curious about projects of personal and collective forgiveness, including the "Truth and Reconciliation" process taking place in Africa. Our focus was first on self-forgiveness, followed by the long, slow struggle to contemplate forgiving all human beings for their ignorance, complicity, self-interest, and indifference. Jenny remained unsure whether she could extend her compassion to her family, but neither of us ever proposed this as the end goal.

During this time I told her a relatively well-known Buddhist tale that I had heard at a dharma talk years ago at a Buddhist meditation center. A teenage girl falsely accused a monk of impregnating her. She did this to conceal from her parents a relationship with a boyfriend of whom they disapproved. Everyone in the village believed the girl's story and turned against the formerly beloved monk. Following his public humiliation and rejection, the monk remained in his hut on the edge of the village continuing the same daily activities he had performed before these upsetting events. With each allegation, the monk's only response was "so it is." When the young girl's child was born she could not take care of it, and in a moment of anger the parents dumped the child on the ostracized monk's doorstep. Again, his response was "so it is." The monk raised the child with great love and devotion and the child prospered under his care. Seeing this, the mother of the child became angry and envious and demanded the child be returned to her, even though she had had almost no prior interest or contact. The parents and other villagers supported the girl's wishes and the happy child was removed from the care of his devoted "monk-father" and the monk's retort was "so it is." When the child's mother became irritated with caring for him and decided to return the child to the monk again, he responded as he always had: the now familiar "so it is." Eventually, the girl and her boyfriend, the actual father of the child, decided to come clean and confessed the truth to the parents and to the entire village. With a deep desire to make amends, the girl, her family, and the other villagers approached the hut of the old monk to publicly apologize for the wrongdoing and disgrace that had been unfairly heaped upon him. Holding the healthy young boy in his arms, the monk nodded unflinchingly, and while gracefully refusing all of the material offerings of the family and villagers, gently bowed his head and said, "so it is." When I finished telling Jenny this story, she began to sob convulsively for the first time in therapy. Her defensive armor cracked open and a new connection with the "outside world" was born. The moment of rupture of encapsulated perpetrator states is unpredictable. Sometimes it can happen through resolution of an enactment or abreaction of a memory. Sometimes a breakthrough occurs in response to a film, a novel, or a shared story. Jenny's catharsis in this moment was a turning point in our therapy and in her ability to lift herself to a higher awareness of her journey.

Jenny worked to understand one of the central teachings offered in several spiritual books she had been reading – not to take things personally. The shift from an entrenched victim position to the transpersonal understanding of her place in the entire human experience – with the necessary gut-wrenching struggles with narcissistic injury – was an important achievement in Jenny's therapy. She no longer felt a need to exert her will on the world or to defend herself from the world. Her ruthlessness could be detoxified, owned, de-linked from her family of origin, and placed in the service of her healthy developmental strivings and ambitions. Most notably, a profound connection to a source of inner wisdom and guidance evolved within Jenny that left her actively participating in an ongoing, redemptive and mystical dialogue with aspects of herself and her understanding of God.

Jenny was eventually willing to cringingly express regret for some of her prior behavior (in contrast to the self-indulgent shame response which had wreaked havoc on her psyche for so many years). Her dignity seemed to be restored by a courageous yearning for the truth, regardless of what that truth might reveal about her. Conscious courage replaced repetition of unconscious cowardice internalized from her family system. Toward the end of therapy, this led to interpersonal as well as intrapsychic recalibrations and to reconciliation events. On the heels of emblematic kerfuffles that took place in stores Jenny patronized, involving the classic combination of perceived disrespect and reactive righteous indignation, Jenny returned to these same businesses with more openness and humility. Her return to the literal scene of humiliation was something that she would have previously regarded as a self-betrayal. Because her courage was occasionally met by others with openness and gratitude, and she witnessed vulnerable acknowledgments of the imperfections by the other persons in these interactions, Jenny's belief in the cyclical mutual nature of forgiveness, gratitude, and healing became palpable and vivid sources of guidance and reparation.

As her ability to acknowledge her perpetrator patterns took precedence over her steadfast clinging to the justified, but imbalanced, view of herself as a victim, Jenny began to intensify her interests in a variety of areas that eventually brought about a new experience of herself and the world. She delved into literature about slavery and the African-American experience, found deep meaning from hiking in nature and observing animals, non-dualistic spirituality, and re-awakened her interest in and deep love for music. Our therapy discourse further expanded to interweave even more material from novels, films, and history. Jenny's sense of isolation and alienation seemed significantly relieved by contextualizing her journey in the wider frame of human struggles with oppression and liberation. When she read material about slavery, she no longer indulged in viewing herself only as a slave. When she hit rough passages in her day-to-day life, she sincerely looked for what those experiences could teach her rather than using the experience to further substantiate a victim narrative. Whenever she felt confused, distressed, lonely, or lost, she consulted her inner source of guidance which always responded with soothing compassionate awareness and patience. She told me that she had begun to pray to God to let her be "part of the solution and not part of the problems," and to help her see the ways in which she was remaining part of the problem.

Jenny developed compassion and gentleness toward herself. She demonstrated a stronger ability to forgive others for their lack of awareness or integrity. She began to have direct experiences of the everyday effects of gratitude, a state that she began to live in more frequently in the later years of treatment. As she described her relationship with inner guidance during our later years together, I realized how essential this aspect of recovery is for all trauma patients. That is, it is important that each trauma survivor establish an active ongoing relationship with some sort of benevolent internal guidance – whether that guidance is described as intuition, a guardian angel, nature, a particular deity or saint, a voice, a totem or an animal, or as a formless, pervasive, accessible redemptive presence. One of the greatest sources of damage to the human psyche caused by coerced and internalized perpetration is the evisceration of the victim's natural connection to his or her own self-protective inner-guidance system. This natural mechanism becomes deeply corrupted by malevolent injunctions, programming, and diabolical catechisms. In C.S. Lewis's (1963) comments on the subject of human evil, he referred to something akin to this process as "diabolical ventriloquism."

From direct experience (as opposed to conceptual conjecture), Jenny came to realize how gratitude multiplies, how condemnation boomerangs, and how accepting and meeting whatever is in front of you with full presence was more important than getting what you think you want from a situation, especially from other people. Jenny began to have moments of enlightened awareness which were never valorized or used to defer suffering or pain. In fact, Jenny began to accept and understand how psycho-spiritual integration and awakening processes by their very nature often see-saw between periods of great openness, serenity, and joy and periods of profound suffering, as layer upon layer of unconscious patterning of pain and shame surfaced for reflection and release. As I watched Jenny become more familiar with accepting this organic healing and spiritual maturation process, I experienced moments of awe and grace. I may have helped to initiate Jenny's spiritual journey with my therapeutic efforts and interventions but her path was truly her own, going in its own unique but fully comprehensible direction, occasionally showing me aspects of the healing processes I had never before witnessed. To me, the humbling experience of participating in this kind of authenticity is one of the greatest gifts a patient can offer a therapist.

Development and maturation of faith

The archetypal theme of the synthesis of opposites can help patients to realize how faith can emerge from doubt – especially faith not rooted in mere conformity. Similarly, patients can draw upon archetypal lore to understand how genuine virtue is not merely compliance generated by fear of retribution. Throughout treatment, the patient's urges for abdication, retaliation, concretization, and self-destruction wrestle with his or her internal forces (and the therapy relationship's forces) of compassion, wisdom, and the "refusal to participate in anything that diminishes or disconnects sentient beings from one another" (Grant, 1996:153).

"Faith as well as knowledge, opens doors of perception that unleash disturbances. Faith that is merely comforting is probably as deleterious to growth as knowledge that is cut off and schizoid" (Eigen, 1998:62). Integrating both mystical and psychoanalytic traditions, Eigen (1998) claims that the inevitably calamitous nature of faith passages that give birth to truly transformative experiences cannot be shortcut by way of simplistic pathways. From a Jungian perspective, the potential for a maturing faith capacity is inherent in the inner world of the archetypal self-care system. As described by Kalsched (1996), this potential for a refined relationship between psyche and Spirit is activated by the humanity and sensitivity of the therapist's approach – especially in navigating the therapeutic zones of disillusion and limitation. Jungian and transpersonal psychology concern themselves in part with changes in consciousness brought about by the ego's contact with transpersonal psychic energies – both sublime and demonic – which temporarily overwhelm the self. The traumatically-conditioned self-care system of a dissociative trauma survivor may initially trigger coping/defensive patterns based on fantasies of omnipotence. But these patterns can be replaced by the patient's learning to resort to a non-defensive, balanced transformational use of the numinous.

If evil can divest and denude the world of meaning, then faith rooted in symbolization can be an undoing of evil (Alford, 1997). Neo-Kleinian psychoanalytic perspectives on the capacity for faith seem particularly compatible with archetypal perspectives. Central to Bion's (1965; 1967; 1970) ideas on faith is his use of the term "O" as a signifier for faith in the unknown, and faith in the emotional truth of a given moment or experience in all its mystery and limitless potentials. According to various interpreters of Bion's work, faith in O, can be viewed psychologically, transcendentally, or both. Faith in O also implies faith in the preservation of good objects even in their absence; this is a faith, that in the presence of terrible trauma and pain, believes redemption or "the good breast" will arrive (Eigen, 1993; Ferro, 2005; Symington and Symington, 1996). Psychological faith, including receptivity to the infinite, faith in the possibility of beauty, grace, awe, wonder, and spiritual benevolence can come to replace omnipotent defensive strategies, perpetrator patterning, and the rigid attitudes that comprise much of the pre-treatment psychological organization of the dissociated self. Contemplating faith, Bion points to a receptivity to that which lies beyond representation – beyond our sense-derived mental functions – toward an intangible core of experience that nourishes the symbolizing process itself. In a position of mature faith, this receptivity is coupled with an acknowledgement that truth always lies beyond the self and can be only partially apprehended through symbols (Chassay, 2012; Eigen, 1993). Faith in O is essentially faith in the possibility of transformation.

By contrast, a lack of faith can be expressed by self-righteousness, arrogance, and contempt. A rejection of faith offers the allure of certainty and conviction in the face of the unknown or the ambiguous. According to Chassay (2012), attention to emotional truth and receptivity to inspiration requires a certain independence from the regulation of pleasure/pain and fear/dread in order for the self to be available for the creative leap that takes the individual beyond his or her neurophysiology – a leap beyond dissociative management of the self and others. "The faithless self substitutes itself for the object, and depends upon that which can be mastered: knowledge rather than inspiration, being right rather than telling the truth, making sense of things rather than having access to feelings that can be transformed into infinite elaborations of meaning" (Chassay, 2012:15). Faithlessness is operationalized in the quest for power to overcome dread which inevitably results in a sense of numbness and failed creativity; it is characterized by preoccupation with self-management instead of a quest for self-awareness (Alford, 1997). In a faithless approach to life, as Chassay (2012) describes, cynicism substitutes for faith in a bunker-like state of mind marked by isolation, secrecy, and a finely honed internal propaganda system designed to hold the vulnerable self hostage to the pathological self-organization. In contrast, the path of faith requires waiting for the voice of the interior to speak, welcoming vulnerability. This is a rejection of the restraining balm of omnipotence, and a rejection of the notion that one's personality cannot be shaped by forces outside of the self's control. This process of shifting from a consolation-based psychotherapy to an inspiration-based psychotherapy, through the rehabilitation of faith, fosters the leap from subjugation to free will, and from alienation to a partnership with all fellow beings.

A clinician needs to communicate and negotiate with all aspects of a trauma survivors' self-experience. Archetypal psychology specifically encourages therapists to help patients to dialogue – rather than identify – with archetypal energies. The therapist must guard against becoming overly frustrated or seduced by the patient's dance with grandiosity and/or nihilism. Assaults on the therapist's faith and the survivor's defenses against malevolent introjects and programmed states need to be acknowledged and challenged as part of this process. The therapist's own vulnerability and limits around destructiveness and exploitation, combined with his or her patience and fortitude, can serve as a bridge for the survivor to discern and break free of polarized archetypal identifications. This therapuetic stance helps the survivor to negotiate his or her way back to less grandiose or more vulnerable feeling states. It can also serve as a model of how a person can find a balanced relationship with transpersonal energies and meaning systems that generate authentic faith.

In this stage of integration, the therapist must provide support to help offset the discomfort of sitting with the ambiguity inherent in the patient's passage through the uncertainty that must be endured to ascend to a higher, non-dualistic level of truth. Relative truths that must be contrasted include what really took place in the traumatic experiences, in opposition to the self's dissociative rearrangements or the perpetrator(s)' distorted versions of that process. The patient should be guided toward "higher truths" that relate to the existential and spiritual re-contextualization of unbearable life events. This guidance is possible only if the therapist has proven himself or herself a reliable and compassionate guide. Therapists can bring support merely by being consistent in their trust of the therapy process, while remaining receptive to any hesitation, advance or retreat. The therapist should be mindful to maintain a state of relaxed hopeful expectation, as distinct from detached waiting. This clinical posture fosters a patient's capacity to ascend from goals and identities based on automatic compliance and defiance – which can withstand neither formidable moral pressure or self-doubt – to higher-level self-directed and self-adjusting patterns that are the basis of sustainable independence.

The therapist should model "holding the space" – tolerating the discomfort of ambiguity, including not knowing if the patient can make the passage. This space needs to leave room for archetypal narrative's counterintuitive and paradoxical contradictions. He or she guides the patient to a point where the patient's momentary uncertainty no longer triggers dissociative reflexes because uncertainty is re-contextualized as essential to the development of emotional, intellectual, and spiritual maturity. Self-doubts can now signal to the individual that his or her awareness has caught sight of an archetypal opportunity to expand his or her confidence. Using this integrative framework, the survivor moves beyond shuttling between cynical resignation and naïve optimism. As the increased sense of harmony and balance finally begins to appear, the survivor can realize – even celebrate – that authentic wholeness necessarily includes all the messy, chaotic, and uninvited events of one's life.

According to relational and archetypal psychology, one of the hidden tragedies of trauma is that the ego distorts reality in an attempt to protect itself against further expected assaults (Bromberg, 1994, 1998; Kalsched, 1996). Almost magnetically, trauma begets more traumas. The survivor flees from trauma and its rippling effects using faulty efforts at self-protection and self-restoration. With this overreaction of the psyche to trauma, Kalsched points to a tendency for trauma survivors to blur the boundaries between the personal and archetypal realms, leading at times to omnipotent identifications. "When the traumatized ego becomes the 'client' of a transpersonal daimon or god, this daimon or god protects the stress-ego with the ferocity of a mother bear with her cubs" (Kalsched, 1996:179). When this stress-induced protection happens, the caretaking side of the numinous energies usually gives way to the destructive side. When the therapist approaches the defensive use of the numinous in a two-stage process in which the negative daimonic side of the numinous realms is first sensitively unmasked, and systematically explored, this then frees the patient to embrace and benefit from the positive numinous dimensions of life. Care must be taken that the patient does not identify with the positive numinous forces but rather is informed by them. The relinquishment of an inflation or identification with an archetype, which according to Kalsched, *both* Jung and Freud, each in their own ways, viewed as essential, "does not unmask the numinous as *illusion* (Freud) but breaks the husk of the ego's *identity* with the numinous and opens the way for surrender, gratitude, and a relationship with the numinous – both dark and light – which is the essence of religious life" (Klasched, 1996:209). Humility and acceptance of the partiality of cure is one way for the therapist and patient to remain vigilant against omnipotent identifications with the numinous.

Because self-indulgent/defense-based exploitation of spirituality can be used to avoid the difficult demands of the transformation process, the therapist needs to challenge the dissociative patient's flights or regressions into spiritual formulas based on separatism, elitism, anesthesia, escapism, and self-righteousness, while also making it clear that spiritualities based on relationality, equality, vulnerability, and inclusivity can enhance integration and support spiritual maturity. Many successfully individuating trauma survivors who have reclaimed their spirituality tend to have formed hybrid spiritualities, borrowing bits and pieces from diverse traditions, making their relationship with the divinity of their understanding their own. Such eclecticism represents the need within the human experience to construct (or re-construct) a meaningful representation of the world that sustains a healthy rebellion against perpetrators' dictatorial spiritual injunctions. Though varying in content, such perpetrator belief systems are characterized by the insistence on a hierarchy of power, contempt for compassionate relationships, and dualistic separation consciousness.

From a basic psychodynamic perspective, the reconstruction of the survivor's faith always begins with faith in the therapist and faith in the therapy relationship itself, based on accrued "emotionally corrective experiences" (Alexander and French, 1946). There are many types of such experiences: successfully negotiating difficult enactments (Aron, 1996; Bromberg, 1998; Ehrenberg, 1992; Maroda, 1999); "transmuting internalizations" (Kohut, 1971); "surviving destruction" (Winnicott, 1971); relinquishing omnipotence and defensive autonomy to face excruciating emotions such as dread, shame, and hate; mastering memory and deprogramming work (through restored affectivity); the experience of psychic relief through an enhanced capacity for restorative fantasy and reverie (Bion, 1967; Peoples, 1992; H. Schwartz, 2000); the ability to experience joy and wonder; and the comfort of an emotional and physical human embrace. The faith regenerated within the therapy container may eventually be extended by the patient-therapy dyad to others, and/or result in more openness to the possible existence of future benevolent mystical and spiritual experiences.

Case example: Miriam

Miriam's trauma history was revealed over time to include family violence, neglect, incest, child prostitution, pornography, involvement in snuff films, ritual abuse, mind control, assassin, courier, espionage, and psychic training. She was frequently depressed, and at times appeared to be barely hanging on to life, yet maintained a steady and committed work life in various helping professions. In spite of an extensive complex trauma history that included assaults on all aspects of her mind, body, and spirit, Miriam retained a connection to her own integrity and compassion for other people. In addition to massive early childhood trauma, Miriam had also been a victim of a male therapist's sexual boundary violations, and soon after that she experienced an unexpected traumatic loss due to the premature death of a female therapist helping her recover from the former therapy trauma. Much of her early therapy with me included inevitable transference fears, tests, and enactments. Our work together was shadowed by these adult traumas in earlier therapy while trying to find effective treatment for her childhood experiences.

Although polyfragmented and highly dissociative, Miriam had managed to maintain a strong conceptual and experiential connection to benevolent archetypal spirituality, even through the worst of her torture and trauma history. These connections involved strong intuition and access to various forms of compassionate transpersonal guidance. Unlike many trauma survivors, for whom revelations of atrocity and coerced perpetration are the most difficult, what most terrified Miriam was remembering and revealing the secrets of what she regarded as divine intervention in her own life, including during organized perpetrator activities and rituals. Miriam maintained benevolent connections with a munificent, wise guidance system in spite of the fact that her primary perpetrators seemed to be on a "search and destroy mission" to ascertain if she had experienced any "angelic" contact during her torture experiences. Miriam revealed how she had dissociatively "tricked herself" into sustaining not only faith in redemptive spirituality but sustained a reasonably balanced faith in her personal access to these higher realms of mystical experience.

Later in her therapy, as integration was well underway, Miriam was able to let herself remember and tell me about a powerful archetypal experience. Miriam described how the most excruciating traumas her perpetrators had designed were aimed to break her connection to anything human or loving or liberating. The same torments, designed to create self-states that could be shaped to do a wide variety of her perpetrators' biddings, mysteriously became for her a private pathway to a kind of grace. This experience of grace through brokenness was described by Miriam as tapping into or landing in an indestructible place of great awe and beauty – the same "place" that had saved her life. Differentiating this experience from dissociation, omnipotent fantasy or therapist seduction/gratification was not difficult in this case since the experiences were presented later in her treatment with little fanfare and great humility. Perpetrator-induced omnipotent fears lingered around these mystical experiences and needed to be worked through. Although she did not believe what was in her mind as she told me about her profound experience of the sacred occurring during out-of-body experiences occurring during torture, Miriam wondered if I could destroy her connection to this experience simply by hearing about it or if I could be destroyed by knowing about it. Working through that transference fear and programmed expectation helped Miriam relax into further explorations and revelations. The fact that I was comfortable discussing these experiences allowed Miriam to understand that I was not unfamiliar with matters spiritual, or mystical. I believe this realization on her part allowed our deepening explorations of these liminal experiences.

Miriam's first access to this transpersonal protected state occurred in childhood after enduring periods of electrocution torture. Miriam was able to recall not only the searing pain, mental disintegration, and perpetrator messages, but unlike many other patients who have described leaving their bodies during torture, she had retained vivid memories of a variety of positive paranormal experiences during and after these torture sessions. These redemptive/protective experiences included her contact with benevolent cosmic beings that seemed to wait for her in some realm between in-between life and death. For most of her life Miriam hid her knowledge and memory of this sacred place. Unconsciously, she believed if she ever so much as thought or remembered these experiences – even within the privacy of her own mind – her recollection alone would somehow make this safe place accessible to her perpetrators for destruction. She feared if she shared this sacred material with any person, the other person would somehow (magically) be hurt or destroyed. Miriam was conditioned to protect herself and others by staying clear of her conscious connections to benevolent sacred realms. This was even as she was trained to find safety and security in identifications with evil and perpetration. Miriam's decision to share this numinous material with me was an important turning point in the integration process. This revelation – harder in some ways for Miriam than her revelations and confessions of perpetration from earlier in treatment – was an important step in releasing the remnants of programmed inhibitions about her relationship with the sacred.

Sharing these extraordinary experiences did not happen, of course, without some negative transference and some fear on Miriam's part that I might be a secret agent working for the perpetrator group she had finally managed to escape. Clearly, she had been trained to fear such things and had been conditioned and retraumatized in prior therapies to expect abandonment and betrayal. However, unlike many patients from organized child abuse backgrounds, Miriam did not dig in her heels around these fears and fantasies. Her experience of my relaxed receptivity in meeting her psycho-spiritual material allowed her to more deeply relax in my presence and to find ease in her own mind, body, and spirit. Although she had been party to diabolical activities, and had kidnapped, procured, tortured, and killed other people, Miriam knew that I was holding her core innocence in my mind and heart while not avoiding facing demonized aspects of her personality.

After a period of relief from her posttraumatic expectations following the initial disclosure of her experiences of the "sacred place" she had visited during torture, we discussed Miriam's bewilderment at how her perpetrators seemed unable to destroy an elemental aspect of her spirituality when they were otherwise successful at fracturing and re-structuring her personality to their specification. Her vague worries about risk to the "sacred place" continued to come in and out of our discourse. A new vision of its safety and durability could only be established through repeated therapeutic encounters with layers of programmed expectancies and their disconfirmation. I reminded Miriam somewhat playfully (this attitude in itself helped demystify the dogma her perpetrators put on spiritual matters), she need not worry about endangering the "sacred place" through remembering and sharing, because this place was beyond the reach of her perpetrators for at least two reasons. First, the perpetrators in their own stolid fantasy of omnipotence could probably not tolerate the possibility that there was any realm they could not invade and destroy. Second, I also theorized that Miriam's perpetrators' entrenched spiritual opposition to the unyielding power of the good rendered them unable to perceive it even when it did appear. Miriam was very heartened by these ideas and seemed to resonate with their potential truth. Whether or not all of her various self-states would agree with my take on these matters, what appeared to be most transformative was that Miriam strongly resonated with, and was alleviated by, my ability to freely play with subversive ideas – ideas that exposed potential gaps and fragilities in the logic and omnipotence of her perpetrators' belief system.

In spite of retaining her redemptive and reparative spiritual connections in some aspects of her personality system, other parts of Miriam's self-system had indeed been sacrificed to hold perpetrator identifications and commit atrocities from these dissociated self-states. Eventually, through continuous contact with diverse personality states in dialogue with me, some of Miriam's split off rage and hate were transmuted into self-protection and mastery of interpersonal and professional challenges. As treatment progressed, Miriam's sacred connections strengthened because some of the implanted "demons" crossed-over and went to work in support of the self and its compassionate spiritual connections, abandoning their allegiances to the perpetrators and their anti-life "traditions." In some cases, perpetrator-identified alters created in cult systems can be exposed to discrepant information and novel relationship experiences, leading to the choice of "conversion" to non-violence and paths of redemption. Some of these types of mutable alters seem to dissolve and fade away over time, while still others hunker down and hide out in the corners of a personality hoping for the eventual "comeback" promised by the perpetrators during years of propaganda and mind control.

Miriam had many intuitive gifts. Over time, as she tested my potential skepticism and my own experience with the numinous, Miriam brought in a great deal of material related to what she considered to be both previous lifetime events, transpersonal revelations, and near-death out-of-body anomalies[2] to add to her recollections of the bizarre and terrifying events of her childhood. My nonjudgmental receptivity to, and understanding of the near-death experiences, "channeling," and "previous lifetimes" she described throughout our work together helped Miriam to feel less alone and less alienated. I was familiar with most of the domains of her metaphysical journey and could converse fluently on the subjects brought in for discussion. Meeting another human being who was familiar with her paths to the diabolical and her paths to enlightenment allowed Miriam to trust the transformational container of psychotherapy which she needed to bring her ordinary and metaphysical selves into a new kind of encounter and integration.

As part of her healing and integration, Miriam shared a great deal with me about her devotional relationship with a well-known female spiritual teacher who embodied a kind of maternal unconditional love. This teacher's commitments involved charitable works around the world, serving the most downtrodden, disadvantaged, and outcast of all people. These charities included rehabilitating street children, AIDS orphans and prostitutes and children of prostitutes – groups with whom Miriam could strongly identify and relate. Miriam even spent some time in the spiritual teacher's native country volunteering to build houses for people whose lives had been devastated by earthquakes and floods. Because I knew of this particular teacher (having seen a couple of films about her life and work, and even meeting her in large open public meetings), I could appreciate and support the value of the teacher's message and contributions.

Miriam's eventual inclusion of this material in her therapy never seemed suspect to me (i.e., seduction, distraction, enactment, omnipotent fantasy) as the maturation of her spiritual life seemed only to follow after Miriam had done some difficult memory work and struggled to understand her chronic patterns of rejecting, betraying, and abandoning objects. Although I supported and respected Miriam's involvement with her inspiring teacher, I sometimes worried that the extensive time Miriam spent in service to the teacher's causes – leaving her own life and work behind for weeks at a time, helping out on retreats, kitchen duty, house building – might have a hidden shadow side with some self-sacrifice, enactment of guilt/reparations, or self-diminishment. I voiced these concerns along with sharing my respect for the teacher and explored the triangle that can emerge when a psychotherapy patient is also consulting a spiritual teacher or path. Miriam was rarely defensive about this subject, and she never used her spirituality as a hideout or a detour. As the years went by, her psychological integration and spiritual evolution coalesced into classical awakening and enlightenment processes, as described in many sacred texts and in the works on perennial philosophy. An essential element of Miriam's therapy process was work with her dreams, her traumatic memories, her mystical experiences, and her past lives.

For therapists unfamiliar with the psychological and spiritual literature on "past-life regression" or working with reports of previous lifetime experiences,[3] it is important to consider the psychodynamic and transpersonal ways of working with this material. Whether held as a transitional experience and/or as a potentially valid metaphysical reality, clinicians can make room for patients' revelations and inquiries into these past-life narratives without humiliating or shutting down the patient, and without feeling like they are working outside of the bounds of their clinical expertise. Like many other patients who have brought this kind of content into treatment over the years (without the use of formal hypnosis, as I predominantly work relationally and experientially), Miriam usually shared scenes of trauma, where she had experienced a wide array of victimization and perpetration events, during different historical periods. Often a given pattern would be replayed in a series of lifetimes as it might be revealed in a series of dreams. Previous lifetime narratives or reflections can allow patients a broader view of the patterns of victimization, complicity, and perpetration that play out in human life, without the excruciating immediacy that reliving traumatic memories from the present lifetime can entail. For some patients the experience of reliving what they view as "past lives" can also have grueling and painful aspects.

The wider-angle lens of multiple lifetimes, a hallmark of many indigenous belief systems, including Buddhism, can help patients integrate many events, dreams, and memories into a more spacious and inclusive identity and a narrative that is not polarized by victimization-perpetration. When the therapeutic focus is on witnessing important meaning structures, emotional triggers, and beliefs operative in the patient's life history, I have found that reviewing this "past-life" material with respect to themes and life lessons can be as valuable as working with dream material or regular trauma memories. This is especially so when the patient is not using "past-life" inquiry/narrative to avoid facing deeper feeling states or to seduce or distract the therapist with mystical theater. For clinicians uncomfortable with concepts of "past lives", I recommend openly sharing their positions and hesitancies with their patients while agreeing to work with the material in an open, non-judgmental manner in the spirit of inclusivity, transitional experiencing, and potential space – a clinical attitude that is deeply honored within contemporary psychoanalytic traditions.

Toward the end of therapy, Miriam allowed herself to remember, and shared with me, another set of positive anomalous experiences based on her witnessing of numerous deaths during her early participation in ritual abuse. Miriam had always felt emotionally and spiritually connected to the victims sacrificed by her group. Over the years, she had separately grieved these experiences, facing the guilt and shame as much as she could. Miriam recalled a type of silent, sacred communion that took place between her innocent empathic spirit and the soul of the dying persons in the process of leaving their bodies in the last moments of their lives. Miriam described a kind of transmission happening through a glance of mutual recognition, witnessing, and respect, somehow soul to soul – in the middle of an insane, violent realm based on torture and execution. Although this memory/revelation can easily be characterized (or psychologized) as restorative and redemptive fantasy and as such, honored as part of a healthy psychological integration process involving the reactivation of imaginal capacities, neither Miriam nor I needed to analyze, interpret, or reduce the revelation. We simply sat with the mystery and acknowledged all the meanings and implications of her finally being able to contain within her unifying self the memories of her own innocence, transcendence, and corruption existing and operating side-by-side throughout the worst experiences of her life.

Miriam later became a gifted teacher, healer, and writer. A quiet sense of joy and liberation replaced the earlier fragmentation and emotional desiccation of her first years in treatment. One day she woke up from a difficult retraumatizing experience that in the past would have sent her reeling for days and heard herself say to herself, "I am no longer a trauma survivor." Miriam eventually decided to formally take the Buddhist bodhisattva vow. This vow is a conscious decision to dedicate one's life to liberating other beings from the suffering inherent in the cycles of birth, death, and reincarnation. The bodhisattva seeks enlightenment not for his or her own sake, but for the sake of all beings. At around the same time, Miriam decided to pursue a different form of human intimacy in her personal life. She began seeking relationships based on equality, power-sharing, and mutual transformation. She mastered several alternative healing arts. She devoted a good portion of the proceeds of her first book to the healing of victims of child abuse, prostitution, and other forms of coerced perpetration.

Forgiveness, suffering, and failure

Forgiveness

The clinical and non-clinical literature on the relationship between forgiveness and reconciliation is sometimes contradictory. Some writers claim that forgiveness is not a prerequisite for reconciliation (Huyse, 2003). Others (Enright, 2001; McLernon *et al.*, 2002) believe that forgiveness is an essential prerequisite to reconciliation. Hamber's (2009) emphasis on reconciliation as a nonlinear process is consistent with relational psychoanalytic perspectives on integration processes with dissociative trauma survivors, underscoring the inevitability of imperfections inherent in the processes of learning to negotiate and tolerate ambiguity. By its very nature, according to Hamber, reconciliation contains paradoxes and tensions due to the constant inconsistency between social, interpersonal, intrapsychic, and political contexts. Instead of conceptualizing reconciliation and forgiveness as outcomes or endpoints in themselves, reconciliation and forgiveness are best understood as a set of ongoing dynamic processes requiring strong capacities for witnessing, tolerance for ambiguity and commitments to inclusivity. Applied to treating the dissociative survivor-perpetrator, internal reconciliation among previously polarized and mutually negating self-states, healing must take place through complex exchanges of anger, moral outrage, repudiation, compassion, forgiveness, and gratitude. One of the main differences between the goals of social reconciliation and personal forgiveness is that the path of societal reconciliation may leave many individuals safely inhabiting a more stable, sane society but with disappointment and a deep feeling of unresolved grief and anger (Hamber, 2009). Forgiveness processes may be thwarted by the unwillingness of perpetrators to confess, feel vulnerable, or make reparations, but social reconciliation can advance the healing of society as a whole. Aspects of individual healing may be bypassed or compromised for the sake of the collective.

From an archetypal perspective, deliberate victimization and forgiveness can be explored with greater equanimity. Naïve, simplistic advice from therapists and misguided cultural pressures on victims to forgive perpetrators as an avenue of recovery should be replaced with more realistic, open-ended approaches to reconciliation (Safer, 2000). Forgiveness in the absence of accountability, social sanctions, or collective remembering may simply be too much to expect of a survivor of coerced perpetration and other forms of betrayal trauma. A survivor of this type of trauma remains vulnerable to various forms of retraumatization through society's (and clinicians') negations, projections, blame, or distortions. In Safer's view, thoughtful non-forgiving can be as much a part of recovery as forgiving, especially in the absence of true contrition or meaningful reparations on the part of perpetrators. According to Grand's (2000) analysis of the treatment of evil, offering forgiveness to the unrepentant not only abandons the victim a second time – reiterating the victim's isolation – but can also serve to solidify the "catastrophic loneliness" of the perpetrator and thus contribute to facilitating, instead of containing, "malignant dissociative contagion." Grand (2000) believes that true forgiveness must include a productive dialogue (one that includes condemnation and repudiation for destructive acts) between the victim, the bystander, and ideally, the perpetrator.

In the analysis of individual and social repair processes that occur in truth and reconciliation commissions, some form of apology or public recognition of wrongdoing by perpetrators is seen as a precondition for forgiveness to be contemplated (Hamber, 2009; Mellor, Bretherton, and Firth, 2007; Shriver, 2001). Reconciliation may be advanced through witnessing, truth-telling, dialogue, information gathering, and restitutive interventions without the appearance of contrition, and confession on the part of perpetrators (Hamber, 2009). Ancient and contemporary spiritual teachers emphasize that forgiving one's victimizers does not depend on what the perpetrator does or does not do or say. From this point of view, forgiveness is an independent, self-preserving, and self-liberating process that reckons with the transient nature of all things, demands nothing of others, and focuses on the rebalancing of the self in relation to itself and the cosmos.

For a dissociative survivor of trauma, a prerequisite for forgiveness or reconciliation is that the parts of the self-system not identified with perpetration must relinquish most forms of collusion (by way of intimidation or by avoidance of encounters) with perpetrator part-selves. It is essential the shared, non-judgmental witnessing of the experiences of victimization, perpetration, and complicity are viewed from the perspectives of different self-states organized around these polarities. During the process, expressions of contempt, grief, sorrow, and indifference may alternate with stony silence and frantic avoidance as part-selves grapple with disowned experiences. For the optimal outcome of self-forgiveness to become manifest, perpetrator-identified states must eventually connect with their underlying vulnerability and culpability. Non-perpetrator parts of the self must identify with their self-protective aggression and their sense of healthy entitlement. Ruthlessness and ambition, previously split off into perpetrator states must be owned and repurposed by other aspects of the patient's self. Each segment of the self must relax rigid coping strategies and embrace their ideological and experiential opposite – at least briefly. This moderation of dissociative oppositions can occur by way of encounters with the therapist's empathy and confrontation, or through perpetrator alters' recognition of the ways in which they were deceived and exploited, or by way of the dialogue where non-perpetrator part-selves express their outrage and repudiation at the actual perpetrators and at perpetrator alters for their destructiveness. The problematic aspect of this forgiveness process is that it involves not a village or a community with separate groups of victims, bystanders, and perpetrators, but all of these groups within a single self.

Reconciliation requires that all voices are given an opportunity for speech, symbolization, and witnessing even if the opportunity is co-opted for further enactments of denial or perpetration. The therapist's steadfast and unflinching acknowledgment of the presence of the majority of the patient's dissociative system will have a positive effect on the reconciliation process, regardless of how the patient's perpetrator self-states use the opportunity for witnessing and reconciliation. Ideally, perpetrator states which have been part of treatment and connected to their own vulnerability for some time will be able to express minimal remorse, contrition or empathy for the suffering they have inflicted on the self and others. However, even without this expression of healthy guilt, the reconciliation process can move forward. Recalcitrant self-states can eventually be encircled by the emerging integration of the majority of the patient's personality system.

Even more challenging at times than the attempts to connect perpetrator part-selves to their own vulnerability and history of betrayal, is the therapeutic activation of moral outrage and repudiation of non-perpetrator part-selves toward the destructiveness and complicity of the other part-selves (and toward actual perpetrators of childhood). This is challenging for three reasons. First, this form of object- related hate has been too dangerous in the past for these previously intimidated or confused part-selves to even contemplate. Second, outrage and any form of hatred are terrifying because these feelings immediately trigger the memories of perpetrators' extreme aggressive and contemptuous enactments. Patients may fear that if they feel something even remotely close to rage and hate they will become just like their perpetrators. Third, this confrontation of destructiveness between alters must counterintuitively coincide with empathy and gratitude on the part of gentler parts of the self for the life-saving functions implicitly enacted (not consciously avowed) by the defiant and malevolent self-states. Ultimately, all parts of the self must come to accept the shared responsibility for all aspects of perpetration, collusion, and victimization.

Most clinicians understand that self-forgiveness is the ultimate, often lifelong challenge for trauma survivors. Self-forgiveness can be more onerous than coming to terms with their perpetrators' culpability. Exposure to some of the archetypal wisdom traditions of nonduality and compassion, in conjunction with sustained immersion in the empathic and compassionate matrix of the therapy relationship, may help erode the entrenched shame and confused pride that serves as a nearly insurmountable obstacle to self-forgiveness. When survivors successfully internalize real compassion and enact self-forgiveness, they inevitably gain a new empathic perspective on their perpetrators' entrapment in, and perpetuation of, a hell of their own making. Often, accompanying these revelations is the survivor's sense that he or she wants to undertake some form of service to humanity. Or the survivor feels inspired to engage in previously foreclosed creative expression. Light and dark elements of the survivor's imagination can be re-channeled into creatively investigating themes of destruction, reconstruction, desolation, and emerging joy.

Suffering

Survivor-perpetrators also face a deeply confused relationship to suffering and failure in the recovery process. The archetypal/transpersonal perspective on suffering and failure contrasts starkly with the dissociative survivor's relationship with pain and shame through the matrix of perpetrator-implanted (and culturally transmitted) programming about vulnerability, loyalty, entitlement, and personal value. Archetypal views of suffering as an essential aspect of psychological and spiritual maturation are perspectives that re-contextualize the intrinsic value of often denigrated, misunderstood experiences. An archetypal frame holds suffering not as a punishment but as a pathway for encountering truth in its starkest forms, a surrender of omnipotent control fantasies, and a potential avenue toward enlightenment (Chassay, 1996; Grant, 1996; Kalsched, 1996). Without the willingness to risk feeling deeply, to risk failure, to experience loss, there is no true capacity to heal or to live life fully, no capacity to face death or deep love with equanimity,

Suffering enlarges our capacity to bear painful experiences and develops our compassion for others' suffering, providing us with a fuller aliveness in the world. From an archetypal viewpoint, suffering is never solely about pain but is always related to the absence of, or a confusion about, the meaning of pain. Most dissociative trauma survivors have been overexposed to perpetrators' conceptions of pain: a means of evacuation, retaliation, annihilation, or a source of humiliation. Because attempts at remembering and re-experiencing pain reinforce traumatic injunctions and perpetrator belief systems, for suffering to become redemptive it must not only be acknowledged (to the extent that it can be shared with another person), it must be integrated into higher orders of meaning (Grant, 1996). The degradation and humiliation aspects of suffering typical of perpetrator systems branded onto the dissociative survivor's mind must be challenged by the therapist's witnessing and empathic commentary. Most importantly, the belief in a life beyond suffering as futile must be exposed as one of the greatest deceptions of the dissociative self-system.

Conscious suffering (including restoration of affectivity) unravels the mechanisms of dissociative flight and undermine programming and perpetrator behavior patterns. Survivors must learn how to consciously embrace suffering rather than let it destroy, fragment, or evacuate their own minds (Bion, 1967). Through conscious suffering, as opposed to dissociating or re-enacting, the individual takes responsibility for metabolizing and releasing – and *not* re-distributing or memorializing – pain. The choice to move toward conscious suffering brings the survivor's sequestered agony into the transformative process of human relationship. Meeting suffering, as opposed to evading or evacuating it, opens the survivor to change, but change of any kind has been what the dissociative system was created to prevent. Repeated experiences of accepting and feeling one's pain in the presence of an empathic other can lead to restoration of the self and its capacities for intimacy and self-awareness. The survivor can come to experience suffering's turbulence and sense of lost control as non-destructive, as honoring the self instead of as betraying the self.

Meeting posttraumatic suffering with awareness and vulnerability is critical for undermining and transforming perpetrator identifications. Most non-redemptive or non-transformational suffering (e.g., addiction, perpetration, repetitive behavior, obsessions, re-enactments, retaliation, self-injury) is based on a limited idea in the mind of the sufferer of who he or she actually is and of what the meaning of the dreaded states of vulnerability in suffering long avoided are all about. All non-redemptive suffering is based on emotional contraction, avoidance, and misrecognition of the meaning of pain through omnipotent fantasy, blame, justification, or dramatization. Most common in perpetrator-identified states (as most common in most perpetrators) is the belief that direct experience of one's suffering is tantamount to defeat or obliteration.

Archetypal traditions regard suffering as honorable and essential to the breakdown of dysfunctional egoic structures that block identification with a higher self, divinity, and felt linkages with fellow humans. Grant (1996) contrasts the limits inherent in a stoic's mastery of pain to the potential inherent in a mystic's embrace of pain. Stoicism may perpetuate omnipotence, while the mystics embrace of pain and surrender may serve as a pathway to revealing a person's deepest nature. To be present and aware while suffering means to consciously recognize the impulse to escape from all pain and suffering and instead to choose and face whatever appears in one's awareness without dissociation – be it grief, dread, horror, loss, sorrow, or revelations about one's most depraved experiences. People who have developed the capacity to tolerate periodic episodes of internal suffering over distraction, escape, fragmentation, evacuation, or various forms of perpetration are able to participate in the human condition rather than bargain with it or try to evade its full reality.

Suffering in the presence of an empathic other can release dissociative patients from their sealed-off states of shame, despair, arrogance, and contempt. I emphasize conscious suffering (in contrast to helpless suffering in sadistic abuse), voluntarily faced, in the spirit of free will and informed consent as the antidote to the ravages of a psyche systematically exploited and disenfranchised by perpetrators. Following catharsis or shared suffering, the accompanying release from internal domination by perpetrator self-states can leave the patient feeling extremely vulnerable and disoriented. If the patient can tolerate this vulnerable state, transforming revelations may emerge. As many mystical traditions instruct, at the core of the vulnerability caused by directly feeling one's suffering is a gift, an intuitive apprehension of an archetypal luminosity that can only be gained by penetrating the center of ignorance and fear. This radiance reveals itself to be personal and impersonal, individual and communal. When sharing his or her suffering, the patient touches this profound state of being, and he or she often experiences a deep sense of belonging – an unexpected discovery after a lifetime of profound alienation. When the survivor experiences both suffering and transcendence included within the conceptual field of "all that is," he or she can sense the beauty of his or her own essential nature and begin to forge an enlightened communion with other sentient beings. Having met suffering head-on, having forgiven the self and repudiated perpetration, having expressed gratitude for *all* aspects of his or her coping and survival strategies, the survivor is responding to human destructiveness and evil with a powerful counterforce of resistance and redemption.

Failure

One of the most powerful forces subtly potentiating mind control programming in the psyches of survivor-perpetrators operates through ongoing reinforcement (conscious and unconscious) of an endless sense of failure, worthlessness, and damnation. In perpetrator groups using mind control, intense "failure programming" is utilized to coerce dissociative performance splits, and to punish and bind victims who cannot fully participate in violent activities or maintenance of loyalty and secrecy. Before they are released from the group's control, these "unsuccessful" subjects' self-esteem and life potential is booby-trapped with numerous injunctions predicting and inciting failure experiences that shadow them their entire lives. Even more extreme, Miller (2012) describes internal "garbage dumps" created by perpetrators in the minds of dissociative survivors to hold noncompliant, uncooperative, and allegedly defective self-states.

The failure programming of perpetrators groups is inadvertently but insidiously reinforced by mainstream cultural norms of invulnerability and success that blame and indict individuals for their inability to participate in the omnipresent consumer bounty. Being a failure as a perpetrator/assassin within a cult, only to experience medical and relational obstacles due to professional ignorance of post-traumatic and dissociative symptomatology coupled with society's scorn of the adult survivor is a compound retraumatization for many dissociative survivors. Being a child in Uganda, Myanmar or Columbia who failed to protect loved ones, failed to fight off his or her assailants, who then successfully internalized the violent training and programming to kill others is one set of mind-bending traumas. However, when on top of these experiences, that same child, now an effective combatant, is recaptured by Western helping agents and stripped of his or her cherished identity and held in a treatment center, feared and rejected by his or her own people, and rendered incapable of providing for himself or herself (as well as for her offspring in the case of female combatants who had children from rapes during the war), the sense of failure and retraumatization can be unbearable. A compounded sense of failure and the attending shame are among the most common causes of trauma survivors' rejection of treatment and return to their perpetrators.

The experience of failure can be viewed through the archetypal lens as inherent in the process of evolving and not as an endpoint in itself. Survivors can feel caught between various internalized injunctions of incompetence and worthlessness – for feeling pain or for not feeling pain, for complicity with perpetrators or for defiance of perpetrators, for revealing dissociative structures or for camouflaging them, for achieving societal validation or for eschewing it, for ignoring themselves and "moving on" and for healing themselves and seeing "moving on" as potentiating complicity. These patients can benefit from understanding how they have kept themselves ensnared in various internal and external hostage dynamics. They can also benefit from understanding the absurdity in attempting to appease these contradictory injunctions, and eventually finding humor in this futility.

From an archetypal perspective, failure can never merely be framed as subtractive or negating: it is also additive as part of the education of the psyche and spirit of the individual. Resistance to failure and lack of experience navigating the terrain of failure make the individual less integrated and less personally evolved, and less valuable to the community. Failure experience understood as a fertilizer for innovation and personal and collective evolution undermines the life-and-death, totalitarian view of success and failure operative in most perpetrator groups and in some social structures.

Case example: Sara

Sara's therapy journey called upon all of the clinical wisdom I could muster during my early years treating severely dissociative trauma survivors. Sara is the DID patient whose case is described in Chapter 3, the woman who carved pentagrams on her arms on a locked unit of the hospital where I worked at the time. I was heartened by the fact that before she died, after years of intensive therapy, we managed to heal her spiritual abuse in addition to successfully integrating her extraordinarily fragmented psyche. Sara's treatment involved not only integrating her dissociative structures but accessing, examining, and eventually deprogramming many perpetrator conditioned self-states. These states were sometimes replicas of perpetrators or were diabolical spiritual figures; at other times, these states were organized around tasks of sexual and violent performance, self-monitoring, self-sabotage, and loyalty to the perpetrating system. Sara had given birth to several infants while she was an adolescent girl member of a sex-death cult. Discussing the tragic fates of these children, plus working through Sara's calcified horror, disgust, shame, and guilt occupied considerable time in the early and middle years of treatment.

There were three themes I am especially relieved to have covered in treatment with Sara. First, I tried to honor the extent of her suffering, her courage in treatment, and all that I learned from our work together by impressing upon her that through my therapy with other trauma surviviors, my consultations with other therapists, and my writing, many others had or would be benefiting from her healing journey. Knowledge of this uplifted and gratified Sara. She knew any beneficial effect of her treatment in the world would enrage her perpetrators. Taking rebellious comfort in this knowledge helped restore her dignity and validated her own commitment to service to others in the final period of her life when a fatal illness prevented her from leaving her apartment. This form of vengeance on her perpetrators helped her integrate aggressive elements of her self because it demonstrated a path that did not replicate the kinds of vengeance and spite she was raised to valorize and enact in the cult that victimized her.

Second, through years of inquiry which included many serendipitous discoveries, Sara and I managed to access and defuse most of her "after-death programming" – training aimed at convincing Sara that her soul was entrapped within the malevolent perpetrator system not just in this life, but in all future lifetimes. Such programming seeks to enroll the victim's belief in perpetrators' omnipotent control over all life and death. Sara was continuously surprised to learn the extent to which her perpetrators had booby-trapped not only every aspect of her life, mind, body, and spirit, but her death as well. Over the years, Sara's lack of self-importance and her traumatically shattered self-esteem collided with the deepening understanding and accruing revelations of her considerable economic, psychological, and spiritual value to her perpetrators. I helped Sara understand that all mystical systems, whether based in love/compassion or in hate/fear have something to say about dying and the afterlife. These systems seek ways to either soothe and sanctify the afterlife or corrupt and control it.[4] Consistent with mainstream religions that define the afterlife and what happens or should happen during the dying process, control over Sara's death was apparently as important to Sara's perpetrators as the volume of trauma they could inflict on Sara and get her to inflict on others as long as she lived.

I believe Sara's dying was a little easier for both of us to cope with, knowing that we had removed, as it were, most of the programming aimed at entrapping her in an eternal cycle of hells. Even if the "death training" Sara endured was nothing more than an elaborate implanted fantasy, the fact that Sara did not have this set of traumas and programs lurking in her unconscious mind as she faced her own death represented one of several forms of mastery and independence from the perpetrating system that Sara managed to achieve while still conscious, alive, and operating from the base of her own intentionality.

Third, Sara and I had managed to help her develop and deepen a connection to an internal source of psychological and spiritual inner guidance and sustenance. A key aspect of the restoration of faith in all psychotherapy and psychospiritual enterprises involves helping a person to realign with his or her own innate wisdom. Inner guidance can be understood to be related to a wide range of familiar constructs such as intuition, insight, wisdom, and the collective unconscious (Jung, 1958), but it also correlates to meta-psychological and paranormal phenomena including psychic abilities, guardian and ancestor spirits, remote viewing, channeling, extrasensory perception, astral travel, and shamanic belief systems. Not only were these topics as far from Sara's mind as they could possibly have been due to her conditioned aversion to anything related to organized religion or spirituality, the entire concept of inner guidance had been so undermined by her perpetrators that a mere suggestion to "inquire within" produced instantaneous nausea. I mention this to indicate how Sara's relationship with her internal self-helper and/or spirit guide was not easy to locate or cultivate. Fortunately, neither was her internal guide ever used as an escape route or spiritual short-cut.

Unlike some patients who either glorify their inner voice or consciously or hopefully regard it as evidence of their potential for wholeness, Sara initially refused to identify with or explore any internal benevolent force. For many years, having been bombarded by memories of her own perpetration experiences, Sara could rarely pull herself away from a commitment to an identity as worthless and condemned. The idea of having access to divine guidance was not something Sara could fathom. And when she could be convinced to briefly contemplate it, her formidable sense of worthlessness would immediately sever the tentative connection. Sara's blockade of all things spiritual was composed of two interlocking dissociative self-organizations: her own self-hatred and self-condemnation, and the elaborate programming by her perpetrators, including implanted spies, assassins, and demons trained to obstruct any possible spiritual independence from her perpetrators' Nazi and satanic ideologies.

Sara was eventually willing to try meditation. I introduced her to the concept of the sacred feminine and to female divinities from the East, particularly Quan Yin (Guanyin)[5] who seemed to resemble the inner guide Sara had been occasionally telling me about from the beginning of her treatment. Sara's perpetrator(s) had been quite methodical and systematic in severing her connections with any benevolent Judeo-Christian imagery, but they had neglected to warn her against believing in African, Asian, or Native American divinities. Prior to these psychospiritual "introductions" which I made many years into Sara's treatment, my use of history via films and books gave Sara a context for her inner experience of trauma and benevolence and did not seem to trigger a great deal of opposition. As time went on, Sara went from a state of utter alienation into an understanding of the world where her past experiences, while horrific, were not entirely unique. Sara developed especially strong identifications with the African-American slavery experience, the details of which she began to study to broaden her perspective on the repetitive patterns of human malevolence. All these explorations began with Sara's consent and risked the possibility of arousing Sara's demon-identified aspects which could at any point surface to oppose the new material (as they had been trained to do). Care was also taken on my part to remind Sara of her prerogative to critique or reject any of the material I was presenting (or reject me for presenting the material). These reminders were important as they laid open the danger of re-enacting yet another version of coercive mind control. This free will aspect of the process was likely as helpful to Sara as the content of the new spiritual material.

Sara's openness to examining non-Western spiritual concepts enabled her to expand her capacity for imagination. She showed an increasing ability to fantasize about alternative images and concepts of benevolent and compassionate spiritual forces. Following some initial anxiety and skepticism, the mere idea of a female divinity revolutionized Sara's thinking because in her many perpetrating systems, males ruled the world, the heavens, and everything in between. She savored her freedom to choose and reject concepts and iconography that resonated with her own developing sensibilities. Eventually, Sara began to collect various artifacts – rocks, feathers, crystals, photos of children, animals, and nature – to add to a small statue of Quan Yin I had given her – and created a personal altar. Without prompting, Sara began to be drawn to Native American imagery showing me that she was gradually beginning to follow her own intuitions and inclinations into the realm of the sacred. As she did this for the first time, the notion occurred to her conscious mind that the sacred could never actually be completely destroyed.

Because of Sara's extensive background in perpetration behavior, the idea of compassionate deities was introduced into our discourse by way of the system of "wrathful deities" from the Tibetan Buddhist tradition. The presence of ferocious, terrifying forms known as wrathful deities is an enigmatic aspect of Tibetan Buddhist iconography and philosophy that embraces the shadow in the service of the sacred. While on the surface these hideous, frightening images appear to contradict Buddhist ideals, they are in fact not personifications of evil or demonic forces but rather benevolent gods who symbolize the tremendous effort it takes to vanquish evil (Preece, 2006). The acceptance of violence as a fundamental reality of the cosmos and the human mind is a valuable contribution from the Tibetan tradition of archetypal healing. Instead of dissociating malice and aggression, the wrathful deities' role is to convert aggression into protections – to protect the faithful by instilling terror in evil spirits and evildoers, and to protect the teachings of Buddhism (the *dharma*). Images of the wrathful deities are kept in homes and temples of Tibetan Buddhists to protect believers against evil influences and to remind them to work at dissolving internal destructive forces. Through prayer and mediation, Tibetan Buddhists believe that they can channel the power of destructive energies toward increased wisdom, compassion, and service.

Simply being able to conceptualize these wrathful deities as potential allies who may be fighting for her rather than supporting evil and perpetrators helped Sara and me with some aspects of deprogramming, and provided her with relief from her assumption "that scary monsters always only work for the bad guys." Some of Sara's more receptive perpetrator alters benefited from the "vocational rehabilitation" implied in stories of the great Buddhist teachers and saints whose work included conversion and conquest of destructive demons and spiritual forces and turning them to work for the benefit and protection of all humanity and the liberation of all beings.

Sara's encounters with Quan Yin and the wrathful deities helped her clear a field for recovering redemptive spirituality in a context that was not dominated by the patriarchal narratives drilled into her by her victimizers. As previously mentioned, Sara already had possessed her own version of an inner guide – a figure she called "The Lady in White" – whose energy and characteristics struck me as quite similar to Quan Yin. In spite of her initial resistances and dismissiveness toward this figure, Sara allowed me to support their relationship over time.

"The Lady in White" first appeared in the early years of Sara's post-hospitalization treatment. In some of Sara's difficult memory work and abreactions, this "alter" – who Sara described as a serene and very wise older person wearing a flowing white robe – could comfort, reassure, and ground Sara. "The Lady in White" seemed quite independent of Sara and myself or the therapy. At first Sara spoke of this figure nonchalantly, as if she had always been part of Sara's consciousness. Sara was not very curious about this aspect of herself. It became clear to me that Sara was disconnected from this figure and from the meaning and implications of her relationships with it.

According to Allison (1980), Kluft (1985), Putnam, (1997), and C. Ross, (1997), internal self-helpers are commonly found in DID patients and represent potential for wholeness. These self-states offer both psychological and transpersonal guidance, memory maintenance, and protection. Adams (1989) and Allison (1980), among other clinical contributors to the development of the trauma/dissociation disorder field, recommended elevating these alter personalities to the status of co-therapists as they are highly supportive of the goals and values of the therapy process, and seem to be unusually informed about the individual's life history and dynamics while ignoring the patient's damage and limitations. Although differences exist in the field about the meaning and appropriate use of internal self-helpers (H. Schwartz, 2000), including them in treatment is often beneficial.

I often asked Sara to invite "The Lady in White" into our dialogues as a way to encourage Sara to entertain a perspective not available from other aspects of herself, and to de-condition Sara to her cultivated aversion to consulting an inner guide. I often asked for dialogue between "The Lady in White" and more destructive aspects of Sara's dissociative self-system. For quite some time, the hostile and perpetrator alters either denied her existence or refused to enter into meaningful conversation with her, these alters instead chose to contemptuously mock Sara's willingness to believe in the reality of this self-state. "The Lady in White's" attitude toward this derision was always calm, accepting, and nonjudgmental – this attitude seemed to unnerve the hateful part-selves and surprise Sara. The idea that "The Lady in White" was Sara, or that it could be Sara, or it was devoted to and "there" for Sara had been completely unimaginable.

Sara's avoidance of "The Lady in White" changed into curiosity, then into gratitude and hopefulness – alternating with episodes of anger where she railed at "The Lady in White" for not preventing the trauma. In this way, "The Lady in White" served the additional function of indestructible other and transitional object who could handle Sara's rage and never retaliate, abandon, or withdraw. In states of great grief and rage, Sara sometimes gave "The Lady in White" the "silent treatment." I regarded this as Sara's only possible form of moral outrage and expression of abandonment rage, aside from the expectable early therapy struggles with issues and fears of disappointment and/or abandonment with me. On occasion, Sara became angry at "The Lady in White" and me, for example when the guide and I took a similar position on an issue that challenged Sara's viewpoint. This was the closest approximation to an experience Sara had previously never had of normal adolescent rebellion with loving, unified parents who she knew had her best interest at heart.

As I delved deeper into the history of the "The Lady in White's" relationship with Sara, it gradually became clear that she knew all of Sara's most horrific moments and traumatic passages – not as a prevention-protector, but as a holder-protector. Over time, Sara could make the distinction between protection that helps avoid terrible events, and protection that sustains, strengthens, and bolsters during disastrous experiences. As Sara's rage became less self-destructively oriented, and as she worked through her perpetrator-implanted dissociative matrix "The Lady in White" began to reveal her transpersonal dimensions. "The Lady in White" shared that she was present during specific cult rituals involving death and torture, and specialized in helping spirits leaving their bodies during traumatic circumstances. "The Lady in White" explained that she had operated through Sara's body and consciousness in ways Sara could not understand or completely remember, to disrupt the flow of destructive events and bring what sounded like comedic-angelic relief into the heart of darkness. This had been possible even in the throes of perpetrators' exaggerated self-aggrandizement through orgies of sadistic sexuality, demonic spiritual invocations, and ritual murders. In one instance, "The Lady in White" explained how she managed to hide some very important bones that were essential to the completion of a power ritual. When the disruption ensued, Sara was brutally punished and blamed for hiding the bones even though Sara had no clue or memory where they were hidden, or if she had hidden them, and if she had how she might have pulled it off. In the chaos that ensued following the episode of the missing bones, Sara got a glimpse of the fragility and absurdity of the perpetrator's methods. The memory of this event had been completely dissociated, but it emerged into consciousness at a time in her healing when she could make most use of it.

In another remembered scenario where Sara had been instructed to walk down the center aisle of a ritual in a bloodied white dress and say the words, "I denounce the Lord," she found herself saying the words "I announce the Lord." Pandemonium ensued in the perpetrator group and the ritual space was temporarily disrupted. Sara was punished and forced to repeat the performance. Once again, through a combination of her innocence, stress, and most of all, from the subtle influence of "The Lady in White," Sara said, "I announce the Lord." When the group exasperatedly changed the script for her to say, "I announce satan," Sara erred again and "accidentally" mispronounced the word and said the reverse: "I denounce satan." Although severely punished and relegated to a less prominent role until she could produce an alter that would cooperate, memories of events like these salvaged some of Sara's dignity. Most of her remembered life history prior to these memories involved complete complicity and coerced perpetration. Some of these "The Lady in White" inspired missteps may have been indirectly responsible for Sara's eventual permanent demotion from the higher ranks of the perpetrator group. This development presaged her eventual exit from the group.

"The Lady in White" eventually taught Sara many things about Sara's true nature, the soul's journey, love, death, compassion, faith, and good and evil. As Sara began to identify with this aspect of her personal and transcendent self, the last of her confusion and identification with evil and perpetration began to recede. Sara allowed this integration process to unfold. Sara's allowings of "The Lady in White" became occasions for serenity and grace. Those occasions were a long way from the self-mutilations and re-enactments of her confinement on a locked unit of a psychiatric hospital. Sara had shown me in her own lived experience that there is indeed an indestructible core at the center of the deepest abyss. And that in spite of any feelings or doubts to the contrary, evil is ultimately transient and unstable. Sara's journey showed that love can be fierce, and light in the darkest places is indeed the most powerful light of all. I was at Sara's hospital bedside a few hours before her unexpected passing and as I wept and watched her unconscious body take the last breaths of a truly archetypal life, I knew I was saying goodbye to one of the greatest teachers of my life.

Conclusion

From the archetypal perspective, trauma and transcendence are mutually interdependent forces in psychological life. Grant's (1996) view of trauma treatment posits that the grief and disillusionment resulting from trauma can be transformed to a spirituality of liberation. The successful healing of internalized perpetration is marked by the survivor-perpetrator's "ability to stand with open eyes before the full scope and mystery of life acknowledging both the existence of evil and one's potential for evil" (p. 152). When trauma includes coerced perpetration, the survivor's reclaiming of his or her autonomy, subjectivity, and relationship to archetypal benevolence – choosing love, compassion, and service to others – contributes to the collective healing and maturation of humanity.

The issue of purification often surfaces in the final stages of treatment. In previous stages, the patient may wonder if his or her mind, body, and soul can ever be completely purified from the evil he or she has witnessed or enacted. The therapist can address misconceptions about purification through the reconciling of apparently mutually exclusive identities. Previous fantasies of recovery may have involved the unrealistic eradication of guilt, shame, and signs of physical trauma. Some patients cling to notions of irredeemable damage and eternal damnation as a strange sort of protection against the possibility of further perpetrations. Aspirations for attaining perfection by way of agonizing repentance or through the avoidance of new "mistakes," are rendered unnecessary when viewed within constructs of archetypal psychology.

If life is metaphorically like a painting, a work in progress that can be seen as a tableau of a patient's journey to that point, traumatic experiences and perpetrator self-states stain or tear at that canvas. A simplistic approach to healing would dictate the complete restoration of the painting to be indistinguishable from its original state. An archetypal approach to purification/redemption in treatment includes the acceptance and assimilation of imperfections. The residue of the patient's traumatic past may be seen as pentimenti (vestigial images that have been abandoned and painted over), lending nuance to the canvas in a manner so subtle as to be imperceptible to most onlookers.

With a similar analogy, there is a tradition within Japanese culture known as *kintsugi* (golden joinery) where broken objects (in particular, ceramics) are lovingly repaired by filling in the cracks with gold or silver (Iten, 2008). These objects are considered to be more valuable and beautiful in their state of imperfection than in their undamaged state. Within this tradition of restoration of broken ceramics, it is believed that the original structure of the object partly determines how it breaks upon impact. Although the object's appearance might be altered, its integrity is actually enhanced through the process of mending (Bartlett, 2008).

Bartlett (2008) describes how the altered physical appearance of mended objects does not diminish their appeal. Rather, a new sense of vitality and resilience elevates their beauty and value to even greater heights – "immaterial factors assumed a material presence through the lines of its mending and became an inextricable part of the bowl's appeal"; the repaired bowl stands as "talismanic proof that imagination and language had the power to make ill fortune good" (p. 10). In her view, repaired objects are appreciated for their uncalculated nature and a physical expression of the spirit of *mushin* – often translated as "no mind," related to the practice of Zen. Other Japanese art forms also carry related connotations: full presence in the moment, non-attachment, equanimity amid changing conditions, and the relinquishment of desire to impose one's will upon the world. As Bartlett poignantly concludes, regardless of whether the story of breakage and mending is known, the affection in which the object was always held is evident in its rebirth as a lovingly-mended object.

Reconsidering the metaphor of one's life as a painting in progress, the harms of perpetration can be recontextualized to embrace the history of damage so that the visible repair can position the "trauma" as a potential vehicle for elevation. Importantly, the flaws on the canvas or in the pottery do not in themselves become valuable; their position of honor is derived from the context of respect for imperfections in which they are situated. The wounds themselves are not diminished; yet their meaning is changed as "the canvas" is enlarged and refined – just as the "narrative" or lived-history of the bowl becomes richer through the process of restoration. The repair is successful through the holistic transformation and reconceptualization of the entire work. In depth psychotherapy, the therapist leads the patient toward experiencing a heightened level of grieving and mourning for all that has been lost and destroyed, without losing sight of the proposition that the realm of archetypal understanding and healing is one in which scars of mind and body are worn not as blemishes but as marks of distinction.

Perhaps the most essential reversal in archetypal psychotherapy occurs when a student/seeker becomes the teacher. Such a metamorphosis is possible once a patient has matured to the point of being able to inform the therapist's understanding of the therapist's own life journey. Archetypal transformation of this caliber takes place in the apogee of the most evolved mentor–mentee relationship. (An analogous evolution is apparent when a middle-aged child becomes an elderly parent's primary caregiver or in a system more structurally similar to psychotherapy when a coach's long-term instruction of an athlete crosses a threshold whereby the athlete offers insights that significantly change the way the coach approaches training and the game itself.) This is not merely an inversion in the hierarchy of power. After the patient becomes fully familiar with the dynamics of healing, in some cases he or she comes to occupy a new position in the relational dyad. In rare cases, the patient can come to play a meaningful role in illuminating aspects of the therapist's own personal and spiritual struggles (regardless of whether the therapist chooses to disclose aspects of these struggles). When this exceptional level of mutuality is realized, it can be a very moving experience for the therapist. At the same time, it affords symbolic corroboration and authentication that the patient's painful experiences have been transmogrified into compelling insights with significance beyond the therapeutic dyad.

The archetypal transmutation of opposites may also scale from the interpersonal to the global level through groups of like-minded people. Just as darkness and light are alchemically mutable within individual narratives, the potential exists for collective social narratives to impel broad-based transformation. Personal transformation is a necessary antecedent to social transformation,[6] individuals are the vectors of ideological contagion with the capacity to convert despair and enslavement into hope and liberation in ever-widening circles of influence. As broadening cohorts of clinicians, advocates, and policy makers join forces to systematically combat the pernicious agents of an archetypal shadow force – interposing consciousness and cultivating compassion within it, collectively we can create and sustain greater opportunities for victims of coerced perpetration to become the redemptive heroes of their own life stories.

Notes

1 The alchemy of wolves and sheep

1 Herman (1992) used the term complex posttraumatic stress disorder, attempting to represent the increased severity of trauma-related deficits (i.e., in identity, attachment, and psychobiological systems) not accounted for by the standard PTSD diagnosis.

2 Shay (1995) described the devastating effects of war on men's personalities, revealing how military training combined with the irrational incidents and conditions of war can culminate in complete character deformation, moral deterioration, and severe posttraumatic stress disorder.

3 Anna Freud's (1936) construct of "identification with the aggressor" underscores the child's agency, and *active* identification with authority (i.e., power and aggression) within a self-protective process, eventuating in superego formation. Ferenczi's (1933) view, by contrast, speaks to the child's helplessness, attachment dilemmas, and states of traumatic overwhelm, fueling an initially *passive* identification with abusers/caretakers. Victims' moral, physical, and emotional helplessness leads to automatic, instantaneous mimicry of abusers; illusory positive attachments to abusers are sustained while the malevolence of the abuser disappears as an aspect of the victims' external reality. With repetition, Ferenczi posits, the more active secondary cultivation of agency and mastery takes place.

4 DID is considered a hidden rather than a rare disorder, is frequently misdiagnosed, and is often missed by casual observers and untrained clinicians, especially when switches between personality states occur in a subtle or not easily detectable manner (Kluft, 1984; 1999; C. Ross, 1997). Kluft (2000) reports that only about 6% of patients with DID exhibit overt symptomatology. In many DID cases, various dissociative states and alter personalities may be *layered* – camouflaged behind one another – with those encapsulating deeper trauma organizationally structured behind those responsible for functionality or containment of less intense states of traumatic injury.

5 Luxenberg, Spinazzola, and Van der Kolk (2001) report that trauma-related disorders, including DID, continue to be grossly underdiagnosed due to many patients' tendencies to present a panoply of symptoms not readily recognizable as related to traumatic experiences. Others, like Herman (1992) suggest underdiagnosis relates to cultural and professional biases against trauma and dissociative disorders, along with a lack of clinical training on the part of many clinicians in effective diagnosis and treatment of trauma-related conditions. Sachs (2008) believes that many professionals remain in denial or become fascinated with the bizarre phenomenology of DID not only because of its volatile, confusing

symptom picture but because of the disturbing links between DID and sadistic forms of abuse and crimes revealed by DID patients.

6 According to DSM IV –TR (American Psychiatric Association, 2000), the dissociative disorders, including DID, are best defined by the essential feature of "disruption in the usually integrated functions of consciousness, memory, identity or perception" (p. 519). In spite of the controversies surrounding DID, consistent incidence/prevalence data suggests DID varies between 1.1% to 3% in the general population, and increases significantly in clinical populations (International Society for the Study of Trauma and Dissociation [ISST&D], 2011).

7 Cited in P. Singer (2006), p. 70

8 Cited in P. Singer (2006), p. 3.

9 Cited in Wessels (2006), p. 59.

10 Cited in Schauer and Elbert (2010), p. 318.

11 Cited in Schauer and Elbert (2010), p. 317.

12 Cited in Wessels (2006), p. 50.

13 Howell (2011) makes an important distinction between the terms *abuse* and *trauma*, cautioning against their automatic, interchangeable usage. An individual can endure life-threatening events and terrible circumstances, however, these events may not necessarily be perceived/remembered by the person as traumatic. Numerous variables including overall resilience, prior trauma history, social/cultural context, and having the opportunity and/or ability to communicate about disturbing experiences with responsive and caring others may explain variations in encoding of disturbing experiences.

14 Some traumatic experiences may be more likely to contribute to the development of trauma spectrum disorders. Perpetrator events, witnessing violence, rape, and torture, seem to have a predictive power in terms of likelihood of a victim developing more severe psychopathology; in general, the more violence children have been forced to commit against others, the more intense the symptoms of posttraumatic stress disorder (Schauer and Elbert, 2010; Van der Kolk *et al.*, 1996).

15 Traumatic and non-traumatic experience may be differentially processed by the brain – trauma is encoded (and then evoked when a person enters the mental state in which the trauma was originally most salient) in procedural repertoires and somatosensory modalities rather than declarative memories (Courtois, 1999; Levine, 1997; Van der Kolk, 1996). According to Van der Kolk, extremely high levels of emotional arousal lead to inadequate evaluation of the sensory information in the hippocampus. During traumatic events, in the absence of full hippocampal functioning (due to elevated levels of stress hormones, especially glucocorticoids), memories cannot be stored and retrieved properly. These peri- and posttraumatic neurophysiciological changes may directly decrease a survivor's ability to express feelings in words (Bremner *et al.*, 1997).

16 See Marx *et al.* (2008) for discussion of tonic immobility.

17 LeDoux (1996; 2007) presents neurological and psychological evidence for two long-term memory systems (explicit and implicit). The explicit system relates to the integration of conscious cognitive and verbal stimuli whereas the implicit system corresponds to more emotionally-valent and unconscious information and experience. "Fear conditioning" (LeDoux, 1996:150) takes place when stimuli associated with the danger of trauma leads to learned triggers that unleash quick emotional reactions that bypass the reflective conscious mind and natural inhibitory mechanisms. Because emotional information is subcortically mediated by the amygdala –engineered for fast, automatic and largely unconscious survival responses – the implicit/emotional memory activation system more strongly affects the conscious/explicit system than vice versa.

18 Under conditions of torture, psychological states can be programmed or hypnotically influenced when individuals are in hyper-aroused or switched-off states (Lacter, 2011; C. Ross, 1997, 2000; H. Schwartz, 2000; Vogt, 2008). Vogt (2008) describes how quick reflex reactions may become institutionalized within the victim's psychology and neurobiology, appearing as a panic response, switching off, or of letting things happen absent the engagement of the will. An extraordinary consequence of severe manipulation via torture and mind control is manifest later in adulthood when the dissociative survivor is compelled to think and act in specific perpetrator-conditioned ways: since the origin of these impulses is obscure to him or her, the survivor experiences the impulses as arising from within and proceeds to own and effectuate them (notwithstanding their ego-dystonic character).

19 Lacter (2011) describes how systematic torture induced victims to form alternate mental states including: hyperattentive blank states, desperate solution-seeking survival states, and states that develop more gradually through ongoing conditioning. All three of these perpetrator-engineered dissociative states subsequently may be subjected to perpetrator strategies to define and control perceptions and beliefs, to install directives and effectuate triggers, in order to force victims to think, to feel, and ultimately to act in ways consistent with the perpetrator(s)' agenda.

20 Schauer and Elbert (2010) state that in some conditions ideological commitments may serve as protective functions, reducing trauma symptoms. Victims' cognitive appraisals of traumatic experiences may affect posttraumatic symptom development – strong feelings of guilt and responsibility might actually increase trauma symptoms. Identifications with evil may likewise reduce symptomatology. Perpetrator-identified states in DID patients may adopt abusers' ideologies to regulate fear, shame, and intense states of emotional vulnerability and may act out when their belief systems are challenged; escalation of destructive behaviors may represent efforts to manage feelings of loss of control or to prevent the abrupt surfacing/re-experiencing of painful memories that lie beneath their ideological bravado.

21 Impairments in self formation and certain pathological processes may be set into motion, not only by trauma, but by failures of essential environmental provisions notably: containment, metabolization and symbolization, recognition, attunement, and stimulus regulation (Kohut, 1971; Bion, 1965, 1967; Bollas, 1995).

22 Salter (2003) and Stout (2005) explicate the thinking patterns of various types of perpetrators and sociopaths; H. Schwartz (2000) has developed a typology for classifying perpetrators.

23 According to Vogt (2008) "implant states" appear in the form of activity-specific impulses and automated behavioral properties, directed toward harm of the self or another and spreading the ideology and action programs of the perpetrator(s). Implants invariably begin as perpetrator loyal and perpetrator-identified, emerging within a consciousness so restricted that there is often at least partial amnesia for some impulse actions and fantasies. Complicating the picture is the possibility of encountering multiple formations of dissociated regulation and implant states, several of which may exist side by side, materializing erratically and impulsively within the switching process of a highly developed dissociative identity disorder.

24 This set of the patient's extreme ego-dystonic experiences results from what is commonly referred to in mainstream culture as extreme brainwashing and the creation of "Manchurian candidates" – after Richard Condon's 1959 book, *The Manchurian Candidate* (and the first of two subsequent Hollywood films by that same name). Brainwashing also entered popular consciousness with the famous kidnapping of heiress Patty Hearst in the 1970s by the Symbionese Liberation Army (SLA). Using a devastating combination of rape, torture, and mind control, Hearst's captors transformed her in a matter of months from a debutante to a criminal soldier and they renamed her "Tanya" as part of the reconditioning and

identity alteration process. Bowart (1994), Lacter (2011), Marks (1979), Miller (2012), C. Ross (2000), Thomas (1989), and Weinstein (1990) offer evidence of government sponsored mind-control programs studying ways of inducing complete psychological breakdowns in healthy and psychiatrically impaired individuals, creating new identities/persons and facilitating their ability to bypass moral inhibitions and execute unethical actions.

25 Beah (2007), p. 119.
26 Cited in Wax (2003).
27 Cited in Human Rights Watch (2003), p. 96.
28 Cited in P. Singer (2006), p. 23.
29 Cited in Schauer and Elbert (2010), p. 32.
30 Named after a notorious Swedish bank robbery committed in August of that year.
31 See Noblitt and Noblitt (2008) for a review of various definitional discussions and clinical debates about *ritual abuse*; and Miller (2012) for an extensive review of all aspects of ritual abuse.
32 See Lacter (2011) for a discussion of distinctions between the terms self-state, ego-state, and alter personality. Throughout this paper, I use the term self-state(s) inclusively, referring to *all* variations of dissociative self-experience from mildly integrated to unformulated aspects of self –organization/self-representation; from highly fragmentary states with minimal sense of self, to extremely high functioning alter personalities with significant agency, identity, specific skill sets, and reflective capacities. In accordance with Kluft (1984) and Lacter (2011) the term alter personalities refers to strongly personified dissociative states demonstrating heightened narcissistic investment in separateness and delineated identities.
33 Paradoxically, the perpetrator-identified self-state or alter personality can be considered to be the epitomical victim.
34 "Archetypal" is most often associated with Carl Jung's (1957) view of the existence of universally understood forms, symbols, behaviors, and identifications – prototypes – embodying predictable patterns of experience and emotions, and with Joseph Campbell's (1949) work on mythology, ritual, and modern narratives. In additionto these significations, throughout this book I use "archetypal" as a means of emphasizing alternative forms of contextualizing patients' experiences of trauma and transformation.
35 Observers of the more than 42 wars and armed conflicts world-wide, mostly in developing countries, have noted that the main target of the warring parties is the civilian population; never before in history have child soldiers played such a prominent role, sometimes constituting as much as 80% of the fighting forces (Elbert *et al.*, 2006; Kaldor, 1999).
36 Cited in P. Singer (2006), p. 194.
37 Cited in Wessels (2006), p. 216.
38 Cited in Schauer and Elbert, 2010 (pp. 323–324).
39 Cited in P. Singer (2006), p. 198.
40 The "Middle Path" or "Middle Way" is a key concept in Buddhism relating to the cultivation of wisdom through finding a balance between austerities and self-indulgences, and is a caveat to avoid all extreme conditions (i.e., aversions and compulsions), in order to attain wisdom. With awareness (mindfulness) and liberation as the goal, the "Middle Path," investigates and penetrates the core of life and all things with an upright, unbiased, neutral, and centered attitude (N. Ross, 1980).

2 The child soldier as a model of internalized perpetration

1 Cited in Dith Pran (1999). *Children of Cambodia's Killing Fields: Memoirs of survivors.*

2 Girls were present in fighting forces (government forces, paramilitary/militia, and armed opposition groups) in 55 countries between 1990–2003; in 38 of these countries they were involved in situations of armed conflict. Girls' roles typically overlap and include working as spies and informants, in intelligence and communications, and as military trainers and combatants. They also serve as health workers and minesweepers, and they may conduct suicide missions. Other support roles include raising crops, selling goods, preparing food, carrying loot and weapons, and stealing food, livestock, and seed stock (Elbert and Schauer, 2010; McKay and Mazurana, 2004). Underlying these various roles and activities, girls' participation in military life is central to sustaining a competent force because of girls' productive and reproductive labor. As such, traditional societal gender roles and patriarchal privilege are replicated, whereby girls (and women) serve men and boys (DiCicco, 2009; Inder, 2011; Schauer and Schauer, 2010).

3 For female child soldiers the post-war adjustment is often more complex. Challenges include significant medical and psychosocial difficulties and fewer opportunities for healing and reintegration. After demobilization, sexually-abused females are often rejected by their families and communities. Stigmatization can be more intense if they return infected with sexually transmitted diseases or if they bring back a child from their time in the forests. In many cultural settings, girls are unable to get married or re-married and they find it difficult to enter a new supportive partnership, within which to bring up their children in civilian life (DiCicco, 2009; Inder, 2011; McKay and Mazurana, 2004; Schauer and Schauer, 2010). Hence, displacement, domestic violence, substance abuse, and prostitution have become quite common outcomes. Gender disparities that privilege boy soldiers over girls lead to fewer girls entering or benefitting from rehabilitation programs (Schauer and Schauer, 2010).

4 Cautioning against overgeneralization, Drumbl (2012) describes the considerable heterogeneity that exists among child soldiers regarding their relationship to violence. Some child soldiers lie to and manipulate commanders to avoid killing; others refuse to inflict gross human rights abuses upon third-party or civilians while some torture, rape, and kill. Some child soldiers commit these acts to navigate volatile militarized hierarchies and some commit atrocities gratuitously or to pursue lucre.

5 The systematic transformation of a child into an effective combatant overlaps with the subjugation and brainwashing of prostitutes by pimps (Malarek, 2003; H. Schwartz et al., 2007), mind control used in religious cults (Hassan, 1990; M. Singer, 1995), and the creation of dissociated "cult alter personalities" in ritual abuse and other forms of organized child abuse (Lacter, 2011; Miller, 2012; Noblitt and Perskin, 2000; H. Schwartz, 2000; Sinason, 1994).

6 A brief search through the documentaries and literature on the civil wars in Liberia and Sierra Leone offers an abundance of disturbing evidence of children and adolescents with virulent attitudes of omnipotent entitlement and hatred, wielding the skulls of their victims, grandiosely flaunting guns, and proclaiming their thrill in bloodletting (Huband, 1998; Stack, 2004; #VBS.TV, 2010; BBC, 2010). By contrast, the film *WarDance* (ShineGLobal, Inc., 2006) offers a moving portrait of child victims of Uganda's civil wars and their attempts to recover through performance art.

7 Doctrine, ideology and propaganda, in Wessels' (2006) view, provide a moral buffer against feelings of guilt by dehumanizing the enemy and portraying the conflict as a righteous battle between good and evil or right and wrong. It is well established that military forces throughout the world employ similar training and indoctrination methods to denigrate and dehumanize the enemy, intending to lubricate new recruits' capacity for righteous killing and other efficacious combat behavior (Shay, 1995).

8 Although the emphasis on sexual violence in the child soldier literature stresses the victimization of females, it is likely that rape, sexual abuse, and sexual humiliation of male recruits also takes place more than has been presented in the literature. This inconsistency in reporting may be due to interviewer bias, failure to inquire into male sexual abuse, and cultural norms, shame, and bravado which may limit demobilizing male soldiers from complete revelation of their sexual trauma history.

9 Conway and Siegelman (2005) describe sudden personality changes – unforeseen breaks in the continuity of awareness – in the face of trauma: food and sleep deprivation, prolonged group education/indoctrination sessions, even repetitive chanting and meditation causes detached and confused states and heightened vulnerability to suggestion. These indoctrination methods are regularly used by most cults, paramilitary, and perpetrator groups to form pliable, dissociative mental states that are receptive to incorporating new identities, motivations, skill sets, and ideologies.

3 Dilemmas of dissociative survival

1 See Howell (2011) for a discussion of the important difference between the dissociated and repressed unconscious.

2 See Schore's (2002; 2009; 2011) integration of brain biology research and psychological theory on dissociation. Schore emphasizes that dissociation involves a disconnection of the central nervous system from the autonomic nervous system *and* a failure of integration of the higher right hemisphere with the lower right brain.

3 Kalsched (1996) linked dissociative process with the Jungian concept of trickster figure. In mythology and indigenous societies, the trickster figure plays important roles – an ambivalent, paradoxical, beguiling agent who delivers healing and destruction, deliverance and entrapment, breakthroughs and breakdowns. Tricksters dissemble, dissimulate and defy rules of logic as well as local cultural restrictions. The paradoxical nature of these mythic figures who often appear as clowns, jesters, trouble-makers, pranksters, unusual cultural heroes/liberators, and as two-faced or embodying two opposing aspects, allows them to be guardians of the threshold (Hansen, 2001).

4 See Kluft (1985; 1990; 1995; 1996; 2000) for an understanding and identification of key features and functions of alters in DID.

5 See Dell (2009a;b), Kluft (1999; 2000), C. Ross (1997) for discussions of the diagnosis of DID and its controversies.

6 Miller (2012) covers the complex subject of assessment and treatment of survivors with ongoing, recent, or current contact (i.e., concurrent with psychotherapy) with perpetrators.

7 Child soldiers and others victims of organized child abuse share a deep confusion about issues of choice, responsibility, and self-determination, all of which have beendeformed through years of propaganda and violent indoctrination. This core confusion is one of the major stumbling blocks in treatment for all trauma survivors as well as for law and policy makers (Happold, 2005). International courts have chosen *not* to prosecute children for war crimes, regardless of their crimes or level of involvement (Cohn, 2004). Drumbl (2012) describes the international community's legal propensity to ease the three-dimensional status of child soldiers as perpetrators, witnesses, and victims into a two-dimensional portrayal of child soldiers as victims and witnesses alone.

8 See H. Schwartz (2000) for a classification system illustrating internalized complicity, collusion, and collaboration.

9 Psychotherapy with criminal perpetrators and pedophiles often involves accessing the hidden, split-off victimized child self. In contrast, psychotherapy with trauma survivors often involves accessing the hidden, split-off sadist and violent aspects of the self. However, to identify the victim-perpetrator duality is not to define the two elements as equivalents. Although survivors of torture and sadistic abuse may bring incredible pain and suffering to those who get close to them, they are not predominantly predatory beings. Rather, most of their enactments, outbursts, and manipulations are best understood as desperate efforts either: to attain safety and relief from pain (Salter, 1995); to communicate in the only way they can about the abuses of power in familial or other systems that perpetrated, permitted, or failed to recognize the trauma (Rivera, 1989; 1996); and to enact programmed behavior (Miller, 2012).

10 A distinction can be made between identification with complicity (or collusion) – a type of automatism, a more unconscious, attitude inculcated in trauma, neglect, and acculturation processes – and complicity itself which is a more conscious, self-indulgent use of avoidance, denial, and self-protection for self-interest and at the expense of others.

11 Hesse and Main (1999) explain that many misattuned, unresponsive, or neglectful parents are not necessarily consciously intending to harm or damage their children. Rather, through the process of enacting disconnected procedural relationship models they are unwittingly transmitting unresolved trauma and re-enacting parenting styles from their own childhoods – the basis of unconscious intergenerational transmission of trauma and neglect.

4 Mind control

1 Many dissociative trauma survivors of organized perpetrator groups report that medical professionals were often actively involved in the groups' activities and were utilized by group leaders to perform emergency surgeries and other medical interventions on traumatized children. These interventions were designed to disguise evidence of the abuse or to save the life of a child whose death might have brought suspicion onto the cult or perpetrator group.

2 Miller (2012) explains the existence of "psychiatric symptoms training" (p. 189) as one form of mind-control training aimed at discrediting the survivor to him or herself and to the medical community, once any trauma disclosures occur. Aside from disrupting or confusing helping professionals, or instigating a potentially useless or harmful psychiatric hospitalization, the activation of "psychiatric symptom training" might lead the survivor to become so dysfunctional that he or she might feel compelled to return to the perpetrators to "have things put right." (p. 190).

3 Internalizing the offender's cognitive distortions by buying into responsibility for what he or she did or did not do may actually be a way of preserving some hope of controlling the abuse – an investment in the prospect that if the victim caused it, he or she can prevent its recurrence (Salter, 1995).

4 See Miller (2012) for additional elaboration on perpetrator-implanted injunctions, meaning structures, and belief systems.

5 See Schwartz et al. (2007) for a review of how similar principles of subjugation are used by pimps to create, manage, and control prostitutes.

6 From concepts of influence and imprinting, to introjects, implants, and programs, Vogt (2012) has developed a unique system to illuminate the full range and complexity of potential perpetrator influences and identification patterns

among trauma survivors – tracking seven distinct "regulation states" varying in accessibility, flexibility, and capacity for modification. Vogt believes that much of the confusion and contention in understanding among clinicians treating trauma and mind control is due to the fact that clinicians do not fully understand that differing severity grades of traumatized patients experience and psychological organizations (i.e., regulation states) require different types of intervention (See Vogt, 2012 for descriptions of these states and the appropriate treatment recommendations).

7 This list is excerpted, expanded, and revised from H. Schwartz (2000), Chapter 3.

8 Based on the revelations of a mind-control survivor and programmer who went public, Miller (2012) describes an actual variety of programming called "shell programming", designed to hide the survivor's DID from the outside world.

9 These children, whether born to female sex slaves destined for a life of prostitution, to female child soldiers raped in the bush and destined for a life of sexual and violent trauma, or born to many of our cult survivor patients, offered up by force to the underground worlds where they will serve a variety of slavery functions (i.e., including on the trafficking and black markets) represent the most disturbing "cash crop" known to humanity.

5 Perpetration and perpetrator states

1 Believing that every mind needs another mind to develop, Bion (1965; 1967) used the term Alpha function to represent an undefinable set of mental operations by which Beta elements (raw impressions of emotional experience) are transformed or converted (processed and decontaminated) into Alpha elements. Beta elements are made useful by therapeutic experience transmuting previously unmetabolized material into potentially communicable information and experience.

2 Pagels (1995) views the roots of evil as based on human beings locating the source of their pain and suffering in others, and in their intolerance of difference. She views evil as a sociological phenomenon involving the demonization of others in order to fortify the loyalty of the group – continuously threatened with fear, anxiety, and dissolution.

3 Echoing the influences of Guntrip (1971) and Fairbairn (1954).

4 Of significance here are Buddhist notions of "core goodness/ basic goodness." The Tibetan tradition known as Dzogchen holds the view that the natural, primordial state (and ultimate nature) of all sentient beings is a pure, all-encompassing, primordial awareness. This is considered to be an already perfected state of our original, archaic nature, which needs no 'perfecting', for it has always been perfect from the very beginning. This quality of being is uncreated, yet spontaneously accomplished. According to these and other related traditions, a primordial and inexorable freedom and goodness, and benevolent emptiness exist at the core of all human beings and can *never* be completely or indefinitely lost. With diligence, practice, and perseverance, accumulated pain, delusion, trauma, and reactivity of all kinds can eventually be transformed into wisdom (Norbu *et al.*, 2003).

5 When approaching relatively novel, complex psychological domains, classification systems can serve useful heuristic templates, especially when tempered with an appreciation of the spectrum of individual variations they comprise. In the treatment of many PTSD patients, these distinct dissociative states can present as less personified expressions of the fundamental patterns described.

6 Perpetrators from diverse backgrounds often create conditions of chemical dependency in their victims – usually with opiates and amphetamines or a combination

of the two – as an essential part of the subjugation/initiation process. Induced addictions, sometimes without the conscious awareness or participation of the victim, along with the ongoing threat of imminent excruciating withdrawal symptoms (through withholding of drugs for noncompliance), maximizes long-term cooperation in victims. Then, biologically-induced complicity in their own victimization intensifies the destabilizing effects from other perpetrator manipulations of victims' attachment needs.

6 Transforming perpetration

1 See H. Schwartz (2000) for a classification system of internalized perpetration.
2 See Salter (1995). Duping delight refers to the pleasure taken in deceiving, fooling, or entrapping the other. Duping delight is a key behavioral feature of malignant narcissism and psychopathy.
3 Significant work has been done illuminating "compassion fatigue," "vicarious traumatization" and "secondary traumatization" of therapists treating trauma (Figley, 1995; Grand, 2000; Saakvitne, 1995; Pearlman and Saakvitne, 1995, H. Schwartz, 2000) and the effective use of this experience to empathize with the complexity of patients' experiences and analyze/interpret enactments.
4 Delving into work on perpetrator introjects, implants, or programmed states may be contraindicated with patients who are medically or psychiatrically unstable, have made recent suicide attempts or been hospitalized, have few psychosocial supports, remain subject to various addictions, or are still in regular contact with their perpetrating group.
5 A cloaking device, related to "fail-safes" and "resistance programming" (Miller, 2012), is one type of camouflage that is specifically embedded by perpetrators in victims' dissociative systems in order to create intrapsychic and interpersonal *invisibility*. The concept of a cloaking device – as a form of active camouflage – comes from science fiction and military stealth technology. Cloaking devices cause objects or individuals – or in this case, parts of individuals – to be partially or wholly obscured or invisible to consciousness and reflective witnessing.
6 Implosion or implosion therapy is a technique used in behavior therapy and also in torture. The client or victim is flooded with experiences of a particular kind until becoming either averse to them or numbed to them.

7 Treatment concepts and trajectories

1 Attacks on linking functions (Bion, 1965) are considered hallmarks of both psychotic and dissociative processes.
2 Echoing the value of "cracks and fractures in the field," Ferro states: They "are of fundamental importance because they give rise to cracks or pivots whereby what was previously outside the present relationship in the form of a set of 'undigested facts' can burst into it […] They allow the transference to become the engine of analysis, by contributing raw material from the patient's internal world and history […I]f there are no cracks, the analysis will become sterile, bogged down in an impasse, but if there are too many, all the various forms of negative and psychotic transference will arise. From this point of view the analysis is like a dam controller who must modulate what enters the metabolic cycle" (Ferro, 2005:34).
3 My use of the term phase-oriented treatment is not meant as a presentation of a completely new intervention but rather as a new synthesis of theoretical and clinical principles within a classic model. Within this familiar format, the patient must now (with the emergence of perpetration material and dynamics) revisit the basic

and well-known phase-oriented approach with a specialized grasp on the unique issues of perpetration – its revelation, treatment, and resolution. In a field as complex as understanding and treating internalized perpetration, it can be very helpful to use a template familiar to most clinicians while moving their perspectives and engagements into new territory.

4 Addiction to violence is also an observed outcome of participation in war for both adult and child soldiers (Beah, 2007; Shay, 1995; P. Singer, 2006; Wessels, 2006).

5 This may be related to Klein's (1975) concept of manic glee and Grand's (2000) notion of re-enlivening the deadened self.

6 See Lacter (2011) for an extensive review of clinical interviewing practices to heal victims of torture-based mind control.

7 According to Drumbl (2012) these include: "criminal trials, civil liability (for example private tort actions, restitutionary claims, and public reparations), lustration, community service programs, truth and reconciliation commissions, endogenous mechanisms, public inquiries, and restorative ceremonies. These processes vary considerably *inter se* regarding how and to what degree they allocate responsibility for the acts of atrocity" (p. 25). From the perspective of transitional justice, perpetrators do not necessarily need to confess or atone to accomplish a successful social outcome. To the contrary, Drumbl emphasizes that many endogenous ceremonies seek to redress past wrongs through future-oriented work and cultivation of relationships rather than through punishment, retribution, or penitence.

8 Truth and reconciliation committees in post-apartheid South Africa and post-genocide Rwanda are perhaps the best-known examples of transitional justice efforts.

9 Three excellent resources on children and transitional justice are Hamber (2009), Parmar *et al.* (2010), and Teitel (2000). See also the International Center for Transitional Justice www.ictj.org.

10 In one of his poetic masterpieces, *Illuminations*, Arthur Rimbaud asks, "Is it possible to become ecstatic amid destruction, rejuvenate oneself through cruelty?" Ashbery (2011:35).

8 Using archetypal concepts as a vehicle of integration

1 These concepts relate to Jung's (1958) principle of the transcendent function – a psychological capacity arising from the psyche's success in sustaining the tension between opposites, supporting new productive unions between conscious and unconscious elements and forces.

2 See Cardena *et al.* (2000) for an excellent review of the literature on the varieties of anomalous experience.

3 See Mills and Lynn (2000); B. Weiss (1988, 2004); Whitton and Fisher (1986).

4 The difficult transition between life and death in shamanic traditions is so important that specially trained and highly valued individuals ("psychopomps") and skills must be developed to guide souls in and out of incarnation, in order to protect the soul's journey and to support the soul's positive development and evolution within the cycles of human existence (Eliade, 1964).

5 Some Buddhist legends present this female or androgynous divinity Quan Yin (who was born a male in some versions of the myth) as vowing to never rest until she has freed all human beings from suffering and from the wheel of death and rebirth (Palmer *et al.*, 1995).

6 In some situations, social/political transformation such as the establishment of new democracies or overthrow of oppressive regimes or the process or transitional justice practices can serve as antecedents or fertilizers for individual transformation.

References

Adams, M.A. (1989). Internal self-helpers of persons with multiple personality disorder. *Dissociation*, 2(3), 3–25.

Alexander, F. and French, T.M. (1946). *Psychoanalytic Therapy: Principles and applications*. New York: Ronald Press.

Alford, C.F. (1997). *What Evil Means to Us*. Ithaca, NY: Cornell University Press.

Allison, R.B. (1980). *Minds in Many Pieces*. New York: Rawson, Wade.

Alpert, J.L. (1995). Criteria: Signposts towards the sexual abuse hypothesis. In J.L. Alpert (Ed.), *Sexual Abuse Recalled: Treating trauma in the era of the recovered memory debate* (pp. 63–96). Northvale, NJ: Jason Aronson, Inc.

American Psychiatric Association (2000). *Diagnostic and Statistical Manual of Mental Disorders* (4th ed.). Washington, DC: American Psychiatric Association.

Anthony, C.K (1998). The Philosophy of the I Ching. Stow, Mass: Anthony Publishing.

Aron, L. (1996). *A Meeting of Minds: Mutuality in psychoanalysis*. Hillsdale, NJ: The Analytic Press.

Ashbery, J. (2011). *Illuminations*: Arthur Rimbaud, translation. New York: Norton.

Auerhahn, N.C. and Laub, D. (1987). Play and playfulness in holocaust survivors. *Psychoanalytic Study of the Child*, 42, 45–58.

Ball, N. (1997). Demobilizing and reintegrating soldiers: Lessons from Africa. In K. Kumar (Ed.), *Rebuilding War-Torn Societies* (pp. 85–105). Boulder, CO: Lynne-Rienner.

Ball, T. (2008). The use of prayer for inner healing of memories and deliverance with ritual abuse survivors. In R. Noblitt and P. Noblitt (Eds), *Ritual Abuse in the 21s Century* (pp. 413–442). Bandon, OR: Robert D. Reed.

Bargh, J.A. and Chartrand, T.L. (1999). The unbearable automaticity of being. *American Psychologist*, 54(7), 462–479.

Bartlett, C. (2008). A tearoom view of mended ceramics. *Flickwerk: The aesthetics of mended Japanese ceramics* (pp. 9–14). Munster: Museum fur Lackkunst.

Bateson, G. (1972). *Steps Towards an Ecology of Mind: Collected essays in anthropology, psychiatry, evolution, and epistemology*. New York: Ballantine.

Beah, I. (2007). *A Long Way Gone: Memories of a boy soldier*. New York: Farrar, Strauss & Giroux.

Becker, D. (1996). The deficiency of the concept of posttraumatic stress disorder when dealing with victims of human rights violations. In R.J. Kleber, C.R. Figley and B.P.R. Gersons (Eds), *Beyond Trauma: Cultural and societal dynamics* (pp. 99–109). New York: Plenum Press.

Benjamin, J. (1988). *The Bonds of Love: Psychoanalysis, feminism and the problem of domination*. New York: Pantheon.

Benjamin, J. (1999/1990). Recognition and destruction: An outline of intersubjectivity. In S.A. Mitchell and L. Aron (Eds), *Relational Psychoanalysis: The emergence of a tradition* (pp. 181–210). Hilldale, NJ: The Analytic Press.

Bettelheim, B. (1989/2010). *The Uses of Enchantment: The meaning and importance of fairy tales*. New York: Vintage (originally published in 1976 by Knopf, Inc., NY).

Bion, W.R. (1963). *Elements of Psycho-analysis*. London: Heinemann.

Bion, W.R. (1965). *Transformations*. London: Heinemann (New York: Jason Aronson, 1983).

Bion, W.R. (1967). *Second Thoughts*. New York: Jason Aronson, 1983.

Bion, W.R. (1970). *Attention and Interpretation*. London: Tavistock Publications (New York: Jason Aronson, 1983).

Blizard, R.A. (1997). The origins of dissociative identity disorder from an object relations theory and attachment theory perspective. *Dissociation*, 10, 223–229.

Blizard, R.A. (2003). Disorganized attachment, development of dissociated self-states, and a relational approach to treatment. *Journal of Trauma and Dissociation*, 4(3), 27–50.

Bloom, S. (1997). *Creating sanctuary: Toward the evolution of sane societies*. New York: Routledge.

Bollas, C. (1989). *Forces of Destiny: Psychoanalysis and human idiom*. Northvale, NJ: Jason Aronson, Inc.

Bollas, C. (1992). Violent innocence. In C. Bollas *Being A Character: Psychoanalysis and self experience* (pp. 165–192). New York: Hill and Wang.

Bollas, C. (1995). The Structure of evil. In C. Bollas, *Cracking Up* (pp. 180–220). New York: Hill and Wang.

Bowart, W.H. (1994/1978). *Operation Mind Control: Researcher's edition*. Fort Bragg, CA: Flatland Editions (previously published New York: Dell Publishing, 1978).

Boyd, W. (2007). Babes in Arms. *New York Times: Sunday Book Review*, February, 25, 2007.

Boyden, J. and Gibbs, S. (1997). *Children of War*. Geneva: United Nations Research Institute for Social Development.

Brandchaft, B. (1994). To free the spirit from its cell. In R.D. Stolorow, G.E. Atwood, and B.Brandchaft (Eds), *The Intersubjective Perspective* (pp. 57–76). Northvale, NJ: Jason Aronson.

Brandchaft, B. and Stolorow, R. (1990). Varieties of therapeutic alliance. *The Annual of Psychoanalysis*, 18, 99–114.

Bremner, J.D., Randall, P., Vermetten, E., Staib, L., Bronen, R.A., Mazure, C., Capelli, S., McCarthy, G., Innis, R.B., and Charney, D.S. (1997). MRI based measurements of hippocampal volume in post-traumatic stress disorder related an childhood physical and sexual abuse. *Biological Psychiatry*, 41, 23–32.

Brett, R., and Specht, I. (2004). *Young Soldiers*. Boulder, CO: Lynne Rienner.

Briere, J.N. (1995). Child abuse, memory, and recall: A commentary. *Consciousness and Cognition*, 4, 83–87.

Briere, J.N. (1996). *Treatment of Adults Sexually Molested as Children: Beyond survival*. New York: Springer.

BBC (2010). *Liberia and Sierra Leone: Dancing with the Devil*. BBC Our World Documentary. June, 11, 2010.

Bromberg, P.M. (1980). Empathy, anxiety, and reality: A view from the bridge. *Contemporary Psychoanalysis*, 16, 223–226.

Bromberg, P.M. (1993). Shadow and substance: A relational perspective on clinical process. *Psychoanalytic Psychology*, 10, 147–168.

Bromberg, P.M. (1994). Speak! That I may hear you: Some reflections on dissociation, reality, and psychoanalytic listening. *Psychoanalytic Dialogues*, 4, 517–547.

Bromberg, P.M. (1995). Resistance, object usage, and human relatedness. *Contemporary Psychoanalysis*, 31, 173–192.

Bromberg, P.M. (1996). Standing in the spaces. The multiplicity of self and the psycho-analytic relationship. *Contemporary Psychoanalysis*, 32(4), 509–536.

Bromberg, P.M. (1998). *Standing in the Spaces: Essays on clinical process, trauma, and dissociation*. Hillsdale, NJ: Analytic Press.

Bromberg, P.M. (2003). On being one's dream: Some reflections on Robert Bosnak's "Embodied Imagination." *Contemporary Psychoanalysis*, 39, 697–710.

Bromberg, P.M. (2006). *Awakening the Dreamer: Clinical journeys*. Mahwah, NJ: Analytic Press.

Bromberg, P.M. (2009). Multiple self-states, the relational mind, and dissociation: A psychoanalytic perspective. In P.F. Dell and J.A. O'Neill (Eds), *Dissociation and the Dissociative Disorders: DSM-V and beyond* (pp. 637–652). New York: Routledge.

Bromberg, P.M. (2011). *The Shadow of the Tsunami and the Growth of the Relational Mind*. New York: Routledge.

Campbell, J. (1949/2008). *The Hero With a Thousand Faces*. Novato, CA: New World Library.

Cardena, E., Lynn, S.J. and S. Krippner (Eds) (2000). *Varieties of Anomolous Experience: Examining the Evidence*. Washington, DC: American Psychological Association.

Carlson, E.A. (1998). A prospective longitudinal study of attachment disorganization/disorientation. *Child Development*, 69, 1107–1128.

Caruth, C. (1995). Preface. In C. Caruth (Ed.), *Trauma: Explorations in memory* (pp. vii–ix). Baltimore, MD: Johns Hopkins University Press.

Chassay, S. (1996). Trauma as initiation: A shamanic perspective on sexual abuse. *Shamanic Applications Review*, 2, 3–12.

Chassay, S. (2012). 'Tis beauty kills the beast: Aesthetic and sensory transformations of en-capsulated states. Unpublished paper, presented at the Psychoanalytic Institute of Northern California (PINC), May 19, 2012.

Chefetz, R. A. (1997). Special case transferences and counter-transferences in the treatment of dissociative disorders. *Dissociation*, 10(4), 255–265.

Chefetz, R. & Bromberg, P.M. (2004). Talking with "me" and "not me:" A dialogue. Contemporary Psychoanalysis, 40, 409–464.

Coalition to Stop the Use of Child Soldiers (2008). *Child Soldiers Global Report*, 12.

Cohn, I. (2004). Progress and hurdles on the road to preventing the use of children as soldiers and ensuring their rehabilitation and reintegration. *Cornell International Law Journal*, 37(3): 531–540.

Condon, R. (1959). *The Manchurian Candidate*. New York: Signet.

Conway, A. (1994). Trance formations of abuse. In Sinason, V. (Ed.), *Treating Survivors of Satanic Abuse* (pp. 254–264). New York: Routledge.

Conway, F. and Siegelman, J. (2005). *Snapping: America's epidemic of sudden personality change* (2nd edn). New York: Stillpoint Press.

Courtois, C. A. (1999). *Recollections of Sexual Abuse: Treatment principles and guidelines*. New York: Norton.

Curtis, J. (1997). Psychopathic alters in otherwise nonpsychopathic DID patients. Paper presented at the 14th Annual Conference of the International Society for the Study of Dissociation, Montreal, Quebec, Canada, November.

Dalenberg, C.J. (2000). Countertransference and the treatment of trauma. Washington, DC.: American Psychological Association.

Davies, J.M. and Frawley, M.G. (1994). *Treating the Adult Survivor of Childhood Sexual Abuse: A psychoanalytic perspective*. New York: Basic Books.

Davoine, F. and Gaudilliere, J.M. (2004). *History Beyond Trauma: Where One Cannot Speak Thereof One Cannot Stay Silent*. New York: Other Books.

De Masi, F. (2003). *The Sadomasochistic Perversion: The entity and the theories*. London: Karnac Books.

Dell, P.F. (2009a). The long struggle to diagnose multiple personality disorder (MPD): I. MPD. In P.F. Dell and J.A. O'Neill (Eds), *Dissociation and the Dissociative Disorders: DSM-V and beyond* (pp. 383–402). New York: Routledge.

Dell, P.F. (2009b). The long struggle to diagnose multiple personality disorder (MPD): II. Partial MPD. In P.F. Dell and J.A. O'Neill (Eds), *Dissociation and the Dissociative Disorders: DSM-V and beyond* (pp. 403–428). New York: Routledge.

Dell, P.F. and O'Neill, J.A. (2009). *Dissociation and the dissociative disorders: DSMV and beyond*. New York: Routledge.

Draijer, N. and Van Zon, P. (2013, in press). Transference focused psychotherapy with former child soldiers: Meeting the murderous self. *Journal of Trauma and Dissociation*, 14.

Drumbl, M.A. (2012). *Reimagining Child Soldiers in International Law and Policy*. New York: Oxford University Press.

Egendorf, A. (1995). Hearing people through their pain. *Journal of Traumatic Stress*, 8(1), 5–28.

Ehrenberg, D.B. (1992). *The Intimate Edge of Experience: Extending the reach of psychoanalytic interaction*. New York: Norton.

Ehrenberg, D.B. (1996). On the analyst's emotional availability and vulnerability. *Contemporary Psychoanalysis*, 32(4), 275–286.

Eigen, M. (1992). *Coming Through the Whirlwind: Case studies in psychotherapy*. Wilmette, IL: Chiron Press.

Eigen, M. (1993). *The Electrified Tightrope*. Northvale, NJ: Jason Aronson.

Eigen, M. (1996). *Psychic Deadness*. Northvale, NJ: Jason Aronson, Inc.

Eigen, M. (1998). *The Psychoanalytic Mystic*. Binghamton, NY: ESF.

Elbert, T., Rockstroh, B., Kolassa, I. T., Schauer, M. and Neuner, F. (2006). The Influence of Organized Violence and Terror on Brain and Mind – a Co-Constructive Perspective. In P. Baltes, P. Reuter-Lorenz & F. Rosler (Eds.), *Lifespan development and the brain: the perspective of biocultural co-constuctivism* (pp. 326–349). Cambridge, UK: Cambridge University Press.

Eliade, M. (1964/1992). *Shamanism: Archaic techniques of ecstasy*. Princeton, NJ: Princeton University Press.

Enright, R. (2001). *Forgiveness is a Choice: A step-by-step process for resolving anger and restoring hope*. Washington DC: American Psychological Association.

Fairbairn, W.R.D. (1954). *An Objects Relations Theory of the Personality*. New York: Basic Books.

Felman, S. (1995). Education and crisis or the vicissitudes of teaching. In C. Caruth (Ed.), *Trauma: Explorations in memory* (pp. 13–60). Baltimore, MD: Johns Hopkins University Press.

Ferenczi, S. (1933). Confusion of tongues between adults and the child. In S. Ferenczi (1955), *Final Contributions to the Problems and Methods of Psychoanalysis* (pp. 87–101). London: Hogarth.

Ferro, A. (2005). *Seeds of Illness, Seeds of Recovery: The genesis of suffering and the role of psychoanalysis*. New York: Brunner/Routledge.

Figley, C.R. (1995). *Compassion Fatigue*. New York: Brunner/Mazel.

Fish-Murray, C.C., Koby, E.V. and Van der Kolk, B.A. (1987). Evolving ideas: The effect of abuse on children's thought. In B.A. Vander Kolk (Ed.), *Psychological Trauma* (pp. 89–110). Washington, DC: American Psychiatric Press.

Foa, E.B. and Kozak, M.J. (1986). Emotional processing of fear: Exposure to corrective information. *Psychological Bulletin*, 99, 20–35.

Fonagy, P. (2002/2011). Multiple voices versus meta-cognition: An attachment theory perspective. In V. Sinason (Ed.), *Attachment Trauma: Working with dissociative identity disorder and multiplicity* (2nd edn) (pp. 21–36). New York: Routledge.

Fonagy, P., Gergeley, G., Jurist, E.L. and Target, M. (2002). *Affect Regulation, Mentalization, and the Development of the Self.* New York: Other Press.

Foreman, S.A. (1996). The significance of turning passive into active in control mastery theory. *Journal of Psychotherapy Practice and Research*, 5, 106–121.

Frankel, S.A. and O'Hearn, T.C. (1996). Similarities in response to extreme and un-remitting stress: cultures of communities under siege. *Psychotherapy: Theory, Research and Practice*, 33(3), 485–502.

Freud, A. (1936). *The Ego and the Mechanisms of Defense.* London: Hogarth.

Freud, S. (1930). *Civilization and its Discontents* (standard edn). London: Hogarth Press.

Freyd, J.J. (1996). *Betrayal Trauma: The logic of forgetting childhood abuse.* Cambridge, MA: Harvard University Press.

Gabbard, G.O. (1993). Countertransference and borderline patients. *The Journal of Psychotherapy: Theory, Practice and Research*, 2(1), 7–18.

Galenson, E. (1986). Some thoughts about infant psychopathology and aggressive development. *International Review of Psychoanalysis*, 13, 349–354.

Gerson, S. (2009). When the third is dead: Memory, mourning, and witnessing in the aftermath of the Holocaust. *International Journal of Psychoanalysis*, 90, 1341–1357.

Glenn, J. (1978). *Child Analysis and Therapy.* New York: Jason Aronson.

Goldberg, P. (2000). Locating the sense of evil. *Mind and Human Interaction*, 12, 1–10.

Graham, D.L.R. (1994). *Loving to Survive.* New York: NYU Press.

Grand, S. (2000). *The Reproduction of Evil: A clinical and cultural perspective.* Hillsdale, NJ: The Analytic Press.

Grant, R. (1996). *The Way of the Wound: A spirituality of trauma and transformation.* Oakland, CA: Robert Grant.

Greenberg, J. R. and Mitchell, S.A. (1983). *Object Relations in Psychoanalytic Theory.* Cambridge, MA: Harvard University Press.

Grossman, W.I. (1991). Pain, aggression, fantasy and concepts of sadomasochism. *Psychoanalytic Quarterly*, 40, 22–52.

Grotstein, J.S. (1990). Nothingness, meaninglessness, chaos and "the Black Hole" II. *Contemporary Psychoanalysis*, 3, 377–408.

Guntrip, H. (1971). *Psychoanalytic Theory, Therapy, and the Self.* New York: Basic Books.

Hamber, B. (2009). *Transforming Societies After Political Violence: Truth, reconciliation, and mental health.* New York: Springer.

Hansen, G.P. (2001). *The Trickster and the Paranormal.* Philadelphia: Xlibris.

Happold, M. (2005). *Child Soldiers in International Law.* Manchester: Juris /Manchester University Press.

Harner, M. (1980/1990). *The Way of the Shaman.* New York: HarperCollins.

Hassan, S. (1990). *Combating Cult Mind Control.* Rochester, VT: Park Street Press.

Hedges, L.E. (1994). *Remembering, Repeating, and Working Through Childhood Trauma.* Northvale, NJ: Jason Aronson.

Herman, J.L. (1992). *Trauma and Recovery.* New York: Basic Books.

Hesse, E. and Main, M. (1999). Second generation effects of unresolved trauma in non-maltreating parents: Dissociated, frightened, and threatening behavior. *Psychoanalytic Inquiry*, 19, 481–540.

Hoffer, E. (1951/2002). *The True Believer: Thoughts on the nature of mass movements*. NY: Harper and Row (Perennial Classics).

Honwana, A. (2006). Child Soldiers. In C. Daiute, Z. Beykong, C. Higson-Smith, and L.Nucci (Eds), *International Perspectives on Youth, Conflict, and Development* (pp. 225–244). New York: Oxford University Press.

Honwana, A. (2008). Children's involvement in war: historical and social contexts. *The Journal of the History of Childhood and Youth*, 1(1), Winter 2008, 139–149.

Hooks, B. (1995). *Killing Rage. Ending racism*. New York: Henry Holt and Co.

Hoppenwasser, (2008). Being in rhythm: Dissociative attunement in the therapeutic process. *Journal of Trauma and Dissociation*, 9(3), 349–367.

Howell, E. F. (1997). Masochism, a bridge to the other side of abuse. *Dissociation*, 10(4), 240–245.

Howell, E.F. (2005). *The Dissociative Mind*. Hillsdale, NJ: The Analytic Press.

Howell, E.F. (2011). *Dissociative Identity Disorder: A relational approach*. New York/London: Routledge.

Huband, M. (1998). *The Liberian Civil War*. New York/London: Routledge.

Human Rights Watch (2003). *You'll Learn Not to Cry: Child combatants in Columbia* (New York, September, 2003), p. 96.

Huyse, L. (2003). The process of reconciliation. In D. Bloomfield, T. Barnes and L. Huyse (Eds), *Reconciliation After Violent Conflict: A handbook* (pp. 19–33). Stockholm: International Institute for Democracy and Electoral Assistance.

International Center for Transitional Justice (2009). *What is Transitional Justice?* www.ictj.org.

International Society for the Study of Trauma and Dissociation (ISST&D) (2011). Guidelines for Treating Dissociative Identity Disorder in Adults, Third Revision. *Journal of Trauma and Dissociation*, 12(2), 115–187.

Iten, C. (2008). Ceramics mended with lacquer: Fundamental aesthetic principles, techniques and artistic concepts. *Flickwerk: The aesthetics of mended Japanese ceramics* (pp. 19–24). Munster: Museum für Lackkunst.

Jackson, K.D. (1992). *Cambodia 1975–1979: Rendez-vous with death*. Princeton, NJ: Princeton University Press.

Janoff-Bulman, R. (1992). *Shattered Assumptions: Toward a new psychology of trauma*. New York: Free Press.

Joshi, P. T. and O'Donnell, D. A. (2003). Consequences of child exposure to war and terrorism. *Clinical Child and Family Psychology Review*, 6(4), 275–292.

Jung, C.G. (1958). *The Collected Works of C.G. Jung*. Princeton, NJ: Princeton University Press.

Kaldor, M. (1999). *New and Old Wars: Organized Violence in a Global Area*. London: Blackwell.

Kalsched, D.E. (1996). *The Inner World of Trauma: Archetypal defenses of the personal spirit*. New York: Routledge.

Kardiner, A. (1941). *The Traumatic Neuroses of War*. New York: Paul Hober.

Karpman, S. (1968). Fairy tales and script drama analysis. *Transactional Analysis Bulletin*, 7(26), 39–43.

Klein, M. (1946/1952). Notes on some schizoid mechanisms. In M. Klein, P.Heimann, S.Isaacs and J.Riviere (Eds), *Developments in Psychoanalysis* (pp. 292–320). London: Hogarth Press.

Klein, M. (1975). *Envy and Gratitude and Other Works, 1946–1963*. New York: Delacorte.

Kluft, R.P. (1984). Treatment of Multiple Personality Disorder. *Psychiatric Clinics of North America*, 7, 9–29.

Kluft, R.P. (1985). The natural history of multiple personality disorder. In R.P. Kluft (Ed.), *Childhood Antecedents of Multiple Personality Disorder* (pp. 197–238). Washington, DC: American Psychiatric Press.

Kluft, R.P. (1988). Today's therapeutic pluralism. *Dissociation*, 1, 1–2.

Kluft, R.P. (1990). Incest and subsequent revictimization: The case of therapist-patient exploitation with a description of the sitting duck syndrome. In R. Kluft (Ed.), *Incest-related syndromes of adult psychopathology* (pp. 263–284). Washington, DC: American Psychiatric Press.

Kluft, R.P. (1995). The confirmation or disconfirmation of memories of abuse in dissociative identity disorder patients: A naturalistic clinical study. *Dissociation*, 8(4), 253–258.

Kluft, R.P. (1996). Dissociative identity disorder. In L.K. Michelson and W.J. Ray (Eds), *Handbook of Dissociation: Theoretical, empirical, and clinical perspectives* (pp. 337–366). New York: Plenum Press.

Kluft, R.P. (1999). An overview of psychotherapy of dissociative identity disorder. *American Journal of Psychotherapy*, 53(3), 289–319.

Kluft, R.P. (2000). The psychoanalytic therapy of dissociative identity disorder in the context of trauma therapy. *Psychoanalytic Inquiry*, 20, 259–286.

Kohut, H. (1971). *The Analysis of the Self*. New York: International Universities Press.

Kornfeld, E.L. (1996). The development of a treatment approach for victims of human rights violations in Chile. In R.J. Kleber, C.R. Figley, B.P.R. Gersons (Eds.), *Beyond Trauma: Cultural and societal dynamics* (pp. 115–130). New York: Plenum Press.

Krystal, H. (1978). Trauma and affects. *The Psychoanalytic Study of the Child*, 33, 81–116.

Lacter, E. (2011). Torture-based mind control: Psychological mechanisms and psychotherapeutic approaches to overcoming mind control. In O.B. Epstein, J. Schwartz and R.W. Schwartz (Eds), *Ritual Abuse and Mind Control: The Manipulation of Attachment Needs* (pp. 57–142). London: Karnac.

Laub, D. (1992). Bearing witness, or the vicissitudes of listening. In S. Felman and D. Laub, *Testimony: Crises of witnessing in literature, psychoanalysis, and history* (pp. 57–74). New York: Routledge.

Laub, D. (1995). Truth and testimony: The process and the struggle. In C. Caruth (Ed.), *Trauma: Explorations in memory* (pp. 61–75). Baltimore, MD: Johns Hopkins University Press.

Laub, D. (2005). Traumatic shutdown of narrative and symbolization. A death instinct derivative. *Contemporary Psychoanalysis*, 6, 302–326.

Laub, D. and Auerhahn, N. (1989). Failed empathy – a central theme in the survivor's Holocaust experience. *Psychoanalytic Psychology*, 6, 377–400.

Laub, D. and Auerhahn, N. (1993). Knowing and not knowing massive trauma: forms of traumatic memory. *International Journal of Psychoanalysis*, 74, 287–302.

LeDoux, J.E. (1996). *The Emotional Brain: The Mysterious Underpinnings of Life*. New York: Touchstone.

LeDoux, J.E. (2000). Emotional Circuits in the Brain. *Annual Review of Neuroscience*, 23, 155–184.

Leowald, H.W. (1980). Psychoanalysis as art and the fantasy nature of the psychoanalytic situation. In H.Leowald, *Papers in Psychoanalysis* (pp. 352–371). New Haven, CT: Yale University Press.

Levenson, E. (1972). *The Fallacy of Understanding*. New York: Basic Books.

Levine, H.B. (1990). Introduction. In H.B. Levine (Ed.), *Adult Analysis and Childhood Sexual Abuse* (pp. 3–20). Hillsdale, NJ: Analytic Press.

Levine, P. (1997). *Waking the tiger: Healing trauma*. Berkeley, CA: North Atlantic Books.

Lewis, C.S. (1963). *The Screwtape Letters*. San Francisco, CA: Harper Collins.

Lifton, R.J. (1961). *Thought Reform and the Psychology of Totalism*. New York: Norton.

Lindemann, E. (1944). Symptomatology and management of acute grief. *American Journal of Psychiatry*, 101, 141–148.

Liotti, G. (1999). Understanding the dissociative process: The contributions of attachment theory. *Psychoanalytic Inquiry*, 19, 757–783.

Liotti, G. (2004). Trauma, dissociation, and disorganized attachment: Three strands of a single braid. *Psychotherapy: Theory, Research, Practice, Training*, 41, 472–486.

Liotti, G. (2006). A model of dissociation based on attachment theory and research. *Journal of Trauma and Dissociation*, 7, 55–74.

Liotti, G. (2011). Attachment disorganization and the clinical dialogue: Theme and variations. In J. Solomon and C. George (Eds), *Disorganization of Attachment and Caregiving* (pp. 383–413). New York: Guilford.

Loewenstein, R.J. (1996). Dissociative amnesia and dissociative fugue. In L.K. Michelson and W.J. Ray (Eds), *Handbook of Dissociation: Theoretical, empirical, and clinical perspectives*. New York: Plenum.

Lyons-Ruth, K. (1999). Two-person unconscious: Intersubjective dialogue, enactive relational representation, and the emergence of new forms of relational organization. *Psychoanalytic Inquiry*, 19, 576–617.

Lyons-Ruth, K. (2003). Dissociation and the parent-infant dialogue: A longitudinal perspective from attachment research. *Journal of the American Psychoanalytic Association*, 51, 883–911.

Lyons-Ruth, K. (2006). The interface between attachment and intersubjectivity. Perspectives from the longitudinal study of disorganized attachment. *Psychoanalytic Inquiry*, 26, 595–516.

Luxenburg, T., Spinazzola, J. and Van der Kolk, B.A. (2001). Complex trauma and disorders of extreme Stress (DESNOS) diagnosis part 1: Assessment. *New Directions in Psychiatry*, 21(25), 373–394.

Main, M. and Solomon, J. (1986). Discovery of a new, insecure-disorganized/disoriented attachment pattern. In M.Yogman and T.B.Brazelton (Eds), *Affective Development in Infancy* (pp. 95–124). Norwood, NY: Ablex Press.

Main, M. and Solomon, J. (1990). Procedures for identifying infants as disorganized/disoriented during the Ainsworth Strange Situation. In M.T. Greenberg, D. Cicchetti and E.M. Cummings (Eds), *Attachment in the Preschool Years* (pp. 121–160). Chicago, IL: Chicago University Press.

Malarek, V. (2003). *The Natashas: Inside the new global sex trade*. New York: Arcade.

Mam, T.D. (1999). Worms from our skin. In D. Pran (Ed.), *Children of Cambodia's illing Fields: Memoirs of survivors* (pp. 11–18). New Haven, CT: Yale University Press.

Marks, J. (1979). *The Search for the Manchurian Candidate: The CIA and mind control*. New York: Times Books.

Marks, R.P. (2012). When the sleeping tiger roars – Perpetrator introjects in children. In R. Vogt's (Ed.) *Perpetrator Introjects: Psychotherapeutic diagnostics and treatment methods* (pp. 87–110). Kroning, Germany: Asanger Verlag.

Marmer, S.S. (1996). An outline for psychoanalytic treatment. In J.L. Spira (Ed.), *Treating Dissociative Identity Disorder* (pp. 183–218). San Francisco, CA: Jossey-Bass.

Maroda, K.J. (1991). *The Power of Countertransference: Innovations in analytic technique*. New York: Wiley and Sons.

Maroda, K.J. (1999). *Seduction, Surrender, and Transformation: Emotional engagement in the analytic process.* Hillsdale, NJ: Analytic Press.

Marx, B.P., Forsyth, J.P., Gallup, G.G., Fuse, T. and Lexington, J.M. (2008). Tonic immobility as an evolved predator defense: Implications for sexual assault survivors. *Clinical Psychology: Science and Practice,* 15, 74–90.

McKay, S. and Mazurana, D. (2004). *Where are the girls? Girls in fighting forces in Northern Uganda, Sierra Leone and Mozambique: Their lives during and after war.* Montreal: Rights and Democracy.

McLernon, F., Cairns, E. and Hewstone, M. (2002). Views on forgiveness in Northern Ireland. *Peace Review* 14(3), 285–290.

Mellor, D., Bretherton, D. and Firth, L. (2007). Aboriginal and non-aboriginal Australia: The dilemma of apologies, forgiveness and reconciliation. *Peace and Conflict: Journal of Peace Psychology,* 13(1), 11–36.

Meltzer, D. (1973/2008). *Sexual States of Mind.* London: Karnac.

Miller, A. (2012). Healing the unimaginable: Treating ritual abuse and mind control. London: Karnac.

Miller, F.A. and Katz, J.A. (2002). *The Inclusion Breakthrough: Unleashing the real power of diversity.* San Francisco, CA: Berrett-Koehler.

Mills, A. and Lynn, S.J. (2000). Past life experiences. In E. Cardena, S.J. Lynn and S.Krippner (Eds), *Varieties of Anomolous Experience: Examining the evidence* (pp. 283–314). Washington, DC: American Psychological Association.

Minow, M. (1998). *Between Vengeance and Forgiveness: Facing history after genocide and mass violence.* Boston, MA: Beacon Press.

Mitchell, S.A. (1993). *Hope and Dread in Psychoanalysis.* New York: Basic.

Mitchell, S.A. (1995). Interaction in the Kleinian and interpersonal traditions. *Contemporary Psychoanalysis,* 31(1), 65–91.

Nachmani, G. (1995). Trauma and ignorance. *Contemporary Psychoanalysis,* 31(3), 423–450.

Nachmani, G. (1997). Discussion: Reconstructing methods of victimization. In R.B. Gartner (Ed.), Memories of Sexual Betrayal: Truth, fantasy, repression and dissociation (pp. 189–208). Northvale, NJ: Jason Aronson.

Nathanson, D. (1992). *Shame and Pride: Affect, sex, and the birth of the self.* New York: Norton.

Nijenhuis, E.R.S. (2003). Looking into the brains of patients with dissociative disorders. *The International Society for the Study of Dissociation News,* 21(2), 6–9.

Nijenhuis, E.R.S. (2004). *Somatoform Dissociation: Phenomenon, measurement, and theoretical issues.* New York: Norton.

Nijenhuis, E.R.S., Van der Hart, O., Kruger, K. and Steele, K. (2004). Somatoform dissociation, trauma and defense. *Australia and New Zealand Journal of Psychiatry,* 38, 678–686.

Nin, A. (1939/2007). Winter of Artifice. Troy, MI: Skyblue Press.

Noblitt, J.R. and Noblitt, P.P. (2008). *Ritual Abuse in the 21st Century: Psychological, forensic, social, and political considerations.* Bandon, OR: Robert D. Reed.

Noblitt, J.R. and Perskin, P.S. (2000). *Cult and Ritual Abuse: Its history and recent discovery in contemporary America* (revised edn). Westport, CT: Praeger.

Norbu, C.N., Clemente, A. and Shane, J. (2003). *Dzogchen: The self-perfected state.* Ithaca, NY: Snow Lion.

Ogawa, J.R., Sroufe, L.A., Weinfeld, N.S., Carlson, E.A. and Egland, B. (1997). Development and the fragmented self: Longitudinal study of dissociative symptomology in a nonclinical sample. *Development and Psychopathy,* 9, 855–879.

Ogden, T. (1989). *The Primitive Edge of Experience.* Northvale, NJ: Jason Aronson.

Orange, D., Atwood, G. E. and Stolorow, R.D. (1997). *Working Intersubjectively: Contextualism in psychoanalytic practice*. Hillsdale, NJ: Analytic Press.

Orwell, G. (1949). *1984*. New York: New American Library, Signet Classic Edition, 1949.

Pagels, E. (1995). *The Origins of Satan: How Christians demonized, Jews, pagans, and heretics*. New York: Random House.

Palmer, M., Ramsay, J. and Kwok, Man-Ho (1995). *Kuan Yin: Myths and prophecies of the Chinese goddess of compassion*. San Francisco, CA: Thorsons.

Parmar, S. (2010). Realizing economic justice for children: The process of transitional justice in post-conflict societies. In S. Parmar, M.J. Roseman, S. Siegrist and T. Towa (Eds.), *Children and Transitional Justice: Truth-telling, acountability, and reconciliation* (pp. 365–401). New York: UNICEF/Human Rights Program at Harvard University Law School, Cambridge, MA.

Parmar, S., Roseman, M.J. Siegrist, S. and Suwa, T. (2010). *Children and Transitional Justice: Truth-telling, accountability, and reconciliation* (NY: UNICEF).

Pearlman, L.A. and Saakvitne, K.W. (1995). *Trauma and the Therapist: Countertransference and vicarious traumatization in psychotherapy with incest survivors*. New York: Norton.

Peoples, K.M. (1992). Unconscious dominance and submission. In E. Cardena (Chair), *Consciousness, dissociative alterations of consciousness and trauma*. Symposium Conducted at the Centennial Convention of the American Psychological Association, Washington, DC, August.

Perry, B.D. and Pollard, R. (1998). Homeostasis, stress, trauma, and adaptation: A neurodevelopmental view of childhood trauma. *Child and Adolescent Psychiatric Clinics of North America*, 7, 33–51.

Pizer, S.A. (1998). *Building Bridges: The negotiation of paradox in psychoanalysis*. Hillsdale, NJ: The Analytic Press.

Pran, D. (1999). *Children of Cambodia's Killing Fields: Memoirs of survivors*. New Haven, CT: Yale University Press.

Preece, R. (2006). *The Psychology of Buddhist Tantra*. Ithaca, NY: Snow Lion.

Putnam, F.W. (1989). *The Diagnosis and Treatment of Multiple Personality Disorder*. New York: Guilford.

Putnam, F.W. (1992). Discussion: Are alter personalities fragments or fictions? *Psychoanalytic Inquiry*, 12, 95–101.

Putnam, F.W. (1997). *Dissociation in Children and Adolescents: A Developmental perspective*. New York: Guilford.

Rabin, H.M. (1995). The liberating effect on the analyst of the paradigm shift in psychoanalysis. *Psychoanalytic Psychology*, 12(4), 467–481.

Rivera, M. (1989). Linking the psychological and the social: Feminism, poststructuralism, and multiple personality. *Dissociation*, 2(1), 24–31.

Rivera, M. (1996). *More Alike Than Different: Treating Severely Dissociative Trauma Survivors*. Toronto: University of Toronto Press.

Rorty, R. (1989). *Contingency, Irony, and Solidarity*. Cambridge: Cambridge University Press.

Rosenfeld, H. (1971). A clinical approach to the psychoanalytic theory of the life and death instincts: An investigation into the aggressive aspects of narcissism. *International Journal of Psychoanalysis*, 52(2), 174–190.

Ross, C. A. (1989). *Multiple Personality Disorder: Diagnosis, clinical features, and treatment*. New York: Wiley.

Ross, C.A. (1991). Epidemiology of MPD and dissociation. *Psychiatric Clinics of North America*, 14, 503–517.

Ross, C.A. (1995). *Satanic Ritual Abuse: Principles of treatment*. Toronto: University of Toronto Press.

Ross, C.A. (1997). *Dissociative Identity Disorder: Diagnosis, clinical features, and treatment of multiple personality.* New York: John Wiley and Sons.

Ross, C.A. (2000). *Bluebird: Deliberate Creation of Multiple Personality by Psychiatrists.* Richardson, TX: Manitou Communications.

Ross, C.A., Norton, G.R. and Wozney, K. (1989). Multiple personality disorder: An analysis of 236 cases. *Canadian Journal of Psychiatry,* 34, 413–418.

Ross, N.W. (1980). *Buddhism: A way of life and thought.* New York: Vintage.

Saakvitne, K.W. (1995). Therapists' response to dissociative clients: Countertransference and vicarious traumatization. In L. Cohen, J. Berzoff, and M. Elin (Eds.), *Dissociative Identity Disorder* (pp. 467–507). Northvale, NJ: Jason Aronson.

Sachs, A. (2008). Introduction. In A. Sachs and G. Galton (Eds.), *Forensic Aspects of Dissociative Identity Disorder* (pp. 1–8). London: Karnac.

Safer, J. (2000). *Forgiving and Not Forgiving: A new approach to resolving intimate betrayal.* New York: Harper.

Salter, A.C. (1995). *Transforming Trauma: A guide to understanding and treating adult survivors of child sexual abuse.* Thousand Oaks, CA: Sage.

Salter, A.C. (2003). *Predators, Pedophiles, Rapists, and Other Sex Offenders: Who they are, how they operate, and how we can protect ourselves and our children.* New York: Basic Books.

Schauer, E. and Elbert, T. (2010). The psychological impact of child soldiering. In E. Martz (Ed.), *Trauma Rehabilitation After War and Conflict: Community and individual perspectives* (pp. 311–360), New York: Springer.

Schauer, M. and Schauer, E. (2010). Trauma-focused public mental health interventions– A paradigm shift in humanitarian assistance and aid work. In E. Martz (Ed.), *Trauma Rehabilitation After War and Conflict: Community and individual perspectives.* New York: Springer.

Schore, A.N. (2002). Advances in neuropsychoanalysis, attachment theory, and trauma research: Implications for attachment theory. *Psychoanalytic Inquiry,* 22, 433–484.

Schore, A.N. (2009). Attachment trauma and the developing right brain: Origins of pathological dissociation. In P.F. Dell and J.F. O'Neil (Eds.), *Dissociation and the Dissociative Disorders: DSM V and beyond* (pp. 107–141). New York: Routledge.

Schore, A.N. (2011). Forward. In P.M. Bromberg, *The Shadow of the Tsunami and the Growth of the Relational Mind* (pp. vii–xxxvii). New York: Routledge.

Schwartz, H.L. (1994). From dissociation to negotiation: A relational psychoanalytic perspective on multiple personality disorder. *Psychoanalytic Psychology,* 11(2), 189–231.

Schwartz, H.L. (2000). *Dialogues With Forgotten Voices: Relational perspectives on child abuse trauma and treatment of dissociative disorders.* New York: Basic Books.

Schwartz, H.L., Williams, J. and Farley, M. (2007). Pimp subjugation of women by mind control. In M. Farley, *Prostitution and Trafficking in Nevada: Making the Connections.* San Francisco, CA: Prostitution Research and Education.

Schwartz, R.W. (2011). "An evil cradling?" Cult practices and the manipulation of attachment needs in ritual abuse. In O.B. Epstein, I. Schwartz and R.W. Schwartz (Eds), *Ritual Abuse and Mind Control: The manipulation of attachment needs* (pp. 39–56). London: Karnac.

Shay, J. (1995). *Achilles in Vietnam: Combat trauma and the undoing of character.* New York: Simon and Schuster.

Shengold, L. (1989). *Soul Murder.* New Haven, CT: Yale University Press.

ShineGlobal, Inc. (2006). *Wardance* (Fine Film Productions, directed by S. Fine and A.N. Fine; Request Harbor Studios).

Sholem, G. (1974). *Major Trends in Jewish Mysticism*. New York: Shocken Books.

Shriver, D.W. (2001). Forgiveness: A bridge across abysses of revenge. In R.G. Helmick & R.L. Petersen (Eds.). *Forgiveness and Reconciliation: Religion, Public Policy, and Conflict Transformation* (pp. 151–167). Radnor, PA: Templeton Foundation Press.

Simpson, M.A. (1996). What went wrong? Diagnostic and ethical problems in dealing with the effects of torture and repression in South Africa. In R.J. Kleber, C.R. Figley and B.P.R. Gersons (Eds.), *Beyond Trauma: Cultural and societal dynamics* (pp. 187–212). New York: Plenum Press.

Sinason, V. (1994). *Treating Survivors of Satanic Abuse*. New York: Routledge.

Sinason, V. (2011a). What has changed in twenty years? In O.B. Epstein, J. Schwartz and R.W. Schwartz (Eds.), *Ritual Abuse and Mind Control: The manipulation of attachment needs* (pp. 1–20). London: Karnac.

Sinason, V. (2011b/2002). Introduction. In Sinason, V. (Ed.), *Attachment Trauma and Multiplicity: Working with dissociative identity disorder* (2nd edn) (pp. 1–12). New York: Routledge.

Singer, M.T. (1995). *Cults in our Midst: The hidden menace in our everyday lives*. San Francisco, CA: Jossey-Bass.

Singer, P.W. (2006). *Children at War*. Berkeley, CA: University of California Press.

Smith, A. (2010). Basic assumptions of transitional justice and children. In Parmar, S., Roseman, M.J., Siegrist, S. & Towa, T. (Eds.), *Children and Transitional Justice: Truth-Telling, Acountability, and Reconciliation* (pp. 31–65). New York: UNICEF/ Human Rights Program at Harvard University, Cambridge, MA.

Smith, M. (1993). *Ritual Abuse: What it is, why it happens, how to help*. San Francisco, CA: Harper.

Soskis, D.A. and Ochberg, F.M. (1982). Concepts of terrorist victimization. In F.M. Ochberg and D.A. Soskis (Eds.), *Victims of Terrorism* (pp. 105–135). Boulder, CO: Westview Press.

Spezzano, C. (1993). A relational model of inquiry and truth: The place of psychoanalysis in human conversation. *Psychoanalytic Dialogues*, 3(2), 177–208.

Spezzano, C. (1995). "Classical" versus "contemporary" theory: The differences that matter clinically. *Contemporary Psychoanalysis*, 31(1), 20–46.

Spiegel, D. (1990). Trauma, dissociation, and hypnosis. In R. Kluft (Ed.) *Incest-related Syndromes of Adult Psychopathology* (pp. 247–262). Washington, DC: American Psychiatric Press.

Stack, J. (2004). *The Liberian Civil War* (Film Documentary).

Steele, K., Dorahy, M.J., Van der Hart, O., and Nijenhuis, E.R.S. (2009). Dissociation versus alterations in consciousness: Related but different concepts. In P.F. Dell and J.A. O'Neill (Eds.), *Dissociatoin and the DissociativeDisorders: DSM-V and beyond* (pp. 155–170). New York: Routledge.

Stolorow, R.D. and Atwood, G.E. (1992). *Contexts of Being: The intersubjective foundations of psychological life*. Hillsdale, NJ: Analytic Press.

Stolorow, R.D. and Atwood, G.E. (1994). Toward a science of human experience. In R.D. Stolorow, G.E. Atwood, and B. Brandchaft (Eds.), *The Intersubjective Perspective* (pp. 15–31). Northvale, NJ: JasonAronson, Inc.

Stolorow, R.D., Brandchaft, B. and Atwood, G.E. (1987). *Psychoanalytic Treatment: An intersubjective approach*. Hillsdale, NJ: Analytic Press.

Stout, M. (2001). *The Myth of Sanity: Divided consciousness and the promise of awareness: Tales of multiple personality in everyday life*. New York: Penguin.

Stout, M. (2005). *The Sociopath Next Door*. New York: Broadway Books.

Straker, G. (2007). A crisis in the subjectivity of the analyst. *Psychoanalytic Dialogues*, 17(2), 153–164.

Sullivan, H.S. (1956). *Clinical Studies in Psychiatry*. New York: Norton.

Symington, J. and Symington, N. (1996). *The Clinical Thinking of Wilfred Bion.* New York: Brunner/Routledge.

Tarnopolosy, A. (2003). The concept of dissociation in early psychoanalytic writers. *Journal of Trauma and Dissociation*, 4, 7–25.

Teitel, R.G. (2000). *Transitional Justice.* New York: Oxford University Press.

Terr, L. (1990). *Too Scared to Cry: How trauma affects children and ultimately us all.* New York: Basic Books.

Thomas, G. (1989). *Journey Into Madness: The true story of secret CIA mind control and medical abuse.* New York: Bantam Books.

Unger, R. (2004). *False Necessity: Anti-Necessitarian social theory in the service of radical democracy* (revised edn). London: Verso.

United Nations (UN Population Fund) (2003). State of World Population: Making 1 Billion Count (New York: UNFPA).

Van der Hart, O., Nijenhuis, E.R.S. and Steele, K. (2006). *The Haunted Self: Structural dissociation and the treatment of chronic traumatization.* New York: Norton.

Van der Kolk, B.A. (1987). *Psychological Trauma.* Washington, DC: American Psychiatric Press.

Van der Kolk, B.A. (1989). The Compulsion to Repeat the Trauma: Re-enactment, revictimization, and masochism. *Psychiatric Clinics of North America*, 12(2), 389–411.

Van der Kolk, B.A. (1996). The complexity of adaptation to trauma: Self-regulation, stimulus discrimination, and characterological development. In B.A. Vander Kolk, A.C. McFarlane, and L. Weisaeth (Eds.), *Traumatic Stress: The effects of overwhelming experience on mind, body, and society* (pp. 182–213), New York: Guilford.

Van der Kolk, B.A. (2005). Developmental trauma disorder: A new rational diagnosis for children with complex trauma histories. *Psychiatric Annals*, 35(5), 390–398.

Van der Kolk, B.A. and Van der Hart, O. (1989). Pierre Janet and the breakdown of adaptation in psychological trauma. *American Journal of Psychiatry*, 146, 1530–1539.

Van der Kolk, B.A., McFarlane, A.C. and Weisaeth, L. (Eds.) (1996a). *Traumatic Stress: The effects of overwhelming experience on mind, body, and society.* New York: Guilford.

Van der Kolk, B.A., Pelcovitz, D., Roth, S., Mandel, F.S., McFarlane, A. and Herman, J.L. (1996b). Dissociation, somatization, and affect dysregulation: The complexity of adaptation to trauma. *American Journal of Psychiatry*, 153, 83–93.

VBS.TV (2010). The Vice Guide to Liberia (8 parts).

Vogt, R. (2008). *Psychotrauma, State, Setting: Psychoanalytical-action-related model for a treatment of complexly traumatized patients.* Germany: Psychosozial-Verlag.

Vogt, R. (2012). Dealing with the problem of introjection on a professional and everyday level. In Vogt, R. (Ed.), *Perpetrtor Introjects: Psychotherapeutic diagnostics and treatment models* (pp. 13–74). Kroning, Germany: Asanger Verlag.

Waites, E.A. (1997). *Memory Quest: Trauma and the search for personal history.* New York: Norton.

Wax, E. (2003). "Toting AK-47s Instead of Bookbags," *Washington Post*, August 25, 2003.

Weinstein, H.M. (1990). *Psychiatry and the CIA: Victims of mind control.* Washington, DC: American Psychiatric Press.

Weiss, B. (1988). *Many Lives, Many Masters: The true story of a prominent psychiatrist, his young patient, and the past life therapy that changed both of their lives.* New York: Fireside Press.

Weiss, B. (2004). *Same Soul, Many Bodies: Discovering the healing power of future lives through progression therapy*. New York: Free Press.

Weiss, J. (1993). *How Psychotherapy Works: Process and technique*. New York: Guilford.

Wessels, M. (2006). *Child Soldiers: From violence to protection*. Cambridge, MA: Harvard University Press.

Wessels, M. and Monteiro, C. (2004). Healing the wounds following protracted conflict in Angola. In U. P. Gielen, J. Fish and J.G. Draguns (Eds.), *Handbook of Culture, Therapy, and Healing* (pp. 321–341). Mahwah, NJ: Erlbaum.

Whitton, J. and Fisher, J. (1986). *Life before Life*. New York: Warner/Doubleday.

Winnicott, D.W. (1947). Hate in the countertransference. In D.Winnicott, *Through Pediatrics to Psychoanalysis* (pp. 194– 204). London: Hogarth Press.

Winnicott, D.W. (1971). *Playing and Reality*. New York: Basic Books.

Young, W.C., Sachs, R.G., Braun, B.G. and Watkins, R.T. (1991). Patients reporting ritual abuse in childhood: A clinical syndrome. *International Journal of Child Abuse and Neglect*, 15, 181–189.

Index

12-step programs 140, 151

abandonment 30, 36, 52–3, 65, 78, 84, 124, 142, 151, 160, 164, 182, 185, 193–4, 199, 201, 212, 227
abduction 1, 4–5, 15, 29, 31–3, 36
abortion 30–1
abreaction 145, 177, 179, 181–2, 204, 226
accountability 31, 34, 51, 116, 140, 144–5, 191–2, 202, 216 *see also* culpability; responsibility
acting out 25, 31, 38, 42, 60, 70, 75, 79, 111, 113–14, 145, 153, 157, 172, 174, 177, 179, 233
Adams, M.A. 226
addiction 30, 32, 37–8, 40, 57–8, 64, 111, 118, 122, 153, 166, 171, 177, 181, 220, 238–9
adolescence 7, 30, 32–3, 37, 42–3, 154, 222, 227, 235
advertising 86, 104
affectivity 128, 167, 170, 176, 179, 184, 210, 219
after death programming 103, 223
aggression 1–2, 4, 8, 12–13, 18, 24, 32, 40, 57, 64–71, 74–5, 111, 124, 133, 145, 171, 173–5, 177, 189, 199, 217–18, 223, 225, 231 *see also* appropriate aggression
AIDS 214
Alford, C.F. 10, 109–10, 117–18, 207–8
alienation 10, 39, 47, 56, 78–9, 111, 130, 140–1, 145, 164, 177, 188, 191, 205, 208, 213, 221, 224
Allison, R.B. 226
Alpha functions 110–11, 238
alter personalities *see* self-states

ambiguity 20, 26, 50, 56, 64, 70, 75, 113–14, 130, 139–41, 155, 159, 161–2, 164, 171–3, 176, 179, 184–5, 188, 190–1, 197, 207–9, 216
amnesia barriers 10, 13, 85, 101, 151, 155, 233 *see also* coerced amnesia; memory loss
amphetamines 125, 238 *see also* drugs
anger 18, 51–2, 60, 65, 90, 101, 124, 163, 171, 174, 185, 204, 216, 226
Angola 41
animal alters 85, 96
animal cruelty 16, 19, 28, 78, 82, 98, 122, 137
annihilation 7, 10–11, 22, 47, 60–1, 66–7, 74, 81, 87–8, 108, 110–11, 119–20, 126, 129–31, 147, 160, 178, 180–1, 185, 194, 219
anti-attachment programming 58, 83, 106, 180
anti-God programming 102, 180
antisocial behaviors 4, 111
anti-therapy programming 58, 106
anxieties 7, 11, 13, 19, 34, 36, 53, 58, 61, 67, 71, 73–5, 93, 101, 110, 114, 116, 123–4, 130, 132, 139, 157, 159, 161–2, 166, 171, 178, 184–5, 188, 201, 225, 238; anxiety management techniques 32, 68, 130, 178, 186; apocalyptic anxieties 110, 112, 194
apocalyptic cults 100
appropriate aggression 24, 64, 141
arrogance 13, 33, 60, 67, 124, 126, 128, 147–8, 159, 177, 188, 207, 220
assassins 68, 80, 98, 100, 153–4, 210, 221, 224